This book is a study of the relations between the body and its technologies in modernism. Tim Armstrong traces the links between modernist literary texts and medical, psychological and social theory across a wide range of writers, including Yeats, Henry James, Eliot, Stein, Poe, Nathanael West, Dreiser, Mina Loy, Djuna Barnes, and Pound. Armstrong shows how modernist texts enact experimental procedures which have their origins in nineteenth-century psychophysics, biology, and bodily reform techniques, but within a content in which the body is reconceived and subjected to new modes of production, representation and commodification. Drawing on a wide range of disciplines, Armstrong challenges the received oppositions between technology and literature, the instrumental and the aesthetic, by demonstrating the leaky boundaries and complex interconnections between these domains. The book offers a cultural history of Modernism as it negotiated the enduring fact of the human body in a period of rapid technological and scientific change.

MODERNISM, TECHNOLOGY, AND THE BODY

To the memory of my parents, Dorothy and Jack Armstrong

MODERNISM, TECHNOLOGY, AND THE BODY

A *cultural study*

TIM ARMSTRONG

Royal Holloway, University of London

CAMBRIDGE
UNIVERSITY PRESS

PUBLISHED BY THE PRESS SYNDICATE OF THE UNIVERSITY OF CAMBRIDGE
The Pitt Building, Trumpington Street, Cambridge CB2 1RP, United Kingdom

CAMBRIDGE UNIVERSITY PRESS
The Edinburgh Building, Cambridge CB2 2RU, United Kingdom
40 West 20th Street, New York, NY 10011-4211, USA
10 Stamford Road, Oakleigh, Melbourne 3166, Australia

First published 1998

Printed in the United Kingdom at the University Press, Cambridge

Typeset in 11/12½pt New Baskerville   [SE]

A catalogue record for this book is available from the British Library

Library of Congress cataloguing in publication data

Armstrong, Tim, 1956–
Modernism, technology, and the body: a cultural history / Tim
Armstrong.
p.   cm.
Includes index.
ISBN 0 521 59004 3 (hardback). – ISBN 0 521 59997 0 (paperback).
1. American literature – 20th century – History and criticism.
2. Modernism (Literature) – United States.   3. Literature and
science – United States – History – 20th century.   4. Body, Human, in
literature.   5. Technology in literature.   6. Psychology in
literature.   I. Title.
PR225.M63A89   1998
810.9'112–dc21   97–8815 CIP

ISBN 0 521 59004 3 hardback
ISBN 0 521 59997 0 paperback

Contents

Illustrations

Acknowledgements

This book began with work on Yeats and Dreiser which seemed to suggest the possibility of a short study of modernist conceptions of the re-energized body. It has overspilled its original boundaries, and taken me into a range of issues in Modernism which I never anticipated. I have, however, been lucky to enter a field which has been reinvigorated by a range of historical and cultural studies by such authors as Friedrich Kittler, Mark Seltzer, and (from the perspective of cultural history) Jonathan Crary, Janet Oppenheimer, Anson Rabinbach, Hillel Schwartz, and many others. At the same time, a major reappraisal of literary Modernism has taken place, with critics such as Ann Douglas, Jane Marcus, Peter Nicholls, Bonnie Kime Scott, and Steven Watson reforming our views of the field. I have been particularly stimulated by the London Modernism Seminar , and by the Modernism conferences, beginning in Cambridge in 1993, which have provided a sense of community of effort in the UK.

Among those I would like to thank for reading work, providing materials, references, ideas, and other forms of help are Howard Booth, Jayna Brown, Claire Buck, Jonathan Burt, Matthew Campbell, Roger L. Conover Valerie Cotter, Stephen Fender, Anne Fogarty, Alex Goody, Warwick Gould, Lee Grieveson, Rainer Herrn, Paula Krebs, Laura Marcus, Peter Nicholls, Norman Page, Andrew Roberts, Jonathan Sawday, Mark Seltzer, Erica Sheen, Sally Shuttleworth, David Trotter, and Pamela Thurschwell. Above all, I would like to thank Sue Wiseman for putting up with all this in Sheffield and London.

Earlier versions of sections appeared in *Textual Practice*, the *Yeats Annual*, and in the collection *American Bodies*; my thanks to publishers for permission to reprint. I would also like to thank the organizers of conferences which gave me the opportunity to test ideas: Modernism and Gender, Cheltenham; Modernism conferences at King's College, Cambridge, Southampton, and London; Bodily Fictions, Brunel; BAAS 1994; Literature and Addiction, Sheffield; and seminars at Cork, Sussex, Nottingham, Birmingham, and Royal Holloway. I am grateful to staff at the University of London Library; the University of Sheffield Library; the British Library; the Beineke Library, Yale; and at the Magnus Hirschfeld Gesellschaft.

For permissions to quote, I would like to thank the following: A. P. Watt Ltd and Simon & Schuster, on behalf of Michael Yeats, for permission to quote from the works of W. B. Yeats; Roger L. Conover, Literary Executor to the Estate of Mina Loy, and the Beineke Library for permission to quote from manuscript material in the Mina Loy collection at the Beineke and from *The Last Lunar Baedeker* and *The Lost Lunar Baedeker*. For permission to reproduce photographs, I would like to thank the British Library, London; the Magnus Hirschfeld Gesellschaft, Berlin; the Prinzhorn Collection, Heidelberg; and the Philadelphia Museum of Art (Walter and Louise Arensberg Collection). Otto Dix's 'The Skat Players' © DACS 1997 is reproduced from the painting in the Staatliche Museum, Berlin, photograph © bpk, Berlin, 1996.

Introduction

In 1930, a man travels to Berlin. A Danish artist resident for a number of years in Paris, he has been in the habit of cross-dressing and acting as a model for his wife's fashionable paintings. In Berlin he meets Magnus Hirschfeld, the eminent sexologist, who helps arrange a series of operations which will change his sex. In 1934, a Nobel prize-winning Irish poet has the rejuvenating 'Steinach Operation', performed by another sexologist, Norman Haire. In the period that follows, his work is revitalized. In 1922, two Americans who regard themselves as the vanguard of Modernism exchange letters on glandular extracts and a wife's menstrual problems. In 1906, a British-resident American novelist begins to chew every mouthful methodically. He masticates in solitude for years and lunches with Horace Fletcher, the inventor of the technique. In 1919, a modernist poet invents her own beauty system, labelling it 'Auto-facial Construction'. In 1899, a young American researcher in psychology publishes two papers on automatic writing before leaving for Paris, where she establishes a salon and becomes a self-declared genius; in 1934, she is forced into a dialogue with the behaviourist B. F. Skinner on the meaning of those experiments. In 1927, sound film arrives and precipitates a European debate on the relation between writing and speech; Hollywood dubs the technique of adding sound to films 'goat-glanding' and a British woman novelist laments 'the Film Gone Male'. In 1900, a naturalist novelist celebrates an electric body in American life; twenty-five years later he depicts those same electric energies as they are oppressively located in the electric chair.

This book is a study of relations between the body and its technologies in Modernism. It is a topic traced across those described above – W. B. Yeats, 'Lili Elbe', Henry James, Mina Loy, Gertrude Stein, Dorothy Richardson, Theodore Dreiser, T. S. Eliot, Ezra

1

Pound – and others including Edgar Allan Poe, Nathanael West, and Djuna Barnes. My aim is to pursue the links between modernist literary texts and medical, psychological, and social theory, working in the spirit of Raymond Williams's observation that consciousness is 'not only knowledge . . . In cultural production . . . the true range is from information and description, or naming and indication, to embodiment and *performance.*'[1] The desire to embody and perform is an important part of the story here, a corporeal equivalent of Modernism's slogan 'No ideas but in things'. In the modern period, the body is re-energized, re-formed, subject to new modes of production, representation, and commodification.

Why is the body so important to Modernism? To answer that question we have to notice, first, a revolution in perceptions of the body in the nineteenth century. At the beginning of the century, the body was the machine in which the self lived; the site of an animal nature which required conscious regulation. It was also a boundary: a doctor in 1800 would listen to a case history, with examination by touch; the live body could not be penetrated safely. A little later the same doctor might subscribe to phrenology, which let interior states be 'read' off from lumps on the head. By the early twentieth century, however, a range of changes had taken place, culminating in 'Flexnerian medicine' – the research-oriented, specialized, scientific medicine codified in the 1910 Flexner Report in America. The body could be penetrated by a barrage of devices: the stethoscope, ophthalmoscope, laryngoscope, speculum, high-intensity light, X-rays. Its physiological rhythms could be followed in the pulse, temperature, and respiration chart; its blood-pressure monitored; its bacteria examined by powerful microscopes. Entering it became safer after 1857 with Lister's antiseptic surgery and the use of chloroform.[2] The body was resolved into a complex of different biomechanical systems, conceived in thermodynamic terms. Other technologies were applied to it: drugs, inoculation, electricity; as well as various external regimes designed to improve its make-up, shape, and the flow of energies through it. The science of work – well established before Frederick Taylor published *The Principles of Scientific Management* in 1911 – attempted to maximize the performance of the body in relation to machine culture. Eugenics sought to govern reproductive potential.

At the same time, the body harboured a crisis. Darwinian science suggested a substrata of primitive material within the body and brain, and aroused widespread fears of regression, destabilizing relations between self and world.[3] The body became a more contingent mechanism, incorporating evolutionary survivals, and with a perceptual, neurological, and performative apparatus whose thresholds constantly reappear in late nineteenth-century psychophysics, and in studies of work and motion. As Friedrich Kittler argues, 'Psychophysics . . . investigated capabilities that in everyday life would have been called superfluous, pathological, or obsolete.'[4] Or, as another writer puts it, 'with the recognition that the anatomical–physiological vicissitudes of the human body might well underlie all knowledge, human beings acquired in their own eyes a new, unaccustomed finitude'.[5] Such a body might be out of step with the modern, technologically advanced, world: diagnoses like hysteria, neurasthenia, even constipation and eye-strain, registered the stress placed on the body by civilization, and suggested that compensatory action was necessary.[6] Even those who wished to offer the body as the site of authenticity were forced to posit a return to an atavistic substratum which created a temporal discontinuity in their idealizations, a fantasy of primitivism. In this book, we will see a parade of cures offered for this default: electro-therapy, dietary regimes, eye-therapy, manipulation, hormones, surgery. Modernity, then, brings both a fragmentation and augmentation of the body in relation to technology; it offers the body as lack, at the same time as it offers technological compensation. Increasingly, that compensation is offered as a part of capitalism's fantasy of the complete body: in the mechanisms of advertising, cosmetics, cosmetic surgery, and cinema; all prosthetic in the sense that they promise the perfection of the body. Indeed, in this study, cinema comes to signal the terminal point of a certain form of prosthetic thinking.

How are these shifts related to modernist texts? Recent critics have suggested that the turn of the century saw an alliance between naturalist writing and an emerging scientific, rationalizing world-view, with a shared concern for the nature of the human subject, the regulation of bodies, for forensic investigation, and for a taxonomic objectivity.[7] If we advance the picture a frame, from the turn of the century to the period of literary Modernism, the situation becomes more complex, and the relationship

between cultural production and social and technological modernity more contested. One influential thesis has suggested that literary Modernism is largely a reaction against modernity. For
Theodor Adorno, the hermeticism and difficulty of artistic
Modernism is a reaction against a commodified and packaged
mass culture and the brutality of state bureaucracies; an attempt
to create a space for the self outside power in which the relation
of the aesthetic sphere to history is, perforce, a negative one.[8] If
that is a line of argument which, for very different reasons, also
appealed to the conservative traditions of the New Criticism, a
number of recent studies of Modernism have reversed the trend,
stressing the way in which, rather than being a reaction against or
escape from the forces of modernity, cultural Modernism is implicated in numerous ways with the scientific, technological, and
political shifts which characterize the modern era. As Jonathan
Crary observes: 'Any effective account of modern culture must
confront the ways in which modernism, rather than being a reaction against or transcendence of processes of scientific and economic rationalization, is inseparable from them.'[9] For Lisa
Steinman, Cecelia Tichi, Bruce Clarke, and others, modernist
writers found their aesthetics on contemporary science and technology: on the new physics, on vitalism, on engineering.[10]

To be sure, a broad survey of early and late Modernisms, like
that recently undertaken by Peter Nicholls, includes a Modernism
which is anti-technological and conservative. Equally, David
Porush distinguishes between those writers who embrace a 'technology of style' and those who make technology their subject.[11]
Such distinctions are useful, but this study suggests that modernists with quite different attitudes to social and technological
modernity saw the body as the locus of anxiety, even crisis; as
requiring an intervention through which it might be made the
grounds of a new form of production. It is, as Anthony Giddens
puts it, no longer a 'given', it is 'reflexively mobilized' in the way
in which the self is.[12] This is not to say that the body was ever 'innocent' or a stable category; its meanings are always socially constructed. But it does seem clear that, for reasons suggested briefly
above, in the late nineteenth century it begins to harbour and
reveal secrets and ambiguities, becoming the site of obscurity and
experiment. Modernist texts have a particular fascination with the
limits of the body, either in terms of its mechanical functioning, its

energy levels, or its abilities as a perceptual system. The subject-matter generated at this point ranges from pathologies requiring treatment (neurasthenia, sexual dysfunction, waste products) to the creative effects produced by 'automaticity' in experiments which test the limits of attention. Even film can be seen in these terms: as a visual illusion which exploits the limits of perception, but which also offers the cinematic body as recompense for the fragmented body of technology.

Two related tendencies can be distinguished here: regulation and clarification. The regulation of the body involves attempts to create equilibria, maintain energy flows, hygiene, etc. The clarification of the body involves the rendering-conscious of states of interiority, or of those limit-phenomena described above, in the name of a scientific aesthetic. (That aesthetic is often gendered: repeatedly we will see states of interiority coded as 'feminine' succumbing to a 'masculine' intervention seen as 'surgical'.) I would like to offer two figures as emblematic of this concern with regulation and clarification. The first is Hugo Münsterberg, the German psychologist who William James brought to Harvard in the 1890s, hoping that he would inculcate a new experimental rigour in America. Münsterberg is, in this study, a more pervasive presence than Freud, appearing as Stein's research director; exposing a medium; administering the first electric lie-detector test; as a pioneering industrial psychologist testing individuals for their suitability for different types of work; as a writer on advertising, and author of the first major psychological study of film. Throughout his career, Münsterberg was concerned with the calibration of the human physiological apparatus in relation to the crisis of modernity.

A second emblematic figure is F. M. Alexander, originator of the Alexander Technique, praised by pragmatist philosopher John Dewey. Alexander was concerned, in the first decades of this century, to produce a body cure which moved beyond a dualism which opposed the mind and the body, the mystical and the mechanical; which neither attacked problems in piecemeal fashion, nor had recourse to a power outside the self (God or Nature). Instead, Alexander sought a technique with which to deal with the body as a total entity and produce a new set of conscious bodily habits which would enable the balanced, dynamic, freely moving body which Hillel Schwartz has recently described as being characterized by *torque*, by the flow of movements outward from a core of the self – an alternative to the machine-body of robotic fantasy.[13] This is a pragmatics of self-expression and conscious control (the Alexander Technique has always been popular with actors) akin to many literary interventions.

Modernism is, then, characterized by the desire to *intervene* in the body; to render it part of modernity by techniques which may be biological, mechanical, or behavioural. The idea of intervention – implying a causality, a direct relation – is a difficult one. Questions of relations between body and text will always stand over a study such as this. How do events in the world, like an author embracing a chewing-regime or having an operation, relate to texts? Is the body internal or external to the practice of writing? The field which recent theory has labelled 'writing the body' often occludes and dehistoricizes those questions, ignoring a history of philosophical meditation on embodiment which is itself part of modernity. Jean-Luc Nancy's insistence that there is an incommensurability between body and discourse is a useful focus here. Nancy argues that mention of the 'written body' obscures the fact that 'the body is not a locus of writing'; there is no 'graphosomatology'. He argues that, while the body is not simply a sign, it is that which 'gives sense a place', the 'finitude of sense'.[14] There is, then, no dialectical relation between text and body that this study can use to reach towards a viable synthesis. We can, however, trace the unstable movements between body and text which are themselves central to Modernism, and, in particular, the will-to-power involved in those moments where modernist writers seek to link text and body, to resolve that constitutive uncertainty.

The interesting thing here is that versions of graphosomatology *are*, historically, a part of the field of modernist bodily interventions, from late nineteenth-century attempts to elaborate a 'physiological aesthetics' to the preoccupation with 'dermographism' in hysterics described by Janet Beizer; from the analysis of the somatics of handwriting (discussed in chapter 7 below) to the widespread belief that silent film provided a language of the body (chapter 8).[15] The body cannot be written, yet writing demands its presence. Writing is itself a bodily technology which, in the modern period, is increasingly considered in operational terms, producing textual technologies which directly negotiate between the body and the production of discourse. Handwriting –

to take one example – appears here in automatic writing and graphology, in before-and-after photographs of the effects of a rejuvenation-operation, and then again in sexual reassignment surgery, in each case evidence of a re-education of the senses which produces textual evidence.

In that sense, modernist interventions in the body are pragmatic, moving into the world of embodied thinking which Pierre Bourdieu calls the *habitus*. Bourdieu writes of 'those complexes of gestures, postures and words ... which only have to be slipped into, like a theatrical costume, to awaken, by the evocative power of bodily mimesis, a universe of ready-made feelings and experiences', providing a metaphorical basis for all understanding and social identification.[16] The tradition which has, from William James to Merleau-Ponty, attempted to define this penumbra of semi-conscious embodied thinking, is itself another version of the modernist desire for clarification. But it also means that the reciprocal relations between body and writing are grounded in practices which cannot readily be described as either cultural or material. We see, in this study, concepts which seem like embodied metaphors; but also others which take metaphor and its bodily location as a subject. If one consider the idea of the 'body electric', for example, it is almost impossible to clearly assign a metaphorical status to the term 'electric'. The body was seen as energized by actual electric flows in the nineteenth-century; but that conceptualization produced more diffuse effects, including, for example, a sense of gender as bipolar and of the body being like a battery, with limited charge. The coupling represented by techniques which hook up bodies to generators in the interests of 'stimulation' seems metaphorical, in the sense that modern science does not see any general revitalization as possible; but, at the point where the generators involved produce 2,000 volts and the aim is to kill, the linkage is literal – though here, too, social metaphors are being *created* rather than simply 'reflected'. Ian Bell's reference to 'the interstitiality of the corporeal and the non-corporeal that was the habitation of the modern writer' is a happy phrase here, given the location of the effects of Yeats's Steinach operation (chapter 5) in the so-called 'interstitial tissue' of the testes.[17] Modernist writing does not simply incorporate bodily metaphors, it operates on them.

My pathway through this field pursues, in the main, the first of what Foucault describes as the two axes of 'bio-power': one which concerns itself with various active interventions in the body (medical, judicial, sexual), and a second which concerns itself with the calculus of populations in a statistical and genetic sense, as in eugenics.[18] Late Victorian and modernist interest in eugenics has been considered in detail by a number of writers (Laura Doyle, William Greenslade, John Carey, David Bradshaw, David Trotter, among others); I touch on it only briefly here.[19] My primary focus is, rather, on the individual application of bodily techniques, with the aim of offering a historicized account of their textual meanings. In a number of cases (and this is closer to the spirit of Foucault's later work on the 'care of the self'), the writers become their own experimental subjects, transforming their own literal and literary corpus. A useful distinction here is offered by a text which signals the beginning of a modern sense of relations between the body and textuality, Grant Allen's *Physiological Aesthetics* (1877). Inspired by Spencer and Helmholtz, Allen attempts to locate aesthetic feelings in 'certain definite nervous states'. He distinguishes between two kinds of pleasurable and painful stimuli related to the conception of the body as a machine: the 'Acute' and the 'Massive'. Acute pains are generated by injury (his example is the loss of a limb), that is damage done to the machine. Massive pains relate to fatigue and lack of energy, that is to do with limits in the normal running of the body considered as a human motor – the thermodynamic apparatus recently described by Anson Rabinbach.[20] Acute pleasures relate to stimulation of one bodily organ; Massive pleasures to general physiological performance, the smooth action of the motor.[21] This taxonomy – which Allen then applies to aesthetic experience – suggests that what I would call aesthetic prosthesis might involve both the replacement of a deficit and a general stimulation. We will trace both of these functions, noting a series of paradoxical relations between the fragmentation and integration of the body suggested by these terms.

Finally, a note on consumption. In writing this book, I repeatedly experienced an uncertainty about the placing of a discussion of economic transformations in the period; of a shift variously conceived as replacing production with consumption, the commodity with the image. The issue circulates, at one moment acting as 'cause', at another as 'effect' or topic, entering discussions of energy, of the image, of agency, even of weight. This mobility suggests that it is less important as 'fact' than as an expression of the anxieties of modernity in relation to flows of desire and capital. Pointing out that 'the move to "periodize" the fall into consumer culture takes the form of a standard, and remarkably portable, story', Mark Seltzer argues that this 'story' needs to be subsumed to 'the general problem of periodizing or historicizing bodies and persons'.[22] This claim seems to lie in a distinctly American tradition, with its origins in Emerson as much as Veblen, subordinating a general logic of capital to the conceptualization of the 'person' – even, perhaps, in Seltzer's Foucaultian version. But Seltzer is surely right to insist that the status of the body in consumer culture is central to the argument – not simply because a desublimated appetitive body seems to be the engine of economic modernity (as Lawrence Birkin argues), but because each new development in media seems to involve the grafting in of fresh productive and receptive capacities.[23] Again, it is important to notice the gendered status of the body here: repeatedly we see a flow of energies – often conceived of as excessive, wasteful, unearned – which is coded as 'feminine', opposed to disciplines coded as masculine. This ranges from the critique of the film star to Skinner's attack on Stein's language; from Yeats's surgical excision of the feminine to the stabilization of gender in Lili Elbe's sexual reassignment. It is towards a problematics of the commoditized body and the gender-politics of Modernism as a whole – the subject of so much recent work – that such examples direct our attention. We can also return, here, to a historicized version of Adorno's argument: if modernist writers often respond enthusiastically to, or incorporate, technology, an increasing cultural paranoia comes to surround popular forms of mechanical reproduction, generating a situation in which the critic struggles to define its effects in progressive terms – for example in the attempts of Sigfied Krakauer and Walter Benjamin to characterize modern life and the cinema by terms of their 'shock' effects.

This book is divided into four parts, each of two chapters, which are designed to reflect some of the ways in which the modern body is resolved into different systems, fragmented and augmented, and reintegrated via technologies which may be surgical or representational. Part 1, 'The regulation of energies', considers flows of energy and nutrition through the body, with a chapter on the electrification of the body and another on the regulation of consumption and waste. The first chapter of Part 2, 'Reshaping the body', examines the issue of the body–machine interface in terms of prosthetics, and offers something like a historical and theoretical context for the book as a whole; it examines the replacement of bodily parts, organ-extension theories, and the organologies of war and advertising. The second chapter in this part examines physical culture in relation to gender. Part 3, 'Technologies of gender', deals with the increasingly interventionist gender technologies of the twentieth century, characterized by hormone-therapies, rejuvenation operations, and early transsexual surgery. Each of these issues is related to literary texts via a range of linkages, from writing about the body to the stimulation of the authorial corpus; from technologies of writing and representation to fears of the impact of those technologies. Part 4, 'Interruption and suture', deals in a systolic and diastolic fashion with experimental procedures at the very limits of perceptual organization: with automatic writing and its conceptualization, and with the cinematic apparatus which, with the coming of sound, attempts to reintegrate the fragmented modalities of two separate technologies, offering a commercialized total prosthesis which disappoints modernist hopes for the silent film.

PART I

The regulation of energies

CHAPTER ONE

Electrifying the body

'I know a man that went to see an electrocution', Henny said through half-closed mouth, 'I don't know what he went to see.'

Christina Stead, *The Man Who Loved Children*[1]

Here are two stories about electricity and death. The first concerns an execution in Augusta, Maine, where, in January 1835, Joseph Sanger was hanged, having poisoned his wife. As a local historian remarks, 'the events that followed . . . were remarkable by any standard'.[2] His body was taken from the gallows by friends who tried to revive it by 'galvanic means', paralleling Frankenstein's revivification of dead flesh in Mary Shelley's novel.[3] The attempt was unsuccessful, though it is nice to imagine that the scientific well-wishers got the odd threatening muscular twinge. They gave up and buried him. The second story is also of an execution, this time at Auburn Prison in New York on 6 August 1890. The prisoner was William Kemmler, who was to be the first man to die in the electric chair. The impending execution had been the occasion of much controversy. The *New York Times* commented: 'Here is a man to be legally killed by electricity, still a new enough force to furnish an almost unploughed field for scientific discovery', adding, a day later, 'There has been so much talk of the killing of Kemmler here that his death has come to be looked upon, not exactly as the end of a life, but rather as the climax of the long contest that has been going on over the beginning of electrical execution.'[4] A crowd of over a thousand followed the scientists and official observers to the prison. The execution went badly; the voltage used was too small, and the electrodes were applied inefficiently. To the horror of observers, the prisoner seemed to remain alive, though unconscious, following the first application of current. Eventually he was killed, after a further protracted dose. Newspapers the next day proclaimed that it was 'Far Worse Than Hanging'; overseas papers ridiculed this American innovation, 'a revolting exhibition' (pun unintended, presumably).[5] Despite the setbacks and the outrage, further electrocutions took place at Sing Sing the following July, and the use of the electric chair was established.

Both incidents are evidence of the nineteenth-century fascination with the application of electricity to the human body, for medical, scientific, and, ultimately, legal purposes. They also suggest a duality in electricity: seen as duplicating the motive forces of the nervous system and perhaps even the 'spark' of life itself, it was at the same time becoming part of a network of power which transcended the scale of the human body and could kill. Its mobile energies seemed like an index of modernity (particularly American modernity), as the enthusiastic social commentator Gerald Stanley Lee suggested in 1913, articulating its ability to connect the individual and the *polis*: 'We have the electricity – the life-current of the republican ideal – characteristically our foremost invention, because it takes all power that belongs to individual places and puts it on a wire and carries it to all places.'[6] This use of electricity to metaphorize power – as portable, networked, and flowing between individuals and the state – illustrates a habit of analogy with which we have become comfortable; indeed, Foucault's conception of power as network is cognate with turn-of-the-century physics.[7] What I wish to examine here is the cultural work done by such metaphors; the circuitry of desire which they generate – though we should note that the term 'generate', which we often use in cultural analysis, is itself contaminated by electrical thinking, by implications of a flow from a core and work at the extremities on the part of ideology. First, however, some history.

ELECTRIC PEOPLE

The invention of electric systems had a number of effects on perceptions of the body. Galvani's experiments in 1791 created widespread interest in the theory of nerve impulses. What Galvani called 'animal electricity' or 'nerveo-electric fluid' replaced the old idea of 'animal' or 'vital' spirits. While Vitalism – with its doctrine that life possesses separate properties from the rest of matter

– persisted throughout the nineteenth century, often incorporating electrical thinking, the emerging paradigm was thermodynamic, involving concepts of *kraft* or energy. According to Helmholtz, Spencer, and others, life could be resolved into a range of organized physical and chemical forces within the general context of a bioenergetic model – the idea, recently explored by Anson Rabinbach, of the 'human motor'.[8]

The *application* of electricity began early. Interest in electrotherapy was linked to technological developments: the invention of the Leyden jar sparked off the first medical experiments in Germany and Switzerland in the 1740s. By the 1780s, 'medical electricity had achieved a certain measure of official recognition in Britain'.[9] In the nineteenth century, interest was stimulated by the discovery of faradic (alternating) currents and of voltaic piles. The heterodox James Gully used galvanism as a 'stimulant' to the nervous system in the 1830s, like later practitioners suggesting that the characteristic nineteenth-century malady of nervous weakness could be cured with electricity's nerve-like energy.[10] Technique advanced to the point where the practioner could choose from a range of devices and impulses, applying them to stimulation points mapped in Hugo von Ziemssen's *Die Electricität in der Medizin* (1857) and described by Beard and Rockwell, the American authorities, as an 'Electro-therapeutical anatomy' (Figure 1). The development of neurology is closely linked to the growth of electrical science, with the tracing of neural pathways in the 1860s and 1870s. Imputs were matched with functions: galvanic (continuous) currents were 'sedative and pain-relieving'; faradic (variable) currents 'stimulating and nutritional'; sinusoidal currents produced 'natural' contractions.[11]

Electricity was also a fertile ground for popular 'fringe' medicine. Methodist founder John Wesley, in *The Desideratum; or, Electricity Made Plain and Useful* (1759), reported treating thousands; in France, Jean-Paul Marat, doctor and revolutionary, explored the effects of negative electricity. Popular electricity flourished in the nineteenth century with a variety of patent devices, galvanic belts, electric baths, for purposes including the control of headache, paralysis, the stimulation of organs, skin, and muscles, urinary and sexual problems, constipation, the treatment of hysteria[12] (and so on: in the 1980s Margaret Thatcher's energy was reportedly sustained by electric baths). The pseudo-scientific

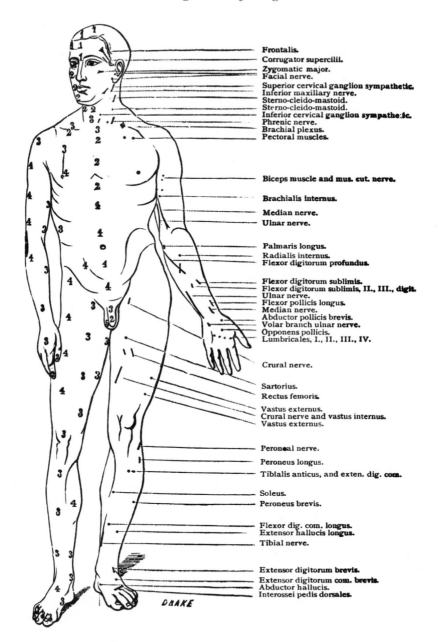

Frontalis.
Corrugator supercilii.
Zygomatic major.
Facial nerve.
Superior cervical ganglion sympathetic.
Inferior maxillary nerve.
Sterno-cleido-mastoid.
Sterno-cleido-mastoid.
Inferior cervical ganglion sympathetic.
Phrenic nerve.
Brachial plexus.
Pectoral muscles.

Biceps muscle and mus. cut. nerve.

Brachialis internus.

Median nerve.
Ulnar nerve.

Palmaris longus.
Radialis internus.
Flexor digitorum profundus.

Flexor digitorum sublimis.
Flexor digitorum sublimis, II., III., digit.
Ulnar nerve.
Flexor pollicis longus.
Median nerve.
Abductor pollicis brevis.
Volar branch ulnar nerve.
Opponens pollicis.
Lumbricales, I., II., III., IV.

Crural nerve.

Sartorius.
Rectus femoris.
Vastus externus.
Crural nerve and vastus internus.
Vastus externus.

Peroneal nerve.

Peroneus longus.

Tibialis anticus, and exten. dig. com.

Soleus.
Peroneus brevis.

Flexor dig. com. longus.
Extensor hallucis longus.
Tibial nerve.

Extensor digitorum brevis.
Extensor digitorum com. brevis.
Abductor hallucis.
Interossei pedis dorsales.

DRAKE

Figure 1 'Electro-therapeutical-anatomy'

exploitation of electricity continued to irritate: Sinclair Lewis's idealistic doctor, in *Martin Arrowsmith* (1925), scorns the 'New Ideal Panacaeatic Electric Cabinet' as window-dressing.[13]

In popular electro-vitalism, as in scientific thinking, electricity seemed to duplicate the body's fundamental energies. As early as 1774, its application to the apparently dead was suggested, and a Glasgow doctor attempted to revive the drowned. In 1819, a Dr Ure experimented with the body of a murderer, producing chest movements.[14] By the turn of the century, *Dr. Foote's Home Cyclopedia of Popular Medical, Social and Sexual Science* has sections on 'nervous telegraphy', 'animo-vital electricity', 'social magnetism', 'therapeutic electricity', and 'individual electricity'. The benevolent Dr Foote even suggests that married couples should sleep apart in order to avoid 'an equalization of those magnetic elements which . . . produce physical attraction and passional love'.[15] In such texts, a range of functions – biological, social, and sexual – become electrical.

Electricity also implied a bodily economy. A central figure in the conceptualization of bodily electricity is George M. Beard, author, with A. D. Rockwell, of the standard text on electric medicine in the 1870s and 1880s, and theorist of 'American Nervousness'. Beard was at the centre of widespread worries over nervous breakdown and the debilitating effects of modernity, and popularized the term 'neurasthenia' or nervous exhaustion – the most common psychiatric diagnosis of the late nineteenth century.[16] He saw the nervous system as powered by a fixed reservoir of energy. The fact that there is a limited quantity available is important: demands on nervous energy produced by the complexity of modern life and its speed of locomotion, work, and information flow (as well as factors like the use of stimulants, luxuries, the education of women) resulted in neurasthenia. The disease could manifest itself in a bewildering variety of symptoms: 'general malaise, debility of all functions, poor appetite, abiding weakness of the back or spine, fugitive neuralgic pains, hysteria, insomnia, hypochondriases, disinclination for consecutive mental labour'.[17] Beard's work influenced a range of psychologists (Silas Weir Mitchell in America, Henry Maudsley in England, Fernand Levillain in France), as well as Freud's early work on neurosis.[18] Non-medical writers on modernity also used the concept, including Max Nordau and Willy Hellpach, author of *Nervosität und*

Kultur (1902); the spectrum includes both anti-modernist critics of the effects of contemporary urban culture, and reformers who saw the possibility of a more fruitful integration of body and speeded-up world.[19] Neurasthenia permeates the literature of the period: evoked by Proust; its symptoms listed by Dreiser and Lewis; critiqued in Charlotte Perkins Gilman's *The Yellow Wallpaper*.

Beard singled out one person as most responsible for neurasthenia: Thomas Edison, with whom he worked, and whose marvellous inventions imposed numerous demands of 'change, speed, and complexity' on the nervous system.[20] His thinking is prosthetic: as the body is plugged into such external systems as the telegraph and railway, its energy needs rise (his treatments aimed to actively 'top up' energy by doses of electricity). The metaphor which he uses is of a generator powering 1,000 lamps, which dims if an additional 500 lamps are added – a detail which uncannily anticipates the Kemmler execution, and suggests that, in both cases, we are dealing with systems which comprise an integrated totality organized by polarities, resistances, and loads.[21]

Inevitably, rethinking physiology also altered conceptions of motivation. In post-Darwinian thought, sexual energy, conceived in electrical terms, becomes the force behind life, constantly seeking discharge. The body was resolved, in the new biophysics, into a system of impulses and flows, circuits, and blockages. A number of psychologists, like Moritz Benedikt, author of *Elektrotherapie* (1868), began to utilize models and procedures in which, as Frank Sulloway puts it, 'the human mind works by virtue of mental "forces" and "energies" following patterns of investment and displacement similar to those in a complicated electrical apparatus'.[22] Freud's theories are heavily electrical in this way, using a vocabulary of 'excitation', 'discharge', 'sexual current', which persists even as he moves away from physiological explanations.[23]

The impact of electricity on the image of the body also extends to more general perceptions of human nature. Electrical metaphors create a new sense of the body – as in *Frankenstein*, in which the boundaries between life and death are problematized. Chris Baldick argues that the 'twitchiness' and grotesquely driven nature of many Dickens characters is accentuated by their 'galvanism'.[24] Dickens, like many of his contemporaries (the Brownings, Tennyson, Harriet Martineau), was fascinated by mesmerism, which implies that bodily energies are part of a more extended field. Poe explores mesmerism, galvanism, and the electrical resuscitation of the dead; Emerson writes on the soul as a dynamo in 'Circles'; and Whitman sings the body electric, pulsating with democratic desire and attraction, in a way which reflects his interest in mesmerism.[25] But literary texts do more than simply reproduce such metaphors. For a range of modernist writers, electro-vitalism provides the energies of modernity; a science both of the body and, following Whitman, of literary transmission. Ezra Pound, who sometimes used the pseudonym 'Helmholtz', deploys electromagnetism in his theories of the 'Vortex', noted that 'the electric current gives light where it meets resistance' – literary production is incandescence.[26] The work of Dora Marsden, Lawrence, Williams, and others is permeated by electricity, generating a world pulsating with energy.[27] It offers a model for communication, for the energies of the text, transferred via a series of relays to the reader. Modernist texts are electrical, plugging into a scientific rhetoric which channels flows of energy and information.

Other effects of electricity on the literary metaphorization of the body are more general. We could postulate that it speeds up the pace of desire and allows it to flow more promiscuously through social networks – leaping past barriers and across distances, as in Pound's likening (in 1912) of sexual energy to a spark jumping a gap, even piercing 'a heavy book cover'; or reappearing as a sublimated radio-like energy 'in the invisible aether'.[28] And if passions could 'flare' and 'blaze' under gaslight, with electricity they are instantaneous: 'turned on', 'cut off', 'short-circuited', or be 'in full current' – in Stevie Smith's *Novel on Yellow Paper* (1936) – or a flood of 'electric passion' from one person to another, as in Lawrence's *Women in Love* (1921).[29] Desire may be figured as the 'circle of warm, delightful fire and lamplight' which Katherine Mansfield describes in 'Psychology' (1919), but such terms become progressively more nostalgic. Mansfield herself sees desire as electric in 'Bliss'.[30]

Lawrence's use of electrical metaphors suggests their easy applicability to sexual desire: electricity and magnetism are, as heterosexual desire is said to be, bipolar. It is even possible to suggest that gender is bipolar on the model of electricity and magnetism rather than vice versa, since (if one accepts Thomas Laqueur's periodization) the shift towards a fully bipolar model of

gender is coextensive with the development of theories of electricity.[31] Otto Weininger's *Sex and Character* (1906) conceives the germ plasm in these terms; a later writer explicitly argues that electricity involves two sex-like 'affections of forces' on the atomic level: 'the female comparatively inert and passive and body-producing . . . the positive electricity or nucleus. The male, its energetic and revolving negative counterpart' – an atomic version of Patrick Geddes's 'active' sperm and 'passive' egg.[32] If Freud also tends to see desire as electrical discharge, that may help explain why, as Judith Butler argues, he sees our original bisexuality as 'the coincidence of two sexual desires within one psyche' so that, 'within Freud's thesis of primary bisexuality, there is no homosexuality, and only opposites attract'. At the same time, electric desire also suggests a shared, universal source of energy, as Lawrence Birkin argues; rendering inevitable the extension of sexuality to women and children and its progressive individualization.[33]

We can see some of these effects at work in the shaded contrasts between the descriptions of emotions in the following two examples, the first a description of Verena in James's *The Bostonians* (1886):

these words, the most effective and penetrating he had uttered, had sunk into her soul and worked and fermented there . . . They had kindled a light in which she saw herself afresh and, strange to say, liked herself better than in the old exaggerated glamour of the lecture-lamps . . . She was to burn everything she had adored; she was to adore everything she had burned . . . It was simply that the truth had changed sides; that radiant image began to look at her from Basil Ransom's expressive eyes. She loved, she was in love – she felt it in every throb of her being.[34]

The figures here are those of penetration, fermenting/transmuting and burning ('the fire of her spirit' in the same paragraph); of a fluid and of its concomitant lighting-effects, the oil or gas-lamp. Polarity is present ('the truth had changed sides'), but simply as a transfer of position. Verena – whom, as Richard Godden argues, threatens to enter the 'promotional' or public economy of stage-lighting – is incorporated by Basil within a domestic love-exchange.[35] The second example is from a book written twenty years later, H. G. Wells's *Tono-Bungay* (1909). This is at the end of the affair between Beatrice and George:

'I've wanted ————' she went on. 'I've talked to you in the nights and made up speeches. Now when I want to make them I'm tongue-tied. But to me it's just as if the moments we have had lasted for ever. Moods and states come and go. To-day my light is out . . .'

To this day I cannot determine whether she said or whether I imagine she said 'chloral'. Perhaps a half-conscious diagnosis flashed it on my brain. Perhaps I am the victim of some perverse imaginative freak of memory, some hinted possibility that scratched and seared. There the word stands in my memory, as if it were written in fire.[36]

Here, the pulse is faster; a series of flashes, as well as the reference to chloral (morphine, a 'toxin' often linked to neurasthenia) suggests the context of what Wells calls 'the conductivity of the nerves'.

One metaphorical source which has received little attention is the first major application of electrical technology: electric lighting, and the development of the utilities and grids which supported it. With Edison's production of the domestic light bulb in 1879, and the introduction of arc-lights in public spaces in the 1880s, a revolution took place. What was involved was more than just a technological shift; it suggests an alteration in what Félix Guattari calls the 'social chemistry of desire', the means through which desire and motivation are articulated and transmitted. If the social and the individual body are intimately related, then the programmes for the wiring of houses that gathered pace around the turn of the century find parallels in the wiring of individual bodies, and in the way in which states of attraction, animation, incandescence are figured. But a more extended example is needed to explore the flow of desire in an electric world.

LIGHTING AND DESIRE IN 'SISTER CARRIE'

Theodore Dreiser explores, perhaps better than any other writer, material culture at the turn of the century. His work describes changes in technology, finance, production, and consumption, as well as shifts in gender and class relations.[37] There is a textbook description of neurasthenia in his novel *Jennie Gerhardt* (1911) – note the stress on the 'flash' of media:

The tremendous and complicated development of our material civilization, the multiplicity, and variety of our social forms, the depth, subtlety, and sophistry of our imaginative impressions, gathered, remultiplied and disseminated by such agencies as the railroad, the express and the post office, the telephone, the telegraph, the newspaper, and, in short, the whole machinery of social intercourse – these elements of existence combine to produce what may be termed a kaleidoscopic glitter, a dazzling and confusing phantasmagoria of life that wearies and stultifies the mental and moral nature. It induces a sort of intellectual fatigue through which we see the ranks of the victims of insomnia, melancholia, and insanity constantly recruited. Our modern brain-pan does not seem capable as yet of receiving, sorting, and storing the vast arm of facts and impressions which present themselves daily. The white light of publicity is too white.[38]

Electricity and electric lighting were among the subjects he covered as a journalist. A piece on 'Electricity in the Household' dealt with H. Barrington Cox, inventor of the thermo-electric generator, a technological dead-end which in 1899 seemed to promise a privatization of electricity generation: 'the securing of electricity direct from coal . . . has been carried to the point where an ordinary dwelling-house can be illuminated by it with incandescent lights'.[39] Rather than being in the control of the two giant American corporations, electricity would be domesticated. Moreover, the thermo-electric generator offered a means of mediating between heat-based systems and the new electrical technology; a transition which Dreiser's *Sister Carrie* (1900) explores.

Sister Carrie describes the newly lit world of the department store and the theatre in Chicago – the city whose World's Fair in 1893 had a huge 'Electricity Hall', and which, by 1910, had the best power system in the world. Throughout, there is a circuit of lights which are switched on, off, on again; which attract, destroy; enliven some, and leave others in darkness. The differentiation of light/lustre and darkness/poverty is constantly present, particularly in the metaphor of the 'light in the eyes'. The lightening of an eye is so much a cliché that it is easy to miss the way that in *Sister Carrie* it acquires a signalling function and informs the novel's structure: it is in the eye that the novel's concern with the specular meets with its analysis of the commerce of the heart, of bodies and the gazes which commodify them, the switching of allegiances, and the transfer of energies. The light in the eye moves, in the course of the novel, from the private and domestic sphere to the public stage, the theatrical market-place within which the power to radiate desire can be exploited.

The intercourse of eyes begins when Carrie meets Drouet, who is to be her first lover, on a train: she looks at him 'out of the side of her eye' and flirts.[40] On arrival in Chicago 'She smiled into his eyes' (11) before parting. This eye-play parallels the developing contrast between the 'burden of toil' and a vision of a lighted world of material possessions: 'Says the soul of the toiler to itself, "I shall soon be free. I shall be in the ways and the hosts of the merry. The streets, the lamps, the lighted chamber set for dining are for me"' (10). Carrie's sister is, literally, lack-lustre, 'cold reality . . . No world of light and merriment' (11). The tragic structure of the novel is figured within this exchange of light and darkness. Carrie's movement towards 'that gilded state which she had so much craved' (377) is a journey into the light of gilded dining-rooms, but also of public acclaim, of representation as spectacle. The play is which her acting career begins is an effect of lights: supported by businessmen who are 'the lights of a certain circle', and orchestrated by Hurstwood, 'a light among them' (178–80). Carrie quickly masters the medium: 'The fact that such ability should reveal itself in her – that they should see it set forth under such effective circumstance – framed almost in massy gold and shone upon by the appropriate lights of sentiment and personality, heightened her charm for them' (187). It is through the management of light-effects that she plots her upward path. After the play, the balance of power changes: Drouet 'was feeling the shadow of something which was coming' and his question about the source of her dramatic power releases 'a flood of light on the matter of superiority. She began to see the things which he did not understand' (198–9). Drouet departs into 'shadow' as Hurstwood, radiating power, moves into the light.

Yet, ultimately, Hurstwood's fate is the same. In New York, dispossessed of his comfortable Chicago position, he falters: 'Bad thoughts had put a shade into his eyes which did not impress others favourably' (344). At his nadir in the final chapter, he walks the street: 'At Broadway and 39th Street was blazing, in incandescent fire, Carrie's name. "Carrie Madenda", it read, "and the Casino Company". All the wet, snowy sidewalk was bright with this radiated fire. It was so bright that it attracted Hurstwood's gaze. He looked up, and then at a large gilt-framed poster-board on which was a fine lithograph of Carrie, life-size . . . "That's you", he said at last, addressing her' (493–4). If Carrie ends up as a commodified image at the centre of radiated light, Hurstwood ends in a 'small, lightless chamber' where he dies in 'blackness, hidden from view' (472, 499).

The novel is thus structured around the polarities of light and darkness. There is an almost mathematical precision in the rise of Carrie and the fall of Hurstwood within what is sometimes called an hour-glass construction, but which could, perhaps more aptly, be related to the sinusoid of alternating current; it is as if a polarity is at work, within a closed system like Beard's. The exchange of energies is figured as economics – the movement of bills from safe or purse is listed with precision – but more fundamentally in terms of light and desire (Carrie ends up transcending money: she is given free accommodation to advertise a hotel and has little cash for Hurstwood on their last meeting). One example: Hurstwood returns home to find it dark. Carrie has moved out, but Hurstwood, not realizing this, lights the gas-fire and sits down before finding her note. He walks from room to room, lighting the gas as he does so, and then returns to the kitchen 'leaving the lights ablaze' (439). Its domestic warmth has vanished. He sells the furniture and sets off for a cheap hotel. Carrie, meanwhile, sits in her comfortable room, his 'gloom' behind her. She finds a notice of her part in the theatre pages, reading it 'with a tingling body' (442). Soon after, she gains a more important role as the 'little Quakeress' and upstages the chief comedian, the appositely named 'Mr. Sparks'.

The contrast between light and darkness is not simply an opposition of structuring polarities, it is a product of the novel's figuration of desire. Light is bodily presence in those who can 'radiate' or 'flash' energy. The competition for Carrie which takes place between Drouet and Hurstwood involves attempts to almost literally 'turn her on'. The masculine necessity to direct Carrie's gaze – towards books, sights, commodities – is emphasized where she is captured or transferred between men. This most scopic of novels begins with a whisper in the ear; but a whisper which directs the eye: '"That", said a voice in her ear, "is one of the prettiest little resorts in Wisconsin"' (4). Hurstwood's attractiveness is based on his ability to create an interchange of atmosphere and light: 'Carrie was dwelling in the atmosphere which this man created for her. Already she was enlivened and suffused with a glow.' She cannot resist 'the glow of his temperament, the light of his eye'. Indeed, there is little to Hurstwood but his eyes: 'His face and body retained utter composure. Only his eyes moved and they flashed a subtle, dissolving fire' (204–7). Such effects produce an almost tropic fascination in the novel. Consider the scene in which Carrie leaves Hurstwood to go to a nightclub with her swell neighbours, the Vances. The New York dining-room is, like the stage, defined by lighting: 'On the ceilings were colored traceries with more gilt, leading to a centre where spread a broad circle of light – incandescent globes mingling with glittering prisms and stucco tendrils of gilt. The floor was of a reddish hue, waxed and polished, and in every direction were mirrors – tall, brilliant, bevel-edged mirrors, reflecting and re-reflecting forms, faces and candelabra a score and a hundred times' (332). The technology (incandescents, i.e. electric lights) is specified, despite the fact that in the 1890s the gas-mantle was a common alternative. The contrast between the two technologies is carefully defined, with gaslight being associated with Hurstwood and his wish to retain Carrie within the muted lighting of domestic settings. The melodrama in which she first appears is Augustin Daly's popular *Under the Gaslight* (1867); 'gaslight' signals the sentimentalism of her suitors. In contrast her ability (as one critic puts it) to 'electrify' her audience, to turn her talent into a commodified product, a 'name in lights', signals the liberation of desire from the domestic sphere and its deployment in the marketplace.[41] The 'flare of the gas-jets' is part of the evocation of 'theatre' in the amateur production, but the building itself is aligned with nearby 'brightly lighted shops', anticipating the later blaze of Carrie's name on Broadway. Hurstwood, in contrast, kills himself with 'a small gas jet'; he dies by that outmoded technology whose passing – and whose obsolescence in the scheme of modern desire – the novel registers.

Carrie's connection with light is almost comically present in her final 'private' destiny, as well as in her public status. In the penultimate chapter it appears that she may be heading for marriage with Bob Ames. His return is announced by Mrs Vance:

'Do you know', she said one day, 'Cousin Bob is making quite a strike out west. You remember Cousin Bob, don't you?'

'Of course', said Carrie, turning eyes that showed that they could lighten clearly. 'What has he done?'

'Oh, he has invented something or other – I forget what. It's a new kind of light, though.' (478)

Mrs Vance continues that 'He's just as bright as he can be.' Ames, too, is a light-effect: his white shirt-front makes 'the line of his face seem brown and strong'. At table they all talk 'lightly'. Their love-

making is another dialogue of lights, eyes, and currents: 'Their
eyes had met, and for the first time Ames felt the shock of sympa-
thy, keen and strong.' An intimate moment involves Ames's
description of Carrie's eyes as those of a comedy-actress: 'There's
a shadow about your eyes, too, which is pathetic. It's in the depth
of them, I think.' The climax of his meditation on self-regulation
is 'Every person according to his light' (485).

This declaration can be brought to bear on Walter Benn
Michaels's argument that Robert Ames's 'anti-materialistic' sobri-
ety is an anachronism in the novel, where identity is a product of
the manipulation of image and its projection. But there is more to
Ames's attempts to educate Carrie than stolid idealism. Ames is an
Edison, the inventor of a light.[42] His insight into her skill as an
actress is based on being able to see her as an object of desire
already present to an audience, not simply as someone he might
desire; he understands her as part of a technology of dissemination (on meeting they say that they have been reading newspaper
accounts of each other). The only difference between them is his
attempt to moralize their roles: she should 'express the world's
sorrows and longings . . . You and I are but mediums.' But this is
because, without the external world, her powers atrophy: 'The
moment you forget their value to the world, and they cease to
represent your own aspirations, they will begin to fade' (485–6).
They are part of a cycle of generation and exchange, of reciproca-
tion and reflection, which must be regulated. Carrie is more than
simply a human being, a body; she becomes a desiring-machine
whose energies are understood by the engineer. That is the real
scandal of *Sister Carrie*, that a human being should became a system
for sustaining and disseminating desire. Dreiser's novel looks
forward to the Hollywood-star system, when the electric image
began to rule the world.

ADDICTIVE PLEASURES

The fact that desire and bodily energy is figured in electric terms
is indicative of the regulation and stimulation of desire in modernism (in a subsequent chapter we see cinema described as 'electricity in its relation to the arts'). A problem which emerges in *Sister
Carrie* is that of addiction, a reversal which enables the product to
dominate the person. The possibility that electric desire might be

transferable and addictive is explored in J. Maclaren Cobban's *Master of His Fate* (1890), a novel indebted to *Dr Jekyll and Mr Hyde*, as well as Maturin's *Melmoth the Wanderer* (1820), Balzac's 'The Elixir of Long Life' (1830), and Eliot's *The Lifted Veil* (1859). It begins with two mysterious cases attended by Dr Lefevre, who has studied at the Salpétrière under 'the famous Dr Charbon' (modelled on Charcot): 'Like the great Charbon, he made nervous and hysterical disorders his speciality, in the treatment of which he was much given to the use of electricity.'[43] He has some of the power of touch of the mesmerist, as well as subscribing to up-to-date theories of electrical treatment – reflecting Charcot's work on hypnosis as neo-mesmerism or biomagnetism.[44]

In both cases, the patients delivered to his London hospital have had the life-force drained out of them by the touch of an elderly foreigner. Lefevre restores them by an electrical 'psycho-dynamics'. The first victim, a handsome young Dragoon, is treated with 'a simple machine . . . on the model of the electric cylinder of Dubois-Raymond, and worked on the theory that the electricity stored in the human body can be driven out by the human will along a prepared channel into another human body' (55–6). The second victim is the beautiful Lady Mary Fane (to whom Lefevre is later engaged); here he contrives a new method using waves modulated by a tuning fork, anticipating electro-vibration techniques popular a decade later.

The main plot concerns Lefevre's relation with the mysterious Julius Courtney, a brilliant student with him in Paris, now a famous talker at the club, a man who 'could do anything he chose' (5), but in fact does nothing but practise, as Wilde's Lord Henry was to do a year later, a decadent philosophy of connoisseurship in the art of living: ' "To live", said Julius, "is surely the purpose of life. Any smaller, any more obvious purpose, will spoil life, just as it spoils Art" ' (24). Julius goes on to compare his life to a sculpture or poem. With an inevitability which gives the plot a certain leadenness, Lefevre discovers that the old and mysterious foreigner is Julius. He has learned to suck the electric energy from others, becoming a degenerate electro-vampire, driven from victim to victim in search of energy. His brilliance waxes and wanes as the 'charge' runs down; at the novel's climax on his yacht on the Thames he accepts only enough from Lefevre to finish his story before throwing himself overboard.

For all that the novel includes two heterosexual pairings (Julius and Lefevre's sister Nora; Lefevre and Lady Mary), the subtext, as in *Dracula,* is a chain of homoerotic desire. Lefevre and his fellow clubmen are charmed by the mysterious Julius: by the 'lustrous softness' of his hair, by the smoothness of his skin, by his 'bright vivacity of eye' and 'eloquent flashes' (19). In the encounter of the old Julius and the Dragoon, the former offers a cigar camply named 'Joy of Spain', and 'exercised a charm over the younger such as he had never known before in the society of any man'; the scene culminates in the energy-sucking touch on the knee, in which 'a thrill shot through him as if a woman had touched him' (64, 66). Homosocial interchanges are also apparent in the circulation of energy from Lady Mary to Julius, then from Lefevre to Lady Mary.

Yet the energies here also relate to women and what they engender in men. Julius tells us that the energies he steals are the life-force, part of 'that simple, passionate, essential nature which lies beneath the thickest lacquer of refinements in our civilized societies' (227). *Master of His Fate* struggles with the radical Darwinian idea noted earlier: that all desire may be *equal.* Lefevre sees Lady Mary as an elevated soul 'above passion', and, in treating her, he postulates that 'the electric force of a man varied vitally from that of a woman' (128). This theory is refuted: the transfer of energies from a nurse fails, and Lefevre comes up with his 'electrical transfusion' technique using a vibrating wire, pumping his *own* energies into her. The text oscillates between a model in which energies are exchanged between, and policed by, men, and a more general model of desire.

The addictive paradigm is also present in *Sister Carrie.* To suggest that it is a novel about addiction may seem odd, since there is no obvious addict. Nevertheless, addiction is central to its depiction of desire and the city – firstly, in Hurstwood's decline. Though he has 'no vices' (396), his closeness to the drink trade hints at a displaced alcoholism. He manages an establishment in Chicago; later he works at less salubrious bars in New York, where there is constant reference to the possibility of a job from the brewery. The pattern of his decline, with his inability to energize himself, his shabbiness, poverty, and hopeless anger shading into apathy and death, seems alcoholic – perhaps unspeakably so and 'invisible', as the disease often is. Certainly he is addicted to his old life, to an established pattern of pleasure. At the mid-point of his decline, he escapes a fight with Carrie and has an expensive dinner he can ill afford: 'Like the morphine fiend, he was becoming addicted to his ease. Anything to relieve his mental distress, to satisfy his craving for comfort' (373).

But there is a second, related, strand of addictive thinking in *Sister Carrie*, linked to what we have come to call the 'buzz' of the city rather than to its depletive effects:

> Walk among the magnificent residences, the splendid equipages, the gilded shops, restaurants, resorts of all kinds. Scent the flowers, the silks, the wines; drink of the laughter springing from the soul of luxurious content, of the glances which gleam like light from defiant spears; feel the quality of smiles which cut like glistening swords and of strides born of place and power, and you shall know of what is the atmosphere of the high and mighty . . . It is like a chemical reagent . . . A day of it to the untried mind is like opium to the untried body. A craving is set up which, if gratified, shall eternally result in dreams and death. (305)

Here, the city itself is addiction: the craving for light, luxury, commodities is a poison; the individual is 'plugged in' to its energies, desires, and rewards. Within this second addictive pattern, it is the upwardly mobile Carrie who is addicted, in her constant phototropism. The speeded-up and commoditized world is suggested by the first large electric sign on Broadway which Dreiser reported seeing in the mid-1890s, 1,500 lights flashing:

SWEPT BY OCEAN BREEZES

THE GREAT HOTELS

PAIN'S FIREWORKS

SOUSA'S BAND

SEIDL'S GREAT ORCHESTRA

THE RACES

NOW — MANHATTAN BEACH — NOW[45]

An example of similar effects in the novel is a passage which follows the description of a restaurant cited above. Notice here the branded commodities and the waiter's 'yes', paralleling the sign's 'now':

> The tables were not so remarkable in themselves, and yet the imprint of 'Sherry' upon the napery, the name of 'Tiffany' upon the silverware, the name of 'Haviland' upon the china, and over all the glow of the small red-shaded candelabra, and the reflected tints of the walls on garments and faces, made them seem remarkable. Each waiter added an air of

exclusiveness and elegance by the manner in which he bowed, scraped, touched and trifled with things. The exclusively personal attention which he devoted to each one, standing half-bent, ear to one side, elbows akimbo, saying 'soup – green turtle, yes – One portion, yes. Oysters – certainly – half-dozen – yes. Asparagus! Olives – yes'. (332–3)

There are thus two types of addiction in *Sister Carrie*: that associated with alcohol and degeneration; and that associated with the lustre of the modern city and its commodity culture. In this and other novels in the period, there is a shift in the paradigm of addiction, from the romantic portrayal of degeneration to a modernist analysis of commodification and desire. In the earlier paradigm, the addictive substance's price, distribution, etc., is less a focus than the 'weakness' of the individual (with a fascination with the squalid areas of the city where the 'fallen' congregate). The result of opium addiction in literary terms is the dream-visions which represent an Oriental decadence. In the second addictive paradigm, emerging in *Sister Carrie*, the 'content' of the addiction, its flow into the body, is identical to its mode of presentation; like the neurasthenic, the addict simply plugs in and becomes part of what she desires.

It is not as if there is an alternative. In Arnold Bennett's *Riceman Steps* (1923), the *refusal* of electric desires is figured as itself anorexic and pathological: the grim bookseller, Mr Earlforward, constantly polices 'the burning of electric current' and will not replace bulbs; he disapproves of his new bride, Violet, having his house and shop vacuum-cleaned (a new technology) as an 'insane expenditure of electricity', frightening evidence of 'the potentialities of [her] energetic brain'.[46] He has no telephone, and his dim shop is contrasted with the well-lit and thriving modern emporium next door. Earlforward effectively starves himself and Violet to death, embodying the refusal of modernist energies as a paranoid defence of the self. As Eve Kosofsky Sedgwick has recently argued, in the twentieth century, addiction – 'sexual compulsiveness', 'co-dependency' – becomes a seemingly inescapable paradigm applicable to all desires, and to the exercise of will or choice itself.[47]

The realist mode plays an important a role in the formation of this discourse of addiction because of its commitment to the depiction of individuals in terms of tropisms and biological laws. In *Social Statics* (1851), Spencer had struggled with this opposition between individual will (which drives the Darwinian struggle) and the social contract: 'the ultimate man will be one whose private requirements coincide with public ones. He will be that manner of man, who in *spontaneously* fulfilling his own nature, *incidentally* performs the functions of a social unit; and yet is only enabled to fulfil his own nature, by all others doing the like.'[48] This uneasy formula figures social cohesion as a by-product; simultaneously declaring its centrality as a precondition. The discussion of Eugene's errant desires in Dreiser's *The Genius* (1915) is similarly paradoxical. 'Tendencies', the author comments, 'are involved in the chemistry of one's being', and what appears to be will can on close inspection be like the operation of protozoa, 'the inevitable action of definite chemical and physical laws'.[49] Dreiser nevertheless pursues his analysis of his character's individual 'genius' and path through life in terms of a series of acts of will – a 'genius' which, even more paradoxically, expresses itself in the world of mass-tropisms, of advertising and magazine-production. The novel negotiates in this way between addiction and individual will, between the typical and the individual. But that, in turn, raises questions of regulation: what happens when such tropic desires – rendered inescapable *and* addictive in the naturalist novel – become transgressive, when their free flow threatens social order?

ELECTRIC DEATH

'The American constitution is more susceptible to electricity than the English or German.' So wrote Beard and Rockwell in 1884, defending the use of electricity for cases of hysteria.[50] If, on the one hand, electricity was used for treating 'hysteria' (variously pictured as a nervous lassitude or overexcitation), in 1890 it began to be used, in a technique supported by medical practitioners, for killing the judicially condemned. These two usages are connected within a disciplinary framework which seeks to regulate human energies within a set of external and internal practices. Electricity was used as early as the Georgian period 'to subdue unruly maniacs'. By 1907, it was being used for investigation of the self, Hugo Münsterberg using a plethysmograph and galvanometer to administer a lie-detector test to the mass-murder Harry Orchard.[51] The development of electro-convulsive therapy by Ugo Cerletti in 1938 represented an extension of such procedures: the high voltages of ECT were designed to deaden areas of neurological confusion, to 'kill' a pathological part of the self in order to save the rest, just as the electric chair removed a social danger. In fact, the development of E C T was inspired by techniques which Cerletti saw used on pigs in Italian slaughterhouses; its conceptual model *is* the electric chair.[52]

If we see the electric chair as the 'treatment' of a pathological component of society, a 'clean' way of solving the problem of transgressive behaviour, it is part of a continuum of applications. As part of the emerging technologies of medical control, electricity is applied to a variety of subjects (hysterical women, criminals, schizophrenics), using techniques which now seem overtly punitive.[53] The procedures developed in medicine were adopted for the electric chair, including wet sponges and skull-caps – Beard and Rockwell's 'Central Galvanization' technique is suggestive in this respect (Figure 2). Indeed, Rockwell (Beard had died) was asked to advise on technique and apparatus for the first killings in 1890–1, writing an account which displays a mixture of scientific fascination and moral disgust.[54]

The possibility of an 'electric death' was, once again, linked to technological developments: with the use of high-voltage alternating current for transmission, electricity became more dangerous. The first accidental death in America was in 1881; and one of the main advocates of the electric chair in New York, the dentist, Alfred Southwick, began his campaign after seeing a man killed instantly by a live wire.[55] The move from accidental to judicial death was rapid, and produced a curious inversion: the word 'electrocution', which we think of neutrally as signifying *any* death by electricity, in fact emerged from the search for a term for the judicial technique used on William Kemmler in 1890. Modelled on 'execution', it carries a forgotten punitive impulse.

The association of the rapidly expanding electric systems with death was particularly potent because the first electrocution was implicated in (and in a sense produced by) the fight for the monopoly over electricity supply in the USA. Kemmler was, famously, caught up in the 'Battle of the Systems', the dispute between Thomas Edison's company with its D C systems and the Westinghouse A C systems. The current used for the executions was A C, provided by Westinghouse generators surreptitiously acquired via an intermediary in Rio. The reason for the subterfuge was Westinghouse's total opposition to its equipment being used for

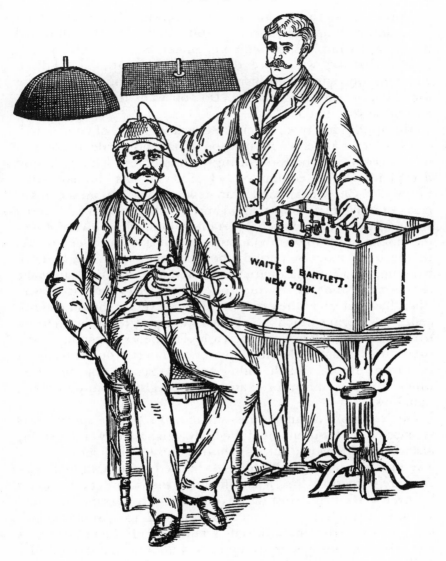

Figure 2 'Central Galvanization'

this purpose (to the extent of secretly hiring a lawyer to defend Kemmler in his appeals), because of the suggestion, promulgated by the rather unpleasant mining engineer, Harold P. Brown, and others, that AC was more dangerous than DC. The Edison company, who stimulated Brown's activities, attempted to exploit the situation with slogans like 'Do you want the executioner's current in your home?'[56]

The application of electricity to executions was, of course, part of a search for an 'efficient' method of state homicide, in contrast to the crude and body-distorting technologies of hanging and decapitation.[57] A committee, chaired by the humanitarian Elbridge T. Gerry, examined a range of options. We can see this as part of the Victorian reformation and systematization of the penal system. But perhaps more important is the way in which the new technology shifts the symbolic structure of state-produced death. In the early modern period, the deformation of the body in hanging, drawing, and quartering served as a theatrical spectacle representing the way in which offenders, particularly at treason trials, had disturbed the order of being.[58] Even in the nineteenth century – during which executions were progressively removed from the public sphere and increasingly repelled spectators – the spectator is distanced by ritual: power operates through an alienation from the pain of the other and that scopic objectification which Thomas Hardy, for example, still registered in describing hangings.

Electrocution changed this situation: a public spectacle is replaced by a chastisement of the body which silently and invisibly absorbs the individual into a scientific and technological system. Two provisions in the Bill which introduced electrocution in New York are suggestive: first, it specified that the victim's body should be given to medicine (institutions queued for tissue samples); and, secondly, the old dispensation of hanging was to be replaced by a semi-private ceremony with only scientific and official observers and a ban on newspaper accounts. So little information was officially released that at the second set of electrocutions (four men at Sing Sing) a Vatican-like system of coloured smoke was used to signal each death to the press. The only other signal was a dimming of the prison lights: as Arnold Beichman reports of Kemmler's death, 'the execution was to take place before 7am, for it was feared that the 1,200 convicts at Auburn would be unduly disturbed by a sudden shut down of the electric power while they were at work in the machine shops'.[59] This *topos*, repeated in Dreiser's account of electrocution and elsewhere, again emphasizes that the death becomes part of a total system whose purpose is general: industrial and domestic as well as disciplinary; and used, above all, for the conveying of information.[60] A related detail reinforces the point, as well as echoing George Beard's description of the body as a generator driving 1,000 lamps: the failure of the first attempt to electrocute Kemmler may have been attributable to the drain created by the bank of lights used to signal the system's working.[61]

Death, then, is a matter of information, and the debate on electric death included a battle over information. The attempt to seal the prison failed: a Western Union telegraph office was wired in opposite, and the published extended descriptions of Kemmler's execution were defiantly illegal. In fact, the reporting ban stimulated interest, producing hundreds of column inches, and causing the anti-publicity law to be withdrawn. The effect was to make executions media events rather than public ceremonies, reported via the wires in London, Paris, and Berlin. Death, at the heart of a technological apparatus within the body, becomes an invisible cipher and so is distanced from the public, whilst at the same time being made available to a wider audience via an information technology. It was this simultaneous effacement and incorporation of death which William Dean Howells objected to in his 1904 article 'State Manslaughter'.[62] He caustically describes how 'the culprit would be cheerfully seated, somewhat as the subject of photography is, and assuming as cheerful or as submissive an expression as possible, would be thrilled into the other world with the touch of a button, or the turn of a key, by the hand of a scientific gentleman, or at least an educated electrician, on the other side of a wall or screen'. He likens the electric chair to a telegraph which converts the body into a message ('beam me up Scotty!') – a possibility realized in Conan Doyle's story 'The Disintegration Machine' (1929), in which the molecular disperser which sends people into the ether (and, if desired, reassembles them) is a wired-up chair which the narrator compares to an electric chair he had seen at Sing Sing.[63] Howells contrasts this picture of 'killing by electricity as next to no killing at all' with accounts of bungled electrocutions.

In fact the 'thrilling' of the subject into eternity was precisely what was aimed at: 'the translation from life to death is quicker than thought' (Rockwell).[64] Electrical death allows the modern state to penetrate the mind. One of the most upsetting aspects of Kemmler's execution is his complicity in the 'scientific' process of his own extinction, his dignified desire to 'make it work' despite the fact that he is the victim of a technique so experimental that only in 1899 was the actual cause of death, heart stoppage, established.[65] Kemmler's body, subject of a corporate battle, turned over to science for autopsy, becomes the final object of a system which absorbs the individual into its structures, reproducing it as a signal, an on–off switch marking the limits of desire.

'AN AMERICAN TRAGEDY' AND THE ELECTRIC CHAIR

If the brave new world of electricity is, in general, figured positively in *Sister Carrie*, there is one point at which the high-voltage dangers of the system are suggested. Hurstwood's only real attempt to rally his fortunes is as a motorman for a streetcar company during a strike, in an episode often seen as unrelated to the rest of the novel. The streetcars are linked to an electric utility using the Westinghouse system. The passage in which Hurstwood is instructed in how to drive the car mirrors the novel's own patterning of rise and decline: '"You see that handle", [the instructor] said, reaching up to an electric cut-off, which was fastened to the roof. "This throws the current on or off. If you want to reverse the car, you turn it over here. If you want to send it forward, you put it over here"' (416). Hurstwood's attempt to 'reverse' his fortunes collapses, however, in the violence of the strike; his opinion that the strikers 'can't win' mirrors his own fate.[66]

Over twenty years later, Dreiser's work sees the implications of the equation of electric systems and the human body played out in deathly form. Dreiser had, in the meantime, consolidated his commitment to a biomechanical world-view, influenced by Jacques Loeb and others.[67] In his unpublished 'Notes on Life', probably begun shortly after *An American Tragedy* was published in 1925, he compares the body to the electrical system of a sawmill. He concludes, 'But what is electricity? . . . Can the eye see it? No. Can the nerves feel it? Yes, but fatally, if in too great volume . . . Will it cure anything? It is thought to stimulate tired muscles, but no one is sure. It is also thought by some to be life itself – the body or force of the organized totality of energy called *Life*.'[68] Ideas latent in *Sister Carrie* are expressed systematically: the body is implicated in industrial systems with which it shares its impulsions and dangers.

The first half of *An American Tragedy* is concerned, like *Sister Carrie*, with the production of desire, beginning with a family which 'presented one of those anomalies of psychic and social reflex and motivation such as would tax the skill of not only the psychologist but the chemist and physicist as well, to unravel'.[69] Dreiser plots attraction as electromagnetics, as in the description of Clyde and Rita: 'There was . . . a kind of ray or electron that intrigued and lured him' (227); or of Sondra: 'her effect on him was electric – thrilling' (242). Again, this is carried in the eyes: he meets Sondra with 'small white electric sparks in his eyes' (483). Like Carrie, Clyde encounters the need to switch lovers in order to rise in class. But, if the naturalistic novel plots an upward path, *An American Tragedy* takes a different route. After Roberta's 'murder', the focus shifts and narrative is largely replaced by a forensic discourse in which competing social discourses struggle to define the meaning of the act. The naturalist novel, with its focus on individual struggle, gives way to some of the generic uncertainty of the modernist text.

In particular, Dreiser explores the way in which Clyde's desires find a pattern which, unavailable in reality, is in a sense confirmed by the telos of 'the chair he had so often seen in his dreams' (870), the fetishized end-point of bodily electrification. The textual engines of the novel, that is, share a certain schematic interest in polarity, reversed polarity, discharge, which generates a plot which is *confirmed* by the electric chair; and which it must seek to humanize. Dreiser is particularly interested in the disposition of execution. The novel's Death House is based on Sing Sing, which he inspected. A small cell block incorporating the execution room, it is 'a room [which] by its arrangement, as well as by the rules governing the lives and actions of the inmates, was sufficient to bring about this torture'. It is a place defined by light and electricity: by night 'glistening incandescents of large size and power . . . flooded each nook and cranny of the various cells' (816). The integrated nature of the network is stressed: the electrocutions dim the lights in the cells, 'an idiotic or thoughtless result of having one electric system to supply the death voltage and the incandescence of this

and all other rooms' (830) – a familiar *topos*. The structure of the Death House is also interesting:

It was a room thirty by fifty feet, of stone and concrete and steel, and surmounted some thirty feet from the floor by a skylight. Presumably an improvement over an older and worse death house, with which it was still connected by a door, it was divided lengthwise by a broad passage, along which, on the ground floor, were twelve cells, six on a side and eight by ten each and facing each other . . .
There was, however, at the centre of this main passage – and dividing these lower cells equally as to number – a second and narrower passage, which at one end gave into what was now known as the Old Death House (where at present only visitors to the inmates of the new Death House were received), and at the other end into the execution room in which stood the electric chair. (816)

This space is divided by an axis with life (visitors) at one end, death at the other. Yet there is also a reverse polarity, since the visitors' room was the old Death House. And Dreiser describes how, prior to death, the prisoner is taken from his cell to one of the more private cells in the old Death House/reception area, before being 'compelled at the final moment, none-the-less (the death march), to retrace his steps along this narrower cross passage – and where all might see – into the execution chamber at the other end of it' (818). This same path must be walked to see visitors. The prisoner is tortured by a constant rehearsal of the movement from life to death, confronting the systemic 'reversed polarity' of the institution.

The end-point of the narrative is the electric chair which is given such iterative force: 'that chair' (815) which is the focus of the system. The specifier 'that' gestures towards it constantly: 'that cap', 'those straps' (830). In the first execution, Clyde sees it is: 'that man! His prayers! And now he was gone. His cell over there would be empty and another man would be put in it – to go too, later. Some one – many – like Cutrone, like himself – had been in this one – on this pallet. He sat up – moved to the chair. But he – they – had sat on that – too' (831). 'That' operates to assimilate all individual agents to a system in which all parts are repeatable (prayers, men). The death room, is never described, it is simply a door which Clyde enters. Electric death is, once again, an absorption of the body into the centre of a system, the moment visible only in the dimming lights.

An American Tragedy suggests the way in which judicial electrocution subordinates the human being to a system of production, reflecting, in the larger context of the novel, the irrelevance of guilt or innocence to the law (Clyde's 'real' crime is *planning* the death of Roberta: a thought-crime punished by technology 'faster than thought'). It is as if Dreiser is playing out the significance of the electrification of desire depicted in *Sister Carrie*, at the point where desire interacts with the systems that produce it. Clyde's desires, we are told throughout the novel, are simply those energized within him by a society which demands (as in Carrie's trajectory) upwards aspiration; but, at the point where those desires liberate dangerous energies, the system kills him. The chair answers a question raised by the novel: if all desire is electric, what is to prevent it becoming a free-floating energy, short-circuiting barriers of class, race, and morality in order to follow its desired pathway?[70] The answer, implicitly, is that such energies are not in fact 'private', that their control is a function of the state. Power flows through networks which must be regulated systematically. The text depicts both the pathways of individual power, and the containment of power within an apparatus – the same apparatus.

SHOCKING EXAMPLES

In their refiguring of human potential, Dreiser's texts stand at the threshold of that awareness of the body as circuitry which was, within his own lifetime, to enable Norbert Weiner's cybernetic models.[71] The dual aspects of the postmodern body – its exteriorization as body-map and circuitry; and its interiorization of the 'desiring machine' of fashion – is the product of that erosion of bodily boundaries which begins, in part, with the commodification of desire produced in *Sister Carrie* by the electric city. Dreiser's texts follow the linkages between the conceptualization of the body and personal, commercial, and state power, as do later novels like Pynchon's *Gravity's Rainbow*, with its plastic prosthesis and multinationals (*Gravity's Rainbow* includes the virtuoso episode of 'Byron the Bulb', the immortal lightbulb who escapes the global cartel which limits any bulb's life via the mysterious organization 'Phoebus').[72] These novels enact a circuit of energization and containment within which social and textual energies are both deployed (*Sister Carrie*) and controlled (*An American Tragedy*) –

processes which Deleuze and Guattari label 'deterritorialization', the production of desire according to new generative possibilities and flows, and 'reterritorialization', the containment of individual freedoms enabled by those new possibilities.[73]

A supplementary question, which has also to do with the status of *this* text, concerns the use to which such material as the electrification of human beings is put in literature. In the case of executions, we are used to the question being asked of Renaissance texts, since the New Historicism has found in the rituals of punishment potent examples of the theatricality of power and its inscription on the body. There is something to be suspicious of here: some of the rhetorical interest of New Historical texts comes from their use of shocking examples, sometimes moving towards violence (and 'subversion') as theatrical simulacra. But modernist texts share this danger in their incorporation of the powers of scientific and economic modernity. The reader is placed in an ambivalent position: energized by the text but 'thinking it' from the outside, as if at the point where power operates it were suddenly an external mechanism. We can refer this spectacle to the discussion of addiction earlier in this chapter. As Adorno suggests in 'The Stars Down to Earth', modern dependency can result in an identification with the systematic forces which engender it, projected as a 'higher' force which may be both inescapable and ironically distanced (his example is astrology). The electric forces of modernity may analogously be what Adorno refers to as not simply an 'expression of dependence', but an 'ideology of dependence', *demanding* rather than simply implying a sacrifice of the individual – a sacrifice which symbolically enacts fears of a loss of autonomy.[74] For Adorno, authoritarianism and paranoia are implicit in modern dependency.

If the specularization and virtuality of violence is a danger of our cultural criticism, that danger begins with the era of the electric chair. Kemmler's death, as we have seen, was converted to signal, telegraphed around the world in an on–off rhythm. Modernist representational techniques quickly incorporated electric death. Edison's one-minute film *Electrocuting an Elephant* (1903) was both an 'experiment' to show the power of his electrical apparatus, and a waste of flesh on a deliberately gigantic scale, staged for the camera. Since human executions could not be filmed, re-enactment was used: Edwin Porter's *The Execution of Czolgosz* (Edison,

1901) recreated the execution of the president's assassin at Auburn State Prison, with test bulbs on the chair and other paraphernalia of execution (it also included a section on the electrical spectacles at the Pan-American Exposition in Buffalo, where McKinley was killed).[75] Recent proposals to televise executions confirm this sense that the human body can only be fully incorporated into our virtual existence at the cost of its erasure. In a situation in which, in the wake of the temporary halt brought about by the Furman decision, America is killing criminals at an accelerating rate, identification with the structure that transmits the message rather than the human subject represents a horrifying possibility.

CHAPTER TWO

Waste products

'"Oh yes", she rejoined in answer to his exhibition of the degree in which what was before him did stir again to sweetness a chord of memory, "oh yes, food's a great tie, it's like language – you can always understand your own, whereas in Europe I had to learn about six others".'[1] These are the words of the nurse, Miss Mumby, in Henry James's unfinished novel *The Ivory Tower* (1917), having just fixed lunch for the novel's hero, Graham ('Gray') Fielder. She articulates a connection between food and language which stresses the distinction between the natal or natural and what one acquires by dint of education or choice. Gray, brought up in Europe, sees that 'the so many things she had learned to understand over there were not forms of speech but alimentary systems'. Alimentary systems, organized ways of eating which are like ways of talking, were very much part of James's thinking as he began *The Ivory Tower* in 1910. Formerly the famous eater-out whose large appetites embellish Elizabeth David's cookery-books ('the eggs were so good that I am ashamed to say how many of them I consumed . . . It was the poetry of butter, and I ate a pound or two of it'[2]), he had just abandoned the austere dietary procedures recommended by the American health reformer Horace Fletcher, which he had followed since 1904. What I want to consider is the nature of the link (if any) between writing and Fletcherizing in James's work – a link which is tantalizing because it does not seem to appear in any systematic way; because it always seems held at arm's-length by that simile, eating being 'like' a language. The notoriously abstract late James seems a limit case of the connections between bodily reform and literary texts – a case that we will build on in examining Eliot and other modernists.

HENRY JAMES, FLETCHERISM, AND REVISION

The charismatic and influential Horace Fletcher, 'The Great Masticator', was one of a number of American dietary reformers in the Progressive era who aimed to maximize bodily efficiency. Others include J. H. Kellogg, with whom he had rivalrous links in the period of his greatest activity, 1903–10, and, later, C. W. Post, inventor of Grape Nuts.[3] The aim of Fletcherism was complete mastication to the point where an automatic swallowing reflex ('nature's food filter') intervened. Chewing to a liquid would produce perfect digestion, 'internal antisepsis', and avoid over-consumption and the 'auto-intoxication' caused by waste lodging in organs. The theory of auto-intoxication, developed in England in the 1890s (and persisting since), took extreme forms: surgeon William Arbuthnot Lane favoured the removal of the colon; F. A. Hornibrook, author of *The Culture of the Abdomen*, wrote of the individual 'walking about with a putrefying mass of ordure in his colon, the decomposition of which is poisoning him constantly'.[4]

The most fundamental aim of Fletcherism was the elimination of waste. Fletcher was fond of the comparison between bodies and sewerage systems, practising internally what Victorian hygiene campaigners had advocated externally.[5] He was obsessed with the purity of Fletcherite faeces, which were to be like factory-made pellets, so well processed that they could cleanly be expelled into the hands and even mailed to interested parties (unlike Kellogg's bulky fibre-based diet, his dairy-intensive diet aimed at minimal throughput, producing 'Economic Digestion Ash'). He also claimed that his technique reduced weight and produced immense bodily resistance, demonstrated in fatigue tests against college athletes. Maximizing efficiency and minimizing waste, the Fletcherite body is like a scientifically managed factory. In his *Glutton or Epicure* (1899), Fletcher compares the body to a power-plant in which the engine is the heart, the dynamo the brain, and so on; a section on 'unprofitable management' making clear his ideological convergence with Frederick Taylor. As James Whorton points out, he also provided an economics of the body: 'deposits of food and rest, and withdrawals of exertion and self-neglect'.[6] This might seem to suggest the steady-state system of earlier psychologists (Herbert Spencer, for example, wrote that 'what in commercial affairs we call profit, answers to the excess of nutrition over waste in a living body'). But, like other progressive thinkers, including William James in 'The Energies of Men', Fletcher is more optimistic, aiming to boost energy levels through efficiency.[7]

Fletcher, dressed in his clinically white suits (Figure 3), lectured messianically to business and popular audiences. His boosters included progressives like John D. Rockefeller and the economist Irving Fisher (with whom he founded the Health and Efficiency League of America), S. S. McClure (of *McClure's Magazine*), and Bernarr Macfadden, publisher of *Physical Culture*. In England, Eustace Miles preached a similar doctrine in his journal *Healthward Ho!*.[8] Literary fans included Henry and William James, Upton Sinclair, who wrote books on fasting and diet, as well as his attack on the meat industry in *The Jungle*, and Conan Doyle; Arnold Bennett and H. G. Wells adopted Hornibrook's related stomach-culture. Gertrude Stein's brother, Leo, was a Fletcherizer, and she could use the terminology.[9]

However, James's adherence to a reformist American dietary cure sits oddly beside his ironic distance from American enthusiasms and technological Modernism, even his chronic constipation predisposed him to a cure. James's prose is not readily compared to the stylistic mechanism epitomized by Alfred Kazin's comments on Dos Passos's *U.S.A.*: 'the wonderfully concrete yet elliptic prose . . . bears along and winds around the life stories in the book like a conveyor belt carrying Americans through some vast Ford plant of the human spirit'.[10] On the contrary, James seems closer to his brother's parallelism, with mind as a constantly elaborating epiphenomenon in a deterministic universe. So what did Fletcherism and its stress on bodily efficiency mean for James and his writing?

Begin with the timing. James's Fletcherism started in May 1904, as he was finishing *The Golden Bowl*, his last major novel. Extolling 'the divine Fletcher' and boasting of making a modest meal last almost an hour, he chewed slowly for almost six years, lunching with the Great Masticator himself in 1909 (one would have liked to be a fly on that wall), and only abandoning the habit on medical advice in early 1910. The period coincides closely with the most famous of James's late tasks, the rewriting of his corpus for the New York Edition – a project which had been in the air for some time, and was negotiated at the end of the American tour undertaken for *The American Scene*, in June 1905. The revisions were finally off

Figure 3 Horace Fletcher, 'The Great Masticator'

his hands in the summer of 1909; by the time James abandoned Fletcher he had begun to sketch out *The Ivory Tower*.[11]

It is tempting, given this chronology, to hypothesize a prima-facie equation between the two tasks: Fletcherism and the 'chewing-over' and purification of James's corpus; literal and figurative rumination. Is this a link that critics writing on James's revisions have considered? The answer is no.[12] Philip Horne, in his study of the New York Edition, *Henry James and Revision*, runs through several metaphors for revision implicit or explicit in James's writings without considering 'chewing-over' – those he discusses include restoring a painting, the cosmetic beautifying of a face, rereading, unconscious process, following one's own tracks, tidying up his 'uncanny brood' for the drawing-room, revivification. Anthony Mazella's recent survey of criticism on the revisions is as silent on the issue as eating should be in polite company.[13] And Hershel Parker's ringing cry, in 1984, for attention to biography mentions only James's social and publishing obligations. Is something lurking behind this flagrant disregard for the alimentary? Or is the suggestion of a connection between Fletcherism and revision perverse, like the food-obsession of the anorexic?[14] What's wrong with talking about food?

For the suggestion is there. In the New York Edition preface to *The Golden Bowl*, which contains James's most extensive comments on the process of revision, he writes:

The 'old' matter is there, re-accepted, re-tasted, exquisitely re-assimilated and re-enjoyed – believed in, to be brief, with the same 'old' grateful faith (since wherever the faith, in a particular case, has become aware of a twinge of doubt I have simply concluded against the matter itself and left it out); yet for due testimony, for reassertion of value, perforating as by some strange and fine, some latent and gathered force, a myriad more adequate channels.[15]

This 're-tasting' or rumination is consonant with Fletcherism; the channels and perforations through which matter is conducted (and through which it is voided) are at least partly those of the digestive tract. The metaphor of eating occurs throughout the prefaces: he 'tastes again' the feel of a work; he 'bites into' a character; his imagination is a *pot-au-feu* mixing flavours; writing is like making jam, or a 'residuum of admirable "stock"'. He writes of keeping down the 'space-hunger' of his material in 'Daisy Miller', in order to achieve an economy of form.[16] In particular James expresses a Fletcherite disapproval of the incomplete digestion of material in early works: he laboured 'too greedily' for truth, he took 'too prompt a mouthful . . . of the fruit of the tree of knowledge' into 'so juvenile, so *generally* gaping a mouth', he was 'fed at every pore'. The pace of *Roderick Hudson* was 'too fast . . . Roderick's disintegration . . . swallows two years in a mouthful'. Elsewhere, bodily metaphors are implicit: he comments of *The Tragic Muse* 'I delight in a deep-breathing economy and an organic form' before considering the girdle and waistband. Similar terms are present in later essays: the meditation on 'the slice of life' in 'The New Novel' (1914), for example, with its description of 'matter into which method may learn how to bite'.[17] James equates perception and writing with ingestion – as F. R. Leavis did when he accused James of a 'malnutrition' of the 'deep centre' of his being. Reception of his work has often centred on metaphors of taste and consumption.[18]

A tantalizing link is thus proposed. If we consider the conditions of creation of the New York Edition, there are further links between revision and Fletcher's project. James's letters on the two share a stress on solitaryness: the Fletcherizer eschewed company as conducive to bolting; the edition required the avoidance of other tasks. A letter of 25 September 1906, in which James recommends Fletcherism to Mrs Humphrey Ward, is a crucial piece of evidence, explicitly linking feelings about interruptions and the technique. He begins by praising solitude: 'The letters of life, in general, become more and more its *poison*, moreover, surely – and are a matter against which, for myself, my heart is rapidly encasing itself in impenetrable steel'. He then moves on to Fletcherism: 'Fletcherize hard . . . Am I a convert? you ask. A *fanatic*, I reply.' He concludes by returning to the steel bands, which are now located firmly around the dietary technique rather than writing: 'Grapple it [Fletcherism] to your soul with hoops of steel. I rejoice to know that you've begun.'[19] The 'poison' of involvement in life and letters modulates into the toxins which the Fletcherizer avoids.

A letter to Edith Wharton reinforces the point about solitary discipline. Writing of her marital problems in October 1908, James is uncertain: 'I move in darkness; I rack my brain; I gnash my teeth.' Nevertheless the teeth-gnashing produces some advice on emotional hygiene, the relation between inner and outer. (It also reiterates Strether's 'Live all you can' in *The Ambassadors* in a more controlled form):

> Only sit tight yourself *and go through the movements of life.* That keeps up our connection with life – I mean the immediate and apparent life; behind which, all the while, the deeper and darker and the unapparent, in which things *really* happen to us, learns, under that hygiene, to stay in its place. Let it get out of its place and it swamps the scene; beside which its place, God knows, is enough for it! Live it all though, every inch of it – out of which something valuable will come – but live it ever so quietly; and – *je maintiens mon dire* – waitingly![20]

Patience, going through the movements, hygiene are James's literary and physical preoccupations. Dorothy Richardson commented in 1924 that James's writing involves material and physical discipline, calling his punctuation 'a spiritual Swedish Drill'.[21] We might even see here a flight from the feminine 'swamp' and from the swelling female body, which Camille Paglia sees as implicit in James's late style: 'James describes states of *waiting*. He seeks fullness, retention, rumination in the bovine sense. The unexpressed is an endemic engorgement, a male pregnancy without issue . . . The prose resists us with its weight and opacity . . . It is a large, humming, *hovering* mass.'[22] Mass, waiting, passivity: Paglia's terms are redolent of the 'anabolic' energy which Patrick Geddes ascribed to the feminine in *The Evolution of Sex* (1889); and, while they seem essentialist in the late twentieth century, they fit well with modernist preoccupations with the 'scientific' elimination of waste often coded as feminine.

As we watch James self-consciously move between a bodily economy and a general economy in which the world impinges too much, we see what the discipline of Fletcherism could represent: a rationale for self-concentration. Accumulating material for his books means being abroad in the world (as in the dinner parties which irked him on his 1905 American tour) and accumulating that surplus of material which James describes in 'The Lesson of Balzac' (1905) in terms of waste: 'It is in the *waste* – the waste of time, of passion, of curiosity, or contact – that true initiation resides.'[23] Revision is a different matter, a self-consuming reformation in which, Thomas Leitch comments, he becomes 'his own ideal reader'.[24] To contemplate a shape, to turn from the big novel to the corpus and to reproduce that corpus in a streamlined form, to adopt a solitary discipline, all these factors find a convergence in this period, and are embodied in Fletcherism.

One motivation for the reformation of corpus and body was fear of death. Sir James Mackenzie, the heart specialist whom he consulted in 1909, compared James's anxiety to the horrors of *The Turn of the Screw*: 'it is the mystery that is making you ill. You think you have got angina pectoris and you are very frightened lest you should die suddenly.'[25] Mystery can make the heart stop, body acting in tandem with literary effects. As he neared the end of his revisions, the New York Edition itself became a blockage for the 'corpulent, slowly-circulating and slowly-masticating' author.[26] In August 1908, he wrote to W. D. Howells: 'I could really shed salt tears of impatience and yearning to get back, after so prolonged a blocking of traffic, to too dreadfully postponed and neglected "creative" work; an accumulated store of ideas and reachings-out for what even now clogs my brain.'[27] Voiding himself of the Edition, James could return to more productive work; to the late autobiographies and his last two novels. And he abandoned the chewing cure.

DISCIPLINING THE CORPUS

To say that the project of Fletcherism is 'linked' to that of revision is to open the question of the links between conceptualizations of the literary and textual corpus which allow James to move so easily from one to the other in his letter to Ward. If we ask what Fletcherism *does* for James in terms of the project of revision, we immediately enter the area in which both body and text are constructs, amenable to a pragmatics which seeks to regulate flows and accumulations in the name of an ideal. William James's writings on consciousness are a useful context here, since they address the paradoxical position of the mind–body complex in Modernism, at once an object of systems and science which remove its authority, and the focus of ideologies which assert its centrality. The older James opposes any dualism. He writes that '"outer" and "inner" are not coefficients with which experiences come to us aboriginally stamped, but are rather results of a later classification performed by us for particular needs'. The body, in particular, is 'the palmary instance of the ambiguous' here: it can be thought of either as 'part of outer nature', and treated as an object; or it can be thought of as 'me', in which case 'its breathing is my "thinking", its sensorial adjustments are my "attention", its kinesthetic alterations are my "efforts", its visceral perturbations are my "emotions"'.[28] It is in intentional activity, in 'doing', that these categories are resolved: the body which acts and has consequences cannot be seen in dualistic terms, it *works* on a world which is neither entirely nature or culture.[29]

Henry James's writings express similar ambiguities over the internality or externality of the body in relation to writing. He tended to see writing in two ways. In one, it is organic, a bodily production – using 'a bellyful of fresh and nutritive impressions', for example; or praising the sculpture of Hendrick Anderson for its blood-flow '*under* the surface', an 'internal economy' including bladder and belly. His work is progeny, flowering seed, a 'living affair'. Revision may thus be a rebirth or a God-like 'breathing' upon 'old wounds and mutilations and disfigurements'.[30] Readers notice a similar embodiment of characters: in 1920, Gilbert Seldes commented 'always, in whatever he wrote, the bodily presence of his characters and the effect of their presence on others are tremendously rendered'.[31] On the other hand, James could refer to the 'veiled and disembodied' author, with an accompanying stress on technique, manipulation, system (a 'particular degree of pressure on the spring of interest'), the working out of a 'scheme', the weaving of a carpet. This is James the artificer, even engineer, and in this scheme reworking can be patching a superstructure, lubricating a machine, or restoring a picture.[32]

Mark Seltzer provides terms for this opposition between the organic and the mechanical in what he calls the 'realist machine'; a discursive mode which reproduces the tensions and relays in modern society between the organic and the mechanical, between bourgeois individualism and rationalized industrial production.[33] Seltzer's terms are, in part, derived from Thorstein Veblen; in *The Theory of Business Enterprise* (1904) and elsewhere, Veblen argued that the real opposition in American society was not between traditionally defined classes, but between the engineers or managers, whose aims were science and efficiency, and the business classes for whom power and wealth were priorities. These opposed conceptualizations, in Seltzer's view, are constantly in tension *and* in relation, typically in an oscillation between ideas of self-possession and of abandonment to social process.[34] A version of this opposition is constantly present in James, for whom the market is a fraught issue. James, Seltzer suggests, presents us with bodies which are 'natural' and integral while also registering their nature as artifacts. His own texts are alternately a matter of craft (production) and of pleasure (consumption).

Fletcherism attempts to resolve these uncertainties: it is an *organic discipline*, a technique which works on the bodily self, aiming to restore a state of 'natural' hygiene. It resembles a religion – William James used Fletcher as one example of 'the religion of healthy-mindedness' in *The Varieties of Religious Experience* (1902), and of 'ideas considered as dynamogenic agents' in 'The Energies of Men' (1907)[35] – yet it also makes claims as a science, linked to other reform movements: eugenics, the body-building of Macfadden and Sandow, Boy Scouts, mass-exercise movements, calorie-counting.[36] Henry James's attitudes to the New York Edition suggest a similar mix of idealism and pragmatism: in Leon Edel's account, the Edition is a Temple of Art, the perfected version of his self; but it was also, as recent critics have stressed, what James hoped would ensure an income – 'the bread of my vieux jours', from which he would continue to feed.[37] The body needs food, and the work needs sales. Yet James could also imagine a corpus which needed no food, no truck with a market, writing in 1902 that 'my work insists upon being independent of such phantasms [as a public] and on unfolding itself wholly from its own "innards"'.[38] This self-consuming body is the literary self, a private entity.

As with William James, one way of resolving this opposition was to *do* something with the body of his work in order to re-present it on the market. James's most fundamental metaphor for revision, Mazella suggests, is the 'religion of doing' described in the preface to *The Golden Bowl*: 'the whole conduct of life consists of things done, which do other things in their turn', so that 'to "put" things is very exactly and responsibly and interminably to do them . . . these things yield in fact some of its most exquisite material to the religion of doing'. The 'innards' here are the 'vast smothering boa-constrictor[s]' of proofs with which he was struggling in 1908.[39] Fletcher's religion of 'doing' lends weight to the sense of the 'innumerable acts' which might reform a life or a corpus, innards or proofs, bringing together technique and body.

What kind of corpus is produced by this technique? Hillel Schwartz, in his fascinating history of food, fat, and diets, argues that the period after 1900 saw a revolution in attitudes to body size: 'Between 1880 and 1920, gluttony (freed from its association with

[dyspeptic] thinness), would be bound to fatness, fatness to inefficiency, inefficiency to lack of energy and loss of balance, and imbalance to overweight. This knot of relationships would hold as well for housewives as for dancers, and in the home as in the heavens.'[40] The aim of a variety of disciplines, including Fletcherism, fasting, and thyroid-medication, was a balanced, regulated, and lighter body. Fashion followed a similar course after 1910, with lines which emulated the forms of modern design – Stuart Ewen writes of 'an emerging ideal of mobile immateriality', evidence of the 'increasingly abstract trajectory' of capitalism itself.[41] The modern regime of bodily self-control was born. Calorie-counting was pioneered by Irving Fisher, the eccentric economist responsible for what came to be the Consumer Price Index. For Fisher, fatness and inflation were conceptually linked. In *Stabilizing the Dollar* (1920) he wrote: 'Imagine the modern American business man tolerating a yard defined as the girth of a President of the United States! Suppose contracts in yards of cloth to be now fulfilled, which had been made in Mr Taft's administration!'[42] The 300 pound Taft – the last president (1908–12) whose size public perception equated with solidity, Schwartz argues – becomes an index of deflationary possibilities which Fisher tries to stabilize with his 'commodity-dollar', an index-linked currency whose value would remain steady while its weight in metal was adjusted as necessary.

The shift in attitudes to the body which Schwartz describes can be related to the literary corpus, beginning with Elaine Showalter's contrast between the 'poisonous volume' of the *fin de siècle* and the Victorian triple-decker.[43] James had written novellas before returning to the sprawling late novels, and, like his readers, sometimes saw them as overinflated. Size was a double burden, encompassing body and book: *The Golden Bowl* was 'too big and the subject is pumped too dry'; the English edition was 'fat, vile, small-typed, horrific'.[44] The New York Edition offered the possibility of reforming the corpus; pruning works, radically recasting others, reissuing the result in a 'handsome' new form. That itself posed problems, as Michael Anesko points out: 'with comfortable margins and attractive type, all those hefty Victorian triple-deckers burst the seams of a one-volume format'.[45] What emerged was related to the heavy ranks of the collected editions which were James's models, but the difference was that corpus is disciplined *as a whole*. The external constraints of the format (the Uniform Edition) are less important than internal consistency. Peter Wollen notes that the 'new look' exemplified by Coco Chanel 'involved adopting a new set of disciplines, internal rather than external: exercise, sports and diet, rather than the corset and stays'. The point is to present a shape to the world.[46] Other writers might make minor revisions for a Collected Edition; James would rewrite his with a thoroughness never seen before, eliminating the unevenesses of chronology in favour of overall balance and tone, recreating and remarketing himself. His elimination of early works set in America, and others he considered poor, consigns them to the status of waste. 'By the mere fact of leaving out certain things', he wrote, 'I exercise a control, a discrimination, I treat certain portions of my work as unhappy accidents.'[47] Like the Fletcherized body, the corpus succumbs to technique.

TASTE AND THE REGULATION OF CONSUMPTION

James's regulation of his own textual body is also, as we have already seen, an act of self-consumption. In its mediation between production and consumption in the name of a balanced corpus, it traverses anxieties associated with the production/consumption cycle. The period from 1880 to 1930 saw a significant shift in the way in which the economic was conceptualized, from an analysis governed by scarcity, in which problems of production dominate, to one governed by abundance, in which consumption replaced production as the main focus.[48] American economists like Simon Patten and Irving Fisher grappled with this new order: Fisher's self-regulating 'commodity-dollar' was an attempt to tune the currency away from the steady-state model implied by the gold standard.[49] Horace Fletcher's theories – like the sexual science which attempts to regulate the individual desires liberated in modern life – sought to regulate consumption in an emerging age of abundance, in which eating too much was suddenly a problem.[50]

Like Fisher, Fletcher proposes an internal governor that will regulate consumption: *taste*. Taste is 'the most important of all the faculties man possesses', the infallible indicator of nutritional value which should keep us chewing pleasurably until there is no taste left and an 'involuntary swallowing' mechanism intervenes, leaving only a fibrous residue which is spat out.[51] Taste allied to chewing to the point of fatigue is the key mechanism of self-control, a 'sentinel' preventing over-consumption in an economy of abundance, tuning each body via a kind of internalized aesthetics. In post-Taylorist studies of industrial efficiency, fatigue signals the point where the system of production must not be pressed further; in Fletcher's system what we could call 'taste fatigue' signals the limits of consumption.[52]

James proposes a comparable mechanism. In the passage which follows the remarks from the preface to *The Golden Bowl* on 're-tasting' cited earlier, James notes that revision retraces

the whole growth of one's 'taste', as our fathers used to say: a blessed comprehensive name for many of the things deepest in us. The 'taste' of the poet is, at bottom and so far as the poet in him prevails over everything else, his active sense of life: in accordance with which truth to keep one's hand on it is to hold the silver clue to the whole labyrinth of his consciousness.[53]

Taste guarantees the process of revision; as in Fletcher, it is 'active'. It is central to our consumption of literature in producing a *regulated* demand for our attention, 'when we feel the surface, like the thick ice of the skater's pond, bear without cracking the strongest pressure we throw on it'. It is an index of pleasure, of 'my and your "fun"', in which the writer's sense of 'luxury' or even 'a delightful bargain' at self-consumption parallels the reader's.[54] James on revision thus shares with Fletcher an understanding that the mechanism of taste will regulate the flow of materials, preventing the malnourishment of cheap literature or the overstraining of the system. The revision process can be seen as a response to the shift towards economies of consumption, with 'taste' as a key point of mediation ('nature's filter') between the luxury of reading and the managerial imperative which regulates the process. Yet it must be noted that the 'fit' here between works and consumer is solipsistic; James's actual relations with his market were fraught, and the New York Edition failed as a commodity.[55] In a market culture, 'taste' is difficult to regulate, and best controlled via such external mechanisms as advertising.[56]

In order to see these issues of the market, consumption and art at work, we can return briefly to the uncompleted late novel *The Ivory Tower*: the only novel for which there is a full set of working notes, a 'formula for building a novel' as Pound put it.[57] In the 'Notes', James writes of his work as a machine with a series of major premises and crises: 'What I want is to get my right firm *joints*, each working on its own hinge, and forming together the play of my machine: they *are* the machine' (296). This is the novelist as engineer, performing a social calculus on characters: 'I see that I really am in complete possession of him, and that no plotting of it as to any but one or two material particulars need here detain me' (329).[58] The construction is described in terms of an ideal of compaction and the elimination of waste: 'my action', he reflects approvingly, 'will strain my Ten Books, most blessedly, to cracking' (270). Later he adds: 'and what has the very essence of my design been but the most magnificent packed and calculated closeness? Keep this closeness up to the notch while admirably *animating* it, and I do what I should simply be sickened to death not to! Of course it means the absolute exclusively *economic* existence and situation of every sentence and every letter' (338).

If the 'Notes' suggest writing as engineering, the text of the novel as we have it proposes a crude embodiment of financial status in its characters. Rosanna is fat, tasteless, has a vast inheritance, and is 'morally elephantine' in the positive sense of having huge reserves of moral force. She rejects 'the most expensive modern aids to the constitution of a "figure"' – that is, she does not diet, Fletcherize, or take Thyroid extracts; she represents happy accumulation matched by old money. Gray is small in stature, 'light and nervous', and resists his inheritance. He is cosmopolitan and may, we are told, become a writer. His friend Horton is tall, fleshier, authoritative, and wants capital – to give his figure the bulk it deserves. In this equation, the characters embody social values in which, as Seltzer puts it of Newman in *The American*, there is a perfect 'equation of interior states and economic conditions'.[59] As with the commodity, what you see is what you get – a perfect example being Gray's comment to Horton: 'Well, you're simply a *figure* – what I call – in all the force of the term; one has only to look at you to see it' (227). 'Figures' are a kind of coinage; their appearance embodies a cash value or marketability. Disembodiment, on the other hand, is associated with the more etherial Gray and the writerly consciousness which watches the plot unfold. The plot centres on Gray's inheritance of his uncle's fortune, whose dubious acquisition is, we understand, exposed in the letter lodged in the ivory ornament which gives the novel its title. Gray places the money in Horton's management, tacitly acquiescing to being swindled. In the speech which James imagines Horton making to Gray, their differences are expressed in terms of embodiment, wealth, and toxicity: 'You *mind*, in your extraordinary way, how this money was accumulated and hankypankied, you suffer, and cultivate a suffering, from the perpetrated wrong of which you feel it the embodied evidence, and with which the possession of it is thereby poisoned for you. But I don't mind one little scrap' (333). The equation of excess with 'poison' is Fletcherite in its desire to eliminate what the novel codes as weight. It allows taste to be moved from the world of consumption – in which it is in danger of becoming conventional and self-perpetuating, 'heavy' – towards the solitary technique of the writer.

In the last pages of the novel as we have it, Gray walks around his inheritance:

> He circled round the house altogether at last, looking at it more critically than had hitherto seemed relevant, taking the measure, disconcertedly, of its unabashed ugliness, and at the end coming to regard it very much as he might have eyed some monstrous modern machine, one of those his generation was going to be expected to master, to fly in, to fight in, to take the terrible women of the future out for airings in, and that mocked at *his* incompetence in such matters while he walked round and round it and gave it, as for dread of what it might do to him, the widest berth his enclosure allowed. (259)

In a set of dialectical contradictions, Gray desires to be weightless, yet eschews the machine that would let him fly, like the aeroplane which wins the girl in Wells's *Tono-Bungay* (1909). The house is a machine to be hated, yet the 'modern machine' is also James's well-knit novel; the Ivory Tower is both a symbol of craft and the repository of a dirty secret. Machine-products, like bodies and books, are inevitably commodified; there is no place for the Veblenian engineer outside the market. The novel presents a character who wishes to be disembodied (like those other modernist avatars, Kafka's Hunger Artist and Melville's anorexic Bartelby); to resist accumulation.[60] But the text equates the body both with capital (flesh equals inherited wealth) and with the idea of an 'animated closeness' in text, writing itself. Similarly, James's edition can be neither pure product of the maker, the reformed corpus, nor a commercial entity embodying a particular commodified taste (the two poles of criticism of the New York Edition); it is condemned to expose the interdependence of the two.

This has, to be sure, been a wilful reading of James's project in terms of its 'innards'. I have said nothing about what is in the guts; the content of his revisions. But neither do the metaphors of picture restoration and 'tidying up a brood'. What they reveal is James's sense of what it was to write and read. James himself commented, in 'The Art of Fiction', that it was the naive reader who thought that 'a novel is a novel, as a pudding is a pudding, and that our only business with it could be to swallow it'.[61] Yet how it is made, and swallowed, and digested is a different matter, in which rumination becomes a metaphor for the art of fiction and the science of criticism; for a kind of consumption which might be moderated within a discipline like Fletcherism.

If the gross materiality of eating as consumption is one aspect of its critical invisibility, a more important issue is James's involvement in a Progressive project which reforms the body. Dana Ringuette suggests that revision is, for, James a *pragmatics* in which the subject is constantly reconstituted, 'a developmental principle revealing an expanding consciousness, constantly revealing growing relations'.[62] Revision becomes a metaphor for writing itself: as William Spengemann puts it, James's later novels aim to 'burst the settled bounds of the author's prior intentions and propel the action beyond the well-kept paths of literary intention into the unpredictable, morally ambiguous world we all inhabit'.[63] But the pragmatics of revision, I would argue, also includes Fletcherism, which seeks to discipline rather than expand, which aims to regulate taste. In answer to our opening question about a simile (writing being 'like' eating), it is difficult to see James's late writing as 'like' Fletcherism because, in a sense, it *is* Fletcherism – 'like' it in its self-description as 'hygiene', its elimination of waste; but becoming in James's letters the thing itself in its solitary economy and self-preoccupation, its obsession with technique. No other writer before James had undertaken what he now did, moving over an entire body of work and making it anew; eliminating some works; altering the texture of the whole in the name of a desired shape. In the Progressive era, the disposition of the body becomes a moral duty; stepping outside of a plot in which it expands comfortably with age and prosperity, suffering from the infirmities that time brings, it becomes forever an indicator of moral rectitude and vitality, implicated in a technological praxis. In taking on that praxis as he revised, James reminds us that the body (like the corpus) is always the site of work, always constructed, and that its attempts to free itself from history and the market-place are as contradictory as Gray's in *The Ivory Tower.*

DISCOURSES OF WASTE: VEBLEN TO BURKE

If Fletcherism represents a conservative approach to the production/consumption cycle, regulating consumption, the discourse of waste takes a different direction in the twentieth century. I want at this point to detour into social theory in order to explore the way in which the conceptualization of 'waste' pervades economic and social thinking in the twentieth century, and in particular to look at the way that it becomes a more positive term. In a mode of thinking inherited from the nineteeth century, waste could be linked to zones of social pollution. In *Anticipations* (1901), H. G. Wells describes the 'pauper masses' as a 'bulky irremovable excretion' produced by the body politic, requiring a eugenic hygiene.[64] But others saw waste as a more general problem, a term for the frustration of social 'efficiency' in a variety of contexts: economics, eugenics, production, materials, food, land, failures of standardization, even light (the British daylight-saving pamphlet *The Waste of Daylight* went through several editions 1908–14).[65] A selection of titles suggests the pervasiveness of the term: *Luxury and Waste of Life* (1908), *Wealth from Waste* (1908 and 1918), *National Waste* (1911), *Poverty and Waste* (1914), *Reclaiming the Waste* (1916), *A Garden in the Waste* (1918), *Millions from Waste* (1919), *Waste v. Wealth* (1922), *Waste and Extravagance in Industry and Government* (1925), *The Tragedy of Waste* (1925).[66]

In many of these texts, waste is not simply the failure of social hygiene; it is bound up with modern modes of production. In the American context, Thorstein Veblen's work provides an important point of reference here. In the *Theory of the Leisure Class* (1899) and subsequent books, Veblen developed what one commentator called 'a synthesis of social waste from the standpoint of biology, psychology, sociology and economics', arguing that 'conspicuous consumption' and 'conspicuous waste' were the inevitable products of modern capitalism, produced by the desire to render economic success visible.[67] For Veblen, 'waste' also applies to the deforming bodily effects of civilization: the tight waist of the middle-class women, the 'substantial and patent waste of time' involved in social life.[68] Such waste is not simply a toxic by-product:

the originality of Veblen's anthropology lies in its vision of waste as a *symbolic* expression of social hierarchy, an insight developed by a number of later thinkers. (Indeed, one could see modern sociology as a response to the problems of social meaning produced by consumer society: Marcel Mauss on gift-exchange, Georg Simmel on money, Werner Sombart on luxury, Emile Durkheim on consumption, and Max Weber on the regulation of society and the self.)

Veblen came to see modern capitalism in negative terms; as calling for a social engineering which would eliminate waste, pointing out the conflict between the interests of the business community and the managerial or engineering community. The former produce 'a conscious withdrawal of efficiency' by keeping production low and prices high, 'sabotaging' the economy. Moreover, Veblen identifies a particular uncertainty of the production–consumption debate: for any modern company the limit of growth is not production or consumption, but *market-share* – producing a wasteful stress on advertising.[69] As Max Lerner comments, the real opposition here is between 'those who perform social functions and those who perform a social waste'.[70] For Veblen, a planned economy is the only antidote: 'the progressive advance of this industrial system towards an all-inclusive mechanical balance of interlocking processes' means that 'it will no longer be practicable to leave its control in the hand of business men working at cross-purposes for private gain'. Engineers replace grasping financiers.[71] These are the contradictions in a market economy supposedly subject to rational control but actually manipulated by individual maximizers. The American ideal of the moral businessman who amalgamates efficiency and fairness was best sustained in analysis of production (as in the case of Ford); in terms of sales, the manipulation of desire enters the picture.[72]

But, if Veblen attempts to divide the economy into productive and non-productive components, his thinking also makes such a division problematic, since the distinction between productivity and waste also applies *within* the individual. The body-time of the worker can be quantified and ordered, rendered concrete in terms of the production of the commodity; but the worker's leisure and consumption is only quantitatively different from that of the leisured classes. At this point the body again becomes important: the desire for luxuries originates in the body, and, for Veblen,

signals the mismatch between an ideal social efficiency and what
human beings (perversely) desire. Above all, Veblen associates the
feminine body with conspicuous consumption, since it is given
over to leisure, to display. This association is a constant of
Veblenian texts. Lorine Prunette's *Women and Leisure: A Study of
Social Waste* (1924), for example, develops Veblen's stress on
femininity as display and, extending his support for the 'new
woman', argues for a countervailing involvement of women in the
workforce. The reactionary sociologist, Werner Sombart, provides
a more historical version of the equation in *Luxury and Capitalism*
(1913). Sombart links a culture of consumption and excess with
the position of women in society (as well as with the figure of the
Jew).[73] He traces the emergence of the 'hedonistic aesthetic
conception of woman': after the thirteenth century, the courtesan
is positioned as object and consumer. For Sombart, 'sexual life' is
at the root of the desire for pleasure, and luxury at the heart of
capitalist modes of production – generating the first factory-
based industries: silk, porcelain, lace, glass, mirrors, carpets, and
tapestries; the sugar trade. A 'decisive transformation' around
1720 inaugurates modern capitalism, with its restlessly shifting
tides of desire and fashion.

Numerous literary texts of the modernist period reproduce the
association of the leisured feminine body with the symbolic
accumulation of waste. Mildred's description of herself in Eugene
O'Neill's *The Hairy Ape* (1922) is consciously Veblenian: 'I'm a
waste product of the Bessemer process – like the millions. Or
rather, I inherit the acquired trait of the by-product, wealth, but
none of the energy, none of the strength of the steel that made
it.'[74] A famous passage in F. Scott Fitzgerald's *Tender is the Night*
(1934) considers the material basis of Nicole's lifestyle. The most
extravagant of her shopping sprees has just been described ('She
bought coloured beads, folding beach cushions, artificial flowers,
honey, a guest bed, bags, scarves, love birds, miniatures . . .'):

[She] bought all these things not a bit like a high-class courtesan buying
underwear and jewels, which were after all professional equipment and
insurance – but with an entirely different point of view. Nicole was the
product of much ingenuity and toil. For her sake trains began their run
at Chicago and transversed the round belly of the continent to California;
chicle factories fumed and link belts grew link by link in factories; men
mixed toothpaste in vats and drew mouthwash out of copper hogsheads;

girls canned tomatoes quickly in August or worked rudely in the Five-and-Tens on Christmas Eve; half-breed Indians toiled on Brazilian coffee plantations and dreamers were muscled out of patent rights in new tractors – these were some of the people who gave a tithe to Nicole, and as the whole system swayed and thundered onward it lent a feverish bloom to such processes of hers as wholesale buying, like the flush of a fireman's face holding his post before a spreading blaze.[75]

Here, the equation of capitalism, luxury, and woman reaches an apocalyptic climax.[76] Fitzgerald's satire explodes Veblen's analysis: Nicole is not simply displaying a male producer's wealth; she is the core of a system. Appropriated labour 'produces' her, but is in fact much more tightly bound to her via the sexualized process of consumption. It is not possible to write Nicole out of this process as 'symbol' of wealth; she is the train and the passenger.

Fitzgerald offers clues to the way that in the inter-war years the discourse of waste had begun to change. The characterization of waste as a problem gives way to a developing awareness of the way in which waste – however deplorable – is intrinsic to an expanding consumption-driven economy. In the 1920s, a new consensus emerges on a range of issues, from a loose monetary policy to expanded consumer credit.[77] The kind of measures promulgated in Keynes's *The Economic Consequences of the Peace* (1919) were the end-product of ways of thinking increasingly influential on both sides of the Atlantic, with America (particularly Harvard, where Irving Fisher worked) leading the way. The populist *Eclipse or Empire?* (1916), by H. B. Gray and Samuel Turner, routinely notes British industrial decline compared to the USA and Germany, but blames lack of consumption rather than British costs; the stimulation of the production/consumption cycle becomes the key to prosperity.[78] Where Veblen had seen advertising as concerned with market-share, in the new economics it is vital to stimulating demand. The result was, increasingly, a perception of waste, in the sense of overproduction, as knitted into the ever-expanding pleasures of modern society. As Ellen Lupton and J. Abbott Miller put it, waste 'was conceived not merely as an incidental by-product of the consumption cycle, nor even as an essential moment in it, *but as a generative force*'; the term 'creative waste' was coined by one American theorist in the 1920s in order to suggest the obligation to consume.[79]

Among the most enthusiastic theorists of this new order was the

American economist Simon N. Patten; associated, in an even more
extreme fashion than Irving Fisher, with a culture of consumption
and abundance. Patten argued that human nature would change
in the new world. He developed a psychology (derived from
William James and J. M. Baldwin), in which ideas were divided into
'sensory' and the 'motor'. The former were linked to pain and
deprivation, the latter to pleasure. An economy of pleasure and
abundance would thus be susceptible to motor ideas: to buying,
consumption, active pleasures. Patten characterized Freud's work
as part of the redundant economy of scarcity; in the pleasure-
economy, non-sexual gratifications would prevail. He even suggested that germ plasm would alter, causing an inheritable
'organic modification' enabling humans to become pleasure-
machines driven by aesthetic enjoyment rather than by urgent
needs. This is a liberation: abundance drives us out of the body
into the aesthetic.[80] Lorine Prunette provides the appropriate
gloss: 'We may now be living in the "pleasure" stage, having gained
such control over nature as to put us beyond the "pain" stage. But
that control is vested in one thing only, in surplus: surplus of
knowledge, of inventions, of energy.'[81] This thinking – which sees
pain as evidence of waste human capacity – was to climax in Gerald
Heard's strange synthesis *Pain, Sex and Time* (1939).

It is to this new order and its uncertainties that much writing on
waste in the inter-war years responds, critiques coexisting with
paeans to consumption. Stuart Chase's *The Tragedy of Waste* (1925)
attacks four 'great channels' of waste: 'vicious or useless goods and
services' like patent medicines, opium, luxury, advertising;
unemployment, and strikes; failures of technique and standardization; waste of natural resources.[82] But he also recognizes the existence of an 'economy of abundance' – the title of one of his later
books. Three years later Gilbert Seldes makes the links between
body and machine – and the confusions inherent in conceptualizations of waste as consumption rather than production – more
explicit:

The human body may be conceived as a machine which creates poisons,
many of which are thrown off; and the industrial body may be conceived
as a machine for making rubbish, part of which serves a useful or agree-
able purpose in its progress towards the junk heap. It sounds wasteful,
uneconomic, immoral; but if prosperity depends on the manufacture of
nine million motor cars a year and only six million can be sold, three
million must be junked.

The first half of this equation belongs to the nineteenth century; the second does not. Seldes goes on to cite Edmund Wilson's description of a furnace which melts down cars, voiding 'molten faeces of gold' – waste returned to the economic.[83] The climax of this critique is Kenneth Burke's essay 'Waste – The Future of Prosperity', published in the *New Republic* in 1930. Burke sees Fordism and social planning behind the culture of excess: the stimulation of desire has become a science. Anticipating Huxley's *Brave New World* and echoing Patten, Burke sarcastically suggests that hormones be used to boost cheerfulness: 'The day may come when a loss of financial confidence will be looked on, not as a problem in economics, but as a lapse in hygiene.'[84] Waste here is inescapable, and, as in so much literature between the wars, the object of horrified fascination.

THE TAYLORIZED TOILET: WASTE AS RESISTANCE

In modernist texts, we can trace the same ambivalence about the status of waste. Many early modernists adopted the slogans of efficiency and their bodily correlatives. The futurist journal, *Lacerba*, would only take commercial advertisements from 'Cooper Roberts of Florence, manufacturers of laxative pills, and they were couched in purgative Futurist language as antidotes to the "ancient dominators" of constipation and lethargy'.[85] For Ezra Pound, the language of engineering – materials, speed, precision – helped define modernity, part of a stress on Aristotelian *techne*. In Imagism, the elimination of textual waste – whether in the form of verbiage or 'sentiment' – was central. The 1913 imagist manifesto promises 'To use absolutely no word that does not contribute to the presentation'. In the 1914 vorticist manifesto:

The vortex is the point of maximum energy.
It represents, in mechanics, the greatest efficiency.
We use the words 'greatest efficiency' in the precise sense – as they would be used in a text book of MECHANICS.[86]

The Russian constructivists issued similar declarations, stressing the alliance of technology and an analytic viewpoint. *The Realistic Manifesto* (1920) declares that 'The plumb-line in our hand, eyes as precise as a ruler, in a spirit as taunt as a compass . . . we construct our work . . . as the engineer constructs his bridges, as the mathematician his formulae of the orbits.'[87] In the works of

William Carlos Williams, Marianne Moore, Rebecca West, and others, this concern for the engineered or 'surgical' is repeated and generalized into a stress on textual efficiency.

Even as he stressed efficiency, however, Pound attacked machine production and industry, in a critique which takes on a Veblenian colouring. *The Cantos* constantly distinguish the craftsman/engineer and the investor; Veblen's term for interference on the part of the moneyed oligarchy, 'sabotage', links Cantos 18 and 19, with a 'big company' buying up and shelving a threatening invention. Neither did he seem to have much time for Fletcher's cult of the regulated body. A doggerel section of a letter to Marianne Moore in 1919 hints that the self-discipline of 'a Malthusian of the intellect' is privative: 'And the wildreness iwll not be healed / either by fletcherizing or by a diet of locusts [sic].' Put on some weight there, Marianne! (She had her revenge later, commenting that in the *Cantos* 'the "singing quality" has somewhat been sacrificed to "weight"'.)[88] Pound's distrust is bound up with his stress on a sexualized 'masculine' creativity rather than the 'utility' and 'extreme economy' he associates with the feminine. Any made object should be a 'natural' extension of the body. The craft of the fisherman's fly in Canto 51 is thus part of 'nature's increase': 'That hath the light of the doer, as it were / a form cleaving to it'. Pound equates that which deviates from such ideal production with bodily waste, hence the scatology of the Hell Cantos, the shit, pus, mud, stench, and maggots, 'the corruptio, foetor, fungus, / liquid animals, melted ossifications, / slow rot' (Canto 14). There is even a parody of industrial production in the 'new dung-flow cut in lozenges' (Canto 15). The oxymoronic 'petrified turd' and 'melted ossifications' represent the commodification and accumulation of material, nature gone awry, as in usury: '*neschek*, the crawling evil, / slime . . .' (Addendum for Canto 798).[89]

Pound's chiding of Moore for aestheticism is reflected in a topos in the *Cantos* brilliantly discussed by Jean-Michel Rabaté: the bellyache. From the legend that Plotinus refused enemas for his colics, regarding the body as dross, the later Pound jokingly makes 'Plotinus, his bellyache' (Canto 99) an index of those who deny the claims of the body. In the Pisan Cantos we have 'San Juan with a belly ache / writing ad posteros' and, Rabaté suggests, Pound realizing that he cannot merely externalize dirt, that there may be reward from 'Whitman or Lovelace / found in the jo-house seat at that / in a cheap edition' (Canto 80). It is Plotinus who leads him out of this excremental hell, imposing 'division' on the dirty mass (a 'division' which is also castration).[90] Pound's 'belly-ache' provides an important clue as to why excretion is a sensitive point in any consideration of the body in terms of production. If creation is on the model of the body, its wastes must be accommodated. In industrial production, waste is minimized; in human activity, it cannot be avoided and may even be pleasurable and productive, as it is for Freud on anal-eroticism and faeces as gifting. Waste-production is the point where the man–machine metaphor fails; where the body declares its irreducible presence, and linear time is replaced by the cyclic time of the body.

It is because of this positioning of bodily waste that the toilet itself becomes such a pressure-point in Taylorist discourse. The first Ford factory was famous for its toilets, which operated on the same principle of regularized and visible production as the factory: 'there are no partitions at all, and when you enter these premises you see two rows of seats facing one another across a space of a few metres . . . But everything is very clean and washed down several times a day.'[91] Satires of Taylorism typically focus on the toilet. In Chaplin's *Modern Times* (1936), Charlie is caught smoking in the toilets by the boss's surveillance camera and sent back to the production line. Upton Sinclair has a Ford overseer in his novel *The Flivver King* (1937) torment his hero Abner Shutt: he would 'put a stop-watch on him and raise hell if he stayed ten seconds more than his three minutes on the toilet'. More factually, Sherwood Anderson reports in *Perhaps Women* (1931) that at one mill invaded by the time-and-motion men it was timing of women's toilet visits which sparked rebellion. A weaver sees his wife clocked and produces a parody of mechanical action: 'He hopped up and down in an absurd jerky way. Cries, queer and seemingly meaningless, came from his throat. He danced for a moment like that and then he sprang forward. He knocked the minute-man down.'[92]

The Taylorized toilet is thus the site of a struggle between nature and culture, dirt and order, invisibility and visibility; between labour and capital, and correspondingly between two types of time, the time of the body and the time of the engineer. 'Waste', like fatigue, signals the point at which the body and the machine cannot readily be reconciled.[93] A double thinking about waste pervades Taylorist thought: waste is that which can theoretically be eliminated from any process (waste motion, gaps in supply), but it is also, at the level of the individual body, the build-up of resistance and toxicity (fatigue, loss of attention) which signals that body's irreducible presence. Psychologically, excretion implies the abject: that which reveals the lack intrinsic in the body, including the cycle of gifting and narcissistic incorporation described by Freud. At the point of excretion, the logic of Taylorism breaks down.

In a number of modernist writers we see a different set of bodily relations to those we saw in James, typified by a pleasure in the production of waste which signals a refusal of the aesthetics of efficiency, and to some extent offering a commentary on the discourse of waste-elimination. Duchamp's famous *Fountain* (1917, Figure 4) is in this respect a joke on the Taylorized Toilet, a ready-made figuring of the industrial waste-control object as art and the art-object as waste, refusing a 'contained' productivity.[94] (A comparable occasion is the 1920 Cologne Dada exhibition, whose entrance was a *pissoir*.) Such work edges towards a critique of the art-work as product and commodity, making 'creative waste' an oxymoronic attempt to short-circuit the cycle of production and consumption. This critique could cut across different positions within Modernism. As Bruce Clarke points out, Dora Marsden, writing in *The New Freewoman* in 1913, attacks the idea of the brain as an efficient machine: 'Good thinking would prevent the formation of thoughts, as a good machine minimizes waste.'[95] For the radical and anarchistic Marsden, waste is like the 'noise' information theorists would later celebrate in literature, a creative imprecision signalling life's tendency to overflow limits. Wyndham Lewis, a sardonic commentator on machine-age enthusiasms, proposed that 'A Philosophy of Dirt' be added to the Kegan Paul 'Today and Tomorrow' Series, countering the hygienic rule of the scientific–domestic with Michaelangelo's *annual* change of underwear.[96]

Gertrude Stein is another example. Her interest in food flourished after her break from her Fletcherizing brother Leo, and counter-alliance with the gastronomically talented Alice B. Toklas, producing the sexually charged food poems of *Tender Buttons*. Despite her acknowledgment of James's influence, Stein's attitude to her texts is radically different. James seeks 'compaction' (for all his lengthiness); Stein, with her notorious refusal to edit, prefers copiousness, and the lack of a centre from which narration can

Figure 4 Waste-production as art-production: Marcel Duchamp,
'Fountain' (1917)

take place. (This is also, as we will see, the aesthetic of automaticity.) As Mina Loy commented, her texts need to produce 'excres-
cence . . . a goodly amount of incoherent debris' to extract the
'radium' of meaning.[97] Leo's arid self-concentration is, as Gilbert
and Gubar suggest, parodied in Stein's *Two*; just as Stein's
'Patriarchal Poetry' (1927) parodies any ordered text: 'Patriarchal
poetry makes no mistake makes no mistake in estimating the value
to be placed upon the best and most arranged of considerations
of this in as apt to be not only to be partially and as cautiously considered as in allowance which is one at a time.'[98] (Compare the

celebration of mistakes in 'Pink Melon Joy': 'In mistakes there is a salutary secretion'.) The 'allowance' here is not only Stein's stipend from her older brother Michael, the inescapable patriarch, but all measured and systematized discourse. The opening of 'Rooms' in *Tender Buttons* (1914) proclaims 'Act so there is no use in a centre. A wide action is not a width. A preparation is given to the ones preparing. They do not eat who mention silver and sweet. There was an occupation.'[99] The occupation of writing is the point, not as discipline but as undiscipline, as a lack of distance which collapses preparer and preparation, which eats its way through language rather than 'mentioning' or subordinating this or that.

If Stein's continuous present locates itself in the process of the lived body, excretions are also productivity. Lisa Ruddick points out that *The Making of Americans* jokes on writing as shitting: 'I am not content, I have not had it come out without pressing the description of Mr Arragon the musician. It should come out of me without any straining in me to be pressing . . . Always each thing must come out completely from me leaving me inside me just then gently empty, so pleasantly and weakly empty.' Stein's texts are, Ruddick comments, 'a form of rhythmic accumulation and release'.[100] She also points out the suggestions of 'anal' gestation in Stein's texts – the dirty baby of so many modernist collaborations. If Veblen had equated women and waste, Stein – the product of an unearned income – renders, like Duchamp, waste-production as the aesthetic itself. There is another possible context here: masculine bodily economies in the nineteenth century stressed seminal retention, not 'spending' excessively. Female bodies, on the other hand, were seen in terms of menstruation and toxicity, and the need for a free flow of waste products.[101] For a masculine version of this hystericized flow of waste we can turn to T. S. Eliot.

ELIOT'S WASTE PAPER: 'MOUTHING OUT HIS OOOOOOZE'

A few years after James abandoned his eating cure, T. S. Eliot reported that 'Christmas day [1914] was passed very quietly' dining with Norbert Wiener, 'a vegetarian and the lightest eater I have ever seen'.[102] This light eating was part of a polite interchange between two Harvard students studying in England; Weiner the mathematician destined to become the 'father of Cybernetics', pioneering the mathematical modelling of biological systems. If, in Weiner, we see a postmodern tendency to resolve the body into information, Eliot is a poet for whom the body is never so comfortably described. Eliot's early protagonists are hyperconscious of bodies, and the reader of his letters and poems repeatedly sees the body and its metaphors intruding, often in ways which are simultaneously exuberant and anxious.

In *The Waste Land*, the discourses of economic and bodily waste described above merge. It is a Veblenian poem in the broad sense of describing a place in which social waste is apparent both in the sterility and luxury of the rich and the indigence and eugenic incontinence of the poor. But it is also a poem which takes pleasure in the production of waste; as Maud Ellmann comments, 'one of the most abject texts in English literature'.[103] The materials of abjection include bodily parts (dirty ears, hands, feet; teeth, parted knees, bones, hair), clothing (underwear), places (dead land, desert), animals (scorpions, bats), acts (rape, abortion, copulation), and actors. The draft is particularly productive of dirt, though Pound and Eliot's editing intrudes here: in 'The Fire Sermon' the 'dirty camisoles' of the draft lose their adjective; the young man's hair, 'thick with grease, and thick with scurf' is excised; his urination and spitting are cut.[104]

Recent criticism has linked the recurrent reference to the body in *The Waste Land* to the hystericization of poet, poem, and of Vivien Eliot.[105] The hysteria here is nominally associated with femininity, as in Eliot's 1921 comments on H. D.'s wasteful copiousness: 'many words should be expunged and many phrases amended . . . I find a neurotic carnality which I dislike.'[106] But F. L. Lucas's comment on *The Waste Land* places Eliot in the same camp: 'we have the spectacle of Mr Lawrence, Miss May Sinclair, and Mr Eliot . . . all trying to get children on mandrake roots instead of bearing their natural offspring'.[107] Eliot's 'cure' at Lausanne in late 1921 was designed to alleviate his own distractedness. From there he wrote to his brother on the lack of 'hygiene' endemic to the family: 'The great thing I am trying to learn is how to use all my energy without waste'; adding 'I realize that our family never was taught mental, any more than physical hygiene, and so we are a seedy lot.'[108]

The hygiene which Eliot seeks is visible in Pound's 'surgical' intervention as editor, which excluded much waste material from a poem which Pound saw as fascinatingly excremental ('It also, to yr. horror probably, reads aloud very well. Mouthing out his oooooooze'). Pound tended, as Forrest Read comments, to see poetry as 'phallic' and prose as 'excremental', related to elimination; a distinction which is part of his assessment of Henry James, and which he put to work in editing the more cloachal passages in Joyce's *Ulysses*.[109] Eliot himself figured Pound's editing as purification: 'It will have been three times through the sieve by Pound as well as myself' (sieving is a process applied to sewage).[110] Pound's advice also applied to the bodies of Eliot and his wife. His recuperation at Lausanne was the culmination of years of worry about the health of both. His letters in the late 1910s and early 1920s weave reports on his progress as a man of letters with comments on Vivien's bodily states: teeth, abscesses, neuralgia, nerves, and menstrual problems. In June 1922, Eliot reported to Ottoline Morrell that Vivien had been finally diagnosed as having a dual source for her illnesses: 'glands', and 'poisoning from colitis'. She was to be treated with animal glands (hormones – Eliot adds 'this at present is purely experimental'), and by 'very strong internal disinfection' (fasting).[111] The diagnosis prompted a series of letters to Pound on glands. In July, Eliot replied to Pound on three occasions that he would be glad to meet Louis Berman, twice mentioning the English endocrinologist Thomas Hogben. Both these letters end with a different glandular transaction, however: with invocations of Pound's own virility, one an ideogram-like transcription of the Nagali *Kama-Sutra*, 'grow fat and libidinous' appended; the other a more direct 'good fucking, brother'.[112] Here, as Wayne Koestlenbaum suggests, is a circulation of masculine energy conducted around Vivien's body, with the injection of glandular matter from Pound paralleling the treatment Vivien was undergoing.

Yet, for all that the Pound–Eliot team might be seen as acting to 'disinfect' waste coded as 'feminine', *The Waste Land* remains a text with a troubling relation to the waste it describes. Notably, there is an absence of any redeeming vision of social order, or of an internal aesthetic of efficiency. As Cecelia Tichi argues, if 'Ezra Pound cut the "waste" from *The Waste Land* in editorial excision' – a task at best partially achieved – 'the poem itself offers no alternative world'.[113] Instead it accumulates detritus. Jean Verdenal – the 'occasion' in part of *The Waste Land* – wrote, on another Christmas day, 1912, that cramming for an examination made his head 'like a department store stocked with anything and everything to hood wink the public'.[114] This is, in fact, the way the poem was seen by many reviewers, particularly in America: as an undergraduate parade of citations. Louis Untermeyer criticized 'a pompous parade of erudition . . . a kaleidoscopic movement in which the bright-coloured pieces fail to atone for the absence of an integrated design'; the poem as window-dressing.[115]

As well as this overproduction of the material of previous culture, reconceived as waste, the poem responds to what it sees as the cheapening of mass culture, towards which it is simultaneously fascinated and repelled. The 'human engine' which waits 'like a taxi throbbing' at the violet hour is a machine not for work, but for leisure – in the seduction scene which follows, and even more clearly in the draft section from which the lines were incorporated.[116] The materials of mass culture are crammed in: gramophones, songs, pubs, convenience foods. The borders of the text are a particularly rich source of such products – a fact reflected in the list of drinks, dinners, cigarettes, prostitutes, cabs in the original opening; or the negative catalogue in 'The Fire Sermon': tonight, 'The river bears no empty bottles, sandwich papers, / Silk handkerchiefs, cardboard boxes, cigarette ends.' The excised 'London' section deals with mass society: 'swarming creatures' driven by social tropisms, 'responsive to the momentary need', puppet-like in their 'jerky motions'.[117] The presence of these objects in the text's margins suggests the way in which Eliot cannot fully incorporate all his materials; his fragments remain undigested. *The Waste Land* thus bespeaks a simultaneous fascination with, and revulsion from, waste. The poem seems to revel in excess, consuming conspicuously in its gratuitous piling of allusions and eclectic cultural borrowings. Like a potlatch, it participates in a paradoxical order, destroying culture in order to reinforce it. The process of waste-production is knitted into its cultural moment: it cannot (and Pound cannot) 'edit out' all the waste, because it *is* waste material; both the abject and a valuable surplus which enables culture to continue, creating its own moment as it orders its abjection.[118] There can be no production without waste.

A more extended illustration of this process is provided by one issue: waste paper.[119] Here Eliot does comment on the 'waste' intrinsic in American capitalism. Late in the war, in April 1918, he wrote to his mother of the limits of frugality across the Atlantic:

'while America is very conscientiously "conserving foodstuffs" etc. she is as wasteful of paper as ever. I fear it would take very serious privation indeed to make Americans realize the wastefulness of such huge papers filled with nonsense and personalities.'[120] He contrasts European carefulness and adds that 'if less pulp were wasted on newspapers, good books could perhaps be printed more cheaply'. Eliot repeatedly links waste paper with the press, from the inhabitants of Hampstead in the drafts of *The Waste Land* – 'They know what they are to feel and what to think, / They know it with the morning printer's ink' – to the press in section v of 'The Dry Salvages'.[121] Pound agreed: if 'The greatest waste in ang-sax letters at the moment is the waste of Eliot's talent', what threatens him is *journalism.*[122]

The Waste Land is caught up in this debate. At least one reviewer called the poem 'a waste of paper'.[123] It incorporates a great deal of 'pulp', the stuff of scandal-sheets and the popular press: 'personalities' like Madame Sosostris and Mr Eugenides, occultism, royal processions, popular songs, scandal, references to polar explorers. In bodily terms, waste paper is also toilet-paper. The abandoned 'Fresca' section equates faeces with the sexually ambiguous literature disparaged by Modernism as Fresca, 'baptised in a soapy sea / of Symonds – Walter Pater – Vernon Lee', shits while reading Samuel Richardson (more direct, Joyce's Bloom wipes himself on the popular press after reading it – in a passage which Pound cut from the *The Little Review*). We might see the same excremental preoccupations in the fears of a chaos of paper which accompanied the poem's creation. In a letter to Mary Hutchinson written in July 1919, in which Eliot expounds a number of the ideas of order which appear the same year in 'Tradition and the Individual Talent', he writes 'I have a good deal to say which would simply appear as an illegible mass of blottings and scratchings and revisions, on paper.'[124] He distinguishes between 'civilized' and 'cultivated', adding 'I certainly do not mean a mass of chaotic erudition which simply issues in giggling.' *The Waste Land* has its own chaotic erudition in a conscious evocation – 'on paper' – of the decadence described above, so hopelessly clotted that Eliot had to hand it to Pound in order that it might find a shape.

At the same time as it mocks pulp, the poem in its publication as a book also involved Veblenian waste in the sense of the gratu-

itous consumption of paper. Famously, Eliot claimed to have provided the footnotes in order to flesh out the pages at the end which
the printers had to put in to get the sections right, an action which
we might see as attempting to cover the 'luxury' of blank pages,
producing a text which balances modesty and value, yet which at
the same time reverses Pound's hygienic editing, reinflating the
text because of the demands of commerce (Horace Liveright, the
publisher, was worried about length, and suggested to Pound that
Eliot add more).[125] Compare Pound lecturing Margaret Anderson
in 1917 on the possibility of expanding *The Little Review*: 'Lady
C[unard] says "DONT make it bigger. DONT make it any bigger,
or I won't have time to read it." C'est une egoisme.' He adds,
however, that 'ON the other hand "the public" likes a lot of paper
for its money. One has to think of it both ways.'[126] Pound was,
admittedly, more boosting to Quinn a few months earlier, writing
that he wanted to publish Joyce and Ford 'after I have succeeded
in enlarging the paper. (That may be nerve, but still one may as
well expect to "enlarge")'.[127] Swelling phallically and creatively for
Quinn, Pound stresses exclusivity when dealing with an aristocrat.
In negotiating to set up the *Criterion* in 1922 – a project which
became involved with arrangements over *The Waste Land* – Eliot
was deeply concerned with economy and not allowing contribu-
tors to overrun; he reported to Pound that he had decided on
'quite a good small format and paper, neat but no extravagance
and not arty'.[128]

Eliot thus thinks of waste in deeply antithetical ways: as that to
be eliminated from the poem; and – less explicitly – as that which
is central to its production. The poem is uncertain of its status: producing waste, yet also curtailing it via Pound's editing, with the
notes figuring explication as a necessarily wasteful supplement.
There is a comparable double-economy in the negotiations over
selling the poem. Lawrence Rainey points out that, on the one
hand, Eliot discussed a 'fair' price with Scofield Thayer at *The Dial*,
noting that George Moore had been paid £100 for a short story;
on the other hand negotiations, under Pound's guidance, bal-
looned to take in book publication and the *Dial* prize, producing
an unprecedented total of $2,800 for the package, as if anticipat-
ing the hectic financial expansion of the 1920s.[129]

We began with Eliot dining sparsely with Norbert Weiner at
Christmas 1914. The first volume of Valerie Eliot's edition of the

Letters ends with a Christmas letter to Henry Eliot, describing Vivien's regime, including 'the most limited and particular diet'. Vivien on a regime; *The Waste Land* packaged and published, and its style behind him; the *Criterion* established – Eliot seemed to be arranging his world, just as he arranged a tradition to bolster it. The later Eliot disliked 'mess', a correspondent warned Djuna Barnes as she submitted *Nightwood*. She was to see the Faber editor take the scalpel to her abject text as Pound had done to his (Barnes reported that she was 'taking out a few "shits"' to aid the process).[130] If *The Waste Land* embodies an overproduction which is a necessary part of its richness, Eliot's late poetry, in contrast, seeks solitude, concentration, and pattern, just as it seeks to curb the hysterical voices of the popular press. The abject body is excluded. The 'indigestible portions' of the speaker which 'the leopards reject' in *Ash Wednesday*, particularly the strings of the eyes, suggest something beyond the body and luxury. There is a point of resolution beyond the inside–outside dialectics of the human engine in the evocation of the dance in the heavens and the earth, and in the search for the still or balanced point in the second section of 'Burnt Norton'. The 'trilling wire in the blood' and the 'dance along the artery' are in the body, yet Eliot's still point is 'Neither flesh nor fleshless':

> The release from action and suffering, release from the inner
> And the outer compulsion, yet surrounded
> By a grace of sense, a white light still and moving,
> *Erhebung* without motion, concentration
> Without elimination . . .

'Elimination' here also means waste; we might even, excrementally, see a pun in 'motion'. Eliot's late poetry, with its fascination with systems, the circulation of messages, feedback, seeks to eliminate the wasteful flows of the early poetry, so that 'dung and death' are subsumed to their proper time. Even where it describes the blood (for example in 'East Coker' IV), it is to evoke the 'wounded surgeon' Christ and his saving sacrifice.[131] Where James had disciplined his textual body, Eliot frees himself from the flesh, from the pain-economy, and seeks an aesthetics of purification, as if the problems of production and consumption and their troubling relation to the body had melted away.

PART II

Reshaping the body

CHAPTER THREE

Prosthetic Modernism

In the first chapter, we saw that the exteriorization of the body in electric systems involved both an empowerment of the self and a dangerous transcendence. This chapter develops some of the implications of this exteriorization. We can begin with Freud's ambivalent discussion of technology in *Civilization and Its Discontents* (1930). Having noted that the body remains 'a transient structure with a limited capacity for adaptation and achievement', he describes the 'omnipotence and omniscience' embodied in the gods as representing 'cultural ideals' now realized by technology: 'Man has, as it were, become a kind of prosthetic God. When he puts on all his auxiliary organs he is truly magnificent; but those organs have not grown on to him and they still give him much trouble at times.'[1] In arguing that 'with every tool man is perfecting his own organs', Freud seems to propound a theory of organ-extension: sight is extended and perfected via the telescope and microscope; hearing via the telephone; memory by the gramophone.

But Freud also writes of technology under the sign of mourning. It supplies deficiencies and makes up for absences, correcting defects in sight, replacing a lost loved one; the house replaces the original loss, the womb. Lost body parts and objects – as in Freud's thinking generally – are compensated for. Writing is, he argues, in this sense prosthetic. Moreover Freud appends a bizarre footnote pointing out the connection between 'primitive' stories of putting out fire with urine and fire as a tool. It is only when the masculine desire to demonstrate sexual prowess in 'homosexual competition' is renounced that fire can be 'carried off'. 'This great cultural conquest was thus the reward for the renunciation of instinct.' The tool is, in this case, less an extension of the body than that which subsumes it to a larger entity; an entity which demands a sacrifice. That Freud himself had a prosthesis by this point – the artificial palate inserted after his operations for cancer, hardly the auxiliary organ of a god – is just one of the many ways in which this essay seems self-referential (one could, for example, consider his Prometheanism; his tendency to see psychoanalysis as a tool involving a 'renunciation of instinct').

The term 'prosthesis' has some of the contradictions raised here in its history: the *OED* lists a first definition, extant from the seventeenth century, as 'the addition of a letter or syllable at the beginning of a word'. The later definition 'that part of surgery which consists in supplying deficiencies, as by artificial limbs', was first noted in 1706. What is grammatically an addition becomes the covering of a lack in the body. 'Prosthetics' is thus a useful heading under which to consider the general field of bodily interventions, technology, and writing in Modernism. But two senses of 'prosthesis' need to be distinguished. What I would label a 'negative' prosthesis involves the replacing of a bodily part, covering a lack. The negative prosthesis operates under the sign of compensation (Freud's 'suffering'). A 'positive' prosthesis involves a more utopian version of technology, in which human capacities are extrapolated. From the nineteenth century, the prosthesis in both these senses is bound up with the dynamics of modernity. Technology offers a re-formed body, more powerful and capable, producing in a range of modernist writers a fascination with organ-extension, organ-replacement, sensory-extension; with the interface between the body and the machine which Gerald Heard, in 1939, labelled *mechanomorphism*.[2]

We need briefly to recapitulate the history of relations between the body and technology here. In the Enlightenment, the body can be compared to a machine, a series of pistons, levers, and cogs.[3] Descartes noted that the body constantly changes and renews itself, but remains the 'same' body, even after amputation. Indeed, the existence of phantom pains in amputated limbs tells Descartes that the limb is disposable, a tool used by the soul; Hooke's 'mechanical muscle' of 1670 confirmed this sense of the limb as mechanical attachment.[4] The nineteenth century reconceptualized the body as a motor rather than simply a machine; its energy levels and the capacity for work conceived in electro-chemical and thermodynamic terms. Late nineteenth-century studies of motion and performance by Muybridge, Marey,

Taylor, and others were carried out within this paradigm, ec .
izing the energies of the body in relation to industrial apparatus.[5]

Marx's critique of the factory system inhabits the anxious interstices of the shift between the tool and the motor. In the chapter
on 'Machinery and Large-Scale Industry' in *Capital*, Marx follows
Hegel in defining the machine as that which is independent of the
human and has an external source of power. The tool, on the
other hand, is knitted to the body, extending its powers. Labour
becomes alienated at the point where a reciprocal relation
between bodily making and being-made by the object is abandoned for the more abstract relations between commodities and
capital.[6] For Marx, the horror of the factory system is that it implies
a reciprocity of persons and machines, subordinating the former
to the latter and 'converting the worker into a living appendage of
the machine'. A 'machine system' yokes such machines together
in a series of interlocking parts, producing 'a mechanical monster
whose body fills whole factories' with 'working organs'.[7] Taylorism
was to posit the body as a component, so that (Bernard Doray comments) the worker 'suffers from the divorce between that part of
his body which has been instrumentalized and calibrated and the
remainder of his living personality'.[8]

Marx proposes a set of relations which associates the body with
production, with the land, and with the tool; the machine with
capitalism and the commodity. The made object carries the trace
of the body, and can be prosthetic in both positive and negative
senses: an extension of the body into the material world, in capitalist production it is dissociated from its maker. But – and this moves
the argument beyond Marx to late capitalism – the commodity
itself invokes the body in its desirability; charged with a sexual
energy by the mechanisms of advertising; in a fetishism which
reconnects Marx to Freud, it offers to make up that which the self
has suffered.[9] This tightly knit relationship between a loss and a
phantasmal reconstitution becomes, as we will see, increasingly
important.

MODERNITY AND ORGAN-EXTENSION

Prosthetic thinking has its origins in the confluence of two elements: the body–machine model, and progressive evolutionary
thought, which projects a future of human adaptation and

the theory of 'organ extension' was developed by Ernst Kapp in his *Grundlinien einer Philosophie der Technik* (1877).[14] Kapp conjectured that primitive tools were conceived as extensions of organs: the club was a projection of the fist, the digging-stick of the arm. Despite the limitations of these ideas, he overturns the Cartesian tradition which simply models the body on the machine. As Jeffrey Herf observes, 'Kapp set a pattern for subsequent [German] authors in placing technical advance in the realm of human anthropology and thus in the sphere of culture as well.'[15] In England, A. Lane-Fox Pitt-Rivers – founder of the Oxford museum – pursued the evolution in tools in a rigid anthropological taxonomy in which tools become semiosis: 'Words are ideas expressed by sounds, whilst tools are ideas expressed by hands.' This mode of thinking reaches one conceptual terminus in Heidegger and Merleau-Ponty, the former conceptualizing embodied thinking in terms of the 'at hand' as opposed to seeing technology in relation to the 'standing-order' of capitalism; the latter writing of 'the transformation of contingency into necessity by an act of a renewed grasp'.[16]

At the end of the nineteenth century, it could still be said that many technological developments were modelled on the body – particularly the deficient body, the telephone emerging from research on the mechanism of the ear; the typewriter from a desire to let the blind write by touch; film from persistence of vision.[17] At the same time, it became increasingly possible in the nineteenth century to posit a more general relation between bodies and machines in which the intentionality of making (the tool) is subsumed to a general logic. In France, E. J. Marey systematically compared machines to organisms with a functional anatomy in *La Machine animale* (1873). If Andrew Ure, to Marx's disgust, could describe the factory as 'a vast automaton, composed of various mechanical and intellectual organs' in 1835, at the end of the century Horace Fletcher could bring home the analogy and see the body as a factory in need of efficient management.[18] A mechanomorphic imaginary links the organic to the mechanical, enabling the body to be seen as a motor, and technological society to be seen in terms of the body. Technologies quickly began to impose systematic demands. With the railroad, mass-production, the machine tool, and electric power, a logic of the machine emerges which transcends any human scale, and which required its own conceptualization in terms of process.[19] Henry Adams, describing the new physics in 'The Virgin and the Dynamo' (1900), commented that 'man had translated himself into a new universe which had no common scale of measurement with the old. He had entered a supersensual world, in which he could measure nothing except by chance collision of movements imperceptible to his senses, perhaps even imperceptible to his instruments.'[20]

Unsurprisingly, early twentieth-century writers who compare the body to a machine are often more attuned to the dynamic and reciprocal nature of the relationship. Arthur Keith's *The Engines of the Human Body* (1919) is one text which tests the analogy. It includes a description of bones as levers, muscles as internal combustion engines, and the central nervous system as an 'automatic version' of the telephone exchange. But the second edition (1925) points out that the automatic telephone exchange had, in fact, been invented in the intervening six years; technology entering into a dynamic relationship with his metaphor. Keith also displays an awareness of the constructed nature of his analogies, arguing that the writer must use 'fresh machinery for the display of old facts', a technology of representation.[21] A surgeon, medical historian (he wrote a history of reconstructive surgery), and rabid eugenicist, Keith is remembered as the validator of the fraudulent Piltdown skull – itself a striking extension of theory into the body, as it provided the 'missing link' by the grafting of an ape jaw on to a hominid skull. The jaw becomes a tool modified by subsequent cultural changes and eating practices.

In the most radical thinking on technology in the modern period, Marx's fear is realized: it is the machine which subsumes and re-forms the human, though not in the pessimistic mode of Forster's 'The Machine Stops'. Thomas Edison told *Good Housekeeping* that new appliances would 'literally force the housewife's brain and nervous system to evolve to be the "equal" of her husband's'.[22] Such energization was celebrated by Gerald Stanley Lee, who wrote on the modern world, mass-society, and economics in *The Voice of the Machine* (1906), *Crowds* (1913), and other texts. *Crowds* mechanizes authorship: in a sublime *mise en abîme*, the conclusion depicts the author amongst huge whirring presses, finishing his book as it is printed. Lee describes three 'characteristic forms' of modern imagination. The first is 'imagination about the unseen or intangible . . . as especially typified in electricity, in the wireless telegraph, the aeroplane'. The second is imagination 'about the future'. The third is 'imagination about people. We are not only inventing new machines, but our new machines have turned upon us and are creating new men. The telephone changes the structure of the brain. Men live in wider distances, and think in larger figures, and became eligible to nobler and wider motives.' Machines 'have become the subconscious body, the abysmal, semi-infinite body of the man'. The genius extends himself through machinery, living in a 'transfigured or lighted-up body'. 'The poet', he continues, 'transmutes his subconscious or machine body into words; and the artist, into colour or into sound or into carved stone. The engineer transmutes his body into long buildings.' Unlike George Beard, for whom technology drains energy, Lee celebrates this process: 'the gearing up of the central power-house in society everywhere is going to make men capable of unheard-of social technique'.[23]

In the UK, speculative essays of the twenties and thirties, modelled on H. G. Wells's *Anticipations* (1901), continue this concern with the evolutionary logic of prosthesis, with a focus on emerging biochemical technologies.[24] Julian Huxley wrote in his *Essays of a Biologist* (1923) of the 'new extension both of knowledge and of control' (the phrase 'extension of control' becomes a keynote) in physio-chemical science, involving 'an alteration of the modes of man's experience'.[25] The influential 'Today and Tomorrow' series published by Kegan Paul, Trench, & Trubner explored these extensions: J. R. Haldane's *Daedalus* (1924) antici-pates genetic engineering and artificial wombs; Ronald Macfie's *Metanthropos, or the Future of the Body* (1928) asks 'Can Man Alter His Future Body?'[26] Macfie is eugenic; more radical speculations include Garet Garrett's *Ouroboros; the Mechanical Extension of Mankind* (1926), and J. D. Bernal's *The World, the Flesh and the Devil* (1929). *Ouroboros* contrasts 'internal evolution' with the use of tools: 'Suddenly man begins to augment himself by an external process. His natural powers become extensible to a degree that makes them original in kind. To his given structure . . . he adds an automatic, artificial member.'[27] In Garrett's view, this augmenta-tion is at the heart of the shift towards mass production, abun-dance, credit and excess, threatening cancer ('tissue growing wild'). Bernal's *The World, the Flesh and the Devil*, a cult book

amongst science-fiction writers, is astonishing in its predictions.
He, too, begins with the tool as prosthesis: 'when the ape-ancestor
first used a stone he was modifying his bodily structure by the
inclusion of a foreign substance . . . there began a series of permanent additions to the body, affecting all its functions and even, as
with spectacles, its sense organs'. He continues: 'the decisive step
will come when we extend the foreign body into the actual structure of living matter', with radical reconstruction via surgery and
physiological chemistry.[28] In a fable of the reconfigured body, he
imagines the discarding of the aging body, leaving a self-repairing
brain in a mechanical cylinder with expanded capacities (X-ray
vision, chemical sensors), possibly even networked to other brains.

   Such utopian predictions work at the level of representation
and the flow of information. Leaping from the tool to the cyborg,
they posit a body outside the body, as it were; the lighted-up or
virtual body of technology. On the ground, a sense of friction was
replacing the tight body–machine fit implied by Taylorism. After
1900, Rabinbach argues, there was a revision of bodily mecha-
nization, with European industrial theorists developing a more
subtle, post-Taylorist, view of the problems of fitting bodies to
tasks. There was an increasing concern with fatigue, which, as we
have seen, marks the limits of the body–machine relation. The new
science of industrial psychology – what the pioneering industrial
psychologist Hugo Münsterberg called *psychotechnics* – sought to
minimize fatigue, to fit apparatus to persons according to their
strengths. A famous set of experiments at General Electric's
Hawthorne Works in the 1920s extended these conclusions, examining group behaviour and supporting a different agenda in the
1930s, the collectivism of the New Deal replacing a mechanical
model of efficiency with a cognitivist and interactional analysis.[29]
The mid-century thus sees a gradual modification of the man-
machine paradigm, culminating in the re-conceptualization of the
body in terms of cybernetics and information flows.[30]

                        MECHANOMODERNISM

To what extent does literary Modernism incorporate mechanomorphism? There is, or course, a range of responses to machine
culture in the period. Speculative fictions which Brian Stableford

labels 'scientific romance' explore the 'extension' of human capacities, without that extension being reflected in stylistic experimentation. Works by H. G. Wells, Arnold Bennett, and Aldous Huxley can be included in this group. Wells deals frequently with bodily modification: the huge head of 'The Man of the Year Million', the wings of 'The Advent of the Flying Man', the speeded-up metabolisms of 'The New Accelerator', the separate development of the Morlocks and Eloi. Bennett's *The Human Machine* (1908), published by the New Age Press, is typical of populist reformism: recommending Annie Besant's *Thought Power*, he urges readers to be 'professionals at living' and raise the efficiency of the body; working through a series of loose parallels with engineering: friction, overheating, fuel.[31] Huxley intervened in his own body, with forays into colonic irrigation, drugs, and other techniques. As David Dunaway comments, 'twice Huxley . . . reconditioned his body when it failed him. Each reconstruction coincided with a major philosophical shift and a rebirth of hope. F. M. Alexander's back-straightening exercises had shaken Huxley from his 1935 depression – and inspired his pacifism. [W. H.] Bates's exercises similarly set the stage for his serious study of mysticism.' Bates's Method for visual reconditioning, Dunaway suggests, was an early version of the cleansing of the doors of perception advocated after mescalin use in the 1950s.[32] Huxley also experimented with mesmerism, making passes over his terminally ill wife Maria. This and his own death – taking a hallucinogenic drug as he felt it coming – recall Poe's 'The Facts in the Case of M. Valdemar', with its mesmerism *in extremis*; a testing of the limits of consciousness.

To be sure, Huxley and others also attacked modern technological society as dehumanizing, stressing the antagonism between technology and the human (the machine dwarfing the human, on the model of Henry Adams's apocalyptic Dynamo, or replacing it, as in Capek's *R.U.R.*).[33] In America, Joseph Slade argues, literature before 1945 generally fails to explore the machine as anything other than negative – attitudes perhaps reflecting an earlier experience of technology.[34] The brutalizing of the self by machine culture is the burden of a range of texts, from *The Education of Henry Adams* to O'Neill's *The Hairy Ape* (1922), Elmer Rice's *The Adding Machine* (1923), and Sophie Treadwell's *Machinal* (1928).

Even Ezra Pound, who was fascinated by forms of prosthetic thought, commented that in Russia they 'started the N.E.P. with disaster / and the immolation of men with machinery'.[35]

Early Modernism in Europe, on the other hand, often aims at a prosthetics which intervenes textually as well as biographically. Relations between body and art in Modernism are often experimental, as the constructivist Theo van Doesburg implied in 1923: 'We are living in the age of the provisional. We assume: that there is no distinction between webbing and backbone, between coitus and art.'[36] Modernist movements celebrated the mechanized body or the body attached to a machine: the fast cars and aeroplanes of the futurists or (more equivocally) the man–machine complex of Epstein's 'Rock-Drill'. The Russian constructivists celebrated a technological self, fully integrated into the forces of modernization ('BE A POSTER! advertise and project a new world' urges the *Disk* manifesto in 1923).[37] Meyerhold advocated a Taylorized acting, using a 'biomechanics' which removed any inefficient gestures.

However, a more reciprocal relationship between man and machine also emerges within Modernism, as in the thinking traced in the previous section, in which neither can be reduced to the other. Wyndham Lewis's campaign against a crude worship of the machine is a good example, coexisting with a keen sense of how technological developments have produced the revolutionary attitudes underlying Modernism. Lewis argues that machine-enthusiasm was appropriate for Russian or Italian Futurism, but inappropriate in industrialized countries like the UK and USA: 'Imagine Ford raving about *machinery* to his workmen!' (His subject, notoriously, was morality.) In *The Art of Being Ruled* (1926), perhaps the most subtle of all modernist responses to the machine age, Lewis attacks Haldane's *Daedalus* – one of the speculative works mentioned above – for its fantasy of 'biologic transformation', and ridicules the futurist machine-body as 'megalomaniac': 'the essence of the futurist form of thought is an accumulation on the *individual* of all the instruments and physiological extensions or "interpenetrations" of which life is susceptible. But if we *control* a thing, it is *us*.' Mechanical extension is beside the point; the real issue is artistic control, and correspondingly technique. Lewis argues that '"machine-mindedness" is able to realize itself far more in rhythm and word-apposition than in the mere mention of rivets, pylons, and driving-belts'.[38] It is in a technology of *writing*, in performative criteria, that the machine age best expresses itself (Lewis's late work was to achieve a close textual alignment with radio).[39] Modernist texts often incorporate discursive technologies in styles labelled 'cinematic' and 'telegraphic', at their most extreme aiming to reconfigure the nature of literary reception. The modernist typographic language promulgated by El Lissitzky and others in the 1920s had similar aims: a reconstruction of vision.

An extreme version of this technology of writing is Bob Brown's prophesy, in *transition* in 1930, of the coming of 'the Readie; a modern, moving, word spectacle'. Brown's reading machine would expand the speed of reading by focusing attention on a moving instantaneously printed tape, with the reader choosing typeface and speed. This 'Bookless Book' anticipates the microfilm (developed by Fiske in the same period) in eliminating waste; it will, he argues, produce more efficient, stripped-down forms: 'Makers of words will be born; fresh, vital eye-words will wink out of dull, dismal, drooling type at startled smug readers. New methods crave new matter; conventional word-prejudices will be automatically overcome, from necessity reading-writing will spring full-blown into being. The Revolution of the Word will be won.'[40] Brown's manifesto resulted in an anthology, *Readies for Bob Brown's Machine* (1931), with typographically challenging texts by Harry Crosby, Robert McAlmon, Stein, Pound, Williams, and others.[41] Brown's *Words* (1931) includes both poems in normal type, and more abstract poems attached in a newly developed typeface so tiny that a strong magnifying-glass is needed to see them:

> In the reading-machine future
> Say by 1950
> All magnum opuses
> Will be etched on the
> Heads of pins.
> Not retched into
> Three volume classics
> By pin heads.

The writer's focus is thus technical and experimental. In the opening poem he portrays himself as a linguistic surgeon, recalling the original link between prosthesis and grammar:

Operating on words – gilding and gelding them
In a rather special laboratory equipped with
Micro and with scope – I anaesthetize
Pompous, prolix, sesquipedalian, Johnsonian
Inflations like *Infundibuliform* . . .[42]

If *Words* seem to call for a new organ of sight, Brown's *Gems: A Censored Anthology* (1931) also experiments with reading. Arguing that censorship actually imports sexuality into a text, Brown suggestively blacks out sections of poems taken from that modernist hate-object, Palgrave's *Golden Treasury*. Typeface is used to attack the dark areas of the censorial psyche: 'Emasculated, ejaculated huddlings of hoarded sexual and excremental rubbish'.[43] Like Stein, whom he admired, Brown explores the reading process in its theoretical and perceptual preconditions.

Brown's poems are, at best, playful, but the appearance of his work in *transition* and its publication by the Hours Press place it in the context of the language experiments which centre on Joyce and Stein (we will discuss the latter's writing experiments in a later chapter). Joyce seems to satirize the literalness of the rhetoric of sensory experimentation in his essay as G .V. L. Slingsby, 'a common reader', in *Our Exagmination*. Outlining the melopoesis of *Finnegans Wake*, he observes that humans are not yet ready for this 'literary Sacre du Printemps for full orchestra', and jests that new organs of reading might be developed: 'Whether or not a public can ever be trained to absorb this kind of thing seems to me extremely doubtful. The sort of person who will spend his time in the exercise of a new set of muscles such, for instance, as for ear wagging, might be interested in developing a new set of brain or receiving cells, always supposing such cells exist.'[44] But Joyce seems only half joking: the *Wake* does demand a conceptual rewiring. (Lewis on Joyce: 'What stimulates him is *ways of doing things*, and technical processes, and not *things to be done*.')[45] Indeed, Pound increasingly found in Joyce's focus on the word as a remembered music and the text as texture a precise reflection of his worsening eyesight – as if he were too close to the surface of the artwork to gain perspective. Pound found support for this view in George H. Gould, the American sight-cure exponent whose advice he sought for Joyce in 1917, sending Joyce a flurry of letters and technical diagrams. Gould's writings suggest another confluence of body-reform and aesthetics: he saw eye-strain as pervasive in the modern world, and as creating a 'myopic' style in many artists, a tendency to vague impressionism. Opposing popular 'muscle-cutting' techniques, he sought to rebalance eyes using corrective lenses. Pound knew his book on Lafcadio Hearn, and reported to Quinn that 'the last [of Gould's works] I remember seeing was a pamphlet on a man who could see a whole page of print at a glance, one eye doing the rim and the other the middle of the page' – a good description of what Vorticist reading might be like.[46]

In seeking to correct Joyce's sight – as he tries to make us *see* from his own position in his criticism – Pound was once again regulating the bodily relations of Modernism. The energizing of the body–machine might appear as a joke, as in a letter on John Quinn's *desiderata* for a wife: 'You want all you say, but you want it coupled to a traction engine, or rather a ten cylinder racing car with all parts reinforced.'[47] But Pound's medical exchanges are pervasive: with Lewis on venereal disease, with the Eliots on glands; with Joyce. Fascinated by the endocrinology of Louis Berman, he reported to Quinn: 'Berman has at least the virtue of having got Joyce's head X-rayed; he found three dental abscesses under the diseased eye.'[48] We ignore Pound's enthusiasm for physiological aesthetics at our peril: he everywhere sought to intervene in the bodies of other modernists, as if to do so were a form of literary criticism.

Pound had, as well as these corrective interventions, a more positive sense of the possibilities of prosthesis.[49] He writes in 'Psychology and Troubadours' that 'Man is – the sensitive part of him – a mechanism, for the purpose of our further discussion a mechanism rather like an electric appliance, switches, wires, etc.' Correspondingly, in 'The Serious Artist', literature is a science seeking 'precision', and the writer a scientist, physician, or surgeon.[50] Pound found a particular ideal in Remy de Gourmont, whose syntheses of biology and philosophy were so influential (F. S. Flint, Pound, Aldington, H. D., and Eliot were all enthusiasts).[51] In *The Natural Philosophy of Love*, Gourmont – following Weininger and other adherents of paedomorphism – saw the male organ as itself a prosthesis, an extension of the more 'primitive' female body; masculinity is 'an augmentation, an aggravation of the normal type represented by femininity; it is a progress, and in this sense a development'.[52] Masculinity as cultural extension was taken up by Pound in his 'Postscript': seminal power is involved in the 'protean capacity' to grow 'new organs' or 'faculties', and to make 'detached, resumable tools':

Man's first inventions are fire and the club, that is to say he detaches his digestion . . . The invention of the first tool turned his mind (using this term in the full sense) turned, let us say, his 'brain' from his own body . . . A single out-push of a demand, made by a spermatic sea of sufficient energy to cast such a form. To cast it as one electric pole will cast a spark to another. To exteriorize.[53]

At once creation, communication, and sexual discharge, this process is also involved in poetry, since Gourmont, in *The Problem of Style*, taught Pound that a poem was a bodily event and style a physiological as well as a poetic construct. Pound writes that 'Sex, in so far as it is not a purely physiological reproductive mechanism, lies in the domain of aesthetics, the junction of tactile and magnetic senses.'[54]

The 'Postscript' is Pound at his most provocative. But the confluence of organ-extension theories and bodily production is common in Modernism, reinforced by evolutionary biology, Vitalism, and the new physics. The futurists saw the body as constantly extending; Boccioni cites photographs of 'emenations' as evidence of the body's dynamic relationship with the space around it, and similar ideas are explored in Mikhail Larionov's 'Rayonism', in which the body was painted with marks representing its radiations. In her 'Futurist Manifesto of Lust' (1913), Valentine de Saint-Point sees lust as 'the expression of a being projected beyond itself', and thus akin to artistic creativity: 'Lust is for the body what an ideal is for the spirit.'[55] In Anglophone Modernism, Pound's sense of the presence of the body in writing is matched by Stein, Sinclair, Yeats, Lawrence, Williams, Joyce, and others. Joyce provides a rigorous example of the confluence of stylistic evolution and bodily production in 'Oxen of the Sun'. Williams reviews a popular medical text and comments 'It seems really the body itself speaking', going on to write of the body as the ground of knowledge and of the danger of 'amputated concepts'. Organ-extension, in Pound and others, enables the writer to move from interiority to literary productivity, to mediate self and world.[56]

NEGATIVE PROSTHESIS IN POE

I want, at this point, to turn away from the 'positive' prosthetics of organ-extension to the 'negative' prosthesis which deals with a body defined by its absences, by hurt. The possibility of replacement ('negative' prosthesis) is again generated by the body–machine model, in which parts can be substituted so long as integrity is sustained. The American Civil War, often seen as the first 'modern' war, prompted advances in the conceptualization of prosthetic limbs; the work of psychologist and neurologist Silas Weir Mitchell on phantom limbs inaugurates the sense of the body held together by a proprioceptive system, a virtual identity.[57] In the wake of his work, artificial limbs became newly mobile and complex. Mitchell was, as it happens, the son of Edgar Allen Poe's physician, and it is with Poe that we can begin an investigation of negative prosthetics. If Poe lies outside the main chronological focus of this study, he was, I would argue, one of the first writers to experience a modern relation to technologies of reproduction.

Poe was fascinated by contemporary science and the body. His work explores the way in which an understanding of life processes seems to render bodily integrity a chimera, to blur the distinctions between life and death. Marie François Bichat, in his *Recherches physiologiques sur la vie et la mort* (1800), had argued that life is not unitary but a collection of interrelated processes, and death as series of moments applying to different systems: respiration, heart-beat, nervous control, consciousness. Poe's obsessive tales of detached organs and live-burial explore the terrible consequences of this dispersal.[58] The body for Poe can be explored, atomized, or mesmerically arrested at the point of death ('A Mesmeric Revelation' and 'The Facts in the Case of M. Valdemar'). It can fall into trance ('Berenice'), or be galvanically revived from apparent death, as in 'Some Words with a Mummy' and 'The Premature Burial'. Its integrity is constantly disrupted, whether through a logic of organ-removal or replacement. In 'A Predicament', dispensability is so extreme that Miss Zenobia reports her own beheading. The body may even be separated from itself; Poe's doubles are in that sense prosthetic, selves distributed across different bodies.

Two tales provide extreme examples. 'Loss of Breath' literalizes the title when Lackobreath ceases to breath. Embarrassed, he leaves town, is violently suffocated, subject to galvanic revival, hung as a criminal, and finally recaptures his breath from his rival Windenough. Other parts are involved: he finds 'a set of false teeth, two pairs of hips, an eye' in his wife's drawer. The setting, an interrupted wedding-morning, implies a lost phallus (Windenough is

'originator of tall monuments – shot-towers – lightning-rods –
Lombardy poplars').[59] Poe's most brilliant exposition of prosthesis, however, is 'The Man That Was Used Up' (1839).[60] The narrator meets General John A. B. C. Smith, returned from fighting the
ferocious 'Bugaboo and Kickapoo Indians' in Florida. He seems
the epitome of manliness – firm calves, swelling chest, flashing eye,
shining hair – yet is mysteriously 'stiff'. The narrator makes
enquiries, but is interrupted each time he is about to learn the
secret. Finally, he confronts the General in his bedroom, and trips
over a bundle on the floor which squeaks and (with the help of a
servant) assembles itself from a variety of prostheses: legs, arm,
chest, wig, palate, eyes, all the while listing the virtues of the makers
(in an early example of product placement, Poe names actual
manufacturers). That is the secret: the General was 'used up' in his
campaigns, like the postmodern Robocop or Six Million Dollar
Man, consumed by the state, and technologically recuperated.
Through what Mark Seltzer terms 'the double logic of technology
as prosthesis', the body is simultaneously the site of productive
work and violent dispersal, with its parts the replaceable components of a machine.[61] Moreover, the linkage of parts to products
commodifies the General; like the advertisement which links cosmetics to areas of beauty and defect, he intimates a false totality.

The General squeaks while dismembered; the change in pitch
from his normal roaring voice pointing towards the thematics of
castration, associated in Poe with passivity and death.[62] The linguistic basis of his integrity is also questioned. The interruption to
the narrator's search for the General manifests itself as a crossed-
wire involving the word 'man', occasioned in turn by the General
himself, a preacher, an actor doing Othello, and a Byron enthusiast:

> '– you know he's the man –'
> 'Man alive, how do you do?'
>
> 'he's the man –'
> 'Man', here broke in Doctor Drummummupp,
>   at the top of his voice . . . 'that is born of woman . . .'
>
> 'why, he's the man -'
> '– mandragora / Nor all the drowsy syrups of the world . . .'
>
> 'why, he's the man –'
> 'Man-*Fred*, I tell you!' here bawled out Miss Bas-Bleu'

The linguistic slippage reinforces the point: in a return to the original meaning of 'prosthesis', 'Man' finds a series of completions which mimics the bolting-on of parts, metonymically destroying the integrity of the word as masculine bodily integrity is deconstructed.

This observation points us towards a *general* problematic of linguistic replacement and fragmentation in Poe.[63] His obsessive essays on Longfellow and plagiarism dwell on misplaced parts; substitution is integral to the patterning of poems like 'Ulalume', and to Poe's interest in ciphers. This logic of disarticulation and substitution has often been seen in psychological terms (Lawrence commented on Poe's fascination at 'the disintegration-processes of his own psyche').[64] But, as the discussion above implies, it is in the intersection of bodily and textual terms, and in the exploration of forms of production and work, that Poe's literary prosthetics operate. His career as a hack reviewer and short-story writer was dominated by the dream, realized only briefly, of editing a literary magazine and exploiting the emerging periodical market.[65] There was little opportunity for the expanded sense of authorship, of ownership of a world, available to the novelist; indeed, we can see Poe's constant self-publicity as attempting to provide a wider context for his fragmentary efforts. Dickens's comments on his failure to find a London publisher for Poe's *Tales of the Grotesque and the Arabesque* (1840) evoke a predicament: 'I do not believe any collection of detached pieces by an unknown writer, even though he were an Englishman, would be at all likely to find a publisher in this metropolis just now.'[66] Detachment is the problem. Poe's preoccupation with the short form and its marketing enables us to equate his productivity with the logic of the disarticulated piecework. In an essentially modern relation to labour, the author can no more sustain a unified self than General Smith; he is 'used up' by the mechanics of the market – as Poe felt he was by his assistant editorship at *Burton's Gentleman's Magazine,* in which 'The Man That Was Used Up' appeared.[67] The dispersed body resembles the elements which an editor might assemble in a market valuing the 'shocking' detail over the 'rounded' portrait.[68] 'The Pit and the Pendulum' is exemplary: we wait, with the narrator, for the bodily 'cut' which is the end for both of us, only to find that the tale is a fragment of a larger story in another genre ('The Relief of Toledo').

Even Poe's longest fiction – *The Narrative of A. Gordon Pym*
(1838) – is widely recognized as having extraneous episodes
added to increase its bulk, rather than forming an organic whole
(appropriately, the text describes cannibalism, putrefaction, and
other bodily violations). Indeed, Poe's polemic against long works
in 'The Philosophy of Composition' implies such a disarticulation:
a long poem or novel can only be read as a series of parts, across
which attention cannot be sustained. In a famous letter of 1844,
he writes: 'I perceived that the whole energetic, busy spirit of the
age tended wholly to the Magazine literature – to the curt, the
terse, the well-timed, and the readily diffused, in preference to the
old forms of the verbose and ponderous & the inaccessible.'[69]
Correspondingly, genius *vacillates*: 'Alternately inspired and
depressed, its inequalities of mood are stamped upon its labours'
– a formula in which labour is the dispersal of the self implied by
'genius', for all that Poe tried to suggest that his career had direction.[70] Poe's stress on 'unity of effect' and a direct circuit between
maker and consumer in the short work can, paradoxically, be
opposed to a sense of the organic; it is a 'unity' which constantly
struggles to restore an integrity to the disarticulated and mechanical.[71] Like the reel of Freud's *fort-da* game, the short story is a symbolic version of a lost object.

Modernist writers would confirm the fact that style was opposed
to the 'natural' self, even seeing it as a self-mastering mutilation in
which the whole is rejected rather than recovered.[72] William
Carlos Williams described Poe's stress on form as an attempt to
clarify and control, as an anticipation of the modernist aesthetic in
which form is opposed to a vague interiority: 'Constantly he
laboured to detach SOMETHING from the inchoate mass.' Poe's
sense of the detached, for Williams, even works (as in his own
poetry) at the level of the word; comparing Poe to Stein, he comments that his essays have 'a luminosity that comes from a dissociation from anything else than thought and ideals; a coldly
nebulous, side to side juxtaposition of the words as the ideas'.[73]

The body as a system of detached signifiers in Poe thus implies
a new organology as well as a loss of self-presence. His texts demonstrate what Ferenczi called the 'autoplastic function', the facility
for producing symptoms all over the body, but that function is
linked to the operations of an emerging literary market and a
traffic in fragmentary textual bodies. Despite a residual romanti-

cism, he anticipates the investigation of such conditions in modernist writers. Peter Nicholls's comments on Blaise Cendrars are useful here. Noting the constant 'dismemberment of the body' he describes 'a sense of the modern as the occasion for a spectacular disembodiment – once penetrated and expanded by capital, the body no longer offers itself as a privileged object of representation, but exists instead as a source of discrete sensory intensities which elude symbolization'. It is the body *and* work 'penetrated by capital' and given over to 'discrete sensory intensities' which Poe gives us; a corpus in which the whole is placed by the commoditized part. That Cendrars himself lost a limb in the First World War – and was, according to Hemingway, rather too showy about his mutilation – leads us to wider issues.[74]

FRAGMENTING THE BODY IN WAR AND ADVERTISING

Poe's General John A. B. C. Smith's body is 'used up' by war, which serves as an extreme version of the state's subordination of the individual. Elaine Scarry has recently argued that war effects a deconstruction of the body in which the injuries of war 'remember forward' to a totality (the better world the 'good' war will make possible) which justifies the conflict; in which all will be restored – though 'not yet'. The signs reserving seats for the 'mutilés de guerre' on the Paris underground register that fiction.[75] This sense of a delayed totality, in a practice which in fact enforces mutilation even as it promises healing, is useful in relating the body in war to its position in capitalist society.

The masculine body's relation to machinery found a particularly sharp focus in the First World War: in terms of its power to kill and main, in terms of its rupturing of the integrity of the self in shell-shock, and in terms of a wider statistical appraisal of the body and its value.[76] Yet the Great War was also a prosthetic war in the sense of attempting to radically extend human capabilities, whether in terms of perception (the surveillance systems examined by Paul Virilio), or performance (fatigue vaccines tested on German troops).[77] The body demanded by the army is designed for planned action and central control, and modern celebrations of war often focus on the mass-body of the corps – the man–machine fantasy which Reich explores in *The Mass Psychology of Fascism* (1933). Morover the society–machine metaphor, with its ideal of

joint action, was generally accepted during the war.[78] John Dewey's
1918 essay 'What are we Fighting For?' illustrates that point, anticipating a 'better organized world', including an extension of the
technological advances prompted by the war into everyday life
(the 'not yet' of technology).[79]

But war also sees pressure on such thinking, as actual bodies are
scattered and maimed. The man–machine equation seems to slip
readily from positive to negative prosthesis; the body signals lack
rather than efficiency, an absence of meaning rather than an
embodied meaning. Two paintings by the English futurist painter
Christopher Nevinson show the shift from mass to fragmented
bodies. Where 'Returning to the Trenches' (1914) is the futurist
vision of mass-men moving dynamically in space, the disillusioned
vision of 'French Troops Resting' (1916) shows the company
broken up into facets, like a cubist study of detached immobile
objects. The critic H. W. Nevinson, the painter's father, illustrates
they way that the body is invaded by war in his defence of his son's
colleagues in *The Atlantic Monthly* in 1914. He recalls Marinetti's
poem on a train full of wounded in the Bulgarian campaign
against the Turks at Adrianople in Autumn 1912:

Suddenly, the air full of the shriek and boom of bullets and shells; ham-
mering of machine-guns, shouting of captains, crash of approaching
cannon. And all the time one felt the deadly microbes crawling in the
suppurating wounds, devouring the flesh, undermining the thin walls of
the entrails. One felt the infinitely little, the pestilence that walks in darkness, at work in the midst of gigantic turmoil making history.[80]

Bodily terms, a sense of microbial perspectives – these terms,
which were to become commonplace in literary evocations of the
Great War, register a modernity which grounds itself in the fragmented body, or even (in the work of Eliot, Dos Passos, or Mary
Borden) in the decomposing body. 'Quick eyes gone under earth',
as Pound wrote.

Perhaps the best-known images of this dismemberment are
those of Otto Dix, whose wartime paintings depict the trenches as
a distorted space of flailing bodies and exploding shells. 'The War
Cripples', 'Prager Strasse' (all 1920), and other paintings of the
post-war period focus on cripples with prosthetic replacements:
artificial limbs, patched bodies, trolleys. 'The Skat Players' (Figure
5) is an extreme version of Dix's clinical view, which led him to
have bodies and entrails brought to him from a hospital. One

Figure 5 Otto Dix, 'The Skat Players' (1920)

figure has a missing eye, a missing arm, and a prosthetic ear with a
tube to a speaking trumpet; he plays cards with his remaining set
of toes and a wooden hand on the other arm. The other two figures
have artificial legs, neck, skull, jaws, hand, and eyes. A jaw bears the
legend 'Unterkieler. ProtheseMake: Dix'; and, indeed, Dix's post-
war paintings combine the prosthesis as subject with collage and
mixed-media techniques which graft in fabric, newspapers, glass,

and other materials, as if the body can no longer be represented in any unmediated way.

As Poe's example suggests, the maiming of bodies in war is an intensification of a more general consumption of bodies in capitalism – signalled, for example, in narratives of cannibalism, from that in Poe's *Pym* to Upton Sinclair's depiction of severed fingers in the sausage mix at a Chicago meat works in *The Jungle* (1906). Daniel Defoe's list of proposed payments to sailors for the loss of hands, legs, and eyes in his *Essay Upon Projects* (1697) is simply the first step in a process of compensation which attempts to count the cost of a lost integrity. Production subsumes the body, rendering it a breakable tool. American satirists, reflecting on the extremes of *laissez faire* capitalism, have often followed Poe in depicting the fractured body. In Twain's *The American Claimant* (1892), Colonel Sellers aims to resurrect and animate bodies as a cheap police force – from the point of view of Capital, a zombie is an ideal worker.[81] Lemuel Pitkin, in Nathanael West's *A Cool Million* (1934), is progressively 'dismantled', losing teeth, eye, hair, and a leg in work-related accidents; later he is part of a stage act in which his detachable organs are knocked out for comic effect. As in Poe, prosthesis is connected to advertising: Lemuel is hired by a glass-eye manufacturer to lose his eye in swanky locations, so that he might shout its name. Dix's 'Prager Strasse' has a shop-window full of dummies and artificial limbs juxtaposed with a classical torso and women in corsets, registering the prosthesis as a macabre accompaniment to the commoditization of beauty.[82]

The reference to advertising suggests the way in which commodity capitalism is *dependent* upon – as well as producing – a fragmentation of bodily integrity. Indeed, it is fragmentation and the promise of a restored integrity, like that in war, which renders the commoditization of the body possible. Two discourses coalesce: the body in advertising becomes a war-zone, characterized by threats, deficiencies, and deferrals; war is, Marinetti insisted, the 'World's Only Hygiene', clearing out the deficient and decayed to make way for the new. Advertising posits a body-in-crisis, a zone of deficits in terms of attributes (strength, skill, nutrition), behaviours (sleep, defecation, etc.), with matching remedies. These compensations are offered through the medium of the image of the perfected body, a phantasmic version of the 'lit up' body; a prosthetic god which we are always just failing to be. We are, of course, also moving here from the masculine to the feminine body; from the body-as-work to the body-as-display.

Thomas Richards has explored the origins of this prosthetic system in late-Victorian advertising images, and in two factors, the idealization of the female body, and the system of patent medicine advertising which sought to create and remedy areas of concern in relation to a normative body:

> The seaside girl eulogized adolescence and signalled the formation of what we now call 'youth culture'. At one and the same time she marked off the adolescent female body as an object of commodity culture and changed the shape of female anatomy by making that body normative and compulsory. In compact form she realizes what must have been every patent medicine advertiser's dream: every act of consumption now became an act of rejuvenation.[83]

In the late 1910s, a new advertising pattern emerged, focusing on the fears and failings of the consumer and picturing a dangerous world of Darwinian struggle. It is from the 1920s that the instantly recognizable modern body-threat copy dates.[84] The generalized fears of bodily pollution and degradation apparent in earlier literature were atomized and commercialized, dispersed across a variety of bodily parts and the technologies appropriate to them.

Roland Marchand identifies three American advertising campaigns in the 1920s which aimed to create a desire for the product *ex nihilo*, all of them focusing on the body and working through narratives of identification and danger.[85] The Fleishmann's Yeast campaign warned of 'intestinal fatigue'; the Listerine campaign of halitosis. Both products already existed, but were marketed with a new aggressiveness, using a pseudo-medical discourse conditioned by the 1906 Food and Drug Act. The third example, the Kotex campaign, sold a new product, disposable sanitary napkins (the campaign included a photograph of Lee Miller by Edward Steichen). Other campaigns highlighted crowsfeet, bromodosis (smelly feet), comedones (blackheads), sour stomach, office hips, perspiration ('Within the Curve of a Woman's Arm: A frank discussion of a subject too often avoided' runs a 1919 ad for Odorono). Disastrous outcomes resulted from the smallest consumer choice: can bad toilet paper lead to surgery (Scott Tissue, 1931)? Will the jaw atrophy unless exercised with chewing gum (Dentyne, 1934)? Might poor quality bandages lead to amputation (Johnson & Johnson, 1936)?[86] The link between a psychoanalytically conceived

body image and consumption was made in one American advertisement in 1932 for a product to alleviate 'domestic hands': it features what the caption calls 'A photographic representation of
inferiority complex caused by Domestic Hands. Interpreted by
Anton Bruehl' – the hands detached and distorted in surreal
fashion.[87]

This dispersal and violent zonation of the body is reflected in
the explosion in the cosmetic *visibility* in bodily parts in advertising in the interwar period: uncovered knees *c.* 1920; in 1925 the
back of a pair of legs in a hosiery advertisement; the first nude
woman in 1936, photographed by Steichen for Woodbury's Facial
Soap.[88] (We do not see her face: she is shown from behind, rendering the body as synecdoche.) The bodily part is knitted into a
system of virtual prosthetics: a system which both exposes and
remedies defects, implying a 'whole' body which can only be
achieved by technology; a whole which is constantly deferred. One
practice which mediates between the negative prosthetics of
replacement and the advertising/cosmetic system is cosmetic
plastic surgery, developed between the wars with experience
gained from battlefield cases. Rather than replacing a lost part,
cosmetic surgery works on a 'natural' body which it has declared
inadequate, misshapen, or past its prime. One pioneer, Charles H.
Willi – inventor of fat-injection techniques – described his work in
London in the 1920s as 'facial rejuvenation' and linked it to contemporary gland operations. Willi's work is celebrated in Elizabeth
Margetson's *Living Canvas: A Romance of Aesthetic Surgery* (1936),
an account of how she realized that 'systematic beauty culture and
the employment of cosmetics' was insufficiently radical; it was only
after she turned to the 'sculptor of living flesh' that she was rejuvenated.[89]

One moment at which the systematic lack described above is
experienced recurs in the work of women writers in the 1930s, and
can be opposed to the masculine body-extension we saw in Pound:
the moment of looking in the mirror and experiencing the body
as a humiliation (often cosmetics feature in such scenes).[90] Julia,
in Rhy's *After Leaving Mr. Mackenzie* (1930), 'thought she had never
seen herself looking quite so ugly' before rearranging her face; the
nameless character in Storm Jameson's 'A Day Off' (1933) experiences 'dismay' in a toilet before applying powder and stealing a
bag to compensate herself; Stephen in *The Well of Loneliness*

(1928), stares at herself in the glass and sees her body as 'a monstrous fetter imposed on her spirit' before forgiving it. Even the beautiful Elvira in Christina Stead's *the Beauties and the Furies* (1936), having admired her naked body in the mirror, wanders about 'giving her body hundreds of small attentions, using ear and nose syringes, sponges, files, scissors, chamois leather, swan's-down puffs, sticks of orange-wood, creams, powers and the rouge which Oliver had brought her home'.[91] Though it is perhaps a truism to note that such moments are reinforced by the burgeoning advertising and cosmetics industries, it is striking how often the mirror suggests an internalization of such perceptions, a disciplining of the self in the name of its 'true' (ideal) shape.

Rhys's *Good Morning, Midnight* (1939), with its mixture of alienated labour and commoditized femininity, is a particularly bitter example.[92] From an early reference to a shop full of artificial limbs in Bloomsbury – the product of the war – to the final drunken and surreal vision of an 'enormous machine made of white steel' with 'innumerable flexible arms' ending in mascara-caked eyes, Rhys's heroine Sasha constantly experiences her body as failure and dreams of rejuvenation. She reads 'a long article by a lady who has had her breasts lifted' while getting 'new hair' at the hairdressers. She remembers being swaddled by a midwife after childbirth, so 'there is not one line, not one wrinkle, not one crease'. The equation of capital and the commoditized body replaces the biblical injunction to work: 'Now, money, for the night is coming. Money for my hair, money for my teeth, money for shoes that won't deform my feet (it's not so easy now to walk around in cheap shoes with very high heels), money for good clothes, money, money.'[93] This is the 'vicious functional circle' described by W. F. Haug, in which the body constantly reaches for a false totality, undoing experience in the name of youthfulness and a cosmetic self which is in turn commoditized.[94]

THE INFLUENCING MACHINE

Technology thus offers, in the modern era, both utopian possibilities and a wounding and fragmentation of the self which is an incorporation of those possibilities in the form of the commodity; both mechanical extension and systemic subordination. As a way of conceptualizing that wounding and returning briefly to the

psychodynamics of the prosthesis, I will conclude with what seems to me a response to mechanomorphism, Victor Tausk's classic 1919 paper 'On the Origin of the "Influencing Machine" in Schizophrenia'. A rivalrous colleague of Freud, Tausk registers and exteriorizes the fears which surround modern technologies of desire. If Freud was to see a 'prosthetic god' in 1929, he had already seen, in Schreber, a case where technology had been incorporated into delusion.

Tausk considers a belief observed in schizophrenics: that they are influenced or controlled from a distance by a mysterious and complex machine operated by their enemies (Figure 6). Early stages of the complex include self-estrangement, a progressive sense of exterior forces at work, culminating in the hypothesis of the 'influencing machine'. In explaining the origins of the influencing machine, Tausk follows Freud, arguing that 'the influencing apparatus is a representation of the patient's genitalia projected to the outer world'.[95] It involves a regression to 'a stage of diffuse narcissistic organ libido' in which 'the entire body is a genital'. This genital is, however, prosthetic, implying a technological version of the self: 'The evolution by distortion of the human apparatus into a machine is a projection that corresponds to the development of the pathological process which converts the ego into a diffuse sexual being, or – expressed in the language of the genital period – into a genital, a machine independent of the aims of the ego, and subordinated to a foreign will.'[96] The machine-as-genital implies a sexualized, polymorphous body, a totalized fetishism in which anything can stand for the genitals.

The functions of the machine as described by schizophrenics include the creation of pictures, the manipulation of thoughts, the production of unexpected motor phenomena (erections, tics), sickness, and strange feelings. In the case of 'pictures', the machine is 'generally a magic lantern or cinematograph. The pictures are seen on a single plane, on walls or windowpanes; unlike typical visual hallucinations, they are not three-dimensional.' At other times the 'suggestion-apparatus' uses electromagnetic waves or mysterious forces.[97] If Tausk's explanation of the influencing machine relies on notions of projection and distortion, he also registers the way in which it represents an introjection of the technologies of 1919: electric wires, telephones, wireless, and cinema. The *complexity* of the machine emerges from its ability to

Figure 6 Jakob Mohr's 'Proofs': a classic 'Influencing Machine'

incorporate successive additions, like updates of a software
system, as the original inhibition of desire is strengthened; the
machine becomes 'hopelessly complex', and drains off psychic
energy, in an inverted version of George Beard's picture of the
psyche 'drained' by the complexity of modern life.

There is thus a reversibility in Tausk's paper: schizophrenics fan-
tasize that their sexual apparatus is converted into a 'hopelessly
complex' machine; yet the 'evolution by distortion of the human
apparatus into a machine' is also a feature of historical evolution.
In a footnote on the last page of his paper, Tausk notes that
machines are already extensions of the body: 'Indeed, the
machines produced by man's ingenuity and created in the image
of man are unconscious projections of man's bodily structure.
Man's ingenuity seems to be unable to free itself from its relation
to the unconscious.' Tausk edges us towards a more historicized
theory of the implications of bodies and machines in the process
of producing desire.[98] Indeed, his article can be read backwards as
another critique of cultural mechanisms which threaten to genital-
ize the body, even as they vitiate the 'real' channels of desire. If the
schizophrenic can depict the influencing machine as cinematic,
while its psychic function is taken to be the externalization of a
threatening desire, then the cinema and other apparatus can, reci-
procally, be seen as producing a new version of the body as both
familiar and radically self-estranged. The schizophrenic's personal
sense of being influenced from afar thus seems simply a literaliza-
tion of cultural paranoia at the potential of mass media, as well as
a sense of the permeability of bodily boundaries – a possibility later
realized by Adorno, who noted the convergence between the
world as an increasingly inescapable 'system' and 'paranoid
systems of thinking' which place those systems at a distance from
the self.[99] Moreover, in positing the influencing machine as
serving the needs of a primal fantasy of the lost original object
(whether we conceptualize that as Tausk's intra-uterine state or the
Lacanian *petit objet*), Tausk enables us to link the mechanisms
established for the satisfaction of desire (cinema and other specular pleasures, the immediate-access pleasures of telephones, the
slave-power of electricity, commodity culture itself) with the sense
of phantasmal completeness offered by those objects. The cinema,
in particular, becomes an expression of fetishized desire: a screen
on which every erotic scenario may be accommodated. Tausk tells

us that capitalism fragments in order to integrate; converts the body into technology in order to heighten its 'natural' pleasures; and renders paranoia a domestic reality.

Seen in this light, the insistence on the ontological priority of the body which we see in many modernist writers is the opposite of materialism (the same might be argued of the phenomenological insistence on the reality of the body). For Poe, the body appears as a symptom of a wounded self, fragmented and exploded by capital; for later writers like Pound, its imagined wholeness and the status of art as an extension of the body can take on a sloganizing unreality in the face of its ideological construction. William's modernist slogan 'No ideas but in things' (or no ideas but those located in the body) *is* at one level paranoia; a paranoia which attempts to defend the reality of body experience at the point where it is already penetrated by the desiring machines of modernity. In a complementary fashion, seeing technology as extending the powers of the writer or reader in any utopian fashion involves a negation of the body's flawed presence; it is surrendered to the ideal.

CHAPTER FOUR

Auto-facial-construction

In the first decades of this century, the British or American enthusiast for bodily reform could choose among a vast array of
methods, ranging from mind-cure techniques to mechanical
manipulation: Christian Science, New Thought, Alexander
Technique, Fletcherism, the Culture of the Abdomen, colonic
irrigation, electric therapies, among numerous eating and exer-
cising regimes, gland treatments, and mechanical devices. The
body became the site of techniques which operated externally and
internally to regulate and reorganize. Many cures could be found
in the pages of Bernarr Macfadden's *Physical Culture*, founded
1899, and his *Encyclopedia of Physical Culture*. Macfadden 'tried to
change the way Americans ate, drank, sat, breathed, slept, dressed,
walked – even how they had sex', in a programme which slid
towards eugenics (readers of *Physical Culture* in 1921 were recommended to read Madison Grant's *The Passing of the Great Race*).[1]
The technological reformation of the body suggested that it could
be optimized, that it was 'perfectible', as Kenneth Dutton has
recently suggested in his study of physical culture.[2] Modernist
movements like Futurism and the Bauhaus absorbed the ideals of
the gymnasium, and celebrated the efficient, streamlined body.[3]

At the same time, physical culture often elided the question of
the relation between external and internal disciplines, between a
mechanical and a motivational or expressive model of the body.
Would changing the mind radically affect the body (as Christian
Science believed)? Might colonic irrigation remove toxins and
release the brain from their effects? It is the instability of such
questions which produces a stress on *pragmatics*, on actions which
intercede in a zone of uncertain causality, as we saw in Fletcherism.
For William James, the body is a liminal zone, alternately part of
the self and part of the object-world, familiar and strange. What

negotiates between these two aspects of the body is the subject of the fourth chapter of *The Principles of Psychology* – *habit.* James describes habit as thinking which is knitted into the body, inherent in pre-programmed (automatic) actions; it is those functions of the body which are incorporated into the self – a characterization of the body as the penumbra of thought recently expounded by Pierre Bourdieu. Habit is negative only when static; James advocates a conscious extension of the habitual, a training of habit. There is thus both an ethics and a bodily pragmatics inherent in the manipulation of what we could call the 'thinking of the body', a pragmatist stress on the individual's ability to enact purposive decisions in relation to the self, on the *work* of self-creation.

The linkage between progressivism, pragmatism, and body-reform is demonstrated by the pragmatist philosopher John Dewey's championing of the Alexander Technique, invented by the F. Matthias Alexander. Beginning with *Man's Supreme Inheritance* (1910), Alexander argued that evolution had introduced a dangerous gap between the body and consciousness. Like James, Alexander sees *habit* as the point of entry for a bodily pragmatics: 'Mental processes, after they have become developed, accustomed, and habitual, become automatic, and finally purely bodily and mechanical.'[4] The Alexander technique aims to render the embodied thinking of habit conscious and programmable. It involves 'a necessary re-education of the subject', as he put it in *Conscious Control* (1912), in which 'in every case the *means* rather than the *end* must be held in mind'.[5] Castigating the uncertain causality of mind-cure, hypnotism, and other techniques which appeal to an obscure 'higher' or secondary self, Alexander also rejected the end-directedness of mechanical techniques. Instead he sought a middle ground, neither clearly motivational nor mechanical, creating 'a satisfactory standard of general psycho-physical functioning' as a precursor to self-cure.[6]

An exchange in 1918 between Dewey and critic Randolph Bourne is instructive. Introducing a new edition of *A Man's Supreme Inheritance,* Dewey praised Alexander for rejecting terms like 'unconscious' and 'subconscious', which 'express reliance upon the primitive mind of sense, of unreflection, as against reliance upon *reflective* mind'.[7] Bourne reviewed the book in the *New Republic* under the title 'Making Over the Body'.[8] Disabled and unlikely to respond to physical utopianism, he was a hostile reviewer, having split with Dewey and other progressives over American involvement in the war. He admits that Alexander has 'a rare physiological intuition', but disagrees with his 'cosmic and evolutionary philosophy' and rationalism, which the war had proved a chimera. Bourne's final paragraph equates Alexander with Freud: Alexander 'has a psychological technique which is apparently a kind of reversed psycho-analysis, unwinding the psychic knots by getting control of the physical end-organs'. This formula reinserts into the argument the dualism which Alexander seeks to circumvent; a cause-and-effect sequence (though Bourne shares Dewey's sense of the body as the site of work on the self). Dewey's reply in the *New Republic* is a classic assertion of instrumentalism: Alexander's 'principle is experimental . . . proof lies in *doing* it'.[9] For that reason, he argues, the principle has the possibility of being evolutionary: if children are trained in it, new habits will be perpetuated across generations via an implicit Lamarkianism.

BODILY REFORM AND GENDER

The possibility that children will represent an extension of the reworked body raises the general issue of gender and the role of mothering – the perpetuation of bodily relations – in the discourse of bodily reform. We can approach that subject obliquely, via the critique of physical culture provided by Wyndham Lewis (whose complex relation to mechanomorphism we have already noted). Like Alexander, Lewis was a formalist, advocating conscious technique over depth, and criticizing those who explore the 'deep' meanings of the body; like James, he stresses work on the self. In *The Art of Being Ruled* (1926), he insists that art is 'the science of the outside of things'; natural science 'the science of the *inside* of things'. Noting that 'a preoccupation with the *vitals* of things is related to *vitalist* enthusiasms' and to the cry 'Up life! down art!', he attacks psychoanalysis, the 'anthropometrist's obsessions' and those who deal with 'the smoking-hot *inside* of things, in contrast to the hard, cold formal skull or carapace'.[10] In 'Our Wild Body', published in *The New Age* in 1910, Lewis slyly employs the idiom of physical reform in promoting his aesthetic of externality: 'The body is sung about, ranted about, abused, cut about by doctors, but never talked about. If you will give me the licence of a doctor and not keep seizing my hand (not out of pain but modesty) as the patient seizes the dentist's, I will examine one or two points and prescribe treatment. It is not, however, the body that is ailing, but our idea of the body.' Lewis attacks the 'calisthenic quack' exemplified by Sandow, arguing that 'The body of the contemporary man is the prey of mercenary "strong men", he is lured with their muscle manufactories . . . by the mere brute magnetism of size.'[11]

Instead, Lewis sees the body as a surface to be manipulated by the artist, as in his own relentlessly physical renderings of facial mechanics in *Tarr* and *The Wild Body*. Functionalism permeates his work; a sense that the body's physical structure can be moulded at will. His meditation on gender, in *The Art of Being Ruled*, has a radical sense of the relativity of physique which reinforces, though in a counter-intuitive manner, his notorious attacks on the cultural 'feminine'. Gender is *produced* by an act of will:

The large, bloated, and sinewy appearance of the male, again, is partly the result of manual work or physical exercise, but is the result as well of thousands of years of ACTING THE MAN. The more muscular frame of the male, and his greater hardihood, are illusions, like everything else about him, provisionally and precariously realized . . . *He is in reality just the same size, and of the same sort.*[12]

It is only 'functional differences', he concludes, 'that separate one thing from another'. In rejecting a biological engram, Lewis declares that the body is plastic, the proper ground for artistic manipulation.

Apart from its radical relativism, Lewis's conclusion might be seen as another version of the gendered nature/culture opposition as it is configured by the organ-extension theory we saw in the previous chapter: as he argues elsewhere, man produces and woman reproduces. The outlines of the masculine body must be held in place by *actions* which constantly define and redefine it; it is, as de Gourmont implied, already a technology. Indeed, in physical culture the masculine body is more readily conceptualized in terms of work and action, and a scientific pragmatics coded as masculine – even as masculine revitalization. Taylorist analysis of the working body overwhelmingly focuses on men.[13] Women – the equation goes – reproduce bodies and social relations; bodily reform seeks to intervene across that field in a scene of masculine genesis. For related reasons the freedom offered by male bodily reformers to women was limited: women might be liberated from convention and sexual restraint, but not at the risk of jeopardizing their role as guardians of the future. (Indeed, the appeal to eugenic health was often made by women reformers, as a means of deflecting criticism and promoting a feminist agenda.[14]) Even radical texts like Floyd Dell's *Woman as World Builders* (1913), an important point of confluence between early Modernism and feminism, shared many of these assumptions.[15]

Women's role in physical culture is conditioned by this gendered equation of masculinity and work, as well as by the tendency to characterize destabilizing flows of pleasure within the desiring-machines of Modernism as feminine. But one space does remain for the feminine: that of the *aesthetic* reformation of the body, and, in particular, of the body-in-movement. The 'stretch and swing' techniques which, for Hillel Schwartz, characterize the 'new kinaesthetic' of the twentieth century are associated with women: eurythmicists, dancers like Isadora Duncan and Loie Fuller.[16] Women serve as the point of mediation between the natural and artificial, between the being of the body and its shaping – a shaping 'already there' rather than produced (in the case of the masculine body) by visible effort. If the muscular masculine body is constructed by the kind of work advocated in the pages of *Physical Culture*, the feminine body – in the double-bind which endures in advertising – is supposed to achieve perfect shape while remaining 'natural'. Schwartz reports that in the period between 1885 and 1905 in America massage became a largely feminine occupation, so that 'the masseuse was the body's civil engineer', but pummelling it into aesthetic shape rather than building it up. The masseuse mediates between two opposed areas: the *work* of burning off fat, and the feminine ideal of aesthetic reduction implied by the invisible process of dieting.[17]

After the turn of the century, the implications of this concern with aesthetic shape and movement are visible in increasingly popular systematic women's-exercise. By 1918, Suzanna Cocroft, advocate of 'True Functional Harmony', was leading 3,500 women office workers in daily exercises in Washington, and Annette Kellerman, author of *Physical Beauty*, developed an exercise style for women in the 1920s.[18] In England, the climax of exercise-for-women was Mary Bagot Stack's 'stretch-and-swing' technique, promulgated in *Building the Body Beautiful* (1931); a system which demonstrates some of the ambivalence of women's position within physical culture. Bagot Stack describes her technique as applied eugenics: 'Women are the natural Race Builders.' Consequently, 'Woman needs a system of her own – a system suitable for her peculiar needs and not tacked on as an afterthought to some system invented originally for men.'[19]

The 'feminine' stress here includes discussion of fitness and birth, but more markedly produces an emphasis on grace, poise, and both mass and individual display. Bagot Stack's Woman's League of Health and Beauty grew rapidly: by 1931 it was able to mount massive demonstrations in Hyde Park, the Albert Hall, and the Olympia ('4000 legs lifted towards the ceiling'); at its peak in 1937, the League had 220 branches and 120,000 members.[20] The first exercise programme broadcast on British television, in 1936, was of Bagot Stack pupils. *Building the Body Beautiful* is illustrated with photographs from features in the *Daily Mail* and *Times*, including a photograph of the 'famous leap' by star pupil Peggy St. Lo (famous for being famous, it is 'considered by experts to be one of the most beautiful photographs ever taken', Figure 7). Other photographs have a pupil looking at herself in the mirror to test her waistline and various 'artistic' poses, stressing the body as ornament. If the healthy body 'is its "own best doctor", masseur, pharmacopoeia', it also creates 'a glorious sense of daily well-being that colours the whole personality, and creates atmosphere in every woman's home'.[21] The eugenic description of women as 'Architects of the Future' takes on an aesthetic colouring here: the body becomes decor just as the house is, as *habitus*, an extension of the self, a zone of embodied virtue. The pragmatic discourse of intervention in the habitual enters the world of the fashion magazine. The question of gender in relation to bodily reform is implicated in the issues of the perfected image and its prosthetic realization raised in the previous chapter.

MINA LOY AND THE BIRTH OF MODERNISM

If male modernists typically thought in prosthetic terms and sought to engender their aesthetics through bodily interventions, women writers had a different approach to the body, conditioned by an awareness of its visibility. The remainder of this chapter reflects on the relationship between the body and performance in

Figure 7 Physical Culture as publicity: 'Famous Leap by Peggy St. Lo'

two women working in the avant-garde milieu of New York and Paris, Mina Loy, and Djuna Barnes.[22] Both these writers were able to make the body productive of their writing; both engaged with bodily reform movements. In Barnes's *Ladies Almanack*, Loy appears as 'Patience Scalpel . . . as cutting in her derision as a surgical instrument'[23] – a parodic version of the 'surgical' Modernism of Pound and Williams.

Roger Conover reports that, in the 1920s, a rumour circulated in Paris that 'Mina Loy' was a fabrication, forcing her to appear at Natalie Barney's salon to disprove it: *habeus corpus*.[24] The absence of a textual body and the withdrawal of her actual body from the public gaze seem linked, since she was famously *a body*, in the sense that she embodied Modernism. Beautiful, elegant; the lover of Marinetti and Papini; exemplar of the futurist doctrine of non-romantic passion;[25] she was admired in the New York avant-garde after her move there in 1916; the incarnation of 'Modern Woman', according to the *New York Evening Sun*.[26] In recent histories like Steven Watson's *Strange Bedfellows* that iconic role is sustained, even at the risk of a critical fetishism which reproduces Modernism's own use of the feminine: Loy appears photographed by Man Ray or Lee Miller, dressed for the Blindman's Ball in one of her own creations, performing with the besotted William Carlos Williams on the bizarre geometrical set of Kreymborg's *Lima Beans*. She is, above all, a *face*, seen in profile, looking up at a camera; even inserted through a comic backdrop in a fair-ground booth.

The way in which the body 'enters the picture' reflects the gender-politics of the modernist movement as a whole, and the status of many women who were both participants and the object of masculine aesthetics. As Bridget Elliott and Jo-Anne Wallace point out, they often occupy 'an ambivalent place (not quite inside or outside of) the metropolitan avant-garde', often embodying a bohemian aesthetic, yet never accorded a central position.[27] Models for Rodin and later artists, photographed by the Surrealists, they mediate relations between the men who are the official sponsors of the movements; they signify as bodies, even where this role coexists with literary or artistic productivity. Examples, among others, include Louise Bryant, Tina Modotti, Lee Miller, Nina Hamnett, Nancy Cunard – whose heavy African bracelets exoticized a notorious body – and Ethel Mannin, who appears against a geometrical background in her record of iconoclastic youth, *Confessions and Impressions* (1930).[28] An extreme example is the Baroness Else von Freytag-Loringhoven, icon of New York Dada and its aggressive aesthetic. As Watson shows, the Baroness achieved notoriety as a performance-artist *avant la lettre*, making her body a work of art: shaving her pubic hair for a film by

Man Ray, wearing coal-scuttles, sewing kewpie-dolls and lightbulbs into her outfits. She was an incarnation of the muse as distraction-effect, tempting, pursuing, and biting Williams; terrifying Stevens; declaring a hopeless love for Duchamp; stealing Hart Crane's type-writer.[29] Barnes wrote an obituary for the Baroness; Loy wrote pas-sionate tributes to Cunard and Isadora Duncan.[30]

Around such figures, the question of 'for whom?' is always present – a question which does not retrospectively demand that modernist women produce a fully and consistently oppositional aesthetic within Modernism (what space would there be for that?), but which acknowledges that visibility may be compromised within a larger containing aesthetic in which women are objectified.[31] (We should also acknowledge the differences in the positions of women modernists: between the avant-garde circles of Loy and Barnes in Paris and New York and writers of the English 'woman's novel',[32] or between Loy's position in relation to her male support-ers – Pound, Williams, McAlmon – and in the lesbian community depicted in Barnes's *Ladies Almanac.*) In fact, a number of women modernists *do* manage the specular productivity in which they are disseminated, using the body as a means of performing modernity; perhaps even of disrupting its gendered assumptions. We need to reconfigure our picture of Modernism to take in these figures, who often appear in standard histories as the connections between male modernists, with curiously mobile biographies in place of the official 'career'.[33] Nancy Cunard's pose as 'white negro' is one example: at the same time as she publishes the *Negro* anthology in 1934, she performs her attack on race, gender, and class taboos; as Susan Stanton Friedman comments, the 'fetishization of her image was itself inseparable from her notoriety as a radical'.[34] H. D.'s use of her image in Macpherson's film *Borderline* (1930) and elsewhere is another instance.[35]

Loy's position here is interesting, if equivocal. Having been deeply involved in Futurism, she quickly became one of the great satirists of Modernism, always with an eye to the 'fashions in lechery' of male writers.[36] In exploring this role, we can look at two areas – machine culture and birth – which in their interaction inform the gendering of bodily reform. Loy offers, first, a critique of Futurism's machine culture, seeing the body–machine coupling as fetishism. An unpublished poem of 1921, 'The Oil in the Machine?', declares:

> Hear the evangel of the new era –
> The machine has no inhibitions
> Man invented the machine in order to discover himself
> Yet I have heard a lady say 'Il fait l'amour comme
> une machine à coudre', with no inflection of approval.
>
> It is the oil in the machine to which the mystics
> referred as the Holy Dove – – – – – And what could
> we make of the sort of pulpy material the Padre Eterno
> made engines out of
>
> We spasimal engineers
> Whose every re- act -ion of grace is an explosion
> in consciousness.[37]

The 'machine à coudre' is a masculine fantasy. 'The Oil in the Machine?' is typical of Loy's poems on the mechanical in that it resists any simple equation of body and machine. Rather than the machine serving as the desirable replacement for the body, it is a reductive version of the body, while the body is a machine which fails to perform. A later poem 'Brain' (1945) illustrates the latter point:

> radio pulp
>
> stacked with myriad microscopic
> recordings
>
> drumming on Time
> trivia
> of the past . . .
> too fast
>
> Automatic disc-server
> ceaselessly
>
> you sabotage my choice
> of selections
>
> lenient
> lapses of memory:
>
> the obsolete.[38]

The jerky and atomized phrases themselves mimic loss of memory and connection, though Loy also registers the productive nature of confusion. The poem seems a response to Bryher's 'If I am a needle on a disk', published in *transition* in 1927, which pictures the writer as a transcription device:

> whatever voices break across me
> or what shadows,
> knees or shoulders,
> silverpoint the blackness;
> got to play the record out
> till I break or am lifted,
> I don't choose the sound I make,
> you don't choose the groove.[39]

Here the self is fragile, subsumed to technology, if interestingly poised between the 'old silence' and the 'new record'. Loy posits a relationship in which the writer remixes messages; 'sabotage' signals the body's creative resistance. Where Bryher sees a tight fit between machine and self, Loy sees a comic dissonance.

Loy's unpublished manuscript *Island in the Air*, one of a series of partly autobiographical draft novels, similarly dwells on mechanical systems as fantastic internalized objects: 'A kind of short-circuit of being alive occurring in a woman when she simply *cant* go on set my nerves quivering so intensely they inscribed a diagram of their system on my inner sensibility.' A dream after one of the 'entertainments' which obsess her protagonist – 'an early electric power plant open to the public view at Earls Court Exhibition' – provides an almost Kleinian account of fetishism as the maternal–mechanical. She asks her mother about sex:

In the dream I shall dream that night, I meet again with that steel swish and arc-lit iterance of a nerveless automatism engendering exiled moons.

I drag at my mother's towering skirts to entreat her to come away – she takes no heed – Suddenly this dream mother comports herself in the wildest way – She is flinging her arms up, and at once they become steely arms – She is changing – turning – changes into a dressmaker's dummy of ringing metal – with expandible bust – the abdomen full as the curving breast of Lohengrin's oncoming swan. There, where the skirts should have been, all that upholstery dissembling the site of sin – is a forbidding cage of iron wire.[40]

In Surrealist fashion, the mother reassembles into a kind of ready-made mechanical sculpture. The palace of science becomes a threat to the order of reproduction.

A second general area in which Loy satirizes male modernists is sexuality, and the related issue of birth.[41] Her unpublished prose parody on Papini, *Pazzarella*, begins with the artist's interview with the title-figure, a gilded lady who is the object of his violent fantasies: 'Ah, then there was no withholding myself and I did throw myself upon her. In a sadistic delirium of destruction I determined to put an end to her.' The result is bathos: 'When I regained my calm, I found I had only possessed her.'[42] Birth is used both for satire and to create an 'Opposed Aesthetic' (as 'Anglo-Mongrels and the Rose' puts it). She ridicules the male aesthetic which founds itself on the objectified feminine body, or on the 1890s Svengali-plot. Her own role in the gestation of an aesthetic is burlesqued in 'Lion's Jaws', with its futurists 'notifying women's wombs / of man's immediate agamogenesis' – that is, the masculine fantasy of reproduction without sex. These wombs speak back:

> These amusing men
> discover in their mail
> duplicate petitions
> to be the lurid mother of 'their' Flabbergast child
> from Nima Lyo, alias Anim Yol, alias
> Inma Oly
> (secret service buffoon to the Woman's Cause)[43]

The duplication of names reflects Loy's penchant for pseudonyms, but also a fragmentation of the name which precludes patriarchal inheritance: whose baby is this? A more allegorical example is an unpublished story 'The Stomach' (1921). It describes Virginia Cosway, model for a Rodinesque statue 'La Tarentella', famous for its protruding stomach. The pose becomes her life: 'For a quarter of a century, the permanent physical adoption of that Spanish pose had defined the daughter's status – the authorized edition of Virginia Cosway issued by the Master for the international society of the elite parasites of the Arts.'[44] She becomes a totemic figure – as Loy did in Paris, fêted by the Surrealists as Arthur Cravan's widow – performing 'her Hispano-abdominal ceremony' at 'the birthdays of new movements'. 'The stomach had become an arbiter of aesthetics.' Like Picasso's African figures or Mrs Purefoy's womb in *Ulysses*, this is a site of modernity's parturition: 'a brief undulation of the hip, and the adjustment of the forefinger; the stomach outswung to its notable attitude, as if enticing aesthetic culture into her womb to be reborn for her audience'. Virginia is an active participant in this display of maternity, as the end of the story suggests:

> The stomach in its age was become fibrous and rigid.
> And as it proceeded towards me, I would have sworn I could see,
> set in the wrinkled lids of its navel – – – – – – – –
> a calculating eye.

'The Stomach' demythologizes Modernism's myths of sexual conquest and of bodily origins, just as an early poem describes a
Galatea able to deploy her own sexuality.[45]

At the same time, Loy is aware of the possibilities of founding an
aesthetic on pregnancy, even if – as her poem 'Parturition'
acknowledges – any such aesthetic is compromised within a patriarchal order. Her description of birth has some of the ambivalence
of Julia Kristeva's, in which the pregnant body is 'the dividing line
between nature and culture', and the site of a possible reformation
of the structure of gender: 'no signifier can cover it (the maternal
body) completely, for the signifier is always meaning, communication structure, whereas a mother–woman is rather a strange "fold"
which turns nature into culture and the "speaking subject" into
biology'.[46] 'Parturition' – which records that 'I am knowing / All
about / Unfolding' – similarly reverses inner and outer, making
the subject traverse herself as distinctions between inner and outer
experience collapse, and as the experience of pregnancy is imi-
tated in the poem's typographical dilation:

Locate an irritation   without
It is   within
Within
It is without.
The sensitized area
Is identical   with the extensity
Of intension

Initially the poem describes bodily boundaries, including those of
gender, in which identity is forged in terms of a romantic and
Nietzschean aesthetics of opposition. But Loy progressively invali-
dates those oppositions. Just as Kristeva locates an ethical weight
in the intercorporeality of the experience of childbirth, a giving
up of the self, Loy claims that she experiences 'negation of myself
as a unit' and is, after birth, 'absorbed / into / The was-is-
ever-shall-be / Of cosmic reproductivity'. In serio-comic terms,
'Parturition' depicts pregnancy as an opening of the self in which
bodily and intellectual experience, nature and culture, are united,
'Blurring spatial contours / So aiding elision of the circum-
scribed'. It provides one basis for a bodily poetics in which the
extremity of experience described, and the trajectory opened out
through childbirth – from 'I am the centre / Of a circle of pain'
to 'I am knowing / All about / Unfolding' – inaugurates a poetics

of self-abandonment, in contrast to the rigid protection of bodily
integrity characteristic of Futurism. Compare her praise of Stein:
'In Gertrude Stein life is never detached from Life; it spreads
tenuous and vibrational between each of its human exterioriza-
tions and the other.'[47]

There is, correspondingly, a preoccupation in Loy's work with
the opening up of the body's boundaries ('dilation') and the
traffic across boundaries. Often, as in 'Parturition', she uses metaphors which radically reverse inner and outer. An early poem,
'The Dead', describes how 'We are turned inside out' and digest
the cities of the past in our stomachs; and how:[48]

> We have flowed out of ourselves
> Beginning on the outside
> That shrivable skin
> Where you leave off.

A late self-portrait, 'An Aged Woman', has a similar sense of the
body's interior hollowed-out and exposed:[49]

> like moth
> eroding internal organs
> hanging or falling down
> in a spoiled closet.[49]

Loy is fascinated by the skin as a porous membrane, as in the striking image with which she describes the child gathering impressions which are simultaneously psychological and physical from
the mother in a poem from her sequence 'Anglo-Mongrels and
the Rose':[50]

> She is overshadowed
> by the mother's aura
> of sub-carnal anger
> restringent to the pores
> of her skin –
> which opening
> like leaves for rain
> crave for caressings
> soft as wings

The poem describes the effect on the child of 'the parent's solar-
plexus / in disequilibrium' – the kind of thinking which informs a
whole range of bodily culture writing in the period, often allied to
a polemic against repression of the kind implicit here.

Loy uses the body's presence to powerful effect in her early poems. Her 'Love Songs', which had led the first issue of Alfred Kreymborg's *Others* in July 1915, were denounced as 'swill poetry', shocking even to Amy Lowell – whose own body, 'a great, rough, strong, masculine thing', was a prominent part of her performances.[51] The outrage lay in references to the 'Pig Cupid' rooting among 'mucous-membrane', and passages like the following (again with images of birth, imprinting):

> We might have coupled
> In the bedridden monopoly of a moment
> Or broken flesh with one another
> At the profane communion table
> Where wine is spill't on promiscuous lips
>
> We might have given birth to a butterfly
> With the daily news
> Printed in blood on its wings[52]

Years before Joyce's epic of the organs in *Ulysses*, Loy's poetry seeks in the body a source for the 'news' which is Modernism; a body defined in terms of physiology and its tendency to resolve itself into different surfaces and traffic across surfaces: membrane, bag-like skin, abortions, scum-filled nostrils, spermatozoa, disheartening odours, sweat, hiccoughs, orgasm. The body knocks against other bodies; its presence insinuates itself into the rhythms of the poetry. We can say that, for Loy, the body is not the 'occasion' of an aesthetic it was for Futurism; it is actual bodily mechanisms which are involved, and, above all, a sense of the body as anything other than an integral unit. Loy reconsiders the penetrability ascribed to the feminine in Modernism, and offers up the de-objectified body.

AUTO-FACIAL-CONSTRUCTION

Given that Loy satirizes the futurist fascination with the body–machine, it seems almost paradoxical that she was the only modernist writer to actually create her own technique for bodily reform: 'Auto-Facial-Construction'. Published as a short pamphlet in Florence in 1919, *Auto-Facial-Construction* is a modernist hybrid, part manifesto, part advertisement, describing a technique which she would 'teach when not drawing or writing about art'.[53] For all that it seems eccentric, we can see it as emblematic of Loy's determination to represent herself in her own terms; to present a face to the world, a literal version of Yeats's 'Mask'. In Loy's case, it is a mask which knows its own necessary physicality and fragility; where Yeats's shields the self, Loy's both reveals it and registers that it is always already the object of the gaze of an other. Andrew Roberts relates Loy's Paris poems to guide-book descriptions of Parisian attractions available to the male *flâneur* who tours the *demi-monde* with a mixture of desire and condemnation. Loy, he suggests, imagines a look which resists that structure, which negotiates between an identification with women who are on display and a satire of the masculine look which 'places' them.[54] A similar thematics of self-presentation and self-construction are present in *Auto-Facial-Construction*.

As a physical-culture technique, 'Auto-Facial-Construction' can be related to Loy's interest in Christian Science, given concrete expression in her 1920 programme *Psycho-Democracy*, with its stress on 'Psychic Evolution', the conscious human control of biological and psychological functioning.[55] It is also related to techniques like Alexander's (the title anticipates his *Constructive Conscious Control of the Individual*, 1924). Loy stresses self-manipulation:

I will instruct men or women who are intelligent and for the briefest period, patient, to become masters of their facial destiny. I understand the skull with its muscular sheath, as a sphere whose superficies can be voluntarily energized. And the foundations of beauty as embedded in the three inter-connecting zones of energy encircling this sphere: the centres of control being at the base of the skull and the highest point of the cranium. Control, through the identity of your Conscious Will, with these centres and zones, can be perfectly attained through my system, which does not include any form of cutaneous hygiene (the care of the skin being left to the skin specialists) except in as far as the stimulus to circulation it induces is of primary importance in the conservation of all the tissues. Through Auto-Facial-Construction the attachments of the muscles to the bones are revitalized, as also the gums, and the original facial contours are permanently preserved as a structure which can be relied upon without anxiety as to the ravages of time. A structure which complexion culture enhances in beauty instead of attempting to disguise.

Like Alexander, Loy rejects the instrumental man–machine model and instead aims at a general revitalization and the restoration of integrity, writing of the face's 'conservation, and when necessary, reconstruction'. Like many bodily reformers, she aims to restore a 'natural' harmony, to make us to 'look like ourselves'.

On the other hand, the technique involves an aesthetic sense rather than a return to nature. It is artistic training rather than study of anatomy which validates the technique. As in the swirling surfaces of the futurist sculptor Boccioni's 'plastic ensembles', the skull becomes a play of forces in space and time. Those who might benefit include 'the society woman, the actor, the actress, the man of public career' – those who perform. Elsewhere, Loy writes 'The satisfaction of Living is in projecting reflections of ourselves into the consciousness of our fellows'; here she comments 'to what end is our experience of life if deprived of a fitting esthetic revelation in our faces?'[56] Auto-Facial-Construction is both natural and artificial; a cosmetics and an expression of the truth of the self. The ambivalence of the body in modernity is that it signifies both authenticity and the site of work.

Despite the fact that Loy never seems to have practiced the technique, her interest in bodily adaptation was sustained: among the later designs in her papers is a 'corselet or armour' to mechanically correct 'middle-age figure curvature', described as 'an efficient supplement to physical-culture exercises'.[57] Even at the end of her life she invited Jonathan Williams to 'discuss the right design for your face-armour.'[58] The presentation of the self remained a concern, though always with an awareness of aging and the need to tune inner and outer states.

The sense of the body as plastic in 'Auto-Facial-Construction' is visible in a range of Loy's texts, for example in her novel *Insel* (its central character based on the Surrealist Richard Oelze). In descriptions which parallel Wyndham Lewis's in *Tarr*, Insel is 'a skull with ligaments attached'; a constructed Frankenstein-like being: 'A kink near the ear suggested the wire-hung jaw of a ventriloquist's dummy.' At the novel's opening he is 'hoping to sell a picture to buy a set of false teeth'; eating, he develops 'a Dali-like protuberance of elongated flesh with his flaccid facial tissue'. His paintings are 'ectoplasm proceeding from him'.[59] Here, as elsewhere in Loy's work, the body fails: attacked from within and without by age in 'An Aged Woman'; already in 'Love Songs' an entropic machine, a 'clock-work mechanism / Running down against time'.[60] Insel is 'a wound up automaton running down', and the narrator has to constantly replenish his electromagnetic energies.

Another focus of the prosthetic thinking of 'Auto-Facial-

Construction' was the Dada boxer, Arthur Cravan, Loy's lover in New York from 1917 up to his disappearance in Mexico in 1919. Loy's writings on Cravan dwell not only on his attractiveness and strength, but also on his ductility: 'Unique phenomenon, a biological mystic, he traced his poetic sensibility to his power to "think" with any part of his body. His poetry reveals a physical illumination detonating as gun-cotton.'[61] Cravan can absorb anything into the self, even as he extends the self into other things. Because of the 'telescopic properties' which enabled him to 'push his entire consciousness into a wisp of grass', the boxer-flaneur becomes part of the urban spaces he inhabits: 'And when . . . he had engulfed in his regard every pebble, every wish, every perpendicular of sky-scraper, every metallic suspension and every square millimeter of superficies of the city he roamed in his tenacious idleness – a sort of inquietude would invade his motor centres. He could no longer *remain* – "God, how New York has contracted", he would say; "Dieu – que l'Amérique se rétrécisse".' The reference to 'motor centres' is only one of a number series of relays between body and machine: the metallic city is absorbed in the 'regard' of the boxer, contracting as it does so, while emotions located in the city 'invade' the motor centres. Like Loy, Cravan can break down the distinction between inner and outer, re-forming his body by per-forming. He is 'self-generated, immune to evolution'; but, unlike the futurist fantasist, he is mastered by externalities as much as he masters them, a shape-changing escape-artist whose last escape was death.

MODERNIST WOMEN AND THE BOXER: LOY AND BARNES

Loy's fascination with the boxer is mirrored in a number of other women modernists, including Djuna Barnes, Marianne Moore, Mary McCarthy, and Joyce Carol Oates. This seems problematic in the light of the treatment of the subject by male modernists, from the boxing of the futurists and Pound to that celebrated and prac-ticed by Hemingway and Mailer, or Brecht's comparison between drama and boxing. The confluence of writing and sporting meta-phors, particularly in American culture, enables an aesthetic which celebrates the 'hard' and clinical; which codes itself as 'mas-culine'.[62] (The fist-fight in Florida between Wallace Stevens and Hemingway might take the prize, though Hemingway assaulted

many in the name of anti-decadence.) Nathanael West's *The Dream
Life of Balso Snell* (1931) provides an extended example of the
configurations of gender here. Early in Balso's surreal journey up
the anus of the Wooden Horse of Troy, he sees a young naked
woman standing by a fountain. She discourses on the city as female
body: 'Feel, oh poet, the warm knife of thought swift stride and slit
in the ready garden . . . Walk towards the houses of the city of your
memory, oh poet! Houses that are protuberances on the skin of
streets – warts, tumours, pimples, corns, nipples, sebaceous cysts,
hard and soft chancres.' She goes on to talk of 'hysterical women'
and jaded appetites.[63] When Balso leaps on her, she meta-
morphoses into a middle-aged schoolteacher, Miss McGeeney.
Paralyzed, he has to make polite conversation. McGeeney is
writing a biography of Samuel Perkins, the biographer of the biographer of Boswell, Johnson's biographer – a figure who stands for
all effete talk about literature. Perkins is compared with
Huysmans's Des Esseintes, the exemplar of decadent sensation-
seeking: 'He had found in the odours of a woman's body never-
ending, ever-fresh variation and change – a world of dreams, seas,
roads, forests, textures, flavours, forms.' She continues, but 'Balso
had gotten one of his hands free. He hit Miss McGeeny a terrific
blow in the gut and hove her into the fountain.'[64]

   This is a representative moment in Modernism: an impatience
with aestheticism; a thwarted rape; blockage attached to the body
and the flesh; an explosion of violence. American energy counters
Old World effeteness, as suggested by Jacques Rigaut in *La
Révolution Surréaliste* in 1929: 'What a peal of laughter at my mistress's terrified face when, as she waited to receive a caress, I
slugged her with my American right hook and her body fell several
feet away.'[65] If male modernists defined themselves against a 'feminine' aesthetic, as Andreas Huyssen and others have suggested,
then West stages that opposition in near-parodic form. One of
Loy's satires is comparable: two characters, 'Love' and 'Futurism',
box using gloves with red flannel hearts, revealing the futurist aim
of destroying romance as just another form of eros.[66]

   Given the misogynist potential in the cult of the boxer, it is fascinating to consider the confluence of the woman writer and the
boxer in Modernism. One important issue is boxing as spectacle.
Fittingly for a nephew of Oscar Wilde, Cravan was a showman of
the ring and salon, as in the Paris lectures in which he shadow-

boxed and fired a revolver while denouncing his literary enemies. 'Genius', he declared, 'is nothing more than an extraordinary manifestation of the body', and he advised artists to 'Do a lot of fucking or go into rigorous training.'[67] Loy stresses Cravan's self-possession, suggesting that his avoidance of the war was a reluctance to have others use his body. He operates as spectacle: 'His life was unreal, or surreal, in that he never *was* the things he became. He never got nearer to a thing than in so far as a poet requires – to take contact with it. For instance, he became *champion de Boxe amateur de la France* without boxing, because all the challengers sat in a row and he was presented and they all resigned.' This is anything but the combination of force and skill celebrated by Hemingway.

Craven's fights were staged for publicity – like the bout in Spain with Jack Johnson, then in exile in Europe; out of his league, Cravan none the less enlisted the American champion into his perpetual circus. That fight was reportedly filmed, and it is worth recalling the links between boxing and early cinema. Boxing was one of the most popular and contentious subjects: the Veriscope film of the Fitzsimmonds–Corbett fight (1897) made $750,000, and a cycle of boxing films was produced in the period 1900–15. Jack Dempsey appeared in *The Prizefighter and the Lady* and other films, part of the commoditization of the sport in the 1920s.[68] As John R. Tunis noted in 1929:

> The modern pugilist is last of all a fighter. A lecturer, and endorser of belts, underwear, shaving cream and storage batteries he must be. An apt speaker on the radio, a handy man with his pen when contracts are being flourished, knowing in the art of obtaining publicity – these are the gifts which must be cultivated by the pugilist of today. As he will need to contest on an average but one bout a year, his ability in the ring is of far less importance.[69]

Anticipating this film-star boxer, Cravan's Dada lecturing and self-promotion marginalize the 'work' of the ring and place the boxer in the 'feminine' culture of the spectacle.

We can extend this sense of a different engagement with boxing by looking at Loy's friend Djuna Barnes, working as a fashionable reporter in New York and then Paris in the 1910s and 1920s. For all that she later disparaged her early writing, Barnes's work as a journalist suggests that the discourse of the grotesque body in her later work is rooted in popular culture and in notions of feminine performance.[70] As recent critics point out, Barnes's career was at the fringes of journalism, far from the prestigious areas of politics and international affairs. She constantly negotiates between areas of work coded as masculine and feminine: a series of interviews with 'Veterans in Harness' – men who had been in their job for decades – coexists, for example, with pieces on performers, dancers, and the circus. Moreover, Barnes constantly performs her own status as 'modern woman'. A graphic example is 'How it Feels to Be Forcibly Fed', published, with photograph, in the *New York World Magazine* in 1914, in which she subjects herself to the ordeal being undergone by British suffragettes. The article includes descriptions of the sensations of being bound, the insertion of a rubber tube through the nostrils into the stomach. Milk is then pumped down it, in a forced infantilism which Barnes barely counters by reproducing it as a media spectacle which is at the same time political critique. In other pieces, Barnes's work ranges from the daredevil (interviewing a gorilla) to the grotesque (a piece on fashionable methods of suicide) or flirtatious. The body of the reporter is part of the act. In her 1914 piece on being the object of fireman's training, 'My Adventures Being Rescued', she comments 'I was a "movie", flashing transient pictures on a receptive sky.'[71]

Given this stress on her dashing performance as a reporter, it is unsurprising that Barnes wrote on boxing for Macfadden's *Physical Culture* and other journals. Attendance at prize-fights was one of the ways in which independent women might assert their distance from the moral purity of the Victorian mother whom Ann Douglas has portrayed as the *bête noire* of Modernism (the Temperance Union campaigned against the sport). She interviewed 'Cowboy' Jess Willard, Heavyweight champion 1915–19 ('The Great White Hope' who defeated Johnson), and his successor, Jack Dempsey, and wrote on women at fights. Her first interview, in April 1915, was entitled 'Jess Willard Says Girls Will Be Boxing for a Living Soon.' Barnes depicts Willard as an inanimate object: a tree-stump, a Rodin sculpture. The champion responds by jokingly aligning himself with women: boxing is 'scientific playing' and 'women will be doing it for a living next, if it gets much more of a art'.[72] The homophobic Willard jokes about his unmarried state in the idiom of cross-dressing: '"Goodness! I thought you were married. Aren't you?" I asked, innocently. "Nope – not a wife yet, but am looking for the job", he said.' He turns the tables on Barnes, weighing her hand (*gloved* – unlike the boxer's) as she had earlier weighed his, and talking about her prospects of landing a millionaire in the marriage market.

This transvestite flirting implies a connection at the level of bodily production and self-commodification. The exchange which Barnes stages suggests a more important link, which again hinges on spectacle and even (as Joyce Carol Oates suggests) on a violent voyeurism.[73] Barnes's 1921 interview, 'Dempsey Welcomes Women Fans', has Dempsey quipping that he is plucking his eyebrows, as these days, with female fans, boxers need to be pretty: 'Women are – what do you call it – perverse, you see. They like to see a head punched, but they want the head that's punched to have a smattering of seven languages in it and a taste for poetry. I suppose they really like destruction.'[74] Dempsey depicts waste as a feminine excess, where a man is satisfied with 'just physical skill'; he also gives a sexual shading to his status as hired body: 'I like to hear the feminine sigh when it's all over; a man just grunts.'

For all that this is dubious, it finds echoes in a piece written seven years earlier by Barnes, 'My Sisters and I at a New York Prizefight'. The fight is depicted as feminine spectacle rather than as physical action: 'the woman's interest lies not in strength but in beauty' – in 'He has fine eyes' rather than 'Look at the muscles of his back.'[75] But at the end of the fight she sees a man shaken up, and shifts the terms:

Was it, after all, the men in the audience who had been careless and indifferent to pain? Was it the sound of a snapping fan that I had heard? Was it a woman's voice that had murmured, 'He has fine eyes?' A woman's hand that had gripped my arm in the dark? A woman's breath that had ceased so suddenly?

And whose voice was it that had cried out just before the finish – 'Go to it, and show us that you're men?'

Gender-relations here become uncertain, destabilizing the opposition between sweat and pain, on the one hand, and spectacle on the other. Indeed, there is a flicker of *Salomé* as Barnes comments that the men lounge on their seats, while women 'sit rigidly upright, balanced between wonder and apprehension, their faces still set in a fixed smile, as of a man beheaded while a joke still hovered in his throat'. Phallic women, beheaded men; boxing becomes a form of decadence. For Barnes, the original question –

what do women want at a fight? – becomes unanswerable as the whole field of gender resolves into a game of desire.

Barnes's interest in physical culture and performance is also visible in *Nightwood* (1936), for all that it involves a far more sophisticated sense of the body as textual origin. *Nightwood* describes bodies which are constantly on the point of fragmentation, or which are, like the legless Mademoiselle Basquette, mutilated. Heads and eyeballs are detached; Jenny Petherbridge is a person of parts: 'Only severed could any part of her have been called "right"'; Robin Vote's hand is 'older and wiser than her body'; Doctor O'Connor constantly decomposes. The aggressions, incorporations, and turnings-against-the-self involved in love, mourning, and addiction exacerbate the situation – Nora Flood is 'dismantled' and dismembered by the loss of Robin.[76] The novel cannot offer any integrating discourse, written as it is from a position of programmatic marginality in which all gendered constructions of the body are mocked, and abjection used to render a critique of the discourse of the hysteric.[77]

The only bodies which Barnes depicts as 'whole' are the constructed bodies of the circus performers, described in extensive epic asides. However, both descriptions confuse the gender-relations of physical culture. The body of Nikka, the black bear-wrestler, is designed to make him an aesthetic object: he is covered in a compendium of subversive tattoos. Like Otto Dix's portrait of 'Suleika, the Tattooed Wonder' (1920), he embodies an aesthetic of display: 'I asked him why all this barbarity; he answered that he loved beauty and would have it about him.' The body of the trapeze-artist Frau Mann is, in contrast, entirely adapted to the muscular tasks which she performs, as the body of the man is in the discourse of physical culture. Rather than having her skin exposed, it has hardened into the pattern of her costume, and 'the bulge in the groin where she took the bar, one foot caught in the flex of the calf, was as solid, specialized and as polished as oak'. Her 'tightly-stitched crotch' makes her 'the property of no man'. Just as Nikka is uninterested in women, she is 'unsexed'; both their names signal gender-crossing.[78] If these two performing bodies mix the gendered assumptions of physical culture, the doctor's room – in which Nora finds him in wig and woman's nightdress – is also a place where the constructed body meets the displayed body:

From the half-open drawers of this chiffonier hung laces, ribands, stock-ings, ladies' underclothing and an abdominal brace, which gave the impression that the feminine finery had suffered venery . . . There was something appallingly degraded about the room, like the rooms in broth-els, which give even the most innocent a sensation of having been accom-plice; yet this room was also muscular, a cross between a *chambre à coucher* and a boxer's training camp.[79]

The flicker of Barnes's reporting career here – the crossing of mas-culine discipline and brothel – signals the predicament of the woman writer, comfortable neither in the self-commodifying posi-tion of the journalist or in the detached 'making' of the surgical modernist.

In positioning these two women modernists in relation to bodily reform and bodily remaking, we can see that the position exem-plified by Lewis, in which masculinity is constructed by the artist and femininity is conservative, is both incorporated and under-mined. The feminine may also be 'self-generated, immune to evo-lution', as Cravan was, but, for Loy, any pure constructionalism must be placed within the arena in which the fight is a spectacle, in which bodies and capital are exchanged. She invents her own bodily reform movement, but stresses the element of performance and self-commodification in her technique and in that of Cravan, introducing *decor* into physical culture. Morever, Loy's 'opposed aesthetic' engages with the 'natural' productivity which places woman in the position of the Lamarkian transference-device; it is based on the dilations rather than the productivity of maternity, on a bodily plasticity and permeability which dissolves the repro-ductive 'unit'. Barnes also performs the role of modern woman, satirizing the gender-categories of boxing even as she deploys them; in *Nightwood*, physical culture is incorporated as comedy, the boxer planted in the brothel. In subsequent chapters, we will see that it is the clarification rather than the confusion of such cate-gories which is the object of the 'surgical' interventions of other modernists.

PART III

Technologies of gender

CHAPTER FIVE

Seminal economies

If you really believe the time has come for you to stop writing verse you should consult a physician, because there must be something wrong with your liver.
                    Frank Pearce Sturm to Yeats, December 1934[1]

A few weeks after I wrote to you I became well enough for work and pleasure. Haire examined me (I told you I would go to him) and approved my state.
                    Yeats to Ethel Mannin, December 1935[2]

In his own time, the scandal of W. B. Yeats's work in the 1930s was the stuff of Dublin rumour, some of it still circulating among unbuttoned scholars at conferences. Any reader of Yeats's *Letters* notices his candid desire for the young women to whom he writes, personal versions of the more abstract states of excitation in the late poems. Yet that late phase, which Richard Ellmann naturalizes somewhat in calling it a 'second puberty', followed a period of barrenness – of physical and creative impotence. Yeats's last phase was partly 'engineered', the result of a bodily intervention – the Steinach Operation which Norman Haire performed on him in 1934, and which, in Yeats's own account, brought a recovery of energy. The operation, as Ellmann argues, 'symbolized for Yeats his attempt to impose potency upon impotence', and produced an influx of startling new material, 'salted' by a resurgence of sexual energy.[3] In this chapter, I will examine the effects of that operation, placing it within an account of Yeats's ideas about sex and the creative process. Even if the Steinach Operation was, as medical historians insist, entirely 'psychogenic' in its effects, it is possible to establish close links between the medical theory involved and Yeats's work.[4] Moreover, Yeats's involvement with the operation places him on the fringes of the world of modernist sexology in which figures like Havelock Ellis and Norman Haire move, in an intimate relation to the scientific gender-shifting of the period.

One aspect of Yeats's late phase which we need to examine is his attitude to the sexuality of women. The view that the artist is unproblematically hermaphrodite, able to project himself or herself into other roles, is problematic; to claim, as Samuel Hynes did in 1977, that Yeats takes on 'a woman's private sexual identity' in his late work is to pass over the question of what might be involved: how 'private' is sexual identity, and how does he 'take it' – 'like a man', as they say? If Yeats, as Elizabeth Cullingford has argued of the period of unhappiness around the time of his marriage, 'equates the debility of age with exile into the realm of masculinity', what does that suggest about Yeats's late interest in sexuality?[5] The relationship between male poet and female muse was one of Yeats's most common themes, and the struggle between the two is often violent. Moreover, Yeats himself was able to distinguish between what it meant to be 'doubly a woman' and 'but once a woman', between being biologically female and a woman in imagination.[6] We need to consider what is involved when a man attempts to think like (or as) a woman.

SEX AND CREATION

Yeats's interest in sex spans his career, from the often sublimated 'decadent' sexuality of his early work to bawdy late poems. He inherits from the romantic tradition an emphasis on the sexual sources of creativity, visible in ideas like the marriage of self and anti-self, and the ideal of beauty embodied in the dancer or statuesque woman. In a 1906 essay, he writes of the ecstatic union of mind and body in creation, taking organic theories of art to their logical conclusion: 'Art bids us touch and taste and hear and see the world, shrinks from what Blake calls mathematic form, from every abstract thing, from all that is in the brain only, from all that is not a fountain jetting from the entire hopes, memories, and sensations of the body.'[7] While it cannot be said that the 'fountain jetting from . . . the body' is (simply) ejaculatory, in such formulae creative processes find parallels in sexual functions.

Yeats also resembles a number of modernists in his emphasis on male sexuality. He was to read *Lady Chatterley's Lover* with approval in the 1930s, but it was Ezra Pound who was most important here, particularly in the winters of 1913–16 in which the two poets lived together in Stone Cottage on the edge of Ashdown Forest, Pound engineering – or at least sustaining – a decisive shift in Yeats's work.[8] Pound had developed a number of theories about the 'germinal' role of men of genius and the sexual matrix of creation. He translated and commented on Remy de Gourmont's *The Natural Philosophy of Love* in 1921 (Yeats had a copy), as well as reviewing Louis Berman's *The Glands Regulating Personality* in 1922.[9] 'Berman's research into glandular activity', Ian Bell comments, 'confirmed the epistemology that underwrote Pound's use of scientific analogy during his London years; here was the final evidence for the shared physiology of body and soul'.[10] The 'real' of imagist aesthetics enters a discourse which is, as Bell shows, both idealist and embodied; which uses scientific terms to validate gendered categories. Pound used Berman and Gourmont to posit the sexual act as a metaphor for artistic creation, and the brain's fluids as analogous to semen, his metaphors taking on a curiously literal relation to Yeats: 'The thought of genius . . . is a sudden out-spurt of mind' and 'the individual genius . . . the man in whom the new access, the new superfluity of spermatozoic pressure (quantitative and qualitative) up-shoots into the brain, alluvial Nile-flood, bringing new crops, new invention.'[11] The description of Wyndham Lewis as exemplar of vorticist aesthetics is similar: 'Vortex . . . Every kind of geyser of jism bursting up white as ivory, to hate or a storm at sea. Spermatozoon, enough to repopulate the island with active and vigorous animals.'[12] Such images are also implicit in Pound and Eliot's exchange of bawdy verse on *The Waste Land,* in which the poem's genesis is described in terms of a pregnant Eliot with Pound as midwife, while copiously flowing sperm lubricates the process.[13]

In expatiating, even in joke, on the engendering and energizing powers of semen and placing it near the centre of modernist aesthetics, Pound followed a long tradition linking 'genius' to seminal power – within a matrix within which making is, as Wayne Koestlenbaum indicates, 'between men'.[14] There is a similar stress elsewhere in modernist aesthetics, for example in William Carlos Williams's description of the cover design of *Kora in Hell* (1920), for which Pound inspired the title: 'It represents the ovum in the act of being impregnated, surrounded by spermatozoa, all trying to get in but only one successful.' Williams adds a eugenic spin: 'I myself improvised the idea, seeing, symbolically, a design using sperm of various breeds, various races let's say.' Spermatic competitiveness is suitable for a volume including 'all my gripes to other poets, all my loyalties to other poets'. Elsewhere Williams writes of 'the true procreative process which is at the back of all genius'.[15] There is, however, a problem lurking in such metaphors (to which we will return), implicit in the tendency to see both brain-work and seminal production as drawing on limited reservoirs of energy.

Masculinity, creativity, and engendering become an issue for Yeats in the period of relative despair which preceded his marriage. The apology in 'Pardon, old fathers', introducing *Responsibilities* (1914), asks forgiveness that:

> for a barren passion's sake,
> Although I have come close on forty-nine,
> I have no child, I have nothing but a book,
> Nothing but that to prove your blood and mine
>
> (*VP* 270)

Even if aware that a book *is* something, Yeats reveals a nostalgia for physical 'begetting'. The sexual displacement of poems like 'The Cap and Bells' is rejected, as is what we could call (after a famous victim) the 'A. C. Benson syndrome' of the neurasthenic poet.[16] One answer to this crisis was marriage, Pound again intervening (with Dorothy Shakespear) in finding a bride – a role flagged in Canto 83, which depicts 'Uncle William' at Stone Cottage, chanting of 'a great Peeeeacock / in the proide ov his oiye',

> a great peacock aere perennius
>   or as in the advice to the young man to
> breed and get married (or not)
>   as you choose to regard it.[17]

After his marriage, Yeats describes his inspiration in a series of semi-autobiographical poems. In 'The Gift of Harun Al-Rashid', the warrior meditates on old age, and suggests that his energies have been replenished by a young woman who brings 'self-born, high-born, and solitary' truths – like those of George Yeats's automatic writing. His earlier wish to be freed from the demands of the body has been displaced by excitation: 'It seems I must buy knowledge with my peace.' The conclusion links sex and occult wisdom:

> All, all those gyres and cubes and midnight things
> Are but a new expression of her body
> Drunk with the bitter sweetness of her youth.
> And now my utmost mystery is out.
> A woman's beauty is a storm-tossed banner;
> Under it wisdom stands . . .   (*VP* 469)[18]

Marriage allows a sexual energy to be invested in the system of 'gyres and cubes', so that the poet may avoid the merely primary material described in 'The Living Beauty'. The energy which Yeats seeks is incarnated in a woman's body. 'Is pure energy confined to creative genius and to sex intercourse?' Yeats asks his communicators in 1919; they answer 'Yes'.[19]

The process of automatic writing which George Yeats initiated on 4 October 1917 was born out of Yeats's need for fresh material. His records of the sessions demonstrates how quickly he began to organize and set the agenda for discussion with his wife's 'communicators'. It seems that George Yeats's motives were, initially, personal – distracting a brooding husband – though she was an adept, and must ultimately be seen as a co-author of *A Vision*.[20] But that is not Yeats's account. In 'The Gift of Harun Al-Rashid' the old scholar wonders why a young woman chooses his 'crabbed mysteries', and asks whether 'Two contemplating passions chose one theme / Through sheer bewilderment?' (*VP* 466). He explains:

> Truths without father came, truths that no book
> Of all the uncounted books that I have read,
> Nor thought out of her mind or mine begot,
> Self-born, high-born, and solitary truths . . .   (*VP* 467)

What Yeats calls 'bewilderment' is closer to mystification. Instead of a union of the sexes ('her mind or mine'), there is, incipiently, a unity at the level of the text. The feminine is subsumed, dialectically, to the 'truths' which the male poet encodes. Complimentary dreams which Yeats reports in April 1921 illustrate this process:

Lat night after the same question I saw in a dream a hercules – I had no memory of George using that word – lying naked alseap or resting. I wonder how a woman could desire such great coarse strength & then it seemed to me I became a woman's mind & I felt the desire of the strength

& I touched his genital organs, but this did not seem to awaken. The same night George dreamed that she had had intercourse but that it was over [*sic*].[21]

The desire here is Yeats's; it is his word and his act. George Mills Harper suggests that Yeats knew a passage from Sara Underwood's *Automatic or Spirit Writing* which suggested that 'blended power is best', praising a marital context for production.[22] But the product of that blending remains with the poet. Indeed, in all of Yeats's associations with women, there is a suggestion that they are the medium for the release of an unconscious wisdom, whether the automatic writing of his wife, or the dancing of Margot Ruddock, or the poems of Dorothy Wellesley. 'Wisdom', in Yeats's work, is uncompromised by the tribulations of the world, unmediated and possessed entire – a constant, despite changes in its content, from his location of it in 'some one image that is the image of [every man's] secret life' in the 1900 essay on Shelley, to his late explanation to Ruddock: 'not the way of our ancestors, who throng in our blood, not the way found by some act of submission to a church or a passion, to anybody or anything who would take from us the burden of ourselves'. Wisdom is a 'self-possession' like that ascribed to Hamlet.[23] But that perfection is outside time and history. The mechanism by which it enters art and becomes poetry is what Yeats calls *incarnation*.

INCARNATION AND SELF-BEGETTING

The annunciation, the moment of divine insemination (whether it is Christian or pagan), and its physical outcome in incarnation, are figures for that intersection of the eternal and the contingent which fascinated Yeats, appearing in his theories of individual creativity and of history.[24] In *A Vision*, 'annunciation' is the point which marks a shift in historical cycles, whether Christian or the 'annunciation that founded Greece', triggered by a sexual mechanism like the divine rape in 'Leda and the Swan'. For a period, the Yeatses were excited by the possibility that they might be the subject of such a mechanism, that the 'new [Irish] avatar' which A.E. had predicted decades earlier might be their son. In the automatic script they also explore 'impregnating moments' (and the related 'initiatory moments'), individual crises like the inception of the automatic script itself.[25]

A particular interest in incarnation can be seen in the period of Yeats's change of mood in the late 1920s, for example in his short essay on 'The Need for Audacity of Thought', published in *The Dial* in 1926, after *The Irish Statesman* turned it down as contentious. Insisting that 'We must consider anew the foundations of existence', Yeats attacks Christians who could not accept a ballad about Jesus performing a miracle from within the womb (the talking body). The clerics who proscribed it could not, he declares, believe in 'the reality of their own thought', in the Incarnation as anything other than a scholastic doctrine. He, on the other hand, saw in 'The Cherry-Tree Carol' 'all that seems impossible, blasphemous even . . . set forth in an old "sing-song" that has yet a mathematical logic'.[26] This is Yeats's procedure in his late works, with their blasphemy, 'sing-song' and esoteric wisdom. *A Vision* shares this make-up, with its framing device of the bawdy story of Huddon and Duddon, Robartes's tall tales, the attached songs, and the 'mathematical logic' of 'The Great Wheel'.

Stan Smith follows F. A. C. Wilson in tracing Yeats's ideas about incarnation to Thomas Taylor's translation of Porphyry's essay on the Cave of the Nymphs, in which the patriarchal principle is incarnated and enters history through the 'seminal powers' released by divine natures as they enter the realm of generation. Taylor notes that 'the genital parts must be considered as symbols of prolific power; and the castration of these parts as signifying the progression of this power into a subject order'. This is, Smith writes, a metaphor for the creative process in which 'the ideational father is castrated into textual being, culminating in the material body of Yeats's text'.[27] The incarnational process involves, that is, a repression of patriarchal energy, paralleling Freud's account of primal castration in *Moses and Monotheism*.

One problem, however, with Smith's account of the way in which the divine enters time through sex is that he bases his case for the repression of the patriarchal principle on 'Among School Children', and ignores other poems which foreground the process which he claims is repressed.[28] Moreover it is often the maternal rather than the patriarchal role which obsesses Yeats, the female body which experiences the 'act of generation'. This becomes particularly clear when we remember that the incarnational model applies to individuals: 'When a man writes any work of genius, or invents some creative action, is it not because some knowledge or power has come into his mind from beyond his mind?'[29] For the late Romantic Yeats, a woman seemed the essential mediating link in that process; it was only through the intervention of his wife that he obtained the material synthesized in *A Vision*. The 'feminine' stands at a crucial point between the absolute nature of Wisdom and its realization in the world.

At the core of Yeats's creative processes there is thus a paradox. Wisdom is ideally self-sufficient, unmediated. But in order to enter art, it must 'spend' itself, abandoning its unity of being to the downwards pathway to incarnation and time. Poetic creation is sexually mediated, and the poet is subject to all the effects of ageing which Yeats felt after 1925, as well as to the physical 'inhibition' (possibly impotence) described in his letters to Margot Ruddock. One response to this paradox is to actively seek an alliance with the feminine; to shift the self, as it were, onto the ground on which it is mediated. If Yeats had wished to be more 'masculine' before his marriage, his position reversed in the 1920s; a point reinforced in a letter to Mannin, where he adopts 'the style of The Arabian Nights' (a book with a female narrator) to argue that the eternal verities of music, form, and love are the important questions, rather than the masculine sphere of politics.[30] Yeats began to take a particular interest in what underpins the incarnational process: the sexuality of women.

One expression of that interest is 'A Man Young and Old', the sequence published in *The Tower*. Yeats describes a man who has found a stony-hearted lover and himself become 'like a bit of stone', unable to purge his feelings. His recovery comes through 'old Madge', the aged and 'barren' female who nevertheless seems to believe that her piece of stone is a child. The old man mocks her, then accepts her belief, in a stanza which includes the apocalyptic peacock's cry:

> Were I but there and none to hear
> I'd have a peacock cry,
> For that is natural to a man
> That lives in memory,
> Being all alone I'd nurse a stone
> And sing it lullaby.   (*VP* 458–9)

These are the 'old women's secrets' that Madge tells him: 'Stories of the bed of straw / Or of the bed of down'. The sequence as a whole offers a lesson in sexual knowledge for the man; feelings of age and impotence are replaced by an apprehension of the art of spiritual midwifery, the nursing of a stone. What does it mean to nurse a stone? Yeats often refers to having a stone upon one's tongue as being unable to utter; as a type of poetic barrenness, particularly in the face of occult events.[31] The word 'barren', according to some etymologies, has its root in the Indo-European root 'bar', or male: the male cannot give birth. We could see the lesson given by Old Madge as a symptom of that necessity; of a poet's need for the feminine in order to internalize the incarnational process, and to make it a principle of self-renewal.

Yeats constantly sought to renew himself in later life, to overcome his feelings of age and to undergo a re-birth. The Romantic equation of self and corpus in the epigraph to the *Collected Works* of 1908 had suggested:

> The friends that have it I do wrong
> When ever I remake a song,
> Should know what issue is at stake:
> It is myself that I remake.   (*VP* 778)

These lines are echoed decades later in 'An Acre of Grass', where the remaking is more imperative, a way of resisting stagnation: 'Grant me an old man's frenzy, / Myself must I remake . . .' (*VP* 576). As I have suggested, Yeats's work undergoes a crisis in the early 1930s – a crisis including health problems, the death of Lady Gregory, and a greater distance between the poet and his wife; and following the bitter end of his involvement in Irish politics. There are periods of particular tension – in April 1933 he reported that he had written his first poem for a year – but the problem of sustaining his career is endemic in this period, generating a range of strategies. A favourite technique was to undertake different tasks in order to give birth to poems. Yeats said that *The King of the Great Clock Tower* was written in order to produce lyrics, and made the same claim of *The Herne's Egg* in 1934: 'I am trusting to this play to give me a new mass of thought and feeling, overflowing into lyrics.' He undertook the task of editing *The Oxford Book of Modern Verse* in late 1934 that he might be 'reborn in imagination'.[32] *On the Boiler* produced lyrics. In these works it is other types of writing – the play and the essay – which generate poetry. Moreover, each involves a contemplation of endings, either of Yeats's literary tradition, or of the poet, or of civilization, as well as the possibility that he will no longer write poetry: a fear of creative impotence. He later said that he 'warmed [himself] back into life' in the late 1920s (*VP* 831) – a metaphor with maiuetic overtones.

In such cases, Yeats was acting as his own muse and midwife, begetting himself on himself and generating energy from within his own corpus. The iconography of the annunciation and parthenogenesis are applied directly to the poet in poems like 'Sun and Stream at Glendalough':

> What motion of the sun or stream
> Or eyelid shot the gleam
> That pierced my body through?
> What made me live like these that seem
> Self-born, born anew?   (*VP* 507)

'Self'- compounds often signal moments of particular 'blessed-ness' or wisdom in Yeats's work: the 'self-sown, self-begotten shape that gives / Athenian intellect its mastery' of 'Colonus' Praise' (*VP* 446), the 'Self-born, high-born and solitary truths' of 'The Gift of Harun Al-Rashid' (*VP* 467), the 'Self-appeasing, self-affrighting' nature of the soul's 'radical innocence' in 'A Prayer for My Daughter' (*VP* 405), the 'self-begotten' influx of 'Old Tom Again' (*VP* 530). Instead of depending on a sexual mediation, the self acts as its own mate in a narcissistic version of the mystic marriage. In a more Freudian vocabulary, Ego-Libido replaces Object-Libido – the conscious nature of the process circumventing some of Freud's uncertainties about whether the Ego or Id is the reservoir of libido.[33] Desire, for the late Yeats, is firmly located within the field of conscious activity.

In terms of gender, 'self-begetting' implies an integration of the feminine and the masculine. That energy which had flowed through the female, and was released in sexuality, is held within the self, and releases energy to the self. Yeats seeks to beget or bear himself on the model of the God of the 'Supernatural Songs', who alone is a complete family: 'But all that run in couples, on earth, in flood or air, share God that is but three, / And could beget or bear themselves could they but love as He' (*VP* 556). In 'What Magic Drum?', written after the Steinach Operation, Yeats depicts a bisexual deity. Here is a divine birth and annunciation with which the poet identifies:

He holds him from desire, all but stops his breathing lest
Primordial Motherhood forsake his limbs, the child no longer rest,
Drinking joy as it were milk upon his breast.

Through light-obliterating garden foliage what magic drum?
Down limb and breast or down that glimmering belly move his
                     mouth and sinewy tongue.
What from the forest came? What beast has licked its young?
                          (*VP* 559–60)

This poem, with its Hindu source emphasizing bisexual reproduction, is the most explicit Yeats wrote on self-engendering – though we can notice that the feminine is present only as a principle; this 'he' is not bisexual, but takes on motherhood in simile, 'as [if] it were'.[34] With its rhetorical questions emphasizing the mystery of divine influxes, 'What Magic Drum?' is close to late poems of self-creation like 'Sun and Stream at Glendalough' and the 'Supernatural Songs'. They celebrate ideal unions and states of self-delight, like the Swedenborgian 'intercourse of angels' described in 'Ribh at the Tomb of Baile and Aillinn', in which sexual union after death becomes the meeting of 'pure substance' rather than a fall into generation. But, even in this poem, the real epiphany is that of Ribh and his book rather than the two legendary figures – and Yeats's, since he describes two characters from his own poem of 1901. The declaration of 'Ribh in Ecstasy' could serve as a rubric for Yeats's self-renewal: 'My soul had found / All happiness in its own cause or ground' (*VP* 557).

SELF-INSEMINATION AND THE STEINACH OPERATION

In parallel with these poetic efforts at self-renewal, there is the Steinach Operation, the physical means by which Yeats sought to halt the process of aging in 1934. Eugen Steinach was a respected authority on the biology of gender, working in Vienna from the turn of the century; his work on rejuvenation dated from the period 1916 to 1918. With thousands of men undergoing his operation in the 1920s, it is something of a scandal to historians of medicine, with overtones of quackery which seem to compromise Steinach's 'real' work (as does association with Sergei Voronoff, the Russian 'monkey-gland' doctor who established a clinic in Algiers in 1920).[35] In fact, it was only in the 1930s that

androgens and testosterone were finally isolated; Steinach and
Voronoff precede endocrinology in its modern form, and like
most medical practices, their work is only fully intelligible within
the social formations which support it.

The use of hormone extracts dates from the late nineteenth
century. Charles Brown-Séquard injected himself with animal testicular extract in the late 1880s, and such extracts – 'the new elixir
of youth' – quickly became popular in America as restoratives for
neurasthenic patients.[36] Others took thyroid extracts, often to
speed up the metabolism for slimming.[37] Such work can be linked
to wider attempts in the period to increase human energies, for
example Wilhelm Weichard's experiments in Germany in the
1900s, which sought to locate the substances which produced
fatigue and provide an antidote.[38] These *active* attempts to combat
aging and fatigue (in contrast to earlier passive attempts, like Silas
Mitchell's rest cure) are characteristic of modernist medicine. A
typical pamphlet of *c.*1932 from Hancock & Co., chemists in the
Strand who dealt (in plain wrappers) with birth-control and
related matters, is headed 'Rejuvenation' and notes that 'Age is
not a wearing out process but a cessation of glandular activity.'[39] It
is thus amenable to treatments which stimulate the glands or
duplicate their action: Hancock's supplied tonics for a range of ail-
ments, including impotence, neurasthenia, seminal weakness,
nerves, low vitality, sadness, inefficiency, etc. The new 'Glandular
Elixir', the text promises, stimulates the 'ductless [hormonal]
glands' and 'produces results which vie with those obtained in the
experiments with glands of the monkey grafted on to the body of
man', all for 27s a bottle. Self-healers offered to duplicate the same
glandular cures by will-power.[40]

Some writers, like Artaud, took the extracts; others had the
Steinach Operation – Freud had it in 1923 as part of his cancer
treatment.[41] In choosing the 'cut' rather than the pills, Yeats was
taking the high road. His surgeon was Norman Haire, an
Australian who came to London in 1919 and who had established
himself at the centre of English sexology by the mid-1920s. Haire
performed Steinach Operations, including many on artists and
writers, counselled patients, wrote guides and encyclopedia
entries on sex, befriended reformers like Havelock Ellis, and established links with Magnus Hirschfeld's Institute for Sexual Science
in Berlin. An international network developed which began to

organize meetings in the 1920s, with one high point, the second Congress of Hirschfeld's World League for Sexual Reform, held in London in 1929. The Congress suggests the alliance of reformers, free-thinkers, eugenicists, and others involved in the subject: it included George Bernard Shaw, Bertrand Russell, Desmond McCarthy, Naomi Mitcheson, Ethel Mannin, and Dora Russell, as well as professionals in a variety of disciplines, from birth-control exponents like Margaret Sanger and Marie Stopes to surgeons like Schmidt and Haire.[42] Arnold Bennett and H. G. Wells offered written support.

Mannin, radical novelist and journalist, knew Haire well and had already written an account of him as 'rationalist' in her out-spoken *Confessions and Impressions* (1930). In a later volume of autobiography, she recalls him introducing her to Yeats, so that 'the famous poet [could] test out his rejuvenated reaction to an attractive young woman'.[43] She and Yeats became friends. A letter to her in December 1935 (providing an epigraph for this chapter), reporting on his condition a year-and-a-half after his operation, encapsulates the connections between the personal and the medical: 'A few weeks after I wrote to you I became well enough for work and pleasure. Haire examined me (I told you I would go to him) and approved my state.'[44] The meanings here are implicit in a barely recoverable context: in the triangulation, in Mannin's familiarity with the operation and with the world of sexology, with Haire himself, and in the hint of sexual activity which one might deduce from Mannin's evident familiarity with the tempo of the poet's desires. 'He had flashes of wit and a *bawdy* sense of humour. For three years I knew him *intimately*', she reported many years later.[45]

Yeats's reasons for undergoing the operation were complex: a fear of old age, poor health, and worries about declining energy were all present. A wide variety of benefits were said to be pro-duced, including cardio-vascular and respiratory improvements. The best-publicized effect, however, was a return of sexual desire and potency, and Haire is reputed to have encouraged (even arranged) post-operative sexual activity. Other texts call sex 'a restorer of tone' and describe the Steinach Operation as an 'eroticization of the nervous system'.[46] Yeats was well up in the medical theory. According to Ellmann he consulted a borrowed copy of Haire's *Rejuvenation* (1924), which describes a number of

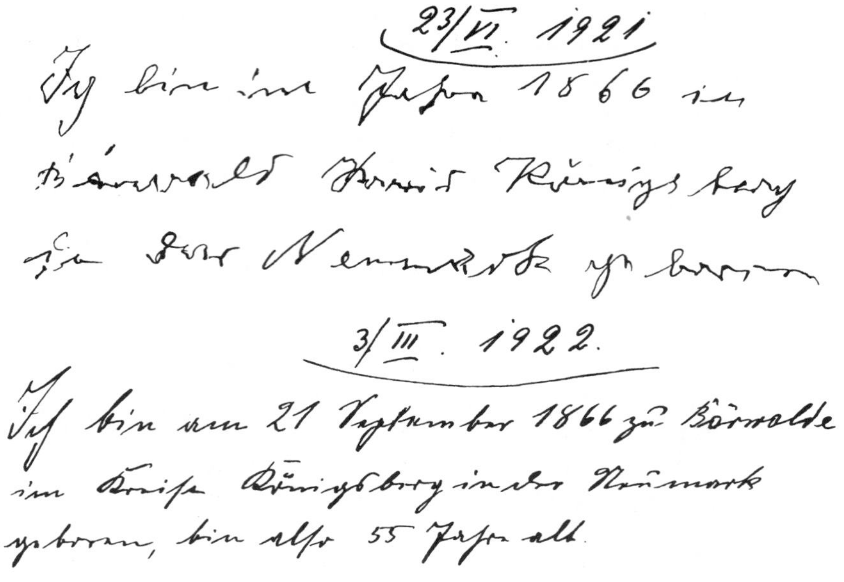

Figure 8 Patient's handwriting before and after operation

successful operations (including one on an unnamed novelist born 1867–8).[47] But the book in Yeats's library, which he recommended to T. Sturge Moore, was the German surgeon Peter Schmidts's *The Conquest of Old Age* (1931). An enthusiast, Schmidt quotes Swift and cites Nietzsche on the will to live: 'All passionate desire longs for eternity.' He uses a standard analysis of personality types: on the one hand, there is the normal, 'pyknic' type, healthy and balanced; on the other hand, the 'dysplastic' type, 'the thin-skinned, the sensitive-nerved, the malcontents, the compassionate, the neurotic, the "crazy"'.[48] The artistic, 'dysplastic' type – for which Yeats would have read his earlier self – is prone to physical or sexual disorders. *The Conquest of Old Age* also includes an attention to the *written* script which places it alongside other physio-textual interventions (Stein's, and the gender surgery described in the next chapter): a before-and-after handwriting sample showing a reduced tremor and new firmness in the rejuvenated hand (Figure 8).

Schmidt's explanation of the operation can be related to the emphasis on self-creation which we have seen in late Yeats. The

Steinach Operation was – it is difficult not to be anticlimactic – simply a vasectomy: the *vas deferens* was severed and sutured. The principle is this:

after the ligature of the vas deferens and the consequent atrophy of the ordinary glandular cells, more space is left for the interstitial tissue, which can now proliferate luxuriously. The interstitial tissue is what constitutes the puberty gland. The enlarged puberty gland secretes more testicular hormone than before, and this, being poured into the blood, produces the effect of which we are in search.[49]

It is this effect, based on the operation of a fictional 'puberty' gland connected to the semen-producing cells, which produces 're-activation'. Energy is diverted from the production of semen to the production of hormone, and the system revitalized via a shift from external to internal secretion (Figure 9).

Why did this process seem so convincing? The clearest explanation lies in two interlocking traditions of thought relating to male sexuality: the idea of the 'spermatic economy' and, less directly, of seminal energy. Nineteenth-century physiology had seen the spermatic economy as part of the closed system of bodily energies which we saw in Beard: excessive expenditure in one area (like the brain or sexual system) causes depletion elsewhere.[50] As Herbert Spencer put it in 1852, 'intense nervous application, involving great waste of the nervous tissues, and a corresponding consumption of nervous matter for their repair, is accompanied by a cessation in the production of sperm-cells'.[51] The equation also worked the other way, producing a vast literature on spermatorrhoea and its depletion of mental energy. The Steinach Operation, while belonging in part to the new theorization of bodily energy in terms of hormones which emerges in the 1920s, seems also to borrow from earlier paradigms: seminal energy is retained within the body, and one organ is made to atrophy in order to energize the adjacent and linked organ.[52]

The explanation of the operation also involves suggestions of self-insemination. A tradition in medical thought had always stressed the role of the 'hotter' fluids of masculine generation in conception.[53] Thomas Laqueur comments that, in the early seventeenth century, 'impregnation . . . becomes metaphorically the igniting of women, setting them aflame as if struck by lightning. Or, in a metaphor even more evocative of the Word . . . it is like the formation of a conception in the brain.' By the nineteenth

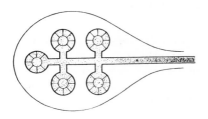

DIAGRAM OF GLAND WITH EXTERNAL
SECRETION

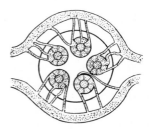

DIAGRAM OF GLAND WITH
INTERNAL SECRETION

The secretion is poured into
the blood

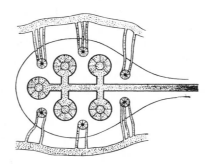

DIAGRAM OF GLAND WITH BOTH EXTERNA
AND INTERNAL SECRETION

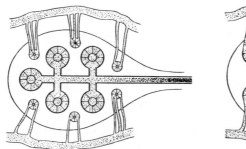

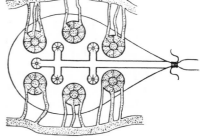

DIAGRAM TO ILLUSTRATE TISSUE CHANGES IN THE TESTICLE AFTER A STEINACH
OPERATION

Figure 9 Explanation of the Steinach Operation

century, he suggests, the link between female orgasm and conception was vanishing, so the power of semen was even greater: 'What emerges is a new and vastly inflated role for semen, which somehow pushes, squeezes, or otherwise excites a woman's insides and which, judging from the silence on the matter, is able to do so without her feeling anything.' Semen could offer a power like electricity, 'coursing through the Fallopian tubes'.[54] Patrick Geddes and J. Arthur Thomson in *The Evolution of Sex* (1889) even saw sexual differentiation as operating at the level of conception: the ovum was feminine and passive ('anabolic'), the sperm active and masculine ('katabolic'). The commonplace nature of ideas of seminal invigoration at the end of the nineteenth century is suggested by Edward Carpenter citing a report which claimed that 'the thriving of girls' after marriage was a result of 'the absorption of semen' – applying the same ideas to intercourse between males.[55] The Steinach Operation represents an involution of these ideas; self rather than the other is stimulated, re-energizing internally: 'Steinach's method is independent of the supply of an external source of energy.'[56]

We might also see the operation as a response to contemporary fears, in America and Europe, of masculine decline, expressed in terms of seminal economy: birth-rates, potency. A 1910 advertising pamphlet for Suspensories of Chicago reiterated the point which Spencer made sixty years earlier: 'the consumption of nerve energy is a direct strain on the spermatic cord . . . the testicles are the barometer of a man's physical and mental condition'. As Harvey Green comments, 'oblique references to "vitality" and "renewed life" were, by the first decades of the twentieth century, code words for sexual potency'.[57] The Steinach Operation draws on such fears by an internalized eugenics in which reproductive potency is sacrificed for greater energy. Schmidt emphasizes that he always, unlike some surgeons (but like Haire), sutures *both* the *vasa deferentia* in order to prevent the fathering of children: his ageing men inseminate and father only themselves. The individual male becomes the receptacle for sexual energy, gaining in energy and weight. There are even overtones of what we could call the transsexual-pathogenic here: Schmidt's book contains before-and-after pictures of men, showing 'healthy' weight-gains suggestive of pregnancy. The Steinach Operation thus fits closely with Yeats's late interest in his own self as the focus for incarnation, providing a physical location for the image of 'self-begetting'. The theory of the conversion of semen into physiological energy, rather than its use in sexual procreation, was a validation of the self-directed nature of Yeats's late sexuality. The 'empty cup' of old age is refilled from within.

IMPOTENCE, AGING, AND THE PURSUIT OF WOMEN

One outcome of the Steinach Operation was that Yeats reported a return of desire. This in turn is connected to the friendships with younger women like Margot Ruddock, Dorothy Wellesley, and Ethel Mannin, so important in his late poetry. Reading through his letters in this period, they are still striking in their obsessions: letter after letter about sexual and intellectual passion, written to women forty or fifty years younger; often women who were bisexual or lesbian. Some include poems about sex, linked, whether imaginatively or factually, to the recipients.

I have suggested that, to some extent, Yeats attempted to act as his own sexual agent in his late works, to get around the problems of 'incarnation', and work from a position of self-sufficiency rather than sexual mediation. What, then, did he hope to gain from these friendships? Clearly, something other than a return of the energy that he had received after his marriage.[58] We need to examine both his feelings about age, and the poetry itself. 'Age', Kathleen Woodward suggests, is imposed on us from without, when suddenly we see our image in the mirror, or others treat us as old.[59] Yeats describes such moments of self-recognition and alienation in a letter to Dorothy Wellesley in 1936: 'Over my dressing table is a mirror in a slanting light where every morning I discover how old I am. "O my dear, O my dear".' The half-conventional phrase 'O my dear' is interesting here. Not only is it the refrain of 'The Three Bushes', but it recurs in Yeats's letters in this period, often in contexts where he writes about aging and women – in particular with Dorothy Wellesley, who had begun writing 'My dear Yeats':[60]

And O my dear, as age increases my chains, my need for freedom grows.

Can I come to you in October? They have fixed my broadcast for Oct. 11. If I cannot come then I will do it from Belfast. But O my dear, my dear.

O my dear, I thank you for that spectacle of personified sunlight. I can never while I live forget your movement across the room just before I left, the movement made to draw attention to the boy in yourself.

My dear, my dear – when you crossed the room with that boyish movement, it was no man who looked at you, it was the woman in me. It seems
that I can make a woman express herself as never before. I have looked
out of her eyes. I have shared her desire.

O my dear, O my dear, do not write. I feel I am in such disgrace. Do burn
the letter about ———.

The phrase conveys affection and a half-mocking admission of
weakness, of an openness to sexual desire in an old man who recognizes her lesbianism. The refrain 'O my dear, O my dear' had
appeared early in Yeats's work, in a song from *The Hour-Glass,* 'I was
going the road one day', based in turn on a folk song translated by
Lady Gregory as 'The Noble Enchanter'. It describes an old man
deserted for a younger man by his wife.[61] Remembering this
origin, we can link the words to a fear of an impotence which slides
towards tiredness and ridicule; a state depicted in numerous late
poems and letters.

But 'O my dear' also, particularly in the fourth letter quoted,
suggests a desire to share or possess a woman's sexual identity: the
emphasis is on the 'my', and the power generated by 'sharing' a
desire which is curiously mobile in its deployment across gender.
The reiterated phrase suggests both the problem and its solution,
both the embarrassments of an aged sexuality and what can be
made of it in terms of the poet's ability to 'enter' the consciousness
of others. However, Yeats remains 'in' the masculine: seeing desire
'through her eyes' is being the boy (man) in Dorothy Wellesley, or
being the woman who is the object of her homosexual desires (that
itself, perhaps, a displaced version of 'being the object of this
woman [whom I desire]'. The movement of the passage is from
the position of the object of a woman's desire to that of the woman
in whom that desire is located – a narcissistic and auto-erotic
oscillation in which Yeats makes himself the object of his own
desire, while (as ever) equating that narcissism and self-sufficiency
with the feminine. Indeed, it is the lesbianism of his correspondent which enables Yeats to keep this narcissism within the feminine: the only man in the picture is the Yeats who writes, rather
than the Yeats who desires and is desired (Yeats parallels Freud,
who formulated the term narcissism to account for the object-
choice of the homosexual).[62] Appositely, while Yeats purchased
Orlando on Wellesley's recommendation, he later admitted that he
had not read it.

This is a route to femininity which takes a Freudian trajectory: Yeats must cripple or maim himself ('Oh my dear') before recovering via a process of self-sufficient autotelic desire which he associates with the 'feminine'. The Steinach Operation, as we have seen, has a similar dynamic. As I suggest in the next chapter, Yeats's two severed-head plays of 1934–5, *The King of the Great Clock Tower* and *Full Moon in March*, dramatize a process of insemination: a passive queen conceives from the blood dripping from the severed head of the player-poet. In each case, there is a trade-off involved: something is cut (off) in order to produce a gain in creativity, to produce lyric, the song produced by or about the queen; another parallel to Steinach's saving 'cut'. With overtones of masculine feminization, even of exploratory transsexualism, the operation can also be linked to the metaphors of imaginative penetration in Yeats's late works. An example is 'The Wild Old Wicked Man', one of the excited poems discussed with Dorothy Wellesley (the object is Lady Pelham):

> I have what no young man can have
> Because he loves too much.
> Words I have that can pierce the heart,
> But what can he do but touch?   (*VP* 588)

The wild old man can do what the young man cannot because he has 'completed' his sexuality in sloughing off 'generation'. Yeats writes, soon after the operation, that the point of his poem 'Ribh Denounces Patrick' is that 'we beget and bear because of the incompleteness of our love'.[63] The better ecstasy is that of the 'completed', that is self-begotten poet, with 'words . . . that can pierce the heart' of a woman, and in so doing confirm his power.

We can see Yeats's late swerve as (despite some important differences) related to modernist aesthetics. Peter Nicholls has recently argued that in Lewis, Pound, Joyce, and Eliot, there is a rejection of the romantic love which modernists associated with the previous century, and which is read as involving a narcissistic over-identification: 'sexual desire produces a sort of lacunae in the subject, a lack which is made good by copying someone else's desire, by finding a relation with another by which one's own self might be mirrored back in idealized form'. That is indeed how Yeats tended to read his earlier fixation on Maud Gonne. Yet the same formula also, paradoxically, *explains* Yeats's exchange with Wellesley, and its mirroring of his self. Yeats overcomes his 'lack' by what Julien Benda (in a passage which, as Nicholls points out, Lewis cited approvingly) disparagingly calls in romantics a 'will to *install themselves inside* things, a kind of thirst to sexually invade everything'.[64] For Yeats, the 'mature' sexuality is defined not by a Lewis-like spurning of identification, but by identification-plus-incorporation; by a remastering of a gendered romantic aesthetics rather than its rejection.

In order see the metaphors of self-creation associated with the Steinach Operation at work, we can examine the production of a central set of poems of sexual life in Yeats's late period, 'The Three Bushes' and its ancillary poems, written in 1936. Yeats's ballad is itself the product of an act of (amicable) usurpation preceding a gestation. Dorothy Wellesley sent Yeats a rather chaste poem for 'improvement'. Yeats initially saw in it the self-born wisdom of woman: 'This is far better than my laboured livelier verses. This is complete, lovely, lucky, born out of itself, or born out of nothing.'[65] But he was soon amending her verse, eventually to the point where she refused to recognize it as her own, and asked for the return of her original draft. Yeats apologized for having effectively taken over the piece ('against my first intention I sent you what I thought a finished version'), but could not conceal the energy which he derived from the exchange: 'Ah my dear how it added to my excitement when I re-made that poem of yours to know it was your poem. I re-made you and myself into a single being. We triumphed over each other and I thought of *The Turtle and the Phoenix*.'[66] This is love as an ideal 'conflagration' like that described in the 'Supernatural Songs' – though the triumph is, of course, Yeats's.

Significantly, the ballad also deals with an Irish mythological topos which Yeats had already used – entwined trees symbolizing love-in-death.[67] Its opening suppositions are similar to those in the 'severed-head' plays. A courtly maiden can only unite with her lover in death. Instead of going to him, the 'lady' uses her chambermaid as sexual surrogate. The mock sub-title, 'An incident from the "Historia mei Temporis" of the Abbé Michel de Bourdeille', refers to the sixteenth-century chronicler Pierre de Bourdeille, who was forced to withdraw from active life after a fall from a horse, and whose *Vies des dames galantes* is, as Patricia Parker notes, preoccupied with impotence and the *défaut* of old age. His name also puns on 'bordel', a fib or humbug, and possibly on 'bordello'.[68] It thus neatly combines the ironies in the life of the old and ailing poet who was developing (or cultivating) a reputation for sexual candour.

If the main body of the poem gains from the inspiration of Wellesley's ballad, the same cannot be said for the supplementary lyrics, which were not suggested by her 'archaic modernity'. The lyrics express what the narrative cannot: the feelings of the participants in the tale, particularly their lust. The fecundity of the theme is suggested by overflow, as the integrity of the original narrative is violated by six additional songs. The language of the songs carries sexual excess, replacing the mannered archaisms of the parent verse with a verbal primitivism: 'Language beaten / Into one name' (*VP* 572). The theme of the poem – that the lover will 'cram love's two divisions / Yet keep his substance whole' – is reflected in the mixing of tenor and vehicle in passages like 'The Chambermaid's Second Song', which itself echoes 'O what may come?', one of the lyrics from *The King of the Great Clock Tower*:

> From pleasure of the bed,
> Dull as a worm,
> His rod and its butting head
> Limp as a worm,
> His spirit that has fled
> Blind as a worm.   (*VP* 575)

The worm serves a complex metaphorical function: both bodily organ and spirit, just as the sexual act is both heaven (for the chambermaid) and hell (for the lady); while it also suggests the reconciliation of the poem's divisions in the grave. The relatively straightforward narrative of the ballad is replaced by an involved meditation on sexuality, love, and death. The grouping as a whole is an example of Yeats generating subject-matter from what is thematically and in origin an 'old tale', producing lyric from uniting himself to a woman's idea which becomes (and in many ways always was) his own idea.

Yeats commented on this process while writing these poems, linking it to a tendency to turn in on himself for his energy: 'I now like my long Ballad of the Three Bushes again. I have written two other poems on the same theme . . . Now that I have shut off external activity (the theatre board & "The Academy" threaten to meet here but so far I waved them off) I live in excitement. A mass of new subjects (not now on sex) are crowding upon me.'[69] Indeed, we could see this principle of textual production as informing much of Yeats's late work: in the proliferating texts of the Rapallo Notebook, with its series of lyrics seemingly spawned by other texts[70] – in particular the drafts of the two 'severed-head' plays.

Sexuality in such cases is not only a 'theme'; it is, rather, a matrix for creative activity, one of the secrets of an old age which manages to both 'lack a theme' and be 'self-begotten, born anew'. Yeats's thoughts about sexuality, incarnation, and rejuvenation find a parallel in the theory of the Steinach Operation, with its overtones of self-insemination. Yeats's own methods in old age involved a similar displacement: the writing of drama, of angry prose, in order that lyrics might be produced. His late energies were often self-directed in the way that the operation was; he made an investment in himself, and internalized the creative energies that he had formerly invested in women. The dream of self-creation in Yeats's late works is matched by a bodily intervention.

YEATS AND EUGENICS

Yeats's sense of blockage at the end of the 1920s has, of course, a historical and political dimension. It came at a point in which his activities in the Senate had culminated in his bitter and doomed attack on the 1925 Divorce Bill. Ireland's post-independence cultural life was dominated, Yeats complained, by a conservative and isolationist Catholicism, imposing censorship and marginalizing Anglo-Irish writers – despite attempts by George Russell at the *Irish Statesman*, among others, to keep open a sense of cultural plurality. Yeats's myth of a true Anglo-Irish tradition, a tradition of bitter satire, matched the satirical mood of other writers in the period.[71] In making himself the 'Gland Old Man', as Dublin gossip jokingly put it, he challenged that consensus at a point of pressure: sexuality.

Yet Yeats's involvement in the world of the Steinach Operation has darker undertones, linked as it was with a desire to reform and reinvigorate the body politic as well as his own body. The work of Steinach and his followers was implicated in eugenics; in broadly based attempts to control gender, sexuality, and reproduction. That was not unusual in a period in which sexual reform and eugenics often went hand in hand: the link is, in different measure, present in Havelock Ellis, Magnus Hirschfeld, Margaret

Sanger, and Marie Stopes, as well as in avowed eugenicists. Norman Haire was on the Council of the Eugenics Society and worked at a clinic in the Walworth Road for the Malthusian League, performing vasectomies, distributing diaphragms, and experimenting with an IUD; he also sterilized mentally 'defective' patients. Stopes authored a controversial British birth-control film which likened human stock to roses in need of pruning.[72] By the mid-1930s, however, the trend was away from the interventionist position, already being discredited by developments in Germany.

Yeats's late interest in eugenics and the work of the Eugenics Society (which he joined in November 1936) has been carefully documented by David Bradshaw, who notes that his hard-line position on issues like compulsory sterilization placed him outside the more moderate mainstream in the 1930s.[73] He was influenced, in particular, by R. B Cattell's *The Fight for our National Intelligence* (1937), incorporating some of Cattell's virulent polemics into the drafts of *On the Boiler*. A concern for breeding is present overtly in *On the Boiler*; in *The Herne's Egg*; and in passages like 'Under Ben Bulben' IV, with its references to 'filling the cradles right' and the 'Profane perfection of mankind'. Misconception, the decline of social order, the debasement of the arts are all part of the coming influx of barbarity, and provoke a countervailing violence in the poet.

Another example of this late violence and its relation to gender is provided by the 'Three Songs to the Same Tune' which Yeats originally wrote for the Blueshirts – songs which Yeats's commentators have spent a great deal of time explaining, thankful for the fact that he disowned them and rewrote them, he said, to make them unsingable.[74] The first song (published in February 1934) is directed against the fanaticism of Ireland:

> Those fanatics all that we would undo;
> Down the fanatic, down the clown;
> Down, down, hammer them down,
> Down to the tune of O'Donnell Abu.   (*VP* 545)

The targets here are not specified clearly; as Yeats said, you could choose them for yourself. But, in the note on the poem which Yeats wrote for *Poetry* in December 1934, the nature of Fascism is spelt out more clearly: 'If any Government or party undertake this work it will need force, marching men (the logic of fanaticism, whether in a woman or a mob is drawn from a premise protected by ignorance and therefore irrefutable); it will promise not this or that measure but a discipline, a way of life.'[75] 'Fanaticism . . . whether in a woman or a mob.' A mob *is* a woman perhaps – a streaming mass of 'ignorant' desires, one of those metaphors which Klaus Theweleit catalogues in Nazi perceptions of the 'Red Woman'.[76] We see the same fears elsewhere in late Yeats: in *On the Boiler*, and in poems like 'Why Should Not Old Men be Mad?', which sees not only the perversion of a 'likely lad' but

> A girl that knew all Dante once
> Live to bear children to a dunce;
> A Helen of social welfare dream
> Climb on a wagonette to scream.   (*VP* 626)

Perversions happen in all directions; a giving way to untoward flows of passion largely attributed to the feminine. The twisting of narrative from its proper channels – no 'finish worthy of the start' has its location in fears of what may emerge from what Yeats elsewhere calls the 'labyrinth' or 'maze' of sexuality. The second version of the song incorporates an anecdote about the Blueshirt neighbour, a woman who summarily drowned her dog after George Yeats complained that a hen was missing. As Cullingford notes, the Blueshirts now appear, ironically, as the index of fanaticism:

> 'Drown all the dogs', said the fierce young woman,
> 'They killed my goose and a cat.
> Drown, drown in the water-butt,
> Drown all the dogs', said the fierce young woman.
>   (*VP* 546)

This parallels Yeats's comments in *On the Boiler* about the Fascist states putting 'quantity before quality' and simply pumping out babies; selection must be discriminating and hierarchical.[77] Drowning *all* the dogs could be called a non-selective eugenics programme, a symptom of feminine irresponsibility rather than rational control. It is, once again, by retaining the power of insemination within the masculine that breeding is regulated.

One could, as a coda, trace the aftercourses of some of the sexologists discussed here and in the next chapter. Steinach was forced out of Vienna by the Nazi invasion, and died in Switzerland in 1944, 'a disappointed man'.[78] Magnus Hirschfeld, in exile in

France, his Institute destroyed in 1931, found himself in the position of having to resist the Nazi appropriation of eugenics – glumly refuting the propositions of Hans Gunther's *Der nordische Gedanke* in his posthumously published *Racism* (1938). He notes, in the baldest possible terms, the final destiny of the Steinach Operation – as instrument of racial hygiene rather than masculine reinvigoration: 'In an enactment which came into force on January 1, 1934 (the Law of Compulsory Sterilization), the Nazi Government provided for the compulsory ligature of the testicular ducts ("Steinach's Operation" which must not be confounded with removal of the testicles or castration) in men, and of the ovarian ducts or Fallopian tubes . . . in women.'[79] For all Hirschfeld's noble liberalism, his own work was not easily disconnected from the modes of thought which had produced such an imperialism, directed at fringe populations and 'degenerate' types. One is tempted, despite a certain reductiveness in the procedure, to say that the same is true of Yeats: with his own Steinach Operation in 1934, the year of the Nazi edict, he purges himself of his lassitude and finds a new violent energy, that of the slain and risen god, celebrating a solipsistic sexuality in the face of the collapse of those metaphorical gender-relations which had sustained his early career.

CHAPTER SIX

Making a woman

What is a woman? It is a question which has, historically, a range of answers. The 1920s, in particular, was a decade of particular attention to the nature of femininity. As Patrice Petro points out, there was a plethora of psychological papers on the subject – by Karl Abraham, Karen Horney, Helene Deutsch, Ernest Jones, Joan Riviere, Sandor Ferenczi, and others, as well as papers by Freud, culminating in 'Female Sexuality' (1931).[1] A wide range of popular and fictional writing examined relations between the sexes. The pressures underlying this interest in femininity include the legacy of the war, enfranchisement, new economic power, the rise of advertising with its basis in a commodified sexuality.[2] What I will consider here is a new, more pragmatic answer to the question 'What is a woman?' which became possible in the period around 1930: a woman is something you can *make*. For it is this period which saw the first transsexual operations; little-known experiments in Weimar Germany more than 20 years before the operations in the USA in the 1950s which are normally taken as the inception of transsexual surgery.

In order to ask how Modernism 'makes' women both within and outside this surgical procedure, I will consider works which might be seen as reworking *fin de siècle* anxieties about gender, particularly those represented in Oscar Wilde's *Salomé*. Wilde asks: what happens when one cuts off a man's head? Or, if one accepts the connection between castration and decapitation made by Freud and Cixous (and by the texts considered here), what happens when a man is castrated? I will examine Yeats's plays in the 1930s and Freud's work, but at the centre of the chapter is *Man into Woman*, the record of what is, so far as I know, one of only three early sex-change operations – a text which stands, in 1931, on the frontier of medical attempts to reconfigure gender. As it turns out, this text also takes us back to Wilde, and forces us to measure the distance between his work and the new creature who steps from the frame bearing the name 'Lili Elbe'.

In *Body Work*, Peter Brooks recounts the story of the Parisian clockmaker treated by Philippe Pinel in the aftermath of the French Revolution. He has become convinced that he has been guillotined and the wrong head replaced on his body. Pinel has another inmate recount the legend of Saint Denis, 'who after decapitation is said to have walked with his head in his hands while covering it with kisses'; he mocks the legend and asks 'what Saint Denis could in the situation kiss his head with – perhaps his ass?'[3] We can take this obsession with decapitation as an index of the hystericized male body and its fears: the bodily hierarchy which places the head at the top is sexualized and degraded, just as Freud's equation of decapitation with castration was to figure the triumph of sexuality over rationality. Pinel's madman is cured by ridicule, but the twentieth century was to find more radical solutions to the problem of displaced bodily parts.

The severed head continued as a feature of nineteenth-century anxieties in texts by Heine, Flaubert, Mallarmé, Huysman, Laforgue, climaxing in Wilde's *Salomé*. The way in which Wilde's text – particularly in the Beardsley edition – challenges Victorian assumptions about the stability of gender and identity has received much discussion.[4] Both the suggestion of castration in the decapitation of the stern prophet, and Herod's incestuous passions and hysteria at the end of the play, suggest an embattled patriarchy. The perversity of the text is enacted at the level of the body, in a series of transgressive acts which offer multiple possibilities: homosexuality, lesbianism, androgyny, the desire of the 'New Woman'.[5] These suggestions can be related to the haunting anxiety which, Ed Cohen has recently shown, attached itself to Wilde's own body, the site of an unspeakable sexuality.

Salomé's choice of the prophet's head, of the male body rather than the jewels, peacocks, and perfumes which Herod offers, is particularly striking in the context of the aesthetics of decadence. As Rita Felski suggests, the tendency of decadent literature is to displace feminine bodies into artifacts, beautiful materials which are the object of the privileged male gaze.[6] If Salomé represents the decadent 'feminization of the aesthetic' and the parallel 'aestheticization of women', then the presence of decapitation in the text – when Salomé demands and gets the prophet's head – threatens to destabilize that aesthetic, exposing the possibility of castration which (male) fetishism denies. That the prophet Iokanaan's body is the primary site of the battle is interesting: an aesthetic which founds itself on the dead or fetishized *male* body sets itself against a dominant focus on the objectified female body.[7] Even more noticeable is the lack of a pay-off in his decapitation: Iokanaan utters his prophecy, but Salomé continues to mock his head and 'red tongue'. (Iokanaan's gains may be important to Christianity, but they are irrelevant to the decadent text.[8]) Salomé is the aesthete here, focusing on the prophet's hair, his lips, the whiteness of his skin, initiating the bodily dispersal of fetishism: 'Thy body was a column of ivory set on a silver socket. It was a garden full of doves and of silver lilies. It was a tower of silver decked with shields of ivory.' She consumes his parts. It is as if the text cannot stand his hypermasculinity; his refusal to 'look at me' (as she puts it) is a refusal to play the part of the aesthete, to absorb enough of the feminine to control it, or enter the decadent world and play with gender and the gaze which allows sexual difference. The play ends with Herod's assertion of power, repressing Salomé's sexuality – 'Kill that woman!' But, as Regenia Gagnier observes, he escapes only at the cost of retiring to his palace and destroying 'his ability to personify the law'.[9] He also ends in near-hysteria. The play thus offers a challenge to patriarchal authority in the name of feminine desire; or, rather, a version of that desire whose potency inheres in its being a masculine fantasy. That it is attributed to the woman is important: as in Freud's account of organ-inferiority, with its emphasis on penis-envy, on the veiling of the female genitals, on fetishism and the denial of castration, this is very much an account of femininity as perceived by the disempowered male.

We will return, admittedly rather circuitously, to *Salomé* via a number of later texts in which Wilde's presence can be traced. Like Elvis, Wilde had a flourishing posthumous career. The myth that he was not dead persisted after his burial. The suspiciously obscure nature of his first interment (before Ross moved him to Père-Lachaise) was often mentioned; he was said to have been seen in Paris and elsewhere. The outrageous Dada boxer, Arthur

Cravan, Wilde's nephew and Mina Loy's lover, reported a secret meeting in 1913 and produced 'Oscar Wilde is Alive!' headlines in New York.[10] The rumours were so persistent that an American admirer wrote a tract protesting the ease with which sensation-seekers could disinter him.[11] Posthumous writings seemed to offer the possibility of a return: the pornographic *Teleny* was advertised in 1903, Neil Bartlett notes, in a catalogue which claimed that 'the writer is stated on good authority to be none other than Oscar Wilde. This becomes the more convincing when we compare the style of his famous *Dorian Gray* with the present lewd but brilliant book.'[12] Style is, of course, precisely what is transferable and problematic in such cases. In the Pemberton–Billing libel trial of 1918, the status of the Wildean style in a wartime production of *Salomé* spilled out into issues of lesbianism, homosexuality, and the audience in a way which both recapitulated the scandal of his trials and made clear that the issue in the play was feminine sexuality – particularly when, in a moment of high camp, the judge had to ask for the word 'orgasm' to be explained.[13] The return of Wilde is associated with bodily disruption, like that of his actual corpse, allegedly decaying before it was cold. The body associated with unspeakable acts and a person who could not be politely named was meant to stay in place, but returns as a symptom of the anxieties which surround it.

We might read the posthumous uncertainty about Wilde, his oscillation between non-person and revenant, as another symptom of the tendency to fictional states which was part of the 'evidence' linking aestheticism to homosexuality – as if the difference between being alive and dead were purely a matter of taste. But, if Wilde did come back, what would he come as? One answer is: he would come as a woman. And he did. In 1923, Wilde spoke through the automatic scripts and Ouija board of Hester Travers Smith [Hester Dowden], well-known medium and author of *Voices from the Void*. Accounts appeared in the *Daily News* and the *Occult Review*, and, in 1924, the full transcripts appeared as *Psychic Messages from Oscar Wilde*. Wilde provided thoughts on his life, on his recent reading, and even on the 'carrion-birds' who peddled stories about his survival. It happened like this. On 8 June 1923, Mrs Smith received a message from the Other Side. She had been experimenting with automatic writing with a friend, 'Mr. V', and her 'control' Johannes. The pen wrote four words before being interrupted:

Lily, my little Lily – No, the lily was mine – a crystal thread – a silver reed that made music in the morning. (Who are you?) Pity Oscar Wilde – one who in the world was a king of life. Bound on Ixion's wheel of thought, I complete for ever the circle of my existence. *Long ago I wrote that there was twilight in my cell and twilight in my heart*, but this is the (last?) twilight of the soul.[14]

Some quick research by Mrs Smith established the Wildean provenance of the italicized passages, and a dialogue ensued. In fact the ghost got better, reappearing at the Ouija-board and producing some tolerable aphorisms in almost twenty seances over the next few months ('Being dead is the most boring experience in life. That is, if one excepts being married and dining with a schoolmaster').[15] Wilde also offered opinions on recent work by George Moore (lacks style), Joyce ('filth'), John Galsworthy, and others – evidently modernist hostility to 'Decadence' was not entirely unreciprocated. The list included W. B. Yeats, a seance-goer who was at that point organizing his wife's automatic writing into the text of *A Vision* (1925); Mrs Smith, who knew him, sent him a report of the conversations. (The connections continued: five years later Yeats used Hester's daughter Dolly for some important automatic writing.)[16]

Wilde also expressed scorn for his middle-brow medium: 'Stop! Stop! Stop! Stop! This image is insufferable. You write like a successful grocer, who from selling pork has taken to writing poetry.' With coaching she improves, but Wilde explains his primacy: 'I think you may reasonably believe you are a living being and I a chimera of your mind. But let me explain that to me you are a chimera, and, in reality, you are less alive than I. For I am still a living soul and mind.' Consigning her to the secondary, Wilde repeats the Aesthetic Movement's tendency to see women as creations rather than creators. But, of course, this Wilde *is* the creation of a woman, and Mrs Smith seems to register the irony. At one point the ghost asks: 'Enquire about Mrs Chan Toon. I had the honour of her acquaintance some years ago.'[17] Mrs Chan Toon, born Mabel Cosgrave, aka Princess Arakan, is (like Cravan) one of Modernism's tricksters: she claimed to have been Wilde's fiancée, married the king of Burma's nephew, and sold forged letters from Wilde and Yeats. As Mrs Wodehouse Pearse she was imprisoned for theft in 1926.[18] In mentioning her, the Wildean text (and its author) seems to joke about its own status. That, incidentally, was not the end of Wilde's ghost: in America he produced *The Ghost*

Epigrams of Oscar Wilde, recorded by 'Lazar' in 1928, though quality declined across the Atlantic.[19]

That Wilde should return in 1923 as a gossipy medium fits well with the modernist tendency to see aesthetic gender-blurring as distasteful – and to disparage spiritualism, particularly of the post-war variety, while remaining fascinated by it.[20] The typical modernist strategy was to remain at one remove from mediumship, disciplining its products as Yeats did with his wife's automatic writing, organizing it into a systematic philosophy. (We will see Hugo Münsterberg exposing a medium and aiding Stein in replacing the occult with an experimental technique.) Pound, in particular, specialized, as Wayne Koestenbaum puts it, in straightening out 'male texts that depended too much on female mediums' – like the Tarot section of *The Waste Land* (which may have been inspired by Mina Loy's more celebratory 'At the Door of the House').[21] Eliot's equation of mediumship and hysteria at the end of 'The Dry Salvages' is representative of this hostility. To 'converse with spirits' or to read fortunes in palms, tea-leaves or other signs, 'To explore the womb, or tomb, or dreams; all these are usual / Pastimes and drugs, and features of . . .'[22] 'Of the press' is Eliot's completion; though 'of women' more readily springs to mind, given those other implicitly gendered ('shrieking . . . scolding . . . merely chattering') voices which disturb the order in section V of each of the *Four Quartets* – like the 'paltry yatter' which Pound excoriates in Canto 99. It is this copious flow of voices that the classicism of the modernist text attempts to regulate – just as, in Koestlenbaum's account, Pound's surgical knife cuts through the clotted mass of hysterical discourse in *The Waste Land* drafts. The 'return of Wilde' thus serves as a metonym for one of the forbidden objects of Modernism; for the circulation of a dubious style. In the sections which follow, I will consider a medical case which, I argue, offers a parallel to the 'surgical Modernism' of Pound, while consciously evoking a Wildean inheritance.

LILI ELBE AND MODERNIST SEXOLOGY

Wilde was able to seize Mrs Smith's pencil because the word 'Lily' is, she said, 'the emblem of the aesthetic movement'. Consider another of the Lilies in this gender-crossing field. Around 1912, the Danish artist, Einar Wegener, and his wife, Gerda, also a painter, arrive in Paris and book into the Hotel d'Alsace in the Rue des Beaux-Arts, having left Copenhagen for a city in which they feel their art will prosper. They are astonished to find – according to Wegener's autobiography – that they have been placed in the rooms in which Wilde died, and spend the next few days reading his works to each other. (Another figure in this book drifts through these rooms: Ethel Mannin, who Norman Haire used to 'test' Yeats's rejuvenation operation, lived there in 1930).[23]

By this time, Wegener is habitually cross-dressing as 'Lili', and is, as a woman, one of the main subjects of his wife's fashionably androgynous art deco paintings, which contrast markedly with his northern and 'masculine' style. They settle in Paris. Years later, Wegener discovers the possibility of treatment in Germany that will change his sex; he undergoes a series of operations in Berlin and Dresden in 1930–31, and Lili becomes an actuality, taking the surname Elbe. She returns to Copenhagen for a brief period before dying from post-operative complications in September 1931. An edited account of her experience is published in Danish and quickly translated into German, and into English as *Man into Woman: The Authentic Record of a Change of Sex* (1933), compiled from diaries and other sources by a pseudonymous 'Niels Hoyer' and introduced by Haire.[24] In the English version, Wegener appears as 'Andreas Sparre' and his wife as 'Grete'.

Man Into Woman is a fascinating text, and has served as an anchor for many subsequent transsexual autobiographies. In Jan Morris's *Conundrum* (1975), she describes a moment of conversion when she (then he) pulled a dusty volume off the top shelf of a bookshop in Ludlow. It was *Man Into Woman*, and suggested a surgical solution to the problem of what is now called 'gender dysphoria'. Other transsexuals, including Richard Raskin (tennis star Renée Richards) found inspiration in the book.[25] Yet *Man Into Woman* and the German experiments with gender-surgery pre-date by two decades what Janice Raymond labels the 'Transsexual Empire' – the medical establishment which licenses and performs transsexual surgery, established, in most accounts, after another Dane, Christine Jorgensen, underwent surgery in America in 1953.[26] How did these operations come about? They were, so far as I know, the third set of such operations in Germany, enabled by advances in plastic surgery made during and after the war – another case of prosthetics modulating from the covering of a lack into a 'cosmetic' intervention which declares the body to be in crisis.

The first subject was a man called Rudolph who changed his name, suggestively, to 'Dora R'.[27] The operations – including Lili's initial operation – were undertaken under the direction of a surgeon, Felix Abraham, attached to the Institute for the Study of Sexual Sciences in Berlin, where Rudolph (alias Dorchen) worked as a housekeeper.[28] Founded by Dr Magnus Hirschfeld in 1919, the Institute flourished within the relatively open context of Weimar Germany, until its suppression by the Nazis in 1933 – providing the book-burning footage often shown in documentaries.[29] At its extensive buildings at In den Zelten, it was a centre for campaigns for sexual tolerance as well as research, lectures, and other activities including public cross-dressing. It is an important site for Modernism. Recalling a stay in the street in the early twenties, Robert McAlmon wrote of the area as one of nightclubs, drugs, sexual freedom, and experimentation, licensed by Hirschfeld's presence. Djuna Barnes was part of a Bohemian group at In den Zelten, 18 in 1921.[30] Auden and Isherwood had connections with the Institute; Isherwood rented a room in its annex.[31] By the 1920s Hirschfeld was part of an international network of sexologists and reformers, including Norman Haire.

Hirschfeld's work drew on an established body of work on the relationship between gender and bodily chemistry, the subject of heightened interest and experimentation at the turn of the century. Biologism was largely uncontested: almost all the major figures in early twentieth-century sexology believed that homosexuality and other issues of gender would have biological origins. One important researcher was Eugen Steinach, whose 'rejuvenation' operations were discussed in the previous chapter. In the 1900s, he seemed to have taken significant steps towards establishing a biological basis for gender, implanting ovaries in male rats and seeing them display female characteristics.[32] He even (reportedly) used an implanted testicle to convert a castrated man who was a 'passive homosexual' and 'feminized' into a 'normal' heterosexual. Others confirmed Steinach's findings, and noted that sex-reversals could even take place spontaneously under certain conditions.[33] Freud praises Steinach's work on the organic determinants of homosexuality, and Haire, introducing *Man into Woman*, refers to his work as a matter of course.[34]

If Steinach represents biological work on gender, Magnus Hirschfeld was, with Havelock Ellis, the pioneer of psychological and sociological study of sexual orientation in the early twentieth century. In *Die Transvestiten* (1910) and other works, he saw transvestitism and homosexuality as part of a group of behaviours practised by 'sexual intermediaries'. Himself homosexual (like Haire) and transvestite, he was less dogmatic than Krafft-Ebing had been, actively exploring the range of available sexual orientations and blurring rather than clarifying gender-distinctions. In a lecture at the International Congress of Physicians at the Albert Hall in 1913, for example, he used a series of slides to demonstrate the difficulty of assigning gender on the basis of facial characteristics, subverting the classifying work of Galtonian science.[35] He attempted to differentiate and defend a range of practices: homosexuality, transvestitism, and transsexualism (in the sense of choosing to live as the 'other' sex). Hirschfeld represented one side of the polarized German debate on homosexuality described by James Steakley.[36] Like Ellis, he saw homosexuals as 'sexual intermediaries', near the middle point of a continuum from the ultramasculine to the ultra-feminine (others were transvestites, androgynes, and hermaphrodites). Confusion and gender-shifting were thus intrinsic to the spectrum, in stark contrast to sexual-differentiation theorists like Hans Blüher, who saw homosexuality as ultra-masculine rather than as masculine–feminine, representing a perfect form of 'virile' ('Greek' or martial) manliness.[37] If Hirshfield validates the gender-shifting of Weimar Germany, Blüher was linked to the proto-Nazi Wandervögel movement with its fear of the cultural 'feminine'.[38]

How would Andreas/Lili and the operations s/he undertook have fitted into this framework? Hirschfeld's attention to sexual intermediaries and sexual ambiguity seems strangely at odds with the idea of 'producing' a surgically constructed woman from a man – even given the claim in *Man into Woman* that Wegener was a hermaphrodite with vestigial ovaries, as well as a transvestite who wished to embody his role. If intermediaries are the middle of the spectrum, why push them towards one pole? One answer lies in the experimental, clarificationary thrust of modern science – the interventionist attitude which sees Steinach as exemplary, which wishes to *produce* the limit cases of gender by a surgical and biological act. But it is also important that what is produced by this violent

divestment is a *woman* (the category which Hirschfeld performed in his own cross-dressing). In the work of Adler and others in the period, gender is a field of struggle, where one tendency must force out the other, with a special anxiety attached to the stabilization of the procreative role of women.[39] Patrice Petro cites an article by Löbel which suggests that, in cases of 'intersexual' women in a marriage, the masculinity of the woman must be driven out: 'she is grateful for the liberation from masculinity. This is the scientific basis for the understanding that beatings are united with love.'[40] The violence inherent in surgery can be justified in a parallel way: as a liberation from masculine gender-anxiety and the stabilization of the other.

Unsurprisingly, other medical experts responded equivocally to the case of Lili Elbe. Haire suggests that Wegener was 'an intermediate sexual type' with vestigial ovaries that could form the basis of a 'true' sexual reassignment; but in contradictory fashion he also uses the case to argue that there are no 100 per cent men or women. Gregorio Marañon, the Spanish sexologist, commented on the case in *The Evolution of Sex and Intersexual Conditions* (1932). For Marañon sexual evolution is directed towards the 'virile' standards of the male, with the feminine as an intermediate or 'hypo-evolutionary' point, 'a phase midway between adolescence and virility. Virility is a terminal phase in sexual evolution.' The suggestion of a regression from the male to the female is, for dominant or single-sex models, alarming, and in an appended note Marañon declares tersely that 'this woman, obviously intersexual, was always a woman'.[41] A woman who is tautologically a woman – there can be no question of regression, much less of choice. But here the contradictory ideological implications of gender-surgery are exposed: Marañon is forced to suggest that Andreas and Grete were 'viriloid' women, their virility proven by their artistic prowess. Their marriage involved 'two intersexuals in which the masculine role was played by the one more virile in character and social attributes'. Marañon attempts to police the boundaries of gender, but he – like the case as a whole – also opens up the possibility that gender is masquerade.

In contrast to Marañon's insistence that Lili was *already* a woman, the medical personnel who superintended Andreas's operation were obviously aware of the necessity for social as well as physical reconfiguration. Lili describes her change as a rebirth –

the clinic is a nursery, and she is initially child-like and helpless. Prior to the operation, Andreas's successful masquerade has been tested on his own mother and father, who fail to penetrate the disguise (91). Lili later comments 'I really had neither parents nor brothers and sisters, as I was born not up here in the North, but down in Germany' (233). A process of de-Oedipalization takes place; she even reads Genesis after her operation, like a New Eve.[42] In postmodern theory and cinema – in the work of Deleuze and Guattari, and of Donna Haraway – such de-Oedipalization has been linked to a utopian liberation of desire, a freedom from gender opposition and the Law of the Father. In this sense, Lili offers a threat to an established structure of gender-division (as Marañon suggests). Yet much of her text is concerned not with the liberation of desire, but with the authority of those who will superintend the process. The 'woman's doctor', Professor Kreutz, who masterminds her transformation is particularly interesting, since he 'fathers' the newly born woman, standing in a synthetic Oedipal position as a 'miracle-man'. His behaviour to her after the operation seems baffling until she interprets it as a parental moulding: 'he sought to evoke her feminine impulses by being alternately mild and stern. Had he not deliberately provoked an eruption of all the primitive instincts of her womanhood?' (183). A young man called Claude who has been attracted to Lili arrives at the 'white nursery' and proposes – she replies that she must ask Kreutz. Lili recapitulates the Oedipus, becoming socially as well as biologically shaped.

Lili's resocialization comes only at the end of a process , with an excited group of physicians in Berlin and Dresden gathered around their 'miraculous' prodigy, a 'constructed-female' (to use Raymond's terminology). But the actual beginnings of Lili have less to do with Steinach and surgery than they have to with the *fin-de-siècle* world of art and literature – indeed, she traces a progress from fantasy and art to medical intervention. To explore that, we must move back from Lili's 'rebirth' in the surgery to her first appearances – as a creature of the studio.

'A GENUINE ACCIDENT OF THE STUDIO'

Throughout *Man into Women*, the protagonist Andreas reflects on the construction of gender as artistic process. His sex-change is refracted through literature – the 'decadent' literature of Wilde, Stevenson, Maeterlinck, and others, its gender-blurring, pre-occupation with the romance-plot and dual identity. In the Hotel d'Alsace, where Wilde died, Lili is born as a Parisian, and *Man into Woman* is, like *Dorian Gray*, the story of a collaborative portrait which comes to life. Like *Dracula*, it is a text with many 'authors', a case history collating information. On the title-page it is subtitled in a manner which suggests both the sensational account of 'monstrosity' and the personal testament of the religious conversion narrative: 'The true story of the miraculous transformations of the Danish painter Einar Wegener (Andreas Sparre)' – providing, in H. J. Stenning's English translation an 'open' pseudonym. Despite this unveiling, the name 'Andreas Sparre' is retained throughout the text, as a kind of vestigial appendage removed only in Norman Haire's introduction to the English translation. The text itself was prepared from the papers of Wegener by 'Neils Hoyer' (Ernst Ludwig Harthern Jacobson), who appears on the title-page as the editor, but who seems from textual evidence to have done rather more than simply compiling the text.[43] His own comments are interpolated with other documents gathered from Andreas's wife and elsewhere. The status of the sex-changed author is also uncertain, subject to multiple assignations of the kind that Marjorie Garber labels 'pronomial dysporia'.[44] She is referred to as a separate person, but photograph captions describe 'Einar Wegener (Andreas Sparre) impersonating Lili. Paris, January 1930'; as in Wilde's 'posing', a truth is both concealed and revealed.

Different explanations of the birth of Lili are offered. Andreas describes Grete and himself as an androgynous couple – like the son of Hermes and the daughter of Aphrodite united in the same body by Zeus, or the Platonic unity in the *Symposium*. But the *moment* of emergence is alarmingly accidental: the actress Anna Larsen fails to appear for a sitting and Einar is asked by Grete to stand in (in costume) so that she can at least work on the body and legs – a cross-dressing masquerade that quickly develops into a game played among intimate friends, then eventually in public, with Grete producing a series of portraits of the person Larsen names as Lili. Thus, 'with an extravagant joke, a genuine accident of the studio, if you like, it started' (65). A joke based on the uncertain status of the body, startling because it suggests that any such random substitution could trigger a change in identification – that the indeterminate gendering of a leg might apply to the whole body.

If Lili is a joint construction, an 'accident of the studio' in which Andreas 'acts' a part, Grete occupies the position of Lord Henry and the painter Basil in Wilde's fable, producing the object of artistic desire: 'for both me and for Grete Lili very soon became a perfectly independent person, in fact a playmate for Grete' (68). In this romance, the portraits which Grete paints bring Lili to life. In one episode, an infatuated Count arrives, having met Lili at a Paris ball, and is introduced to Andreas, who is passed off as her brother. Told Lili is out, he is bitterly disappointed until shown the paintings of Lili in the studio, which confirm (as well as substitute for) her reality – at which point he addresses a proposal for her hand to Andreas as her guardian! The aim, at this stage, is playful masquerade: Lili thrives in the inverted world of the carnivalesque, appearing as a female Cupid in a water-carnival (82).

Grete registers her own sense of Lili's construction through art in a passage from her diary quoted in the book, with a disquiet at the possibility of a return-of-the-repressed like that exacted on Basil in *Dorian Gray*, or on Jekyll by his creation Hyde:

'It often happens', [Grete] continued excitedly, 'that when she poses for me as a model a strange feeling comes over me that it is *she* whom I am creating and forming rather than the girl whom I am representing on my canvas. Sometimes it seems to me that here is something which is stronger than we are, something which makes us powerless and will thrust us aside, as if, indeed, it wanted to be revenged on us for having played with it.' (93)

An imagined being threatens to become actual. Lili's gradual dominance is described as a takeover like Jekyll's, with a similar 'double life' involved, one personality struggling with another. Andreas's growing despair is recorded in melodramatic terms: 'Lili is no longer content to share her existence with me. She wants to have an existence of her own . . . I – I'm no longer any use. Cannot do anything more. I'm finished. Lili has known this for a long time . . . And consequently she rebels more vigorously every day' (16). Lili admits that 'perhaps I am the murderer of Andreas' (166). Just before the first operation, Andreas writes his own imaginary obituary, in a major retrospective section of the text which details his history, at the end of which Andreas departs and is replaced by Lili and her less coherent account. The text becomes progressively more fragmentary, the art no longer being present in its shaping, but rather in the attempt to physically embody the metaphors which it has projected. It is, in that sense, a prosthetic text, written in 'another hand'.

One other aspect of the 'studio' is important: commerce. Writing on Dorian Gray as a consumer of sensations in Wilde's fable, Rachel Bowlby argues that his femininity reflects the status of the new woman consumer.[45] Some of the same economic determinants are at play in the case of Lili, who becomes the centre of the couple's economic success in Paris. In this case, the familiar north–south/masculine–feminine dynamics (and the necessity to travel across borders) which pervade the text have economic significance. In Paris, the southern city, Grete's work, art-deco and stylized, is appreciated more than Andreas's moody northern romantic landscapes; there, the Danish national biography comments, Grete (Gerda Wegener) 'found her real milieu'.[46] Andreas describes his work as 'fundamentally . . . Northern' with 'Teutonic' affinities: 'Whatever masculine force resided in him found its outlet in these strong, somewhat wild and willful pictures' (37–9). Paris is a more 'feminine' city; Lili declares that she is 'born' in the South. A 1925 article in *The Studio* comments 'in her art Mme. Wegener has always been more a child of France than of Denmark'. It continues: 'Although there were some faint reminiscences of Aubrey Beardsley in her earlier efforts, there has always been a certain French piquancy over much of her work. She is endowed with a pregnant invention, unafraid of what a prudish *bourgeoisie* may think of her *motifs*.'[47] Grete's 'pregnant invention' inherits a hint of decadence from the Beardsley whose sexually ambiguous illustrations of *Salomé* help engender Lili. Grete's work for the fashion magazines of Paris exploit ambivalence; her pictures of Lili circulate in *Vogue, Vie Parisienne, Fantasio, Rire*, to the point where an exhibition of the Lili paintings is organized. Subsequently, Gerda Wegener had a successful career, winning prizes and illustrating a number of art-books (including an edition of Casanova's *Une Aventure d'Amour à Venise*). The accident of the studio becomes a commercial reality.

FROM ROMANCE TO ESSENTIALISM

The name 'Lili' was given to Andreas's drag incarnation by Anna Larsen. Her second name she takes to mark her Rubicon: the Elbe flows through Dresden, where she has the last of her operations – the Elbe itself a crossing point between East and West (between the masculine Teutonic and feminine Slavic races, according to Renan).[48] It is the operations which differentiate *Man into Woman* from texts like *Dorian Gray* or *Jekyll and Hyde*, which describe two morally and socially opposed beings struggling within one body, often with overtones of gender-opposition. A friend called Neils Hvide, looking at Grete's portrait of Lili, meditates on the proposed course of action: "'And now the question is, whether that *being* there" – and he pointed to the portrait – "can be summoned into existence and take up the battle of life'" (49). The question might be from Wilde, but the course of action is not, moving the ground of intervention from art to medicine, and the problematics from those of display and concealment to a revelation and liberation of an 'essence'. After surgery, there is no going back. Following the operation, with rumours about Andreas's disappearance circulating, it is suggested that she reverse the masquerade, impersonating Andreas; she is horrified. What the text accepts as 'that abyss which separates man and woman' (270) is crossed by what Lili calls a 'bridge', but it is finally a one-way bridge – as in Joyce's joke, a pier.

The modernist autobiography thus differentiates itself from decadent romance. Lili is at first a 'masquerade', but gradually her performance and presence begins to deform the body and its manifestations, producing a feminine body-language as identity shifts from Andreas to Lili. Eventually Andreas reports that he is 'read' by passers-by and friends as 'a girl impersonating a man' (107). The female body is manifested as displaced symptoms – menstrual nose-bleeds and fits of sobbing, which appear as Lili takes a female part in a ballet: 'At first I thought that I had displaced some internal organ during the ballet performances' (99). A displaced organ is a hysterical symptom, the 'wandering womb'; nose-bleeds have been associated with menstruation since Aristotle.[49] After the first operation (castration) and ovarian implants, the 'blood' which is at the centre of this process becomes Lili's; the voice rises. Lili as masquerade is no longer sustainable; the body changes, and after the ovaries of a woman of twenty-six are implanted she even becomes younger, a rejuvenation-effect reported by later transsexuals.[50] The handwriting changes: the German edition of *Man into Woman* reproduces Einar and Lili's respective holographs (Figure 10), signalling convergences

Figure 10 'Ein Mensch Wechselt Sein Geschlecht' [a man changes his sex]

Lili claims that gender = personality and
biology = destiny = (determina)

between the 'experiment' of transsexualism and the rejuvenation
and distraction-effects described in earlier chapters; the desire to
write 'as' a woman produces a fresh self and its appropriate text.

The irony at this point is that Lili's claims bespeak an essential-
ism which sees gender as determining personality, and biology as
destiny, even as those categories are problematized by their
manipulation. Lili's femininity is stereotyped by a desire to be
Andreas's 'other': 'I veiled completely the character of Andreas.
He was ingenious, sagacious, and interested in everything – a
reflective and thoughtful man. And I was quite superficial.
Deliberately so. For I had to demonstrate every day that I was a
different creature from him, that I was a woman' (235). But Lili
insists that this was 'not merely farcical acting. It was really my character, untroubled, carefree, illogical, capricious.' The essence of
the feminine is thus reaffirmed, even as it is figured as performance, a dance of veils. Lili wishes to create 'with my blood', to
have children. And to do so she abandons art and intellect, as if
cutting off Andreas's head as well as the genitals. 'I feel so
changed', she writes to Kreutz, 'that it seems as if you had operated
not upon my body but upon my brain' (244). Lili associates
Andreas's creativity both with virility and with a masculine desire
to reify nature, which she abandons in favour of simple enjoyment.
Before the operation, Andreas had worried whether Lili would
inherit his 'joy' at transmuting life into art (119–20). Instead she
simply registers that desire as masculine: 'I do not want to be an
artist, but a woman. Hence I must shut all artistic creation out of
my life . . . because I cannot continue the work of the virile artist
who was Andreas' (279–80). Simply to be a woman is enough: a
creation whose 'femininity' is sufficient to its being. Andreas
becomes his own 'Other', but an Other no longer involved in the
problematics of specular desire.

The romance of Lili's creation, within an account which stresses
'accident' and play, thus becomes entangled within an ineluctable
logic which replaces the contingent with the essential, the super-
ficialities of dress with the claims of 'blood', and the metaphorical
shifts of romance with the surgeon's knife. Wegener's operations
anticipate the imperialism of later medical procedures – which can
lead to gender-reassignment after a slip in circumcision mutilates
a penis.[51] Lili suggests that her 'Master' is a modern Prometheus,
moulding the clay of humanity. The sense of fascinated masculine

[margin notes: Like Marilyn Monroe]

[margin note: as you can't be both!]

intervention is particularly the case if one looks at the group gathering around their new creation Lili Elbe: Haire, the translator
Stenning, the compiler, the surgeon Abraham and other medical
staff, 'Kreutz', and, behind the scenes, Hirschfeld himself.[52] It is to
Kreutz that Andreas looks for the solution to the problem of identity on their first meeting in Paris: 'Well, Professor, what am I? . . .
What . . . ?' (25). His answer is that Andreas/Lili is a woman –
though that 'truth' must be surgically revealed. Like Freud,
'Kreutz' believes that a woman is (among other things) a castrated
male.[53] Yet the person courageously agreeing to the operation is,
by all normal definitions, a man – cross-dressing and rather
desperate, but still claiming the privileges of masculinity. We might
see the unsung 'Dora R.' and Lili as modernist (and male) versions
of Freud's resistant Victorian subject, also, of course, named Dora,
reconfiguring the body rather than the psyche within an experimental science which aims, even more fundamentally than Freud,
to make the body display its inner truth within a shape which is
subject to the will, rather than within the gender-play of Wildean
romance.

YEATS: DECAPITATION, CASTRATION, RECOVERY

If *Man into Woman* both evokes and subsumes the art-into-life
dynamics of *Dorian Gray*, we might also read it, perhaps perversely,
as a recension of *Salomé* in which the 'cut' of castration produces
a firmer sense of gender-roles. In order to explore the issue of the
relations between surgical Modernism and decadence, I want to
shift focus radically and pursue the connections between Yeats's
Steinach Operation and the 'severed-head' plays which followed it
in 1934–5 – plays which consciously revise Wilde with the literalizing impulse which we have seen in *Man into Woman*. To do so is
not simply arbitrary. Yeats, as we have seen, has connections with
the reformist community which produced Lili, and the Steinach
Operation is gender-surgery. As in the case of Lili Elbe, we can
read the outcome as a reinterpretation of the uncertainties over
gender associated with the name of Wilde.

An bridging text which Yeats would have known is Ezra Pound's
outrageous 1918 translation of Laforgue's version of the Salomé
story, 'Our Tetrarchal Précieuse'. Altering the original freely,
Pound reads Laforgue as a comic parody of Flaubert. Laforgue's

mystical and absolutist Salomé becomes a spoilt and precocious adolescent, lecturing at bored suitors. Pound downplays the love-interest and Laforgue's suggestion that Jao has 'exorcised' her virginity and impregnated her.[54] This parodic princess is a victim of dated enthusiasms – aestheticism, mysticism – and attempts to revivify the corpse: 'As soon as she had got [the head], Salomé, inspired by the true spirit of research, had commenced the renowned experiments after decollation; of which we have heard so much. She awaited. The electric passes of her hypnotic manual brought from it nothing but inconsequential grimaces.'[55]

Yeats responds to the Pound–Laforgue text to the extent that his version is also anti-aesthetic. But, rather than simply parodying *Salomé*, he produces an allegory of masculine power as he shifts the ground from the biblical setting to the Orphic and Celtic legends in which heads burst into song. His plays exist in three versions: *The King of the Great Clock Tower*, a verse version of the same title, and a much revised play, *A Full Moon in March*. In his preface, Yeats notes two major differences between his plays and Wilde's. The first is that he eliminates, between the second and third versions, the figure of the King, that is the Herod-figure (most have agreed with Yeats in finding it dramatically unnecessary, the final arrangement having 'greater intensity'). The second major difference is that 'in [Wilde's] play the dance is before the head is cut off'.[56] Yeats notes that the dance *with* the head was his real addition to the Salomé-tradition: 'Wilde's dancer never danced with the head in her hands – her dance came before the decapitation of the saint and is a mere uncovering of nakedness.'[57] This is a critique of *fin-de-siècle* veiling and unveiling, of the mere play of representations rather than the actual involvement of the body. Yeats is responding to what Marjorie Garber suggests is central to the Salomé-tradition: 'the essence of the dance itself, its taboo border-crossing, is not only sensuality, but gender undecidability, and not only gender undecidability, but the paradox of gender identification, the disruptive element that intervenes, transvestitism as a space of possibility structuring and confounding culture'.[58] If *Salomé* is replete with images of cross-gender identification, Yeats, placing the dance after the severing of the head and removing an ambiguous spectatorship and focus on the veiling of desire, restores the sexual binary. Instead of the dance of gender, we see a fetishistic version of coitus. Wilde's Salomé dances in order to get what she wants; Yeats's Queen dances with what she knows she cannot have, and endows the head with posthumous power as she is inseminated by the blood of the stroller.

Other differences between Yeats's plays and *Salomé* are also significant: the figure of Salomé's mother and the incest-plots are eliminated from the picture, for example. But the most important changes concern the treatment of the Salomé-figure herself: she is chaste and distant rather than sexually active, and displaced from the centre of the action – we enter with the Stroller, who becomes the protagonist; miraculously, we see his severed head sing. These changes shift the gender-politics. The hysterical male (King) is eliminated in successive drafts, leaving a naked confrontation between powerful Queen and Stroller/Swineherd. The dance, in *Salomé* a means to her getting what *she* wants, becomes part of a bargain which the Stroller/Swineherd sets: his head will be struck off, but the Queen will dance and then kiss it. Moreover, voice is reassigned: where Salomé's usurpation of the prophet's voice is a central issue for Wilde, in Yeats's plays the Queen's songs (as in Noh theatre) are ventriloquized by male attendants. In *The King of the Great Clock Tower*, the head sings of the union of the dead and the living: 'Crossed fingers there in pleasure can / Exceed the nuptial bed of man'. Here, the forbidden union is fruitful – the Queen's shudder signalling the insemination which breaks her moon-like isolation. In the original concluding song, carried over to the final version, the stress is on completion and the overcoming of 'lack'. The question is 'What can she lack whose emblem is the moon?':

First Attendant	Delight my heart with sound; speak yet again;
	But look and look with understanding eyes
	Upon the pitchers that they carry; tight
	Therein all time's completed treasure is:
	What do they lack? O cry it out again.
Second Attendant	Their desecration and the lover's night.[59]

'Desecration' is penetration: 'O, what may come / Into my womb, / What caterpillar / My beauty consume?' The Latin *desecrare* means to consecrate; the antithetical meaning in English is, of course, to violate – both meanings evoked by Yeats.

In Yeats's severed-head plays, the scenario of *Salomé* thus produces a trajectory which overcomes the equation of castration and decapitation through the dance and song of the Queen and of the head. The cut which the Stroller suffers is the saving sacrifice which Yeats called 'the drama of the slain god and the risen god' (Dionysus–Orpheus); the silent and intimidating Queen is moved into song and inseminated. We can note that *Man Into Woman* offers a parallel to Yeats rather than to Wilde here: Wegener's submission to surgery is also figured as 'cutting off his head', in that what Lili sees as the artistic, masculine part, the intellect, is excised in order that she can signify with her body.

Examining the folkloric origins of the image of the severed head in Yeats's stories and plays, Genevieve Brennan has linked the topic to castration fears. F. A. C. Wilson provides a more traditional route to the same conclusion via the castration of Dionysus as described in Thomas Taylor's translation of *The Works of the Emperor Julian*: Dionysus is castrated by the mother goddess in order to prevent the descent into generation which is, we saw, part of the incarnational process.[60] Elaine Showalter points out that 'the Freudian equation of decapitation and castration is itself a product of *fin-de-siècle* culture. The severed head [in *Dracula*] also seems to be a way to control the New Woman by separating the mind from the body. Moreover, the imagery of decapitation/castration, as Wendy Doniger O'Flaherty points out, "may symbolize the loss of the power of imagination".'[61] If a fear of creative impotence underlies some of Yeats's late works, we might follow Hélène Cixous in 'Castration or Decapitation', and read the severing of the Stroller's head in *The King of the Great Clock Tower* and *A Full Moon in March* as a castration which has the paradoxical effect of serving a fantasy of potency. (In this, it is like the Steinach Operation itself: a diversion of sexual energy.) The Queen is inseminated and rendered the player's 'property'. Cixous argues that what she calls 'the Realm of the Proper', or of property, is integral to 'man's classic fear of seeing himself expropriated, seeing himself deprived . . . Everything must return to the masculine. "Return": the economy is founded on a system of returns. If a man spends and is spent, it's on condition that his power returns.'[62] Such an investment is part of the background of these plays (Yeats wrote them in order to see if his power to produce lyrics would return); and of their subject-matter. The Stroller makes a gift of his body, but expects a return in the power of insemination and song. The Queen, who seems to represent a threat to masculinity in her self-sufficient perfection, is reintegrated into a poetic economy which aims to produce lyric. She becomes a test of the poet's desire.

FREUD AND 'ORGAN-INFERIORITY'

I will end with some reflections on the relation of Yeats's rewriting of the *Salomé* plot to Freud's late thoughts on gender – reflections which may help clarify the production of gender in Yeats.[63] For Freud, the defining absence of femininity is absolute – as indeed it tended to be for all of the participants in the psychoanalytic debate on femininity in the 1920s, for whom penis-envy is a given.[64] In the 1925 paper on 'Some Psychical Consequences of the Anatomical Sex-Distinctions between the Sexes', he argues that the little boy may displace or explain away what he sees in a girl's genitals, since it only becomes significant 'later, when some threat of castration has obtained a hold on him', at which point a 'terrible storm of emotion' is released. However, 'a little girl behaves differently. She makes her judgement and her decision in a flash. She has seen it and knows that she is without it and wants to have it.'[65] In this account of penis-envy, the girl is the realist, seeing and wanting – like the modern consumer – where the boy converts the reality of what he sees into something else (disavowal, fetishism, fantasy) before finally becoming aware, at the point of the Oedipal threat, that it is his own potential lack that he sees.[66] For the girl, organ-inferiority thus precedes the Oedipal stage proper, enabling her to swerve away from the mother so she can attach herself to the father, then eventually to a husband, accepting a child as a substitute for the phallus.

That is not Freud's only account of this progression: in the paper on 'The Dissolution of the Oedipus Complex' a year earlier (and elsewhere) he argues that the path to the boy's realization of the possibility of castration is prepared, firstly by the mother's withdrawal of the breast, and then by threats of castration, which only have their 'deferred effect' when he sees the little girl's genitals. In one account, the 'real' is the sight of the genitals; in the other, it is threat of castration. The two are interchangeable, and Freud's texts repeat that uncertainty he ascribes to the boy: is the castration 'real' or not? What is real and what symbolic?

I would argue that, despite the fact that in Wilde's play the focus is Salomé's sexuality and in Yeats's the Stroller's bargain, *Salomé* is redolent of the Freudian theory of the emergence of *masculine* sexuality in its relation to the feminine: that is part of its threatening power.[67] We see this in its veiling of the phallic woman, its Medusa images (particularly in Beardsley's version), its interest in incestuous desire, and its final savage repression of desire in the name of the 'unknown god' – the latter loosely paralleling Freud's account of the end of the Oedipus in the formation of the Superego (for the boy). Yeats's severed-head plays, on the other hand, reminds us more of the position of *feminine* sexuality in Freud's account, that is of a trajectory in which Salomé finds her way to femininity. Yeats writes out the mother in the first version, then the father in the final version, leaving only a heterosexually charged encounter between opposites – paralleling Freud's account of the woman's two-part Oedipus. There is in Yeats's queen(s) a desire for power, for the head, but in his text the unveiling only happens when the Queen holds the severed head and acknowledges her 'lack', finding a 'completion' which can only be effected by penetration and 'desecration'. Finally, Yeats ends his plays with insemination and acceptance of a child as substitute for what cannot be mastered:

First Attendant [singing as Queen]

> Child and darling, hear my song,
> Never cry I did you wrong;
> Cry that wrong came not from me
> But my virgin cruelty.
> Great my love before you came,
> Greater when I loved in shame,
> Greatest when there broke from me
> Storm of virgin cruelty.

The queen dances to tap-drums and in the dance lays the head upon the throne.[68]

Underlying this parallel is, no doubt, Freud's own fetishism and overvaluation of the phallus, which means that, for man, the 'lack' is phantasmal, for the woman clear. Freud's summation of the case for the woman, 'it corresponds to the difference between a castration that has been carried out and one which has been merely threatened', encapsulates Yeats's (as well as the transsexual's) journey towards the literalism of surgery.

In that sense, the male modernist who undergoes the cut –

whether Pound's metaphorical surgery on Eliot, or Haire's minor surgery on Yeats, or Abraham's radical surgery on Wegener – is following the feminine Freudian trajectory, at least in the sense that in actually enacting castration (the 'creation of a woman') the uncertainty which surrounds gender and desire for the masculine subject is dispelled. The fantasy of man-made or constructed femininity has a long pedigree, from Pygmalion to *L'Éve future* and beyond. But it finds a particular focus within modernist aesthetics. The 'surgical' Modernism espoused by Apollinaire, Marinetti, Pound, Yeats, and others attempts to resolve gender-confusions in favour of an 'objectivity' often seen as masculine.[69] That, in turn, involves a repudiation of the threatening decadent sexuality associated with *Salomé*, which modernist writers tended to associate with an immature confusion comparable to that in Freud's account of male sexual development. As we have seen, such a recuperation might involve taking a 'feminine' position (as construed by Freud) in order to clarify and fix gender roles, to answer the question 'What is a woman?' The desire to 'place' femininity helps explains the plethora of male modernist texts which create women, from Molly Bloom to Lady Chatterley, who know their own lack and where it might be completed; who say 'yes, yes' to the bargain of heterosexuality.

To be sure, it can be argued that the transsexual destabilizes or problematizes gender, forming a 'third sex' – whereas my account has moved from Wegener/Lili Elbe to the binary Freudian model. I have taken this approach because of the one-way trip which Wegener undergoes, with its understanding of femininity as divestment, both of organ and intellect; a journey from 'what am I?' to 'I am a woman, and will create with my body.' Judith Butler uses the term 'literalizing fantasy' to describe the process in which particular organs come to be the site of the 'incorporation of an identification', of the denial necessary to maintain gender as binary.[70] She suggests that the transsexual demonstrates the imaginary nature of such assignments: 'very often what is wanted in terms of pleasure requires an imaginary participation in bodily parts, either appendages or orifices, that one might not actually possess'. But, in the actual production of the transsexual body, the opposite is true: organs are made to conform to self-perception, the 'mind trapped in the wrong body' within a context in which 'wrong' presupposes a knowledge of the 'right' configuration. If, as Butler argues (following Wittig) the assignment of 'sex', before even gender, 'is the reality-effect of a violent process that is concealed by that very effect', a process which forcibly configures bodily parts by their naming (language), then the transsexual exposes that process at its most material.[71] That does not mean that transsexualism necessarily reproduces the disfigurement of gender; it is possible to imagine utopian forms of elective surgery.[72] But, in the context of the 1930s, and a 'Man' who wishes to change 'his' sex (as the title of the German edition put it), that is hardly the case. Like the 'bachelor machines' of the Surrealists, Lili is a man's woman.[73] By enabling Wegener's move from art to surgery in pursuit of a real 'sex', by constructing Lili as a woman, by introducing her moving account to the public as a pioneering case of a 'happy' intervention in pursuit of the 'truth' of gender, modernist medicine produces something like Yeats's version of Salomé: a woman for whom destiny is anatomy. This is the literalizing fantasy of Modernism at the level of the organ: 'no ideas but in things'.

PART IV

Interruption and suture

CHAPTER SEVEN

Distracted writing

Like vases that communicate that side's light and noise
into it poured your answering words
words before language a speech as good as birds
Brian Coffey, Advent VII

She smoothes her hair with automatic hand,
And puts a record on the gramophone.
The Waste Land, lines 255–6

Modernity brings with it the reconfiguration and re-energizing of the writing body in a number of different ways. We are, perhaps, most familiar with the positive modes in which the body enters writing, expressing the self as impulse, sexual being, or vehicle for the epiphany. But modes of disconnection are also an important part of this picture, as late nineteenth-century science fragmented the body into competing systems with their respective tolerations, limits, and interfaces. This chapter explores an experimental literary mode founded on disconnection and automatic writing, and visits a moment in the debate on its use, the exchange between Gertrude Stein and the behaviourist psychologist B. F. Skinner in 1934. It traces a shift from a nineteenth-century paradigm in which automatic writing is evidence of a 'secondary personality' to a modernist paradigm in which modes of production – and, eventually, of reception – are the focus. It will, in particular, relate automaticity to the dialectic of *attention* and *distraction* central to turn-of-the-century psychology, and to modernity itself. At the limits of the body considered as a perceptual apparatus, distraction produces the modern artwork.

One focus is the automatic *hand*, one of the prosthetic devices of Modernism, a technology for the extension of the human sensorium (psychic researcher Sir William Barrett coined the term 'autoscope' for devices used for 'communicating with the unknown').[1] The hand as a synecdoche for the writer, for writerly authority, has a long history.[2] In automatic writing, it becomes a mechanism for the production of data whose authority is less certain. W. B. Yeats described the hand as instrument, and was fascinated by an image of a mystic foil: 'What hand holds the point upon you?'[3] But, as Pound noted, discussing automatic painting in his 'Vorticism' essay of 1915, the claim that 'the painting is done without volition on their part, that their hands are guided by "spirits" or by some mysterious agency over which they have little or no control', is itself troubling.[4] Issues of authority centre on the question 'whose hand?' Reviewing the automatic scripts generated by Yeats and his wife, K. P. S. Jochum asks 'how much of it is fake, how much of it is genuine, is there a mixture of both?'[5] That question, for Jochum, is best resolved by the 'hands' in which questions and answers are recorded: he finds an 'orderliness . . . incommensurate with automatism' and chastises the editors for sometimes mistaking George's hand with W. B.'s. This confusion of hands is, however, intrinsic to automatic writing practices, which break the link between consciousness and text, producing material whose source is uncertain.

THE NINETEENTH-CENTURY CONTEXT: AUTOMATISM AND DUAL PERSONALITY

Automatic writing has its origins in two closely linked contexts. The first is Victorian psychic research and the technique's popularization at the seance-table by William Stainton Moses from the 1870s.[6] The second is the psychological experiments conducted by researchers including Pierre Janet and Alfred Binet in France, Boris Sidis and William James in America, and Frederic Myers and Edmund Gurney in England. The demarcation between the two areas was not always clear, and some – like Myers, with Moses a founder of the Society for Psychical Research in 1882 – moved between contexts. Myers's 1885 article 'Automatic Writing', in the *Proceedings of the Society for Psychical Research*, introduced a new stringency to the debate, matched by an article on 'Multiple Personality' the following year.[7] Myers saw mediumship and automatism as evidence for a subliminal self potentially separable from the body; automatism is the writing of that self and mediumship its voice, documented in the voluminous appendices to his *Human Personality and Its Survival of Bodily Death* (1903).

The hypothesis of secondary selves was supported by a Darwinian psychology, developed by Hughlings Jackson and others, which postulated a deeper, atavistic level of conscious, just as anthropologists like Tylor saw 'survivals' of primitive society in the 'civilized'. As Anne Harrington has recently shown, dual personality was linked to widespread interest, stimulated by the French neurologist Paul Broca, in the different functions of the brain hemispheres: the right hemisphere primitive and 'artistic', the left as more developed and rational.[8] Henri Ellenberger notes that 'by 1880 or so, double personality had become one of the most widely discussed clinical disorders'.[9] In 1902, Henry Adams could comment archly that 'alternating personalities turned up constantly, even among one's friends', adding that 'the new psychology . . . seemed convinced that it had actually split personality not only into dualism, but also into complex groups, like telephonic centres and systems, that might be isolated and called up at will, and whose physical action might be occult in the sense of strangeness to any known form of force'.[10]

Adam's linkage between dual personality and the dispersal of communication implicit in the 'telephonic system' – conceived in terms of flows of information – nicely identifies a defining uncertainty in the debate. 'Produced' by techniques like automatic writing and hypnosis, secondary personalities appeared intermittently. Researchers had problems deciding whether the secondary personality was a 'deeper' self or a parasitic effect which could be experimentally produced at the limits of organized selfhood. Binet's *On Double Consciousness* (1890), for example, attacks Huxley and other positivists who suggest that consciousness is an epiphenomenon; he rejects any 'anatomical theory' for automatic writings, hysterical blindness, or unconscious apprehension, arguing that these processes 'reveal a directive process of reasoning and a directive volition'. He posits a 'second consciousness' which can produce automatic writing, hear whispered messages, make calculations and so on without the primary consciousness being aware. The second consciousness is mobile and fluctuating, often incorporating oppositional impulses; it is suggestible, characterized by an impoverishment or 'narrowing of the field of consciousness'.[11]

In the famous cases which made popular reading at the turn of the century, the secondary self emerges as an organized *person* rather than simply as an effect of technique. In the cases of Féilda and Louis V. in France, and Mary Reynolds and the Reverend Hanna in the USA, a new individual is 'born' at particular moments, produced by a fright, a fall from a horse, or simply awakening from sleep. Sometimes it emerges as an infant, relearning language. The second self thus created haunts late nineteenth-century literature – in the strata which respond to passion in *Jude the Obscure* or obey the call of the wild in *Dracula*. For a romantic strain in Modernism (represented by Yeats, Lawrence and others), this self may represent the 'true' being, an atavistic return to origins rather than a parasite. Remy de Gourmont's essay, 'Subconscious Creation', illustrates the way in which artistic process could be depicted in these terms. Gourmont places involuntary processes at the centre of creativity, asserting that 'the subconscious state is the state of automatic cerebration in full freedom, while intellectual activity pursues its course at the extreme limit of consciousness, a little below it and beyond its reach'.[12] The conscious mind may act simply as a scribe: 'With Mozart, the whole process is, therefore, subconscious, and the material labour of execution amounts to little more than mere copying.'[13]

Myers's *Human Personality* includes a letter from Robert Louis Stevenson in Samoa, in which Stevenson – an s p r member – elaborates on his 'Chapter on Dreams' and describes how, during illness, he has felt his experience split into that of two selves, 'myself' and 'the other fellow'.[14] As its author recognized, *The Strange Case of Dr. Jekyll and Mr. Hyde* illustrates double-personality theories. It is, for example, an implication of accounts published by Sidis and others that what underlies many cases is a longing for a life of greater vivacity and freedom, just as Jekyll's motivation for his experiments is that Hyde refreshes the parts that other personas cannot. Hyde is in that sense, a prosthesis; an addition to the body, 'knitted' into its flesh, extending its capabilities. Two aspects of *Jekyll and Hyde* can be singled out: its structuring around the discontinuity between Hyde and Jekyll, and its preoccupation with handwriting. Myers was particularly interested in the way in which different selves alternate and even compete. In *Science and the Future Life* he attacks the continuity implicit in William James's no truth searched for. — Snowman/Jimmy

'Stream of Consciousness': 'we are now learning to conceive of our normal consciousness as representing only a fragment of the activity going on in our brains. We know of cases when a secondary current of consciousness – connected in various ways with the primary current – is always ready to take its place; so that the person lives alternating two different lives, with different chains of memory, and even different characters.'[15] *Human Personality* adds that 'these manufactured personalities sometimes cling obstinately to their fictitious names, and refuse to admit that they are in reality only aspects or portions of the automatist himself'.[16] In double-personality cases recounted by Sidis and others there is a stress – often in the face of considerable uncertainty – on establishing the 'true' person; and in most cases making that person the designated heir of competing forces. Similarly, Lanyon's concern in the novel is to establish the 'truth' of Hyde; though what he is faced with often seems more like an effect, a switching-device rather than a 'core' identity.

There is in Myers's work a subversive suggestion that technique – a specifically textual technique – might create rather than simply discover the secondary self. He considers the way in which a 'secondary chain of memories' might be built up:

Could we persuade some correspondent to write us a letter each time that he was in (say) the maudlin phase of drunkenness, the series of letters would resemble a series of planchette-messages in several ways. In the first place, they would express a character differing from his normal character, but congruous with itself. In the second place, the handwriting would be larger and laxer than his ordinary script. And in the third place, our correspondent, when sober, might very probably know nothing of the contents of the epistles, and might even contest their authenticity.[17]

This recalls the abstemious Jekyll comparing his liberation of Hyde – who 'drinks' pleasure with 'bestial avidity' – to a series of alcoholic binges.[18] More importantly, Myers's description of the secondary self produced by a textual experiment makes Hyde's blasphemous marginal scribbles a form of automatic writing. Although Hyde shares handwriting with Jekyll, in contrast to many reported cases where handwriting altered, Jekyll comments on 'the ape-like tricks that he would play on me, scrawling in my own hand blasphemies on the pages of my books' (96).

In these passages and elsewhere, the metaphorical and actual 'hand' becomes a focus for relations between dominant medical and judicial discourses and Hyde's dissident text. The hand of Jekyll, we are told, is 'professional in shape and size; it was large, firm, white and comely' where Hyde's is 'lean, corded, knuckly, of a dusky pallor, and thickly shaded with a swart growth of hair' (87–8). Evolutionary, class and racial differences indicate a disturbance in the chain of patriarchy – Jekyll remembers 'the days of childhood, when I had walked with my father's hand' – and Jekyll's narrative ends by telling us that one hand will supplant another: 'Here, then, as I lay down the pen . . .' (97). Moreover the transfer of hands operates elsewhere in the text. When Hyde risks arrest for murder if he cannot get to Jekyll's locked-up chemicals, he comments: 'I saw that I must employ another hand, and thought of Lanyon.' He can do this because 'I could write my own hand' – a phrase which, narrated by Jekyll remembering Hyde's action, twice crosses identities (93). Hyde's letter to Lanyon itself insists that he (as Jekyll) would 'have sacrificed [his] fortune or [his] left hand' for his friend, asks him to get the powders on the 'left hand' of the cabinet, and to admit Hyde 'with your own hand' before placing the chemicals 'in his hands'. The letter concludes with an appeal not to ignore the instructions: 'my hand trembles at the bare thought of such a possibility' (74–5). Hyde is what enables Stevenson to suggest that discontinuous narrative which Myers imagines: a narrative of the left hand, of the addictive, automatic self, with that self rendered coherent by a chain of masculine delivery in which writing is passed from hand to hand: wills and depositions, scrawled notes, annotations.

We can return Stevenson to the context of psychic research via W. T. Stead, campaigning journalist turned psychic enthusiast and founder of Julia's Bureau (Yeats was a regular attendee at his seances). Stead was obsessed with the idea of 'the Double' as the visible manifestation of the subconscious self, and wrote a series of articles on doubles for his psychic journal *Borderland* (1893–7), from theoretical pieces to news-snippets like 'A Double in Wandsworth'. Stead's 'Double' is an emanation of the self which can take physical shape; it can be proved to be in different places at the same time, commit crimes, and even be photographed. Stead published an essay on Stevenson in his regular 'Gallery of Borderliners' feature in 1895. The novelist is 'gifted with the power of weaving both the waking and sleeping experiences into a continuous thread': he can, that is, produce the double as an imaginative totality. The double is the most extreme of a range of phenomena: 'If the consciousness of a distinct continuous existence in dreams be the first step towards the discovery of your other Self, automatic-telepathic handwriting may be regarded as the second, and the phenomenon of the Double, whether in dream or in waking life, is the third and most marvellous of all the stages of the dissection of personality.'[19] Stevenson leaps to the third stage of this progress towards ontological certainty, but Stead is condemned to less secure ground, assembling discontinuous evidence and developing the 'telepathic handwriting' by which 'it is possible to make the acquaintance of the Man of the Dream Life'.[20] If Stevenson stands for a direct (but fictional) apprehension of the double, *Borderland* remains in the ambiguous area in which reproductive technologies – spirit-photographs, automatic writing – must produce the object of study.

THE DIALECTIC OF ATTENTION AND DISTRACTION

Myers's experiments with discontinuity and continuity suggest another context, less concerned with the *source* of automatic writing than with the mechanics by which it is elicited. In his *Discourse Networks*, Friedrich Kittler has suggested that the turn-of-the-century saw a shift in the production of discourse, produced by related developments in information technologies and the conceptualization of communication. Beginning with Herman Ebbinghaus's experiments on the memorization of random strings of words in the 1880s, Kittler traces a recurrent fascination with language as pure product, examined through psychological experiments which typically treated the production of discourse as a motor activity and focused on such topics as reaction-times, repetition, memory, automaticity, stimulus, and response. At the same time, technologies such as the typewriter, phonograph, radio, and film disconnected the production of language from time, distance, and the individual body. Correspondingly, Kittler argues, writing is 'disconnected from all discursive technologies, is no longer based on an individual capable of imbuing it with coherence through connecting curves and the pressure of the pen; it swells in an apparatus that cuts up individuals into test materials'.[21] Many speculated on the effects that such changes in production of texts would have on style: would the typewriter produce a different sentence structure? Would journalism produce a 'telegraphic' style (as practiced by the futurists and attributed to Hemingway)? A representative modernist moment is the speech which Aragon's pen makes in his *Treatise on Style* (1928), the author having considered its role as a machine 'from a more physical standpoint'. The pen declares itself tired of being 'the middle term between the peculiarities of their physique on the one hand, and the lack-luster of their expression on the other'. Describing itself as the 'pantograph of the arm', Aragon's pen directs its invective at writers.[22]

The key term in this context is 'distraction'. 'Distraction' is part of a continuum in which the other extreme is 'attention' – that which breaks down as distraction-effects like automaticity intrude.[23] Attention, as Jonathan Crary has recently argued, was one of the fundamental and determining categories of the nine-teenth-century experimental psychology which begins with Wundt; a category which presupposed that the subject is produced by its response to stimuli, and its ability to process information and to maintain fluctuating levels of pyschic energy.[24] William James's definition of the term exemplifies this sense of the self: 'focaliza-tion, concentration, of consciousness are of its essence. It implies withdrawal from some things in order to deal effectively with others, and is a condition which has a real opposite in the con-fused, dazed, scatter-brained state which in French is called *distrac-tion*, and *Zerstreutheit* in German.'[25]

Research in this area often involved an interest in what we might now call multi-tasking: the ability of tasks like listening and computation to be undertaken as 'background' or motor activities while conscious attention is directed elsewhere (typically, a more difficult task was attempted while a 'background' activity was taking place). Popular fascination was directed at prodigies who could write separate words with different hands and feet, while psychological experimenters considered the possibility of forcing conscious process in writing to its limits. Moments of linguistic breakdown or systemic overload and the linguistic pathologies which mark the limits of language-production became crucial. Psychologists posited differing explanations of what they detected: the intercession of a hypnotic passivity; a splitting of conscious-ness; the unconscious 'rhythmatization' of tasks; the intercession of memory or reverie. It was found, for example, that mild distraction could actually increase attention, a 'dynamogenic effect, the stimulation of one sense organ facilitating the functioning of another'.[26]

While the concepts of attention and distraction were differently conceived in different situations, the sense that the human subject could be defined and explored in these terms cuts across different positions. The sense of the self as produced by a process of attention/distraction even applied to spiritualists: the Reverend Moses would recite Virgil in order to eliminate his own consciousness from automatic writing.[27] Attention is an important element in Myers's analysis of the subliminal self; it is that which binds body and spirit together: 'the soul keeps the body alive by attending to it'. Inattention loosens those links, allowing a divided mode of existence: 'in deep states [the spirit] can partially withdraw attention from the organism and bestow it elsewhere, while remaining capable of at once resuming its ordinary attitude towards that organism. Bodily death ensues when the soul's attention is wholly and irrevocably withdrawn from the organism.' For Myers, selective and subliminal attention (distraction) can liberate hidden potential.[28]

For Freud, automaticity and distraction are similarly creative. In his earlier work, he relates them to the pre-conscious rather than the unconscious. In *Jokes and their Relation to the Unconscious* (1905) he describes the mechanism of the joke as 'automatic', utilizing a set response in order to subvert it, switching contexts rapidly. Distraction operates to catch the attention and keep the psyche's defenses occupied while the joke does its work. Freud also links distraction to telepathy and mediumship; the medium's sensitivity is enabled by the distracting astrological paraphernalia.[29] At its most general, distraction is, like hypnosis, a technique for circumventing the censoring devices of the ego. Moreover, Freud implies that distraction in the sense of a dispersal of attention is at the heart of psychoanalysis: the attention (*aufmerksamkeit*) of the analyst should be 'evenly suspended or poised' so that unconscious processes may emerge; the analyst does not direct the analysis in one direction or another. This is a prosthetic process, linking unconscious to unconscious 'as a telephone receiver is adjusted to the transmitting microphone'.[30]

Distraction and attention are, finally, important in terms of mass culture – an issue we will revisit at the end of this chapter. In a brilliant essay on theories of perception in the late nineteenth century, Crary argues that the development of a psychology of attention from 1870 has its origins in a breakdown of a sense of the perceptual field as already organized by perspective or a transparent optics. Instead, the subject is presented with 'a perceptual field newly decomposed into various abstract units of sensation and new possibilities of synthesis' in which various pathologies (hysteria, neurasthenia, aphasia, agnostia, etc.) represent the possibilities that the subject will fail to organize what she or he is presented with. *Attention* is central to that process of selection and peripheral inhibition which allows organization to take place; distractions are eliminated or filtered out. Crary suggests that the emergence of this problematic coincides with a new copiousness in the visual field, linked to the technological feats and requirements of an emergent commercial capitalism. Modernity involves 'a continual crisis of attentiveness . . . the changing configurations of capitalism pushing attention and distraction to new limits and thresholds, with unending introduction of new products, new sources of stimulation, and streams of information'.[31] George Beard, the theorist of 'American Nervousness', saw linguistic breakdown, automaticity, and similar effects as evidence of 'brain exhaustion' brought about by an overloaded psychic mechanism. This is a perspective which allows us to link Taylorism's pursuit of the determinants of attention with the technologies of advertising and cinema; production and consumption can be theorized in terms of attention, distraction, and the anxieties which surround the neurophysiological economy.

It is the shift away from ideas of the secondary personality to this Modernist paradigm for the production of automatic writing that I will consider in the work of Gertrude Stein. But it is also worth noting a transitional figure, W. B. Yeats, whose automatic writing sessions with his wife George Yeats produced that material which was synthesized in *A Vision* (1925). The origins of Yeats's psychic research lie in the nineteenth century, and in discussing the 'communicator' Leo Africanus – a ghost who claimed a dubious connection to Yeats – he carefully considered the thesis of a 'secondary personality'.[32] Yet, as he and George Yeats investigated the process of automaticity in their sessions in 1918, they came up with a set of terms which are close cognates of attention and distraction – 'sequence' and 'allusion', the former that which is ordered and directed; the latter the entry of random and unexpected material, described as 'the creative part of the automatic faculty'.[33] This material was largely written out of *A Vision* – the perfected product bears little trace of its origins – but is nevertheless central to its production and conceptualization.

GERTRUDE STEIN AND AUTOMATIC WRITING

Some of the most important work on automatic writing at the turn of the century was done by two young researchers in the Harvard Psychological Laboratory, Leon Solomons and Gertrude Stein.[34] Stein's work in this area has been the subject of controversy, mainly because of the behaviourist psychologist B. F. Skinner's debunking 1934 article in the *Atlantic Monthly*, 'Has Gertrude Stein a Secret?'[35] Skinner asserted that *Tender Buttons* used the techniques of automatic writing which Stein had explored in the laboratory. Stein herself responded to the accusation on a number of occasions; Sherwood Anderson and many subsequent critics have added their voices against Skinner, portraying his article as crudely reductionist.[36] (Some, on the other hand, saw Skinner's article as vindicating their doubts about Stein.[37]) What I will consider here is the possibility that Skinner's grounding of Stein's procedures in turn-of-the-century psychological experiments may provide useful clues to her work.

Many critics have misinterpreted Skinner's article.[38] Wilma Koutstaal has recently provided a careful description of the contexts of Solomons and Stein's experiments, which helps provide a more nuanced account of their relation to her writing.[39] The Harvard laboratory was supervised by Hugo Münsterberg, then providing a major impetus towards an applied scientific psychology in America. The connection between Stein and William James is usually stressed in discussions of her work at Harvard; it was, however, Münsterberg who directed research in this period, and who would have approved it (here as elsewhere he was written out of the history of American psychology after pro-German activities in the First World War). The Solomons–Stein emphasis on motor automatism reflects Münsterberg's championing of physiological explanations, as well as his work on fatigue and attention. (Münsterberg also exposed a famous medium in 1909, to James's annoyance.[40]) Solomons and Stein aimed in particular to test the established idea, sketched above, that automatic writing accessed a 'secondary personality'.[41] They sought to produce the same effects through a physiologically conceived 'motor automatism' in which the normally functioning mind produced the desired result by being uncoupled from self-consciousness via 'distraction'. Admittedly, in the follow-up article she wrote without Solomons, Stein gives some attention to the 'double-brain' hypothesis in explaining 'Type II' personalities, more 'hysterical'.[42] But the more important Solomons-Stein experiment works towards the opposite conclusion, seeing automatic writing as a rapid alternation of states of consciousness in which those states which produced the automatic writing are not available to memory:

> The consciousness without memory seems to *approach as its limit*, simply a condition in which the subject has not the faintest inkling of what he has written, but feels quite sure that he has been writing. It shows no tendency to pass beyond this into real unconsciousness. It seems to depend on the lack of associations between the different words – one word going out of consciousness before another has come to be associated with it.[43]

'Real unconsciousness' appeared to be an unrelated phenomenon. Automatic writing is produced not by the delivery of a message from within (or elsewhere) but by a disconnection of the link between utterance and intention.

This conclusion can, it seems to me, be linked to Stein's experimental work up to 1930. In 'The Gradual Making of *The Making of Americans*' – a 1935 lecture written in the wake of Skinner's article, Stein argues that what came out of her psychological work was a typology of personalities and their 'bottom nature'. The second article, written without Solomons, offers evidence of that interest (as Janet Hobhouse comments, '*The Making of Americans* was in Gertrude's mind to some extent a scientific work. It was to set forth a theory of behavior'[44]). But, in the lecture, Stein also stresses repetition and the use of a continuous present: 'I began to get enormously interested in hearing how everybody said the same thing over and over again with infinite variations but over and over again until finally if you listened with great intensity you could hear it rise and fall and tell all that there was inside them, not so much by the actual words they said or the thoughts they had but the movement of their thoughts and words endlessly the same and endlessly different.'[45] The stress on the differential and on one moment divorced from another for the purposes of analysis, the eschewal of content or 'depth', the attention to the mechanism of production – all these features carry forward the assumptions of the Harvard experiments. What is important is *writing* – mechanical production – rather than narrative. *The Geographical History of America* (1935) dismisses narrative, with its need for memory and beginnings, middles and endings, founded on the commonplaces of 'human nature'. In contrast, 'Writing is neither remembering nor forgetting neither beginning or ending'; it is generated by 'the human mind' rather than human nature. Given that most texts are narrative, it is only by atomized reading that they can be recuperated:

I found that any kind of book if you read with glasses and somebody is cutting your hair and you cannot keep the glasses on and you use your glasses as a magnifying glass and so read word by word reading word by word makes the writing that is not anything be something.

Very regrettable but very true.

So that shows to you that a whole thing is not interesting because as a whole well as a whole there has to be remembering and forgetting, but one at a time, oh one at a time is something oh yes definitely something.[46]

This is an exact description of distracted reading, taking place amidst other activities and isolating elements of writing ('one at a time').

An important clue to this effect is provided by Skinner. He was fascinated by the automatism reported by Stein in which the 'distraction' effect was obtained not by the usual method of reading another text, but by following her own writing some words behind her pencil. He speculates that the gap between producing and knowing got smaller and smaller, so that a kind of distraction-effect took place at the end of the pencil, the author writing at a distance from herself just large enough to sunder writing and consciousness of writing.[47] This is a gap which we could see as related to the 'temps perdu' which Helmholtz defined as the body's reaction-time, separating motor activity from apperception, and opening up the space into which the investigative technologies of modernity are inserted – experimental physiology, Marey's graphic analyses of motion.[48] In 'How Writing is Written' (1935), Stein notes the centrality of memory to learning and knowledge, yet 'at any moment where you are conscious of knowing anything, memory plays no part'. To write in this way is to enter the continuous present, the world of 'one time-knowledge'.[49] But that time is *not* simply the present: it is time in a loop which approaches the present as its limit: 'I say I never repeat while I am writing because while I am writing I am almost completely, and that is if you like being a genius, I am almost entirely and completely listening and talking, the two in one and the one in two and that is having completely its own time and has in it no element of remembering.'[50] 'Talking and listening all at once' without remembering is separating producing from knowing, watching what one produces only as it is produced. In *Everybody's Autobiography*, Stein comments that her experiments were not 'distracted' enough: 'we always knew what we were doing how could we not when every minute in the laboratory we were doing what we were watching ourselves doing, that was our training'.[51] To know what one is doing only as one is doing it is a different matter; a matter of distraction.

The writing so produced is not, it should be said, typical of 'automatic' texts: all Stein's writings contain elements of organization and intertextual reference. What I am describing is a conceptual framework which validates Stein's textual production. We can see the effects generated by this style in almost any of Stein's works after 1910, while remaining aware of differences in her styles, which often depend on the 'postulates' of the experiment (for example on whether the focus is syntax or *lexis*).[52] Consider the following passage, from 'Miss Furr and Miss Skeene', Stein's 1911 meditation on gayness:

Helen Furr was living somewhere else then and telling some about being gay and she was gay then and she was living quite regularly then. She was regularly gay then. She was quite regular in being gay then. She remembered all the little ways of being gay. She used all the little ways of being gay. She was quite regularly gay. She told many then the way of being gay, she taught very many then little ways they could use in being gay. She was living very well, she was gay then, she went on living then, she was regular in being gay, she always was living very well and was gay very well and was telling about little ways one could be learning to use in being gay, and later was telling them quite often, telling them again and again.[53]

Repetition, gradual increment and variation, a framework of discontinuity/continuity. There *is* an overall direction to this passage, but at the level of the sentence there is process rather than a sense of destination. Stein's techniques relate to the modernist attack on syntax, as in Marinetti's 1913 manifesto 'Destruction of Syntax – Imagination Without Strings – Words-in-Freedom', or the Russian futurist pamphlet of the same year, *The Word as Such*.[54] But Stein's banner is also 'writing without remembering', the banner of automaticity.

In the example cited above, the verbal forms carry the reader; in *Tender Buttons*, as Stein suggested, it is nominal forms which predominate. *Tender Buttons* began with the composition of its third section 'Rooms', which, as Lisa Ruddick argues, has as its recurring theme the paradox of themelessness: 'the unanchored quality of its own linguistic play'.[55] It is possible to read parts of *Tender Buttons* thematically (as Ruddick does) or in terms of latent and manifest content (as William Gass does), and arrive at a range of meanings on such issues as seeing, sexual pleasure, and the construction of patriarchy.[56] Skinner was wrong, too, about its lack of cultural reference, which ranges from the Old Testament to Whitman. But such effects can only, it seems to me, be read in terms of an aesthetic which strips language of an origin and renders it as a series of resonant events.[57] There is no theory of expression at work.

What automatic writing might thus provide was not so much Skinner's 'secret' – a literal technique – as the rejection of a nineteenth-century aesthetics, inherent in the dialectic of consciousness and unconscious on which the theory of automatic writing was founded. We might see the resulting model in terms of Jakobson's linguistic axes: a depth model (the occult word as metaphor, hidden truth) is supplanted by a stress on metonymy and the syntagmatic chain. Her lecture, 'Composition as Explanation' (1926), argues that 'it is very interesting that nothing inside in them, that is when you consider the long history of how every one ever acted or has felt, it is very interesting that nothing inside in them in all of them makes it connectedly different'. In contrast to the multilayered evolutionary self of the depth model, the modern self is a series of fragmented and integrated moments.[58]

A brief comparison between Stein and the Surrealists is useful here. André Breton practiced automatic writing with Philippe Soupault from 1919, and championed it in the first Surrealist Manifesto (1924) and subsequent writings. The technique was linked to his experience of war-shattered soldiers, and his reading of Janet, James, Myers, and Freud. He describes automaticity in terms of attention, interference, echolalia, and other psychological terms, climaxing in the evocation of a 'complete state of distraction'.[59] To some extent Breton regarded his experiments as scientific, varying the speed of writing, for example, to gauge its effects.[60] There is, as in Stein, a radical de-hierarchization of literature, expressed in the doctrine that all automatic writings are 'of equal merit'.[61] Breton stressed speed and a disconnection from sequential logic: 'Write quickly, without any preconceived subject, fast enough so that you will not remember what you're writing and be tempted to reread what you have written.'[62] Automatic writing is pure performance, with the method itself more important than its 'effects'; it liberated writing from the order of the 'beautiful' and 'lucid'.

Yet where Stein sought exteriority and the mechanics of language, Breton also insists on grounding automaticity in the spontaneous values of the 'true' self: automatism reveals 'the actual functioning of thought', as he put it in his famous definition; it is a device to link inner and outer worlds and reunify the self, a *vase communicant*.[63] To that end, he distinguished between Surrealist automatic writing and that practised by mediums who 'act in a wholly *mechanical* way in their execution of letter and line. They have absolutely no knowledge of what they are writing and drawing. Their hand is anesthetized: it is as if it were being directed by another hand.'[64] Similarly, there is a trace of the second-self model in Louis Aragon's remark that Breton and Soupault 'wished to drown all personal responsibility for them by attributing their words to the dictation of some shared parasitical organ'. But Aragon also described Surrealism as a *mechanism* for inspiration, 'limited by fatigue'; as pure technique.[65] And Breton tends to see automatic writing as (at the limit) mechanical:

> writing that is 'automatic', or 'mechanical' as Flournoy would have said, or 'unconscious' as Mr. René Sudre would have it, has always seemed to me to be the limit toward which the surrealist poet ought to strive (keeping in mind, however, that contrary to what spiritualism proposes – dissociating the psychological personality of the medium – surrealism postulates nothing less than the unification of that personality). Which means that for us the question of the exteriority of, let us say again for simplicity, 'the voice', obviously does not even arise.[66]

What happens 'at the limit' is writing itself (Kittler: '*écriture automatique*, the duty of nothing more and nothing less than literature'[67]). Indeed, Breton reports that 'experience has come to verify fully Myer's assertion that automatic *speech* does not in itself constitute a more developed form of motor message than automatic *writing*; and furthermore, it is to be distrusted because of the deep memory and personality alterations it involves'. Sidestepping the issue of the nature of the unconscious, Breton privileges the technique and casts doubts on the idea of a secondary personality, in the end joining Stein in the pursuit of writing.[68]

Earlier modernist texts take on aspects of these experiments. Foucault comments on Raymond Roussel's language experiments that 'the reader thinks that he recognizes the wayward wanderings of the imagination where in fact there is only random language, methodically treated'. This is writing at 'the very edge of consciousness'.[69] Equally, the cognitive double-tasking employed in experiments on distraction can readily be seen in such texts as *The Prose of the Trans-Siberian and Little Jeanne of France* (1913) the six-foot long 'simultaneous' poem by Blaise Cendrars and Sonia Delaunay involving text, painting, and maps; the mind forced to attend to two disparate tasks at once. Marinetti similarly advocated texts written in 'parallel lines' carrying different sensations. As Roger Shattuck comments in an essay on Freud and Valéry, the division between conscious and unconscious process in Modernism may be more typically seen in terms of *speeds* of mental process rather than a depth model.[70]

Indeed, once one begins to look for the dynamics of attention, distraction, and automaticity in modernist texts, they appear widespread. Rebecca West praises Pavlov in her essay 'The Strange Necessity' (1928), commenting that 'It would be entertaining to rewrite [Michael Arlen's novel] *The Green Hat* as a timed record of the administration of stimuli to a subject.' She conducts a distraction experiment, reading Pavlov and talking to an electrician, noting the 'co-existence' thoughts in her mind before concluding that the self exists as a perpetual flux of data, reacting both to itself and to outside stimuli.[71] William Carlos Williams, in his essay on Stein, wrote: 'Movement . . . is for us the effect of a breakdown of the attention', adding that movement 'must always be considered aimless, without progress'. For Williams, Stein's writings address the problem of distributing attention across the process of writing without allowing it to be fixated. His own prose writing, in the period 1918–32, used automatic techniques which he borrowed from Surrealism, and in the Prologue to *Kora in Hell* he writes that most writing depends on easy associations in which 'the attention has been held too rigid on the one plane instead of following a more flexible, jagged resort. It is to loosen the attention, my attention since I occupy part of the field, that I write these improvisations.'[72] Williams was deliberate, but we might see a more oblique distraction signalled in the convalescence Eliot undertook in Lausanne in late 1921, during which part of *The Waste Land* was written. Eliot's rest-cure was intended to overcome the problem (reported to Sydney Waterlow) that he had 'been losing power of concentration and attention, as well as becoming a prey to habitual worry and dread of the future'. *The Waste Land* is itself a distracted text. Eliot was later to comment, in *The Use of Poetry and the Use of Criticism* (1933), on the fact that 'some forms of ill-health, debility or anaemia' might break down 'strong habitual barriers' and 'produce an efflux of poetry in a way approaching the condition of automatic writing'; he stresses that this involves 'not a [mystical] vision but a motion terminating in an arrangement of words on paper' – a perfect description of the automatic.[73] Stein, in this respect, is a central modernist, making explicit the methods which others efface, and opening the way to many later writers who use forms of distracted production.[74]

SKINNER AND STEIN: THE PATHOLOGY OF WRITING AND REPETITION

We might also return to the question of what the confluence of Skinner and Stein in 1934 meant for the behaviourist. Having read Stein's recollections of her experiments in part of *The Autobiography of Alice B. Toklas* published in the *Atlantic Monthly*, Skinner dug up the articles and used them to challenge her reputation – or, at least, to attack *Tender Buttons* and other non-narrative works, which he saw as an 'ill-advised experiment' in non-sense. Skinner pointed out the similarity of method in Stein's reports of her writing and automatic procedures: '(1) *Tender Buttons* was written on scraps of paper and no scrap was ever thrown away; (2) Miss Stein likes to write in the presence of distracting noises; (3) her hand writing is often more legible to Miss Toklas than to herself (that is, her writing is "cold" as soon as it is produced); and (4) she is "fond of writing the letter *m*", with which

. . . the automatic procedure often began.'[75] He focuses in particular on Stein and Solomons's fourth set of experiments, using
'spontaneous automatic writing'. They had reported that:

A phrase would seem to get into the head and keep repeating itself at
every opportunity, and hang over from day to day even. The stuff written
was grammatical, and the words and phrases fitted together all right, but
there was not much connected thought. The unconsciousness was
broken into every six or seven words by flashes of consciousness, so that
one cannot be sure but what the slight element of connected thought
which occasionally appeared was due to these flashes of consciousness.[76]

They add that 'absurd mistakes are occasionally made in the
reading of words – substitutions similar in sound but utterly distant
in sense'. An example Skinner cites from their article is: 'When he
could not be the longest and thus to be, and thus to be, the
strongest'. It is this automatic-substitutive style which Skinner
posits as Stein's 'secret'.

The real focus of Skinner's attack, however, is on the avowed aim
of the Harvard researchers to produce automatic writing without
creating a secondary self, in the developed version he calls 'the
organized *alter ego* of the hysteric'. The secondary personality of
Tender Buttons is 'flimsy' and childlike; 'The writing is cold'; 'our
hypothetical author shows no sign of a personal history or a cultural background'; 'the writing springs from no literary sources'
except the nursery rhyme. Here Skinner spectacularly misunder-
stands Solomons and Stein's work, which, rather than aiming to
produce a 'limited' secondary personality, sought its elimination.
Stein is criticized for her affectless style, as if a secondary self – precisely what she sought to avoid – would have been more interesting. Skinner seems trapped, as critic, within a romantic
aesthetics of self and other, failing to pursue the gains of Stein's
open style from the point of view of the reader. He implies that
meaning must originate from an organized structure of personality and 'cultural background'; it cannot be 'the invention of the
analyzer'. This is 'Literature Without Meaning', as he called it in a
lecture, adding examples from Cummings and Joyce.

The blind spot here is revealing. What Skinner fears is something which his own work might seem to make an obvious subject:
writing as pure behaviour, considered apart from a concept of mind.
We get 'what her arm wrote' (he is quoting Stein), 'and', he adds,

'it is an arm which has very little to say'. Compare a passage in his autobiography which cites a radio evangelist on drinking: 'someone had complained that he could not control his drinking, and [Luke] Rader said something like this: "What do you mean you can't control it? Isn't it your arm that raises the glass to your lips. Do you mean to tell me you can't control your arm?"'[77] A hand or arm which simply writes is to close to addiction, automaticity as programmed repetition. His critique is finally of a writing predicated on the body rather than mind; and in particular of a de-somaticized body, washed clean of 'depth' and acting as a language-machine. Skinner thus provides both an understanding of Stein's automaticity and a negative judgment on its effects.

The oddest aspect of that judgment is its relation to his own discourse as a founder of Behaviourism. Skinner's work, with its origins in Mach, Poincaré, and Watson's 1913 manifesto, avoids reference to mentalist explanations (which Skinner scornfully described as positing a 'man within', an explanation which simply repeats the problem). He writes: 'the position can be stated as follows: what is felt or introspectively observed is not some non-physical world of consciousness, mind, or mental life but the observer's own body'.[78] Operant Psychology dwells on something close to an automatic writing, the stimulus–response curve transcribed from the lever pressed by the rat in the Skinner Box. Skinner also, like Stein, narrowed the time-frame, rejecting the hypothesis of a pre-existing drive or future goals, and describing behaviour within a controlled environment. (Stein: 'I wanted to get rid of everything except the picture within the frame . . . I wanted as far as possible to make it exact, as exact as mathematics.'[79]) Given these parallels, could we say that Skinner's attack on Stein was produced by Stein's exact resemblance to his work?

Two explanations can be offered for this antipathy: one relates to the privileged status of literature for Skinner; the other derives more speculatively from his family romance. *Particulars of My Life*, the first volume of Skinner's autobiography, describes his original love: literature. It ends with his painful decision to abandon a writing career, despite encouragement from Robert Frost and others, and his first steps in psychology in 1928 – at Harvard, where Stein studied three decades earlier. There is evidence of trauma and a lost ideal in a 'Polemic Against Literature' written in the period. Skinner later attempted to heal the rift between his early ambitions and actual career, teaching courses in literary psychology. Yet one could also say that what he calls Stein's 'secret' – that her writing was 'generated' by psychological research – challenges his path in the opposite direction, the abrogation of literature for science, even as it reveals a possible communality between the projects. One might thus detect a double rivalry in Skinner: he gave up writing because he had little to say (an accusation he aims at Stein); and at Harvard he entered a depleted department well after the glory days of James, Münsterberg, and Sidis.

Appositely enough, rivalry is a strong theme in *Particulars of My Life*, in relation to Skinner's younger brother Ebbe. His denials of a battle for parental affection punctuate stories which palpably demonstrate the intensity of competition, via comments on Ebbe's amiability and close relations with his parents. Skinner accidentally shoots him with an arrow, citing Hamlet: 'I have shot mine arrow o'er the house / And hurt my brother'. The rivalry persists until Ebbe's sudden death as a teenager, at which point Skinner – a man with no unconscious, apparently – remarks flatly on his lack of grief. One set of episodes is interesting. With candid detachment, Skinner describes how he showed Ebbe his erection. Ebbe plays with it, which Skinner interprets as aggression: 'At that age, to ejaculate was to be slightly demeaned or defeated, and he was planning to put himself in a superior position. I told him that I could take that kind of stimulation for any length of time without having an orgasm, and he stopped at once, rather petulantly.' This scenario of mastery through control is undone a page later, as the scene shifts from the body to language, and to the stylistic ground on which Skinner was to engage Stein – repetition:

He discovered that he could tease me by repeating what I said. He would start with a remark he thought rather silly, and if I then said, 'Oh, stop it', he would simply echo me: 'Oh, stop it.' If I tried to save myself by saying, 'I don't care if you do that', he would say 'I don't care if you do that.' My protests only supplied him with further material, and my silence was his victory.[80]

Repetition here features as aggression and a loss of (phallic) control: he cannot take linguistic stimulus 'for any length of time'. The parallels with Stein are clear: her repetitive style, like Ebbe's, flaunted the purposelessness of language. One might add that a younger brother represents the dangers of repetition to any first child: one becomes two.

Skinner's autobiographies also suggest a preoccupation with repetition and originality. As a schoolboy he was fascinated by the hypothesis that Bacon wrote Shakespeare's plays, and was himself accused of plagiarism. His literary efforts were emulative or parodic. But he also guards moments at which words come unprompted: he wrote a play in a single day in what was 'very close to automatic writing'; later he produced *Walden Two* in a similar way.[81] 'Automatic writing' in the romantic sense thus remains an area of privileged production for Skinner, like Proustian memory (another interest) – an attitude challenged by Stein. A matrix thus emerges in which Skinner's failed attempts at literature, his idealization of its sources, the threat of secondariness, and even sibling rivalry all converge on Stein's science of literary repetition. We could also say that her work provides a feedback which he could not tolerate: rather than keeping literature as a separate humanist sphere on which the psychologist might comment respectfully, Stein invades it with techniques related to those of the behaviourist.

I would also suggest that Skinner's encounter with Stein prompts a shift in his attitude. His course in 'The Psychology of Literature', taught in the late 1920s, included a range of features suggesting cognitivist leanings: 'Psychological basis of style; nature and function of metaphor; techniques of humour, etc. Unconscious language processes and their use in the production of literary effects'.[82] In lectures on literature in the early 1930s, he was willing to psychoanalyse Lewis Carroll and others.[83] The later 1930s, in contrast, saw a move towards a behaviourist consideration of language which was to climax in *Verbal Behavior* (1959) – the work which Noam Chomsky was to attack for avoiding a 'depth' model of language. In this period, Skinner considered word-association and word-sequence as patterns of behavioural repetition, extending the ideas of George Zipf's *Psychobiology of Language* (1935) 'in the hope of discovering just what effect the occurrence of a sound has in facilitating or suppressing subsequent occurrences'. Language could be seen as a pattern of repetition and difference in which, for example, 'we pick up words from each others in a conversation and use a particular word again and again'[84] – A Steinian pursuit.

STEIN IN THE 1930S: FROM AUTOMATISM TO AUTHORITY

Stein was stung by Skinner's article and responded in a variety of texts, including 'How Writing is Written' and *Everyone's Autobiography* (1937).[85] Her official position was that the most important thing that she inherited from her period as a psychological researcher was a sense of the different types of human character. She reported that the original suggestion (probably from Münsterberg) was 'that we should do experiments in fatigue', and that she became interested in 'the difference between being active and being tired' in relation to the 'bottom nature' of the subjects, and that this led in turn to the idea, expressed in *The Making of Americans*, that 'one could make diagrams and describe every individual man or woman'.[86] Nevertheless, in linking her work to fatigue study – to production rather than content – Stein reinforces the connections between the experiments and her own writing practices. Similarly, when she describes *The Making of Americans* in responding to Skinner in 'How Writing is Written', she echoes a section of her original paper quoted by Skinner:

SOLOMONS AND STEIN (1896): The stuff written was grammatical, and the words and phrases fitted together all right, but there was not much connected thought.

STEIN (1935): I had to use present participles, new constructions of grammar. The grammar-constructions are correct, but they are changed, in order to get this immediacy.[87]

The retrospective nature of that judgment is important here, since in 1935 her work was changing direction. Richard Bridgeman argues that 'before Skinner had made consciousness an issue, Gertrude Stein had felt free to locate her creative efforts apart from it'.[88] In fact, Stein's work had already begun to shift towards a more deliberate stance: in *The Autobiography of Alice B. Toklas* (written 1932), *Four in America* (1932–3), and in the work Stein saw as pivotal, her 1930 poem *Before the Flowers of Friendship Faded Friendship Faded*. In her lectures on *Narration* (1934) she describes the latter: 'Hitherto I had always been writing, with a concentration of recognition of the thing that was to be existing as my writing as it was being written. And now, the recognition was prepared beforehand there it was it was already recognition a thing I could recognize because it had been recognized before I began my writing, and a very queer thing was happening.'[89] The 'queer thing' is a move away from the disconnection of the earlier work. The category of the 'already recognized' reverses the paradigm in which recognition at best approaches the asymptote of the writing hand. In *Before the Flowers of Friendship Faded Friendship Faded*, what was initially a translation of a poem by George Huget took another direction: 'I finished the whole thing not translating but carrying out an idea which was already existing and then suddenly I realized something I realized that words came out differently if there is no recognition as the words are forming because recognition had already taken place.'

This is another moment of modernist mediumship: an intervention from an 'elsewhere' which is fully within the author, preconceived. Admittedly the poem's precognition is not easy to see: it seems one of Stein's more difficult modes.[90] It is partly in the metre, more regular than that of Stein's other 'poems' (as in the line which gives one Stein selection its title: 'Look at me now and here I am'). Rather than using the 'continuous present', it uses co-ordinated tenses which slide into each other, including loops in which that which will happen becomes that which has happened and is happening: 'Between now not at all and after which began / It could be morning which it was at night'. One of the poem's subjects is the difference between three and two; that is, between a dialectic like that of writer, writing, and awareness of subject. In *Everybody's Autobiography* Stein reports that a ventriloquizing effect could impose itself on the process of pure writing: 'On the other hand as I write the movement of the words spoken by some one whom lately I have been hearing sounds like my writing feels to me as I am writing. That is what led me to portrait writing.'[91] Beyond that apprehension lies the portrait and voice of an 'other': 'Alice B. Toklas'; or 'Gertrude Stein', genius and public figure.

Stein had considered the same issue in 'Henry James', one of *Four in America*, using the distinction between 'accident' and 'coincidence', or between 'writing' and 'going to be written'. The former, which Stein equates with Shakespeare's plays in their open form, is unpremeditated; the latter, equated with Shakespeare's sonnets, is writing subsumed within a larger framework of containing forms.[92] 'Henry James' meditates on this distinction: 'If

you who are writing know what it is that is coming in writing, does
that make you keep on writing or does it not.' In particular, Stein
explores the construction of a voice, a conscious setting of the
right words in the right order, as opposed to the automatic paradigm in which each word is separately placed:

There is the writing which is being written because the writing and the
writer look alike. In this case the words next to each other make a sound.
When the same writer writes and the writing and the writer look alike but
they do not look alike because they are writing what is going to be written
or what has been written then the words next to each other sound different than they did when the writer writes when the writer is writing what
he is writing.[93]

The contrast is between knowing-writing and writing-as-writing, in
which a time-lag splits intention from production. The suggestion
that Henry James wrote 'both ways at once' describes a possible
reconciliation between these modes. Stein's 1935 American lectures plot her career in these terms, as a series of shifts between
word-consciousness and pattern-consciousness, climaxing in a
mature sense of self (and of genius). The key term here is one
which Stein had previously downplayed, the *author* in whom voice
is located. In 'Henry James' she writes:

Clarity is of no importance because nobody listens and nobody knows
what you mean no matter what you mean, nor how clearly you mean what
you mean. But if you have vitality enough of knowing enough of what you
mean, somebody and sometime and sometimes a great many will have to
realize that you know what you mean and so they will agree that you mean
what you know, what you know you mean, which is as near as anybody can
come to understanding any one.[94]

The Autobiography of Alice B. Toklas is the fruit of this concern for
voice – a way of writing, ventriloquizing Alice, suggested to her by
a friend. Janet Hobhouse acutely comments that the *Autobiography*
released Stein from the need 'to have writing and writer mutually
unconsciousness of each other and certainly unconscious of any
other audience'.[95] The paradigm set in place by 'motor automatism' is abandoned for the more self-conscious world of Stein's late
works, governed by other considerations than the scientific,
including that of money – an economy which consciously aims for
a market with a narrative of the person, as Stein complains in
Everybody's Autobiography. But that is another story.

THE DISTRACTED HAND: JUNE ETTA DOWNEY

If we wondered what kind of career Stein would have had if she had remained a psychological researcher, we might turn to a psychologist who extended her work. June Etta Downey, a year younger than Stein, spent her entire career at the University of Wyoming, up to her death in 1932.[96] A largely forgotten figure – unlike John B. Watson, with whom she collaborated, she founded no 'school' – Downey seems remarkably attuned to the preoccupations of literary modernity. She investigated two sets of issues in particular: the analysis of handwriting, including both its relation to personality type and the effects of 'distraction'; and the psychology of literature and literary language.[97] The point where these two concerns intersect is automatic writing.

Downey's work began with *Control Processes in Modified Handwriting* (1908), a classic attention–distraction study in which subjects wrote while undergoing such distractions as counting, reading, reading aloud, and listening to lists being read; Downey posited a gradation from alternating attention to full automatism.[98] Like Stein, she sides with the 'grapho-motor' explanation of automatism, rather than a 'detached co-consciousness'. Countering the accusation that her narrowly focused experiments may not cover complex contexts like the seance or literature – 'those cases of automatic writing which issue in such novel and meaningful combinations of words as is held to be explicable only by the presence of a selective [i.e. secondary] consciousness' – she is none the less willing to generalize:

the transition from marginal awareness to complete awareness of writing; the long lapses of writing-consciousness that occurred rarely; the dropping-out at various times of anticipatory report, or memory processes; the occasional loss of the sense of agency bear such close analogy to descriptive accounts of what takes place in automatic writing so-called, that it is difficult to believe that they are the products of wholly different conditions. To the writer, a physiological interpretation of the present test is the only one that has meaning.[99]

In her 1923 article on 'Automatic Writing', Downey pushed this line of thought further, seeing in the disconnections of automatic writing a confirmation of temporal continuity as central to consciousness: 'it was our impression for the whole course of the experiment that a report of unawareness was certainly conditioned by lack of memory-connections and that, possibly, consciousness itself should be phased wholly in terms of connection'. We might see a vindication of Stein's technique in the conclusion that 'all lapses reported were memory lapses which approached as a limit a completely dissociated mental bit'.[100] This, at the limit, is distracted writing.

However, in extending the work of Solomons and Stein, Downey also found more evidence of conscious control under 'distraction' than they had. In her later career she explores how one can work with distraction and integrate it into a literary psychology. If, like Stein, Downey rejects the double-consciousness theory in automatic writing, she was willing to resuscitate it in *Plots and Personalities*, a book on 'training the creative imagination' written with Edwin Slosson. Downey notes that the eliciting of a double or multiple personality is 'common in dreams and literature', a technique which might be used for literary 'character-making', in a creative daydreaming.[101] More importantly, Downey sees a form of distraction as important to the literary trope. In a series of articles culminating in *Creative Imagination: Studies in the Psychology of Literature* (1929), she parallels Jakobson in analysing language according to two axes: that of 'connection' and that of 'substitution'. The former, as we have seen, was the most fundamental basis for analysis of language and thought. Substitution, on the other hand, is the basis for metaphor and is linked to the other postulate to emerge from the automatic writing experiments: it creates a 'double mental context' in which two ideas can be held in tension.[102] In a cognitive double-tasking, performing two tasks at once, the mind is distracted into the axis of substitution, enabling metaphor. The two linguistic axes suggest corresponding literary styles. 'Style swings between vivid word-consciousness and meaning or sentence-consciousness' – a taxonomy which Stein also found herself applying as she summarized her career in the 1935 lectures.[103] In what could be a prescription for *Tender Buttons*, Downey observes that the word 'blossoms' in 'detached consciousness'; whereas in the sentence it is 'held rigid in a given scheme of associations'. Using this scheme (which to some extent remains implicit rather than developed), Downey discusses a range of features at the interface of aesthetics and psychology: the associations of words ('word-physiognomy', which ranges from the shape of letters to onomatopoeia), the cognitive significance of grammar, the ways in which characteristic tonal patterns can be identified in different poets, even the effect of the typewriter on style.[104] She also focuses on the role of the body in literary reception: kinaesthetic effects perform themselves in the body of the reader, through a process of sensory disruption and even invasion ('hypnotic' texts). The reader struggles – ideally – from 'subjectivity of experience' to a state of 'aesthetic objectivity' in which the text's tendency to 'take over' the reader is overcome, often helped by devices in the text which aim to achieve 'psychical distance'.[105]

The stay-at-home Downey thus takes on the psychological career Stein abandoned. She finds a model for aesthetic reception as well as production in the psychophysical dynamics of attention and distraction, the reader sorting through a cluttered perceptual field in search for a point of stability. In her psychology, distraction and automaticity become what they were for Stein: a way of directing attention at aspects of language, seen in terms of failure of sequence ('memory lapses which approached as a limit a purely disconnected mental bit'). Metaphor itself involves such a 'disconnection'; language, at its most creative, is distraction, an act performed on the body of the reader which leaves her struggling for meaning and distance.

CODA: DISTRACTION AND CINEMA IN KRACAUER AND BENJAMIN

I will conclude this chapter with a shift in focus which points the debate on automaticity towards the issue of mass culture, and towards some of the material discussed in the final chapter. In so doing, we can develop and generalize the hints of a theory of a distracted *reception* (rather than production) implicit in Downey's work. If we return briefly to the nineteenth-century context, we see the 'secondary self' being characterized in terms which stress its suggestibility and susceptibility to influence. It was postulated that it could be affected at a distance by magnetism or even 'toxic substances' in test-tubes (prototypes, perhaps, of the 'communicating vessels' of the Surrealists).[106] At the turn of the century, this suggestibility is applied to analyses of collective behaviour: of crowds, cinema audiences, and even of the consumer.

One example is provided by the leading American exponent of the 'subpersonal self', Boris Sidis. In *The Psychology of Suggestion*

(1898) and *Multiple Personality* (1905), the primary self is described as self-aware and striving, whereas the subconscious self is fixated on the present moment.[107] It is shallow, amoral, and capable of a preternatural mimicry because of its tendency to identification (evidence of weak ego-boundaries). This argument is elevated to social theory:

The subwaking self dresses to fashion, gossips in company, runs riot in business panics, revels in the crowd storms in the mob, and prays in the camp meeting. Its senses are acute, but its sense is nil. Association by contiguity, the mental mechanism of the brute, is the only one that it possesses. The subwaking self lacks all personality and individuality, it is absolutely servile; it works according to no maxims; it has no moral law, no law at all . . . [it] has no will; it is blown hither and thither by all sorts of incoming suggestions.[108]

The secondary self's linkage, in Sidis, Le Bon and others, to the mechanisms of fashion and mass entertainment, anticipates the work of American theorists of advertising and film after the First World War, who were to debate whether advertising should address subconscious needs and fears or the rational, conscious mind, and come down firmly on the side of the irrational.[109] Sidis's critique of the subconscious extends also to the technology which releases it. In *Multiple Personality*, he devotes a chapter to 'Hypnoid States or Underground Life' in which 'Crystal gazing is analogous to automatic writing. The subconscious activity brings out visual perceptions which appear as hallucinations to the upper consciousness. The upper consciousness sees the pictures projected by the subconscious in the same way as the automatic writer reads the product of automatic writing.'[110] Yeats's explorations into the mechanism of automatic writing two decades later were to use similar metaphors of screens and projection. He asked 'Why does automatic faculty make pictures that have no apparent relation to the ego?' Thomas replied that: 'The automatic faculty does not so much make pictures as present a surface on which pictures can be reflected & only those pictures which have a correspondence to some portion of the ego's experience can be seen by the ego.'[111] These formula draw us metaphorically towards the cinema, which, in its exploitation of the limits of vision, is conceptually related to experiments with attention and distraction.

The consideration of distraction finds, however, a more positive location in Modernism. If for Sidis and others it signals a cultural danger, in the Weimar essays of Sigfried Kracauer and Walter Benjamin 'distraction' and related terms become more positive, a basis for the progressive understanding of art in the age of mechanical reproduction. Kracauer's 'The Cult of Distraction' (1926) and other essays including 'Boredom' (1924) explore the way in which modern media is received in a state of distractedness: the audience switches from radio station to station, or is shocked out of the seamless narrative of the bourgeois artwork by the cinema's 'fragmented sequence of splendid sense impressions'.[112] His account of film places it in ambivalent relation to modern life, reflecting back at the audience an existence 'deprived of substance, empty as a tin can, a life which instead of internal connections knows nothing but isolated events forming ever new series of images in the manner of a kaleidoscope'.[113] Kracauer's hope was that cinema would denaturalize the bourgeois world-view, making (in the 'Boredom' essay) the 'soul' flow out of itself to become a part of the material world, living, like Dreiser's Carrie, in the flux of advertising and the air-waves, and thus constantly encountering material reality.

Benjamin develops Kracauer's often unresolved lines of thought further. His analysis of distraction and of Brechtian alienation or interruption (*verfremdung*) are often linked to Russian Formalism, but his psychologizing of perception places it close to the psychological discourse of attention and distraction. There is, for example, a stress on the analysis of the disconnected fragment of behaviour. In 'The Author as Producer' (1934), he describes epic theatre as the 'dramatic laboratory' which submits modern man to 'tests and observations . . . The purpose of epic theatre is to construct out of the smallest elements of behavior what Aristotelian drama calls "action".'[114] Benjamin overturns the writer as the source of a work – the guarantor of its genius – in favour of the work of production, with the writer as engineer: 'The mind which believes only in its own magic strength *will* disappear.'[115] In its terminology and focus on perception, Benjamin's 'The Work of Art in the Age of Mechanical Reproduction' (1936) also shows its debts to the analysis of attention and distraction. He evokes Freud's *The Psychopathology of Everyday Life* in order to argue that Freud 'isolated and made analyzable things which had heretofore floated along unnoticed in the broad stream of perception', just as film does.[116] The description of film which follows precisely reproduces the conditions of psychological testing. In the dark, the viewer is subject to a series of distraction or 'shock' effects: discontinuity of 'association' between images, 'changes of place and focus which periodically assail the spectator', the camera's 'lowerings and liftings, its interruptions and isolations, its extensions and accelerations, its enlargements and reductions'. 'The camera', he concludes, 'introduces us to unconscious optics as does psychoanalysis to unconscious impulses'.[117] Benjamin's use of the term 'distraction' is thus closer to the term as it is used by Wundt or Downey than to any sense of mass media as an escape from reality. Described in terms of apperceptive 'tasks', distraction is opposed to a leisured 'attention' to the art-object.

However, in a bold stroke, Benjamin links this technical use of the term to its more commonplace meaning.[118] Exploring Georges Duhamel's accusation that the movie is simply a diversion for the care-worn masses, Benjamin makes 'distraction' central to his theory of mass art. In so doing, he confronts the contradictions inherent in Kracauer's theory of the 'shock' effect of modern media. On the one hand, such media simply reflect back at the viewer an alienated existence; it is the vehicle of a social pessimism. On the other hand, film represents a utopian possibility which might open up new modes of perception. This contradiction reappears throughout the essay: 'the film, on the one hand, extends our comprehension of the necessities which rule our lives; on the other, it manages to assure us of an immense and unexpected field of action'.[119] But where does the latter, utopian possibility come into play, and how does it relate to what he called reception?

The argument here is difficult. Benjamin begins by arguing that art which demands 'concentration' absorbs the audience, whereas 'distracted' art can be possessed by the audience; his example is architecture, which can be in-habited; used, become the subject of habit. He continues with the climax of his piece:

The distracted person, too, can form habits. More, the ability to master certain tasks in a state of distraction proves that their solution has become a matter of habit. Distraction as provided by art presents a covert control of the extent to which new tasks have become soluble by apperception. Since, moreover, individuals are tempted to avoid such tasks, art will tackle the most difficult and most important ones where it is able to mobilize the masses. Today it does so in the film. Reception in a state of distraction, which is increasing noticeably in all fields of art and is symptomatic of profound changes in apperception, finds in the film its true mode of exercise. The film with its shock effect meets this mode of reception halfway. The film makes the cult value recede into the background not only by putting the public in the position of critic, but also by the fact that at the movies this position requires no attention. The public is an examiner, but an absent-minded one.[120]

'Distraction' does a double duty here. On the model of architecture, it signals a mode of democratic familiarity with the artwork, and allows an unconscious problem-solving. But it is also that which must be 'met' by the film, which 'shock' must counter. 'Shock' is a stimulant which seems to imply anything but absent-mindedness: 'the shock of the film', he writes earlier, 'should be cushioned by heightened presence of mind'.

Benjamin seems to imply that film holds the possibility of reconciling these oppositions through its 'unconscious optics', repositioning the subject as part of that which its perceives in such a way that it is not simply absorbed into its systematicity. Such a repositioning involves the body, just as architecture must add 'tactile appropriation' to looking. This issue is explored in 'On Some Motifs in Baudelaire' (1939), where shock is linked to 'the urban masses' and to electric energy: 'Moving through this traffic involves the individual in a series of shocks and collisions. At dangerous intersections, nervous impulses flow through him in rapid succession, like the energy from a battery.'[121] Echoing Kracauer, Benjamin depicts that energy as regulated in the modern city by the pulsations of the traffic signals: 'technology has subjected the human sensorium to a complex kind of training'. He continues: 'There came a day when a new and urgent need for stimuli was met by the film. In a film, perception in the form of shocks was established as a formal principle. That which determines the rhythm of production on a conveyer belt is the basis of the rhythm of reception in the film.' The film spectator is located here at the interstices of the mechanical and the physical. 'Shocks' are the bodily effects which result from the collision of the bodily (perceptive) and the technological (film), and they represent the limits of bourgeois perception.

In proposing this spectator – distracted, plugged into collective energies but demonstrating the dissonance between the mechanical and the human – Benjamin suggests that film both reproduces the rhythms of modernity at a bodily level and provides a model for modern art. A distracted criticism will not seek the values inherent in the classical work of art with its aura; it will, with the 'new perception' inherent in film, reach beyond a discredited language to locate itself in the human body, in a non-moralized version of Dada's assault on the senses. At the limits of the senses, distraction serves – as throughout the story told here – to open the artwork to a new order.

CHAPTER EIGHT

Film finds a tongue

Benjamin's stress on cinema as a technology of distraction, described in the previous chapter, registers its origins in nine-teenth-century explorations of the limits of the body, considered as a psychophysical apparatus. Cinema is, Jonathan Crary suggests, enabled by a rupture in the enlightenment sense of an epistemology founded on vision. In the nineteenth century, the eye comes to be seen as flawed, subject to limits and susceptible to illusionistic effects – one of which, persistence of vision, underlies cinema. Mary Ann Doane comments that 'the early cinema would incarnate a double and contradictory desire addressed to moder-nity – the desire to humanize the machine (by inscribing what are perceived to be flaws in the human body in an apparatus) and yet to simultaneously appeal to it as a supplement of the body, as a prosthesis which makes up for a lack'.[1] Film also allows the exploration of motion and even the spaces of the body in new ways, in the work of Muybridge, Marey and the Taylorist researchers Frank and Lilian Gilbreth, and in early medical films.[2] It is in this sense doubly prosthetic: an extension of a sense and the exploita-tion of its limits. Cinema does this, but does more; it provides a compensatory image of a complete and perfect body – that of the star. If it is founded on rupture, it also sutures the viewer into the perceptive apparatus, into an economy of pleasure.[3] This is the cinematic equivalent of the specular prosthesis considered earlier.

My subject is the culmination in the construction of the cine-matic body with the arrival of sound film in the years 1927–9 – a final suture which arrives, despite the existence of earlier sound technologies, only once what Noël Burch labels the 'Institutional Mode of Representation' is established.[4] One question I will ask is: what anxieties surround the arrival of sound and its realignment of the cinematic body? Film theorists who champion realism have seen 1927 as a temporary dislocation, only briefly producing detrimental effects like the static camera and abandonment of locations. There is some truth in that view. On the other hand, sound *was* perceived by many as traumatic or catastrophic, its absolute nature signalled by the speed of its implementation, in contrast to the uneven development of techniques like colour and deep focus. It is among those intellectuals and writers interested in film that responses to the discursive shift represented by sound are most marked, allowing us to investigate the relations between film, sound, and modernity. In concentrating on writings *about* sound rather than the sound film itself, I have attempted to avoid the kind of Formalism which ascribes meanings and a politics directly to the cinematic apparatus: as we will see, the 'cinematicized' body has a migratory status which sees it appear in literary texts and social commentaries which are in turn recirculated within the cinema.

GOAT-GLANDING: SOUND AND THE BODY

Consider a famous moment at which both the technology creating sound and the 'natural' location of sound are represented. In the final scenes of *Singin' in the Rain* (Gene Kelly and Stanley Donen, 1952), Hollywood's comedy on the coming of sound, the imperious star, Lina Lamont (Jean Hagen), is singing to an enthusiastic audience at the premiere of her first sound picture, which has been hastily converted from silent. Her male producer and co-stars are in the wings, where they haul on a rope which pulls up the curtain behind her, revealing the young Kathy Seldon (Debbie Reynolds) at a second microphone. Not only is Kathy doing the singing, she has dubbed all Lina's lines because the latter's Bronx rasp is not 'phonogenic'. Lina falters as the audience titters; voice and body go out of synch. In another modernist version of Plato's allegory of the cave, Kathy is revealed as the 'true' voice and the silent star humiliated.

Here is another episode, closer to sound's mythic birth in Jolson's cry to his mother. It is Warner's premiere of *Glorious Betsy* on 26 April 1928, with Vitaphone sound in some scenes. For many of the Hollywood elite, this was their first taste of what was widely seen as a passing fad concocted on the East Coast. As director William De Mille recalled it, 'I shall never forget the moment when

André de Segurola . . . playing the part of a military, stood in the middle of the picture to address the people around him. "Ladies and gentlemen", he said. *He said!* A thrill ran through the house. The screen had spoken at last: an operation had been performed and the man, dumb from infancy, could talk.'[5] Here sound is a prosthesis in which a missing organ is supplied – as in the title of one of the first books on the subject, Fitzhugh Green's *The Film Finds its Tongue* (1929).[6] The conjuring up of a miraculous 'operation' recurs in the nickname given to the process, in the period 1928–9, of adding sound to previously produced but unreleased films: 'goat-glanding' – a joking term borrowed from the hormonal implants used by Voronoff, and popularized in America by 'Goat Gland Brinkley', the Kansas 'doctor' who claimed to restore sexual potency.[7] Offering rejuvenation to a youth-driven industry, 'goat-glanding' hints at a gendered argument which we will trace intermittently across the debate on sound – a masculinization and a denial of the 'lack' inscribed within the cinematic apparatus, in parallel to the 'invagination' which Kaja Silverman sees in sound's relation to the female body.[8]

Stories of bodily effects surround the coming of sound. If the *Brooklyn Daily Eagle* described the movies in 1896 as 'Electricity in its application to the arts', in the new organology the body is wired for sound.[9] With Jolson in *The Jazz Singer* it was 'as if an electric current had been run along a wire under the seats'.[10] When the equipment was shown to Harry Warner, 'the effect . . . was electrical'.[11] Such 'thrills' suggest sound film as another modernist technology for the reproduction and dissemination of sensory data. The nineteenth-century psychophysics which gave birth to cinema, the telephone, and the phonograph had fragmented the human subject in order to study perception. Attempts to map sound onto vision – for example in various 'sound-spectra' propounded in the late nineteenth century, or Scriabin's 'colour-organ' – might be seen as a response to that fragmentation, positing symbolic equivalences.[12]

But sound film works differently, offering a *recombination* of the senses. The first successful system, Vitaphone, used discs and synchronizing motors; the yoking of technologies rather than the tighter graft achieved by sound on the optical track. Some early writers stress a separate development: Green locates its biomechanics in the radio and PA system. Warners purchase a radio station to advertise films: 'Sam Warner and [chief electrician Frank] Murphy . . . were fascinated by the new apparatus. They spent hours pouring over the mysteries of vacuum tubes, amplifiers, microphones, monitors, loud speakers. *They were scrutinizing the embryonic ganglia of the Talkies!*' When Benjamin Levinson of Western Electric tries to convince Warner of the possibilities of sound, Warner repeats the conventional wisdom that it is a disaster. Levinson replies: 'You're thinking about the old ones. "Cameraphone", "Kinetophone", all those old things. But this is different. This is a talking picture that works like radio! Vacuum tubes. Amplifiers. Listen, while I explain to you.'[13] The 'listen' (which seems to echo and anticipate Jolson) is directed at a technology yoked to another mechanism (radio). In contrast, James Cameron, a writer on film technology, promulgates what will become the dominant narrative: in *Motion Pictures with Sound* (1929), he ignores Vitaphone and traces sound's origins in experiments in 1905 which used fluctuating beams and light-sensitive selenium cells to transmit sound as light pulses. 'It was found that the electric arc lamp is itself a telephone receiver. The big light which hangs from a pole on the street corner may be made to talk.'[14] In this story, sound is already yoked to the visual.

The epistemological status of sound is important here: early analysis of cinema almost universally linked it to hallucination, dream, and illusion. In contrast, Helmholtz, James Clerk Maxwell, and other nineteenth-century physiologists saw the ear as a more perfect apparatus, and hearing as more reliable.[15] As Kaja Silverman points out, film critics have often echoed that judgment in insisting that filmic sound is 'real' in a way that the two-dimensional filmic image cannot be. Moreover, in sound production, sound and visual tracks had to be equalized, binding film to real-time mechanisms (precise cranking speeds) and offering verisimilitude at the level of diegesis.[16] 'Real' bodies speaking in concrete situations replace the dreamlike bodies of silent cinema: the copy for John Barrymore's first sound film said: '*Yesterday* a speechless shadow – *Today* a vivid, living person – thanks to VITAPHONE'. Cantor Joseph Rosenblatt in *The Jazz Singer* was, the *Moving Picture World* reported, 'to appear as a singer not as an actor' – a presence with none of the taint of fiction.[17] The body which is simply an object among other objects in silent films, Kracauer argued, takes on a material and socially located existence. At the end of Hays's speech in the first screening, the audience applauded – at which point, miraculously, he bowed![18] Even where sound was questioned, its use for documentary – for the recording of the 'actual' – went unchallenged.

Given this narrative of a suture enacted in the name of a revitalized realism, it is important to pause over the uncertainties surrounding the moment of goat-glanding. The reviewer of the third Vitaphone feature in *Variety* saw it as exhausting: 'It must be that the mere knowledge that the entertainment is a reproduction has the effect of creating an altogether imaginary feeling of mechanical flatness, such as one gets from a player (automatic) piano.'[19] Fitzhugh Green commented on the acuteness of eye and ear in relation to synchronization: if lips and sound 'did not coincide perfectly, the movie voice seemed to wander away from its owner and the listener no longer connected it with him; it might be anybody's voice'.[20] The first Vitaphone feature opened with a Will Hays' speech, and one watcher recalled that it was 'like watching a man flying without wings. It was uncanny . . . . His lips moved and sound came forth . . . He seemed to be present, and yet he did not seem to be present. No wonder a scientist the next day called it: "The nearest thing to a resurrection!"'[21] Like an occult voice, it is placed in an absent body, raising issues of ownership, control, and location. Scandals over voice-doubling, particularly of songs, demonstrated that the voice attached to a body might be another's, fracturing the cinematic body into an assemblage of parts (actor, singer, stand-in).

One of King Vidor's anecdotes suggests the way in which linguistic confusion was also generated by the new medium. Describing the making of his first sound film in 1929, he recalls that Bert, the props man, was 'not yet accustomed to seeing dialogue in a script'. Seeing the phrase 'you can't make a silk purse out of a sow's ear', Bert underlines 'silk purse' and 'sow's ear' and dutifully provides them 'along with the other required objects'. If the comedy inheres in a Laputan literalism which cannot recognize a signifier, the joke rebounds: when a burro used in the film proves to have one ear missing, Bert gleefully produces the prop, as if supplying an organ to hear all this asinine talk.[22]

Another symptom of the uncertainty of relations between bodies and voices is the way in which ideas of 'race' became implicated in the musical. The 'original' screen voice was Jolson's blackface; and among the first musicals released in 1929 were *Hearts in Dixie* (Fox) and *Hallelujah* (MGM), both with African-American casts and southern subjects – the latter with Vidor's burro. One reason for the sudden visibility of black performers was the idea that their 'low mellow' voices recorded better than those of white speakers. Donald Bogle records a sudden optimism in the black community, with headlines like 'Talkies May Help Race Artists!' In 1929, Robert Benchley even commented that 'It may be that the talking-movies must be participated in exclusively by Negroes', arguing that the timing of Stephin Fetchit in *Hearts in Dixie* naturalizes the 'essentially phony medium' in which 'a synchronized sound-track . . . winds its way along the side of a photographic film'.[23] Vidor had been trying to persuade studios to make such a film for several years; now he had a new argument, providing 'a list of scenes suitable for an all-Negro sound film – river baptisms, prayer-meetings accompanied by spirituals, Negro preaching, banjo-playing, dancing, the blues'.[24] Reviewing *Hearts in Dixie*, Dorothy Richardson agreed that sound worked best distributed across the screen in the collective choral song of the South, and (implicitly) poorly for bourgeois voices in individual white bodies; she rhapsodizes with unselfconscious primitivism on 'rich Negro-laughter, Negro-dancing, of bodies whose disforming western garb could not conceal the tiger-flow of muscles'.[25] Here the black body is inserted – goat-glanded in, one might say – as a source of vigour at the moment of suture, of an experimental uncertainty in which the African-American signals orality itself, the 'natural' voice. One can also speculate that black actors were more easily risked by the studios than vulnerable white stars, sidestepping the optical qualities – the 'luminous' screen image and white skin – celebrated in the silent star.[26]

As Thomas Cripps suggests, the conceptual model here was the syncopated rhythms of jazz – 'every foot of the film would be "synched" to black music'.[27] But, for all that sound was seen as inherent in the black body, Vidor's *Hallelujah* is celebrated by film historians for the innovative use of non-naturalistic sound, with off-screen noises, post-synchronization, and sound-symbolism; the 'natural' is produced by an experimental Modernism. In these films, sound is also a disciplinary mechanism in the sense that it aligns bodies and music in relation to technology: advertising posters for both show dancers and musicians moving to music, with a shadow-effect – silhouettes of performers on a wall – which mimics the projection of film.[28] In such negotiations and contradictions, the anxieties involved in sound film are visible.

'Goat-glanding' – the adding of sound to Silents – serves as a metaphor for the coming of sound, since it is a technique which both separates and sutures. The first film to be treated in this way was *Don Juan*, shot in 1926. By late 1928, music and sound effects or sections of dialogue were being added to films across a variety of genres: epic (*Noah's Ark*), swashbuckler (*The Iron Mask*), and comedy (*Welcome Danger*). To be sure, problems with second-generation recordings meant that, by the early 1930s, location recording was preferred to post-synchronization, enforcing a realism which sees voice as 'located' in the natural body.[29] But, if the overall direction of Hollywood film was towards Naturalism, there is also, as we have seen, a dislocation at the moment in which the new technology was sutured into the cinematic apparatus. That dislocation was most sharply registered among intellectuals interested in film.

RESPONDING TO SOUND (1): THE AVANT-GARDE

The relationship between cinema and literary Modernism has scarcely received adequate study. Most modernist writers and artists expressed an interest in film; some made films; others borrowed 'cinematic' techniques: the Dada manifesto *Synthetic Cinema of Painting*; Philippe Soupault's 'cinematic poems'; the 'Camera Eye' sections of Dos Passos's *1919*. Gertrude Stein claimed that her 'continuous present' was cinematic, and for the Surrealists cinema represented a royal road to the unconscious, imitating the fluidity of dream. Film also seemed to embody modernist concerns for scientific representation, speed, and attack; the 'shock' effects celebrated by the futurists. Tom Gunning suggests that the links between early film and Modernism are part of a preoccupation with the spectacular: it was 'the exhibitionist quality of turn-of-the-century popular art that made it attractive to the avant-garde – its freedom from the creation of a diegesis, its accent on direct stimulation'.[30]

There is a utopian possibility offered here: that the 'language crisis' of Modernism can be resolved by direct access to the body. In 1926, Virginia Woolf commented, in her one essay on cinema, on its gesturing towards 'some secret language which we feel and see, but never speak'; a language 'rendered visible without the help of words'.[31] Theorists writing from a variety of different perspectives portray cinema in similar terms. In 1913, Georg Lukács commented on the absence of language in the cinema as destabilizing the androcentric world of accepted reality and liberating the fantastic, with its origins in the body; Hugo von Hofmannsthal similarly argued, in 1921, that silence placed cinema closer to the body, pantomime, and dream, than to literature.[32] As Sabine Hake shows, German writers, including the eurythmicist Jo Haïri Peterkirsten, saw cinema as a spectacle in which the body might be liberated: 'the body became the true medium of cinema, endowing its images with the kind of authenticity that was no longer available through, and in, language'.[33] The Surrealists stressed the disarticulation of the cinematic body: for Jean Epstein it is magnified into parts which signify independently – Hayakawa's back, Chaplin's boots. 'Life fragments itself into new individualities. Instead of a mouth, the mouth, lava of kisses, essence of touch. Everything quivers with bewitchment . . . The close-up transfigures man.' Epstein later elaborated the concept of 'lyrosophical' knowing, involving a prosthetic extension of the sensorium: 'bringing the unconscious to consciousness, through the hyper-extension of a single sense – that of seeing'.[34] This is the 'possibility of seeing without boundaries', the 'tele-eye, ray-eye' celebrated in Dziga Vertov's 1924 Manifesto.[35]

The sense of the heightened readability of the body in silent films is sustained by an analogy which sees it as a visual language, and, in particular, as *writing*. If Viktor Shklovsky could describe film tentatively as 'conversation prior to an alphabet', others were already comparing it to hieroglyphics. In France, Louis Haugmard, in 'The "Aesthetic" of the Cinematograph' (1913), argued that cinema 'is a form of notation by image, as arithmetic and algebra are notations by figures and letters'.[36] In 1915, the American populist poet Vachel Lindsay elaborated a pictographic language of cinema, claiming *The Egyptian Book of the Dead* as 'the greatest motion picture I have ever attended' and declaring that 'American civilization grows more hieroglyphic every day.'[37] Sergei Einstein wrote of emulating the 'cuneiform dramaturgy' of O'Neill's *Strange Interlude*. Hieroglyphics imply a language of presence, of direct apprehension. Ernest Betts, in his *Heraclitus, or the*

Future of Films (1928), pointed to a gestural language, and, as Hillel Schwartz notes, silent audiences learned to read 'those subtler motions of the face, shoulder, rib cage and pelvis that reflected inner states but had been scarcely visible from the distant galleries and boxes of "legitimate" theatre, vaudeville or burlesque'. Gesture assumed a heightened readability, as Béla Bálazs suggested when he wrote of a 'microphysiology' of the screen.[38]

An illustration of the convergence of prosthetic experimentalism and hieroglyphic writing is H. D.'s pamphlet on *Borderline* (1930), the silent film by Kenneth Macpherson in which she appeared, and which embodied the aims of the *Close Up* group. She describes the film-maker as a 'Leonardo': 'this name connotes mechanical efficiency, modernity and curiosity allied with pure creative impulse. The film *per se*, a curious melding of mechanical and creative instincts.' The film-maker is a surgeon paring nerves and heart-valves, and the camera 'a monster compound . . . of steel and fibre and final miracle, that delicate crystal lense'. Correspondingly, Macpherson is 'a hard-boiled mechanic, as if he himself were all camera, bone and sinew and steel-glint of rapacious grey eyes'.[39] H. D. stresses his control: he performs almost every task (script, lighting, shooting, editing); he looks through the lens as he directs; he carefully visualizes every scene in advance via 'a series of some 1,000 pictures' attached to his script. The latter forms a 'dynamic picture writing' which realizes his 'inner vision'. The director as *auteur* – as a pictographic *writer* – remains centre-stage. If H. D. stresses the intrinsic demands of cinema, so that literary film-makers are often misguided, film nevertheless fulfills the fantasy of replacing a debased language:

I mean words, as such, have become weathered, the old stamp is obliterated, the image of king or of olive wreath or the actual stars or the actual oak branch have been worn off the coin. Words are all alike now, the words even one feels sometimes of a foreign language have lost 'virtue'. The film brings words back and now much more the actual matter of the drama. Words become again 'winged' indeed. We 'fly' upstairs with Lulu.[40]

The directness celebrated by the avant-garde was, however, not without dangers, since it might imply the redundancy of literature. For Terry Ramsaye, writing in the first extensive history of cinema, *A Million and One Nights* (1926), Griffith's *Intolerance* failed because it adhered to literary modes: 'Allusions, simile, and metaphor can

succeed in the printed and spoken world as an aid to the dim pic-
torial quality of the word expression. The motion picture has no
use for them, because it itself is the event'; it is 'a language instead
of a sign'. Cinema moves from representation to being, from 'it
was' to 'it is'. The laborious discursive techniques of literature are
eliminated: 'In the re-creation of events for the re-enjoyment of
emotions', he writes, 'the film brings just such a short-cut directness as the whole of scientific industry is seeking in every phase of
human concern. Science has remade the world by bringing about
the marvel of work done without human labour.'[41] This is the
pairing of what Aldous Huxley (who later worked at MGM) called
'Taylorized work and mechanized amusement'. Or, as Peter
Wollen puts it, 'a carefully regulated new "soul" is added to the new
Fordized body, a kitsch soul for a machine body'.[42] A dangerous
move from production to (passive) consumption is suggested, and
here further doubts enter the frame. Modernists might praise
Chaplin as a subversive artist, but cinema was capital-intensive and
bound to the needs of commercial distribution. Many modernist
writers sympathized with populist attacks on Hollywood values,
particularly in relation to a mass audience coded as 'feminine' and
suggestible. Elmer Rice's play *The Adding Machine* (1923) is typical,
opening with a long monologue from Mrs Zero on movie scandals
as reported in *Pictureland*; Daisy's ludicrous passion for Mr Zero is
produced by cinema.[43]

Such tension between cinematic and literary modes of production is sharpened at points of crisis. How did the avant-garde
respond to the coming of sound; and how did sound alter the
status of cinema as visual language? Obviously, sound film represented an increase in cost and technological difficulty, making
independent production harder, and undermined cinematic 'universality' by making films language-specific. Beyond that, there is
a variety of reactions. In what follows, I draw on related debates in
the Soviet Union, and in *Close Up*, the 'International Magazine
devoted to Film Art' edited in Switzerland and London by
Macpherson and Bryher from 1927 to 1933. In all these responses
it is voice – sound located in the body – rather than sound *per se*
which is the issue.

As we have seen, early sound produced uncertainties over the
technology. Huxley complained of 'disembodied entertainers ges-
ticulating flatly on the screen and making gramophone-like

noises'.[44] In the USSR, Ippolit Sokolov protested against 'a dis-embodied voice with no intonation' produced by 'bad actors'.[45] Some, like H. G. Wells, argued that sound was suited to musical accompaniment, but not for speech. Rudolph Arnheim refined the case in 'A New Laocoon' (1938), arguing that sound film was derived from unreconciled sources, radio and silent cinema.[46] Such attacks seem aimed at *forestalling* the reintegration of the senses offered by sound cinema. A second set of complaints concern the way sound diminished audience-input and fantasy. For the Surrealists, the dreamlike fluidity and unreality of cinema is disrupted by speech; Crevel and Eluard comment that 'Between creatures purified by silence, speech places a sordid link.'[47] In *Heraclitus*, Ernest Betts argues that 'there is something monstrous about a speaking film', no 'mystery', no imaginative freeplay. Silence heightens attention to the body, providing 'a positive accentuation of the other means – gesture, timing, facial expression and grouping – by which an actor's intentions are expressed'.[48] His book has an addendum slip inserted here, a crisis marker:

Since the above was written speaking films have been launched as a commercial proposition, as the general pattern of the film of the future. As a matter of fact, their acceptance marks the most spectacular act of self-destruction that has yet come out of Hollywood, and violates the film's proper function at its source. The soul of the film – its eloquent and vital silence – is destroyed. The film now returns to the circus whence it came, among the freaks and the fat ladies.

Readability and integrity is replaced by a return to spectacle, to the 'cinema of attractions'.

Related objections concern sound's tendency to push film towards realism. For Horkheimer and Adorno, sound destroys the last possibilities of difference or allegory: as Miriam Hansen puts it, 'the masks of mass culture are all the more terrifying once they begin to talk, once they are naturalized by synchronic dialogue'.[49] Similar conclusions were reached by other theorists, including Hans Richter.[50] A famous crisis-document, 'The Sound Film. A Statement from the USSR' by Eisenstein and others, responded to a threat to the Soviet stress on cutting-rhythm; sound would produce naturalism and 'dramas of high culture', locating sounds in bodies and continuous actions rather than the '*juxtaposition* of fragments' in cutting and montage. 'The first experiments with sound', they urge, 'must aim at a sharp discord with the visual images'. The voice must not be owned, as in bourgeois drama; the camera should produce dialectic rather than mimesis.[51]

A gradual and qualified acceptance of sound ensued. Pudovkin, a signatory of the 'Statement', later argued that the silent intertitle interrupts the flow of a film; he celebrated 'the living full-valued word' over the 'impoverished word or intertitle'. But again this did not mean a naturalistic matching of bodies and action: sound was to be cut contrapuntally *against* visual images, making the technology a component of audience perception.[52] The critic and scriptwriter Viktor Shklovsky also developed his thinking, suggesting that sound functions within a sign-system in which its application as realism simply exposes the point where it is sutured to the image: 'Sound cinema is the cinema of the doubly embellished, doubly switched semantic sign . . . We must fight against scripts that are split in two, against imitative sound.'[53]

A comparable snapshot of modernist uncertainty is provided by *Close Up* – a journal whose existence (1927–33) was in many ways bound up with the sound crisis. In early comments in August 1928, Wilbur Needham pointed out that the sensitive can realize sound, like novels, in their heads, in contrast to the 'raucous howls of the talking films'. In September, sound was an 'unattractive hybrid'; in October, the Soviet statement was reprinted.[54] By 1929, sound's impact was clear: the July editorial complained of 'a voice that takes away all that people put in for themselves'. September 1929, was effectively an 'anti-sound issue': Macpherson's editorial links sound to static cameras, commercialism, and sentimentality, 'the heroine's speech to her sweetie'. Clifford Howard's 'Author and Talkies' asserts that film had 'no apparent latency of speech' before it 'squawked forth into speech and song', and suggests that the writer will be marginalized in Hollywood. Another piece sarcastically describes *The Singing Fool* as 'the greatest contribution to modern art since Ethel M. Dell wrote *The Way of an Eagle*'. Like Betts, the Marxist, H. A. Potamkin, stresses aesthetics over bodily response – though it is important to see that the actual opposition is between active and passive reception, between reading and receiving:

That is purity. That is unity. That is the aesthetic as against the rudimentarily psychologic, which, in the film construction, is a physical attack. The film, on the whole, remains no more than a physical attack, and the talking film, as it is produced today, has further lowered the level of this physical attack. The view of film-making as effect makes for passive (even apathetic spectators), the view of film-making as the strict realization of the intrinsic makes for active, completely participating spectators.[55]

Dorothy Richardson's regular column in *Close Up*, 'Continuous Performance', also expresses doubts. In 'Almost Persuaded' (June 1929), she registers an impact 'comparable to that we should receive if our favourite Botticelli began throwing stones'. For Richardson, silent cinema is the vehicle for a seamless identification with the *camera* rather than with character; the camera opens up a transfigured world, and her focus – as with the Soviets, if to less dialectical purpose – is on its prosthetic possibilities rather than on representation; on production rather than consumption.[56] Her review of *Hearts in Dixie* argues that the need to 'dictate' words to the apparatus reduces actors to ventriloquist's dummies. Song, on the other hand 'got through the adenoidal obstructed and, because the sound was distributed rather than localized upon a single form, kept the medium intact'.[57] The objection, once again, is to the way sound congeals in particular bodies.

Like the Soviet writers, *Close Up* adjusted to sound after 1930, publishing articles on 'Playing with Sound', sound-symbolism, and experimental sound-stages. Nevertheless the magazine's internationalism and dedication to independent production was undermined by sound. Richardson's September 1930 piece, 'A Tear for Lycidas', is an extraordinary elegy for the Silents, which have entered the past as 'a mode of memory' like the lasting images of a life: 'To this peculiar intensity of being, to each man's individual intensity of being, the silent film, with musical accompaniment, can translate him.'[58] Richardson ceased to write on film when *Close Up* folded.[59] Less than a year later she translated Robert de Traz's book on a tuberculosis sanitorium, *Silent Hours* (1934). The title chapter is a paean to the value of the daily regime of two hours' silence. 'Silence should be a slowing up. We prefer speed, which is also sound. We seek the rhythm of our lives in abrupt external excitements, whereas the necessary propulsion, sustaining and prolonging our being, should come from within and from the depths.'[60] The argument must have seemed familiar.

What underlies these attacks? One set of objections is to the way in which the body reappears traumatically in sound cinema, as a maimed or aggressive object: a ventriloquist's dummy, a statue throwing stones, freaks and fat ladies; as a physical 'attack'. It is as if the compact between Modernism and cinema which allows the former to co-opt the latter is ruptured by this speaking device, exposing a monstrously sutured new body at the level of diegesis. An experimental prosthetic extension – 'hyperextension of a single sense – that of seeing', as Epstein put it – is replaced by a total prosthesis at the level of representation, a reconstructed (and commercially exploitable) body replaces a technique of looking which opens up and explores the body. If silent cinema is pros-thetic in the sense that it is looking perfected – providing what Grant Allen's *Physiological Aesthetics* (1877) called 'Acute pleasure', the pleasure of extending a single sense – then sound cinema represents Allen's 'Massive' pleasure, pertaining to a *whole* repre-sented body, its commodification and energization.[61]

Secondly, sound threatens to disrupt the readability of cinema, imposing voice as a catastrophic commentary which reinserts film into the world of human interactions. If *The Battleship Potemkin* demonstrated 'the discovery that an artistic medium practically without words had been found' (Walter Reisch), that discovery was threatened by a return to 'dictated' concepts.[62] Ultimately, sound in the Soviet Union was linked to the authoritarian voice of Soviet realism formalized in the first Five Year Plan.[63] The debate on montage as reproducing the ineffable 'inner speech' of the subject which flourished among the Russian formalists in the 1920s faltered as 'outer speech' asserted its priority.[64] Acutely, Richardson saw a gender divide here. In a 'Close Up' column sub-titled 'The Film Gone Male', she argues that silent film has a 'quality of being nowhere and everywhere' and expressed 'some-thing of the changeless being at the heart of all becoming'. In its uninfected registering of reality, it was 'essentially feminine'. In succumbing to narrative, propaganda, and sound, it is fulfilling a 'masculine destiny . . . The destiny of planful becoming rather than of purposeful being. It will be the chosen battle-ground of rival patterns, plans, ideologies in endless succession and bewil-dering variety.'[65] Epistemology replaces ontology. Implicitly, Richardson compares her stream-of-consciousness technique to the silent cinema, and sees in sound a return to the authoritarian-ism of a patriarchal language, bolstered by a realist aesthetic.

We might see a theoretical rearguard action in Sigfried Kracauer's stress on the 'shock' effects of film in the late 1930s. As we have seen, Betts and Potamkin saw sound as returning cinema to mere 'physical attack'. Kracauer attempts to find a radical perspective from the suggestion that 'the material elements that present themselves in film directly stimulate the *material layers* of the human being: his nerves, his senses, his entire physiological substance'. If film works to extend the human 'sensorium', distraction-effects might produce a new mode of perception.[66] Kracauer was later to argue that sound film shifts the emphasis 'from the meanings of speech to its material qualities', alienating words as it alienates images.[67] This, once again, disrupts the location of sound in bodies: the word becomes, paradoxically, an *object* in Kracauer's distracted realism, and for that reason may be reread.

RESPONDING TO SOUND (2): THE HOLLYWOOD WRITER

Having seen hostility to sound from those for whom film was an experimental rather than a realist medium, we can also look at the response of those writers who wished to exploit the voice – perhaps, even, to recapture lost cultural authority by inserting themselves at the point of the goat-gland. Scott Fitzgerald commented in 1936 that 'As long past as 1930, I had a hunch that the talkies would make even the best selling novelist as archaic as silent pictures.'[68] There was opportunity: the 1928 'sound panic' saw novelists, playwrights, and actors drafted (or perhaps grafted) in *en masse* from the East; Ian Hamilton records that 'by the end of 1931, there were 354 full-time writers in Hollywood'. Classics were adapted wholesale. Briefly, literature seemed to be the model for cinema.[69]

The portents, admittedly, were bad. Hollywood had lionized writers like P. G. Woodhouse as cultural capital, but attempts to actually use them, like Goldwyn's 'Eminent Authors Programme', had largely failed. And, if sound offered new possibilities, its technological demands and scriptwriting teams involved greater subordination to an industrial mode of production. The parade of writers who went to Hollywood – Dorothy Parker, F. Scott Fitzgerald, William Faulkner, Aldous Huxley, Raymond Chandler, Lilian Hellman, and many others – produced a history of mutual abuse. By 1952, Chandler was able to conclude that in Hollywood 'most of your work is wasted', pointing out that the director has creative control and admitting the primacy of the visual: 'The best scenes I ever wrote were practically monosyllabic.'[70] Discursive 'goat-glanding' – the adding of dialogue – thus represents a point of possible engagement between text and film, but also a deepening of the crisis of writerly authority.

That crisis was exacerbated by external mechanisms. Voice, Richardson suggested, pushes cinema into a patriarchal public sphere. In Hollywood, the beginnings of a new mode of censorship via the Motion Picture Producers and Distributor's Association of America, headed by Will Hays, roughly coincides with the arrival of sound (though factors like the rise of Catholic pressure-groups are important to its establishment and progressive growth in importance). Certainly the work of the Hays Office was facilitated by the availability of scripts, and the resulting pressure was apparent in Hollywood's use of transgressive modernist texts in the early 1930s. Film versions of Hemingway's *A Farewell to Arms*, Faulkner's *Sanctuary*, and Lewis's *Ann Vickers* all created controversy, prompting the Hays Office to pre-emptively review novels likely to be bought by studios.[71] *Sanctuary* (1931) is particularly interesting. Richard Gray suggests that Faulkner's entry into Hollywood was an important moment in the imposition of censorship. He was recruited by MGM on the basis of *Sanctuary*'s notoriety, while Paramount adapted it, without his involvement, as *The Story of Temple Drake* (1933).[72] The film was subject to both internal and external censorship aimed at the novel's Gothic sexuality. Even after cuts enforced by James Wingate, the industry censor, the film was opposed by the Hays Office and by New York state censors. A crisis ensued, and the film could only be released after further cuts. Paradoxically, Gray argues, Faulkner's novel both took him to Hollywood *and* helped create a climate which curtailed his work there.

One issue in *Temple Drake* was the rape scene, where the film uses the device of a power failure and a scream in the dark. The presence of corn cobs – in the novel the instrument of the impotent Popeye's sexual assault – in a shot leading up to the rape was contested. Wingate argued that such a shot should be excluded precisely because the audience might know the function of the cobs from the book.[73] Here, on the other hand, the text itself provides points of possible reference with respect to the film. But how would audiences know about the book, which in any case works by suggestion (the rape is not that explicit)? The censors seemed to fear that the book would provide an alternative word-of-mouth commentary, disseminated even among those who did not read modern fiction; a voice *rendered public*, as Richardson had predicted.

A contrast to Faulkner, and the author I wish to relate most closely to sound film, is Nathanael West. A screenwriter for Republic, a minor studio churning out double features, it was only at the point of his death in a road accident in 1940 that his career was taking off. He struggled to sustain *two* careers: as a member of the Screen Writer's Guild, and as a writer of modernist satire; seeking to maintain what screenwriter Milton Sperling called his 'reserve and rock-like integrity', but without the established position outside the institution which Faulkner and Chandler enjoyed.[74] His texts constantly return to the issue of the authority of the (male) artist in relation to mass culture. In his Hollywood satire *The Day of the Locust* (1939), he explores a problem which the sound cinema brings into sharp focus: the spectacle of commodified femininity.

The Day of the Locust has always been seen as a text which incorporates cinematic strategies, and has often, as Thomas Strychacz points out, been criticized because it 'reproduces rather than accommodates the narrative strategies of Hollywood film art, and in so doing loses sight of the narrative framing that constitutes its cultural prerogative'.[75] In fact, the novel meditates on those strategies, and on the status of voice. The novel's successful screenwriter is Claude Estee, the 'master of an involved comic rhetoric that permitted him to express his moral indignation and still keep his reputation for worldliness and wit' – a stance like West's. But Claude offers no critique: he spins plot-lines mechanically, and owns a vulgar reproduction southern mansion. It is the protagonist, Tod Hackett, on whom the issue of cultural authority devolves. A graduate of the Yale School of Fine Arts, Tod works as a set designer, seeing art mocked by Hollywood's collapsing of fiction and reality. His response is 'The Burning of Los Angeles', a panoramic canvas in the satiric tradition of Daumier and Goya which serves as the indexical centre to the novel: 'a picture he was soon to paint, [it] definitely proved he had talent'.[76]

Strychacz argues that here 'the narrator offers proof positive that the projected painting will indeed be completed and that Tod is to become an artist of some talent'.[77] This seems less than clear:

'was soon to paint' can be interpreted as Tod's intention rather than a stable judgment. Moreover, the verb 'projected' alerts us to the *cinematic* fantasy which Tod's painting becomes. The critical distance necessary for such a painting is eroded in the novel, to the point where Tod wonders whether 'he himself didn't suffer from the ingrained, morbid apathy he liked to draw in others' (365). There is no place for art: Tod has no studio, moves distractedly through a series of unreal spaces, and ends the novel being driven to Claude's house. His distractedness and lack of distance culminate in Tod's entry into the picture: trapped outside a premiere, he rearranges it in his head as an 'escape', himself becoming one of its violent crowd.

Tod's incorporation into Hollywood's machinery is suggested most strongly by the scene in which he fantasizes about raping the seventeen-year old actress Faye Greener – the focus of all masculine desire in the text, and of its investigation of the cinematic body:

He knew what it would be like lurking in the dark in a vacant lot, waiting for her. Whatever that bird was that sang at night in California would be bursting its heart in theatrical runs and quavers and the chill air would smell of spice pink. She would drive up, turn the motor off, look up at the stars, so that her breasts reared, then toss her head high and sigh. She would throw the ignition keys into her purse and snap it shut, then get out of the car. The long step she took would make her tight dress pull up so that an inch of glowing flesh would show above her black stocking. (407)

Although this reads like a shooting-script, we cannot simply ascribe it to the screenwriter–author West; it is Tod's fantasy. He is interrupted by a waiter at the climactic moment, and tries to rerun it through his head, like the broken reel of the pornographic film he saw earlier. Cinematicized desire links him to the jaded masses he satirizes. The fantasy is triggered by seeing a customer of Mrs Jennings, the Hollywood madame for whom Faye works, marking Tod as a displaced client. His attempts to persuade Faye not to sell herself result in an incomprehension directed against the aesthetic: 'She couldn't understand the aesthetic argument and with what values could he back up the moral one? The economic didn't make sense either. Whoring certainly paid.' He is reduced to shouting 'like a YMCA lecturer on sex hygiene' (346).

The failure of Tod's persuasion – a failure of voice – signals the helplessness of masculine authority before the spectacle of commodified desire. This becomes a general concern, reflected in a variety of disconnected or hysterical masculine voices. Late in the novel, Homer Simpson, whose name evokes the origins of Western literature, sees Faye making love to Miguel, and in a comic version of the primal scene he regresses in 'uterine flight'. Tod listens as Homer spouts 'a muddy, twisting torrent' of language: 'he realized that a lot of it wasn't jumbled so much as timeless. The words went behind each other instead of after. What he had taken for long strings were really one thick word and not a sentence' (399). Throughout the text, bodies are mechanical, with a matching artificiality of voice: Harry Greener and Homer are disjointed mechanisms, the former with a manic laugh, the latter with a stammer; Abe Kusich is a ventriloquist's dummy. The child-actor, Adore, sings and moves 'against rather than in time with the music', his body telling of a sexuality it cannot understand.[78] When Tod, Faye, and Homer watch a drag artist, a man whose body seems that of a woman, the 'proper' relation of voices to bodies is disrupted.

The disarticulation between voice and body is also figured in Faye, but with a significant difference: her voice is emptied of content rather than hysterical, absorbed into an institution in which the body speaks. Her voice is 'artificial', and, in her only film role, she delivers one line badly, while her body signals sex. Early in the novel, Tod watches her spin out filmic plots mechanically and concentrates on her 'wet lips and the tiny point of her tongue' – on the gland itself – rather than what she says (319). Later, the scene is repeated with all the major male characters watching:

None of them really heard her. They were all too busy watching her smile, laugh, shiver, whisper, grow indignant, cross and uncross her legs, stick out her tongue, widen and narrow her eyes, toss her head so that her platinum hair splashed across the red plush of the chair back. The strange thing about her gestures and expressions was that they didn't really illustrate what she was saying. They were almost pure. It was as though her body recognized how foolish her words were and tried to excite her hearers into being uncritical. (387)

West describes something like the relation between body and discourse engendered by the Hays Code: meaning cannot be spoken; the culling of inflammatory material reduces plots to absurdity, with desire suggested by open mouths and scissoring legs. The men who watch Faye are fascinated by her body, a spectacle disconnected from the voice which spins out clichés, as if she were silent. Indeed, the silent film in the novel *is* pornography: 'Le Prédicament de Marie', shown at the brothel run by the former silent actress Mrs Jennings. The visual and sexual prevails over sound; and sound, throughout the text, is badly matched to bodies. The split between the lascivious bodily action and the dull plots Faye spins out enacts the crisis of filmic speech: to the rhythms of whose voice is this sexually charged body to move? What can be added to the body by the writer?

The answer in West's text is not the male voice. Tod is undermined by a cinematic sexuality which hystericizes the male subject, exposing his lack. The 'economic argument' defeats Tod because in Hollywood he has no authority, no voice, in the face of what he sees and cannot resist. In the final scenes, he is one of a crowd excited by 'a young man with a portable microphone' and yet another 'rapid, hysterical voice' (409). The novel ends with Tod hearing a police siren as he is driven away from the riot, and not knowing whether it is his own voice until he touches his lips and finds them closed, at which point he too hysterically joins in the wailing – an apposite image for a goat-glanded voice as pure uncertainty, as anything other than the imposition of control. West's novel fails in its attempt to impose an authorial voice on his chaos of desire, producing something close to postmodern satire – a satire with no clear position outside its object.

SPECULAR ECONOMIES

Cinema's mechanisms of desire have, of course, always been a subject of anxiety.[79] What the avant-garde saw as the strength of film – its directness of stimulation – was, for critics, a danger. Terry Ramsaye cites an influential article in the *Contemporary Review* in 1925 by the psychoanalyst Barbara Low, in which she relates cinema to Ferenczi's discussion of the childhood period of 'unconditional omnipotence' and 'magic gesture':

It is surely clear that the cinema entertainment must gratify this 'magic omnipotent wish' more than any fairy tale, any novel, picture or drama can do – and does so independently, to a large extent, of the theme of the film. It is the *method* which brings about so vividly the sense of wish fulfillment. It is the cinema's business to show all problems solved, all doors opened, all questions answered.[80]

Low worries about the effacement of 'blood and sweat' from a film of Scott in the Antarctic; time-lapse photography may make children think that plants grow in minutes. The Scott film is little different from a 'crook melodrama', since 'the mechanism at work is much the same or even identical'. Low relates cinema to other forms of modern life: 'short and scrappy journalism and fiction, our rapid dramatic shows, our jazz bands, even our demand for quick lunches and quicker locomotion'. She reports a Birmingham study which concludes – shades of MTV – that 'The Cinema may, even, be fostering a quick and careless way of looking at things, developing the habit of the unseeing eye which never gets beyond the obvious.'[81] Low was writing in a tradition of critique including Hugo Münsterberg's pioneering 1916 study. In cinema, he argues, 'the massive outer world has lost its weight, it has been freed from space, time, and causality, and has been clothed in the forms of our own consciousness'. The cinema is founded on 'omnipresence' and voyeurism, and therefore has 'strong social effects': it can produce hallucinations and influence the weak-willed and neurasthenic, producing 'imitation and other motor responses'. Stressing identification and the image rather than narrative, he argues that 'it is not enough to have the villain punished in the last few pictures in the reel. If scenes of vice or crime are shown with all their lure and glamour the moral devastation of such a suggestive show is not undone by the appended social reaction.'[82] Such thinking was reproduced widely in institutional critiques of film between the wars.

The issue of the 'lure of glamour' became particularly fraught in the 1920s, with the emergence of the spectre of the modern woman who dispenses her sexual favours at will. Best-selling novels of the 1920s featured heroines who, in one way or another, asserted a self-determination: in England, Edith Hull's *The Sheik* (1921), Margaret Kennedy's *The Constant Nymph* (1924), Elinor Glyn's *'It'* (1927); in the USA, Gertrude Atherton's *Black Oxen* (1923), Anne Douglas Sedgwick's *The Little French Girl* (1924), Anita Loos's *Gentlemen Prefer Blondes* (1925), and Viña Delmar's *Bad Girl* (1928).[83] In the words of Lewis Jacobs, writing in 1939, such films as *Male and Female* (1919), *Why Change Your Wife* (1920), *Forbidden Fruit* (1921), and *Manslaughter* (1922) 'attacked the genteel tradition, flaunted sex, advocated new morals, condoned illicit and illegal relationships, set up new ideals, established a new tempo of living, and broke-down pre-war class distinctions with the new emphasis on money, luxuries, material success'. Swanson, Negri, Garbo, and Bow, he continues, were 'prototypes of the ultra-civilized, sleek and slender, knowing and disillusioned, restless, over-sexed and neurotic woman who "leads her own life"'.[84] Dozens of films depicted this new woman: *Blind Husbands, Don't Neglect Your Wife, Flapper Wives, Other Men's Wives, Week-End Wives, Miss Bluebeard, Should a Wife Tell?, More Deadly than the Male, Temptation, Modern Marriage,* and so on.

The preoccupation with sexuality implicit in these titles is matched by other media. Richard Maltby sees, in the 1920s, a crucial stage in the history of the image in which woman is established as 'an object of scophilic desire' via 'the appearance of permissive, auto-erotic images of female sexuality', disseminated in cinema and advertising.[85] The susceptibility of the newly homogenized and 'femininized' urban masses to forms of suggestion and hypnosis, in the social theory of Le Bon, Freud, and others can be linked to the expressed ideology of 1920s advertisers, the 'psychological engineers' increasingly confident in their strategies.[86] More fundamentally, the connection between consumption and sexualized images becomes encoded in cinema itself. Moreover, as Miriam Hansen comments, 'Film spectatorship epitomized a tendency that strategies of advertising and consumer culture had been pursuing for decades: the stimulation of new needs and new desires through visual fascination. Besides turning visual fascination itself into a commodity, the cinema generated a meta-discourse of consumption . . . a phantasmagoric environment in which the boundaries between "looking" and "having" were blurred.'[87] Links between cinema and advertising became increasingly common in the 1920s, cosmetics and fashion tied to ads showing the 'Clara Bow look', the 'Jean Harlow look'.

The cinematic body thus comes to be associated with dangerous categories: commodity-fetishism; the 'unearned' pleasures of the cinematic gaze itself. The traffic between the specular and the economic is thematized in the issue of gold-digging, which crystallizes the exchanges implicit in Hollywood cinema; not the actual selling of sex – which could not be depicted – but rather an equation of glamour, voyeurism, and money. Lea Jacobs describes the way in which the term 'gold digger' becomes current in the mid-1920s, the focus shifting from the moral issues ('will she or won't she?')

to women who successfully commoditize their glamour. With the arrival of the depression, the sense of unease which surrounds these issues is sharpened. The early 1930s saw a number of films linked to prostitution: *Safe in Hell* (1931), *Susan Lennox, Her Fall and Rise* (1931), *Blond Venus* (1932), *Faithless* (1932), and Mae West's *She Done Him Wrong* (1933). Alfred Green's *Baby Face* (1933) is perhaps the most extravagant, offering a fascinated critique of the 1920s aesthetic of excess. *The Day of the Locust* is symptomatic of a fascination with the fringe actress as prostitute; the figure for whom all desire is exploitable; and related to the characterization of the filmic audience – particularly women – as succumbing to instant gratifications.[88]

What does sound bring to these issues? Gilles Deleuze insists that the silent film mediated and naturalized reality, while its intertitle 'took on an abstract universality and expressed in some senses a law'.[89] In contrast, sound film provides an embodied, context-bound voice in which the transactions of gender and class are specific and bounded by the 'self-presence' (as Kaja Silverman puts it) of the voice – a self-presence which locates the voice more firmly within capitalist modes of self-commodification.[90] Alan Williams argues that this helps explain the decline of the melodramatic plot which forms a staple of silent film, since sound film also eliminates expressiveness, particularly in the male lead, with melodramatic sentiment abandoned in favour of cooler, wisecracking styles; 'the liberation of speech brings with it the repression of the body'.[91] But, as West makes clear in relation to Faye, the body is still a danger, and verbal exchanges sharpen the issues: the gold-digger can enter into bargains, banter, even humiliate the men she gulls; her work threatens to become more clearly articulated. Gold-digger films were a focus for censorship: scenes in which money changed hands between men and women for sexual favours were proscribed, and replaced by scenes in which the status of the 'kept' woman was suggested by a shift in circumstances (a move to a penthouse). A displaced visual image replaces the transaction, as if the heroines were rewarded for simply looking good – the economy of stardom. Censorship splits apart sound and the body (as in West's text): the body and its location can signify desire where the voice may not. What the voice can do is to provide the wisecrack, the riposte, verbal features which suggest sexual independence without articulating sexual exchange.

If West fails to do more than register the problems of the regulation of desire, we can see an oblique response to the same problem *within* the industry itself, in the Busby Berkeley musicals of the 1930s, which combine gold-digging with bizarre synchronized dance sequences. Arguably, Berkeley is present in the margins of *The Day of the Locust*, since Faye – long-legged, platinum blond, large-faced – is the type of the Berkeley or Goldwyn Girl. Berkeley's films subsume the specularized body to an engineering aesthetic, with girls arranged in lines, patterns, tableaux imitating flowers, zippers, even genitalia, closer to the choreography of beauty contests and mass-exercise than to dance.[92] His camera represents an almost camp apotheosis of masculine voyeurism: a specially developed gantry swoops through tunnels of legs, dives and soars, enacting a fantasy of total license; mechanisms including censorship are literalized in shorts in which peeking is 'punished' with the closing of a view.[93] Berkeley refused to use multiple cameras and the dispersed gaze which they imply, and there is little shot/counter-shot, with its suggestion of an intersubjective relation (his coy explanation was that coming from the stage he did not know about multiple crews).

In Berkeley's dance sequences, sound serves a regulatory rather than an expressive function, providing the rhythms to which bodies move. Mary Ann Doane has described his work as offering a 'compensatory prosthetic power', a regulation of the body in the name of the male gaze, overcoming the 'lack' inscribed within the cinematic apparatus.[94] If voice implies a negotiation of pleasures in which the object of desire might choose her own disposition, Berkeley effaces voice to produce a masculine economy of pleasure. On the one hand, the pleasures of sound are almost infantilized (the sound cartoon exhibits the same yoking of bodily language and music; Disney's goat-glanded *Steamboat Willie* has its music literally projected onto the body of animals – cow's udders produce whistles, teeth become xylophones, Minnie plays organ-grinder on a goat's tail). On the other, in their engineering aesthetic his films return to the filmic time-and-motion studies pioneered by the Gilbreths in the 1910s. Berkeley's sequences efface the anxiety-ridden middle ground of social interchange and embodied desire represented by sound cinema, 'solving' the problem of the regulation of desire by thematizing it as mechanism.

SINGIN' IN THE RAIN

I will conclude where I began, with Hollywood's own look back at goat-glanding from 1952. *Singin' in the Rain* neatly dovetails the sound panic with the 'backstage musical', recycling the uncertainties of early sound as comedy. The plot hardly needs rehearsing: silent stars Don Lockwood and Lina Lamont are making *The Dueling Cavalier*, their latest historical epic, when the sudden success of *The Jazz Singer* means that it has to be goat-glanded. The urbane Don (Gene Kelly) adapts well, but the process is threatened by the imperious silent star Lina (Jean Hagen). Her Bronx rasp and inability to carry a line signals disaster. The project is rescued by the modest and upscale Kathy Seldon (Debbie Reynolds) providing a voice for Lina.

Lina is doomed by the catastrophe of sound, and *Singin' in the Rain* tells a Darwinian story of technological succession in which the silent film is depicted as an exhausted genre. The revitalization implied by 'goat-glanding' is imposed on the plot: in contrast to the static reality of early talkies, it is the *silent* film which appears stagy, while the sound camera becomes mobile. Moreover, other technological shifts are mapped onto sound. One is the use of colour. Black and white is used for the silent films, and Lina is dressed in silver and white. In contrast, the film moves towards the climactic Broadway Ballet with Kelly and the dancer Cyd Charisse, with its bravura primary colours. Depth of field is also used to reinforce the sound/silent transition. The silent sequences are studio shots; but in the Broadway Ballet there are both painted flats and a final sequence with tremendous depth of field – culminating in a shot in which Kelly is lifted towards the camera, leaving the chorus in the distance, still in focus (it needed MGM's two biggest stages[95]). Both these technological shifts – colour, deep focus – took place gradually and intermittently over the period 1930–1950; here they are incorporated into a general model of a goat-glanded apparatus.

A central issue in *Singin' in the Rain* is the location and grounding of voice in the body. The possibility that voice will be separated from, rather than located in, the body renders sound what Peter Wollen calls a 'potentially free-floating, and thus radically unreliable, semantic element'.[96] The film repeatedly plays with the comic disarticulation produced by the new technology: it drifts away as the mouth crosses the microphone, it registers extraneous thumps like the tapping of a fan; it picks up a heartbeat. Film and disc get out of synchronization and the Don and Lina characters exchange voices and lines, gender-reversal signalling a failure to assign words correctly to bodies. It is this scene which generates the idea of goat-glanding, giving Don's sidekick, Cosmo, the idea of superimposing a voice. The climax of the plot is the recognition of the 'real' voice in Kathy, equating sound with truth. Indeed, Wollen argues – invoking Derrida – that the film works to locate the cinematic signifier in the authority of voice, removing any 'excess' in which meaning might wander.[97]

The disconnection of voice from body is also, in the film's politics, a form of alienation. Lina attempts to co-opt Kathy's goat-glanded voice on a contractual basis, converting her labour into surplus value. She can do this because she is a star: her name and image are commodities; she represents the Hollywood economy which generates value from spectacle. The film's climax reveals the 'natural' source of labour, restoring Kathy's property rights. Hostility to the dominance of the star was, institutionally, part of the shift to sound (just as Clifford Howard argued in *Close Up* that sound was unsuited to 'movie queens'[98]). It is often suggested that John Gilbert's failure was less to do with his voice than with a studio plot to get rid of him; Lilian Gish and others were affected. The new generation of actors that came with sound were subject to greater studio control of salaries and casting than those of the 1920s, while films on Hollywood, like *Stand-In* (1937), satirized the capricious female star and stressed collective effort. In *Singin' in the Rain*, the comic animus against Lina is sustained by the delay in hearing her raucous voice, which we are only allowed to hear after a glittering screen image is established. Lines like 'Am I dumb or somethin'?' and the final misogynist episode in which the men around her publicly expose her signal a hostility to the star-as-image, as specular body, and a relocation of acting ability in the properly modulated, tutored, and controlled voice. The 'free' energy of the feminine star is replaced by the bound energy of the trained voice, overseen by the technicians who supervise its production, from voice coaches to sound engineers. In contrast to Lina's narcissistic lassitude, tantrums, and inability to learn, we have the *work* of Don, who, after initial uncertainties, emerges triumphantly as the director of his own dance sequences. Given that the film also separates the woman who dances and the woman who sings (Charisse and Reynolds), the female star is doubly disarticulated.

In enforcing this gendered division of effort, *Singin' in the Rain* returns to the musicals made by the Freed Unit at MGM in the 1930s (the film is constructed around Freed–Brown songs). The backstage musical stresses the plot of achievement – work, rehearsal, recognition – rather than the static poses intrinsic to Lina's desirability. Interestingly, allusions to the Berkeley musicals of the 1930s reinforce this emphasis: the arrival of sound in the plot is followed by a non-diegetic sequence designed to encapsulate the early musical, climaxing in the 'Beautiful Girl' number (from a 1930s musical, *Going Hollywood*). The style is mock-Berkeley, including a shot of a row of legs dancing, the rest of the body matted out. For all that Kelly disapproved of Berkeley's minimal choreography, the sequence enacts a mechanical control of the body consonant with the film's focus on the technology which aligns bodies and music. If Lina's attempt to 'own' Kathy's voice is exposed, Don's setting of bodies to music is naturalized. The focus on talk in the earlier stages of the film is replaced by a focus on musical spectacle in which the hero becomes a director. Kelly's liberal politics provide a context. Mark Roth argues that the Warners musicals of the early 1930s (in particular *42nd Street* and *Footlight Parade*) were more collectivist than those that followed, reinforcing an ideology which stresses co-operative endeavour, with a strong director at the helm of the musical-within-the-musical – a formula Roth sees as expressing the mythology of the New Deal in 1932–3, with the director orchestrating an upward path like that which Roosevelt sold to the electorate, creating 'the image of a political leader as a large-scale Busby Berkeley'.[99] In *Singin' in the Rain*, Don's work is contrasted with Lina's desire to merely accumulate, equating the silent star with the excess of the 1920s, and sound, once again, with the regulation of desire. In Kathy's voice, Hollywood finds its own solution to the problem of the specular economy.

This is the end of the story of cinema considered as a modernist prosthesis. As sound is 'goat-glanded' in, film as the extension of seeing and as the vehicle for a new language – even, one might say, a prosthetic language – is replaced by the embodied voice, discursively located and owned.[100] The experimental possibilities of writing the body offered by cinema give way to a commercialized desiring-machine with its total (but virtual) prosthesis. Goat-glanding also implies a 'masculinization' in the commentaries which surround it; a regulation of the image and of desire and a return of voice and discursive power to a dominant ideology, enforced by divergent mechanisms which converge in sound: censorship, Berkley's engineering aesthetic, Kelly's dance. But sound cinema, from the modernist viewpoint, is perpetually consigned to reproducing the conditions of its own production, re-enacting, via external and internal censorship, a split between voice and body. Sokolov, Huxley, Richardson, and others heard 'disembodied voices' in the early sound film, and West portrays Faye as unvoiced, not just because the voice was poorly grafted onto the body, but because it seemed grounded in the fundamental inauthenticity of an embodied technology.

Notes

INTRODUCTION

1 Raymond Williams, *Marxism and Literature* (Oxford University Press, 1977), 139.

2 Stanley Joel Reiser, *Medicine and the Reign of Technology* (Cambridge University Press, 1978), ch. 4.

3 See e.g. J. E. Chamberlin and Sander L. Gilman, eds., *Degeneration: The Dark Side of Progress* (New York: Colombia University Press, 1985); Daniel Pick, *Faces of Degeneration: A European Disorder c.1948–c.1918* (Cambridge University Press, 1989).

4 Friedrich A. Kittler, *Discourse Networks 1800/1900*, trans. Michael Metteer (Stanford University Press, 1990), 215.

5 Jan Goldstein, 'The Advent of Psychological Modernism in France: An Alternative Narrative', in *Modernist Impulses in the Human Sciences 1870–1930*, ed. Dorothy Ross (Baltimore: Johns Hopkins University Press, 1994), 207.

6 See e.g. Janet Oppenheim, *'Shattered Nerves': Doctors, Patients, and Depression in Victorian England* (New York: Oxford University Press, 1991).

7 See e.g. Ronald E. Martin, *American Literature and the Universe of Force* (Durham: Duke University Press, 1981); and esp. Mark Seltzer, *Bodies and Machines* (New York: Routledge, 1992). On medicine, Peter M. Logan's 'Conceiving the Body: Realism and Medicine in *Middlemarch*', *History of the Human Sciences*, 4 (1991), 197–222 is useful.

8 See e.g. Eugene Lunn, *Marxism and Modernism: A Historical Study of Lukács, Brecht, Benjamin and Adorno* (Berkeley: University of California Press, 1982); Marshall Berman, *All that is Solid Melts Into Air: The Experience of Modernity* (London: Verso, 1983).

9 Jonathan Crary, *Techniques of the Observer: On Vision and Modernity in the Nineteenth Century* (Cambridge, MA: MIT Press, 1990), 85. On the issues here, see Dorothy Ross, 'Modernism Reconsidered', *Modernist Impulses*, 1–25.

10 Cecelia Tichi, *Shifting Gears: Technology, Literature, Culture in*

Modernist America (Chapel Hill: University of North Carolina Press, 1987); Lisa Steinman, *Made in America: Science, Technology and American Modernism* (New Haven: Yale University Press, 1987); Bruce Clarke, *Dora Marsden and Early Modernism: Gender, Individualism, Science* (Ann Arbor: University of Michigan Press, 1996).

11 Peter Nicholls, *Modernisms: A Literary Guide* (London: Macmillan, 1995); David Porush, *The Soft Machine: Cybernetic Fiction* (New York: Methuen, 1985), 25.

12 Anthony Giddens, *Modernity and Self-Identity: Self and Society in the Late Modern Age* (Cambridge: Polity Press, 1991), 7.

13 Hillel Schwartz, 'Torque: The New Kinaesthetic of the Twentieth Century', *Incorporations* [*Zone* 6], ed. Jonathan Crary and Stanford Kwinter (New York: Urzone, 1992), 71–126.

14 Jean-Luc Nancy, 'Corpus', in *Thinking Bodies*, ed. Juliet Flower MacCannell and Laura Zakarin (Stanford: Stanford University Press, 1994), 24, 29.

15 Janet Beizer, *Ventriloquized Bodies: Narratives of Hysteria in Nineteenth Century France* (Ithaca: Cornell University Press, 1993), 20–9.

16 Pierre Bourdieu, *Distinction: A Social Critique of the Judgement of Taste*, trans. Richard Nice (1979; London: Routledge, 1989), 474.

17 Ian F. A. Bell, *Critic as Scientist: The Modernist Poetics of Ezra Pound* (London: Methuen, 1981), 2.

18 Michel Foucault, *The History of Sexuality*, vol. I, trans. Robert Hurley (London: Penguin, 1981), 139.

19 See Laura Doyle, *Bordering on the Body: The Racial Matrix of Modern Fiction and Culture* (New York: Oxford University Press, 1994); William Greenslade, *Degeneration, Culture and the Novel 1880–1940* (Cambridge University Press, 1994); John Carey, *The Intellectuals and the Masses: Pride and Prejudice among the Literary Intelligentsia, 1880–1939* (London: Faber & Faber, 1992).

20 Anson Rabinbach, *The Human Motor: Energy, Fatigue, and the Origins of Modernity* (New York: Basic Books, 1990).

21 Grant Allen, *Physiological Aesthetics* (London: Henry S. King, 1877), viii, 20–5.

22 Seltzer, *Bodies and Machines*, 60.

23 Lawrence Birkin, *Consuming Desire: Sexual Science and the Emergence of a Culture of Abundance, 1871–1914* (Ithaca: Cornell University Press, 1988).

1 ELECTRIFYING THE BODY

1 Christina Stead, *The Man Who Loved Children* (1940; London: Penguin, 1970), 195.

2 Edward Schriver, 'Reluctant Hangman: The State of Maine and

Capital Punishment, 1820–1887', *New England Quarterly*, 63 (1990), 272.

3 Although the Shelleys knew Galvani's experiments, electricity is only clearly specified in film versions.

4 *New York Times*, 5 August 1890, 1; 6 August 1890, 1.

5 Headline, *New York Times*, 7 August 1890, 1; report in the London *Standard*, quoted in Arnold Beichman, 'The First Electrocution', *Commentary*, 35 (1963), 417.

6 Gerald Stanley Lee, *Crowds* (London: Curtis Brown, 1913), 278, 199. On electricity as American energy, see David E. Nye, *Electrifying America: Social Meanings of New Technology, 1880–1940* (Cambridge: MIT Press, 1990).

7 See Alan Liu, 'Wordsworth and Subversion, 1793–1804: Trying Cultural Criticism', *Yale Journal of Criticism*, 2.2 (1989), 55–100.

8 See e.g. E. Benton, 'Vitalism in Nineteenth-Century Scientific Thought', *Studies in the History and Philosophy of Science*, 5 (1974), 17–48; Everett Mendleson, 'Physical Models and Physiological Concepts: Explanation in Nineteenth Century Biology', *British Journal for the History of Science*, 2 (1965), 201–13; Anson Rabinbach, *The Human Motor: Energy, Fatigue, and the Origins of Modernity* (New York: Basic Books, 1990), ch. 2; David F. Channell, *The Vital Machine: A Study of Technology and Organic Life* (New York: Oxford University Press, 1991). On the gendering of these issues, see Cynthia Eagle Russet, *Sexual Science: The Victorian Construction of Womanhood* (Cambridge, MA: Harvard University Press, 1989), 108–29.

9 Margaret Rowbottom and Charles Susskind, *Electricity and Medicine: A History of Their Interaction* (San Francisco Press, 1984), 7–23.

10 Janet Oppenheim, *'Shattered Nerves': Doctors, Patients, and Depression in Victorian England* (New York: Oxford University Press, 1991), 119ff on Gully.

11 Rowbottom and Susskind, *Electricity and Medicine*, 115–16, 127.

12 See Harvey Green, *Fit for America: Health, Fitness, Sport and American Society* (Baltimore: Johns Hopkins University Press, 1986), ch. 7.

13 Sinclair Lewis, *Martin Arrowsmith* (London: Jonathan Cape, 1925), ch. 15.

14 Rowbottom and Susskind, *Electricity and Medicine*, 23.

15 Edward B. Foote, *Dr. Foote's Home Cyclopedia of Popular Medical, Social and Sexual Science*, rev. edn (New York: Murray Hill, 1901), 1127.

16 Discussions of Beard include Oppenheim, *Shattered Nerves*, ch. 3; Charles E. Rosenberg, 'The Place of George M. Beard in Nineteenth Century Psychiatry', *Bulletin of the History of Medicine*, 36 (1962), 245–59, rep. in *No Other Gods: On Science and American Social Thought* (Baltimore: Johns Hopkins Press, 1978); George Drinka, *The Birth of Neurosis: Myth, Malady, and the Victorians* (New York: Simon, 1984), 184–238; Peter Gay, *The Tender Passion* (New York: Oxford

University Press, 1986), 339–49; Rabinbach, *The Human Motor*, 153–5, and Tom Lutz, *American Nervousness, 1903* (Ithaca: Cornell University Press, 1991).

17 George Miller Beard, 'Neurasthenia, or Nervous Exhaustion', *The Boston Medical and Surgical Journal*, n.s. 3 (1869), 218. This was an opening shot: vast lists of symptoms accreted.

18 Drinka, *The Birth of Neurosis*, 210–28; M. B. Macmillan, 'Beard's Concept of Neurasthenia and Freud's Concept of the Actual Neuroses', *Journal of the History of the Behavioral Sciences*, 12 (1976), 376–90.

19 See note 16 above; and Stephen Kern *The Culture of Time and Space 1880–1918* (Cambridge, MA: Harvard University Press, 1983), 124–30.

20 On Beard and Edison, see Nye, *Electrifying America*, 164–5.

21 George Beard, *American Nervousness. Its Causes and Consequences* (New York: G. Putnam's, 1881), 98.

22 Frank J. Sulloway, *Freud: Biologist of the Mind* (New York: Basic Books, 1989), 61.

23 Freud also used 'Faradization' on Elizabeth von R. and other early patients.

24 Chris Baldick, *In Frankensteins's Shadow: Myth, Monstrosity, and Nineteenth Century Writing* (Oxford: Clarendon Press, 1987), ch. 5.

25 See e.g. Fred Kaplan, *Dickens and Mesmerism* (Princeton University Press, 1975); Harold Aspiz, *Whitman and the Body Beautiful* (Urbana: University of Illinois Press, 1980), ch. 5.

26 Ezra Pound, 'Psychology and Troubadours' (1912), in *The Spirit of Romance*, rev. edn (London: Peter Owen, 1952), 97. On Pound's electromagnetic thinking, see Max Nänny, *Ezra Pound: Poetics for an Electric Age* (Berne: Francke, 1973); Ian F. A. Bell, *Critic as Scientist* (London: Methuen, 1981).

27 See Bruce Clarke, *Dora Marsden and Early Modernism: Gender, Individualism, Science* (Ann Arbor: University of Michigan Press, 1996).

28 Pound, 'Psychology and Troubadours', 93.

29 Stevie Smith, *Novel on Yellow Paper* (London: Jonathan Cape, 1936), 198; D. H. Lawrence, *Women in Love* (1921; London: Penguin, 1977), 353–4.

30 Katherine Mansfield, *The Stories of Katherine Mansfield*, ed. Anthony Alpers (Auckland: Oxford University Press, 1984), 320.

31 Thomas Laqueur, *Making Sex: Body and Gender from the Greeks to Freud* (Cambridge, MA: Harvard University Press, 1990).

32 O. Overbeck, *Overbeck's New Electronic Theory of Life and Rejuvenation* (Lincoln: J. W. Ruddock, 1925), 12,19.

33 Judith Butler, *Gender Trouble: Feminism and the Subversion of Identity* (London: Routledge, 1990), 61; Lawrence Birkin, *Consuming Desire:*

Sexual Science and the Emergence of a Culture of Abundance, 1871–1914 (Ithaca: Cornell University Press, 1988).

34 Henry James, *The Bostonians*, ed. Charles R. Anderson (London: Penguin, 1984), 374.

35 Richard Godden, *Fictions of Capital: The American Novel from James to Mailer* (Cambridge University Press, 1990), 27.

36 H. G. Wells, *Tono-Bungay* (1908; London: Pan, 1964), 321.

37 Rachel Bowlby relates *Sister Carrie* to the new culture of the department store and to the 'economy of spectacular abundance' in *Just Looking: Consumer Culture in Dreiser, Gissing and Zola* (London: Methuen, 1985), 52–65; Walter Benn Michaels positions Dreiser in debates on modernity in '*Sister Carrie*'s Popular Economy', *Critical Inquiry*, 8 (1980), 373–90, rep. in *The Gold Standard and the Logic of Naturalism* (Berkeley: University of California Press, 1987), ch. 1.

38 Theodore Dreiser, *Jennie Gerhardt* (1911; London: Constable, 1928), 116 (ch. 17).

39 Dreiser, 'A Vision of Fairy Lamps', *Success*, 1 (March 1899), 23; 'Electricity in the Household', *Demorest's*, 35 (January 1899), 38–9, rep. in *Selected Magazine Articles of Theodore Dreiser: Life and Art in the American 1890s*, ed. Yoshinobu Hakutani (London: Associated Universities Press, 1987), 137–42.

40 Theodore Dreiser, *Sister Carrie* (New York: Penguin, 1981), 5 (the version 'restored' to its original state, before Dreiser was forced to revise it by his publishers). Subsequent references in text.

41 Hugh Witemeyer, 'Gaslight and Magic Lamp in Sister Carrie', *PMLA*, 86 (1971), 236–40.

42 Ames may also have been modelled on Elmer Gates, the physiologist whose work on brain toxins is evoked in Hurstwood's decline. Ellen Moers, *Two Dreisers* (New York: Viking, 1969), 161–2.

43 J. Maclaren Cobban, *Master of his Fate* (1890; Elstree, Herts.: Greenhill Books, 1987), 76. Subsequent references in text. The book was serialized in *Blackwood's Magazine*.

44 See Anne Harrington, 'Hysteria, Hypnosis, and the Lure of the Invisible: The Rise of Neo-mesmerism in *fin-de-siècle* French Psychiatry', *The Anatomy of Madness: Essays in the History of Psychiatry*, vol. III, *The Asylum and its Psychiatry*, ed. W. F. Bynum, Roy Porter, and Michael Shepherd (London: Routledge, 1988), 226–46.

45 Theodore Dreiser, *The Color of a Great City* (New York: Boni & Liveright, 1923), 119; commmented on by Nye, *Electrifying America*, 5off.

46 Arnold Bennett, *Riceyman Steps* (1923; Oxford University Press, 1983), 95, 100, 274.

47 Eve Kosofsky Sedgwick, 'Epidemics of the Will', *Incorporations* [*Zone* 6], ed. Jonathan Crary and Stanford Kwinter (New York: Urzone, 1992), 582–95.

48 Herbert Spencer, *Social Statics; or, The Conditions Essential to Human*

Happiness Specified, and the First of them Developed (1851; New York: D. Appleton, 1888), 483.

49 Theodore Dreiser, *The Genius* (1925; Cleveland: World Publishing, 1954), 285.

50 George Beard and A. D. Rockwell, *A Practical Treatise on the Medical and Surgical Uses of Electricity*, 4th edn (London: H. K. Lewis, 1884), 386. For background, see Edward Stainbrook, 'The Uses of Electricity in Psychiatric Medicine during the Nineteenth Century', *Bulletin for the History of Medicine*, 22 (1948), 164–75.

51 Oppenheim, *Shattered Nerves*, 119; Jutta and Lothar Spillman, 'The Rise and Fall of Hugo Münsterberg', *Journal for the History of Behavioral Psychology*, 29 (1993), 329.

52 Rowbottom and Susskind, *Electricity and Medicine*, 193.

53 The experience of ECT as both punishment and a 'small death' is common: see Janet Frame's autobiography *An Angel at My Table* (London: Women's Press, 1984), 98–109.

54 A. D. Rockwell, *Rambling Recollections* (New York: Paul B. Hoeber, 1920).

55 Beichman, 'The First Electrocution', 410–19.

56 Thomas Hughes, *Networks of Power: Electrification in Western Society, 1880–1930* (Baltimore: Johns Hopkins University Press, 1983), 106ff; 'Harold Brown and the Executioner's Current: An Incident in the AC-DC Controversy', *Harvard Business History Review*, 32 (1958), 143–65. The episode is fictionalized in Christopher Davis's *A Peep into the Twentieth Century* (New York: Harper & Row, 1971); see Eric Mottram, *Blood on the Nash Ambassador: Investigations in American Culture* (London: Hutchinson Radius, 1989), 145–7.

57 Roger Neustadter reviews press accounts of the case in 'The "Deadly Current": The Death Penalty in the Industrial Age', *Journal of American Culture*, 12 (1989), 79–88, concluding that electrocution reflected 'the popular conception of history in which science, technology, and progress marched hand in hand'. While this is true of official rhetoric, there were many dissenting voices in 1890 and later, and even the 'Battle of the Systems' encompassed contradictory elements (e.g. the fact that Edison wished to discredit Westinghouse technology, even as he supported 'hygienic' death). The metaphorical associations generated by the term 'power' suggest that we need to locate the case within a more general account of the relations between technology and society, and look at the way in which electric death helps generate rather than simply reflect an ideology of industrial production.

58 See e.g. Karen Cunningham, 'Renaissance Execution and Marlovian Elocution: The Drama of Death', *PMLA*, 105 (1990), 209–22; Leonard Tennenhouse, *Power on Display: The Politics of Shakespeare's Genres* (New York and London: Methuen, 1986), ch. 3.

59 Beichman, 'The First Execution', 415.

60 The electrically obsessed Dr Foote condemned the procedure in terms of feedback: 'those who are called to witness the execution are nearly shocked to death themselves'. *Home Cyclopaedia*, 245.

61 *New York Times*, 7 August 1890, 1.

62 William Dean Howells, 'State Manslaughter', *Harper's Weekly*, 18 (6 February 1904), 196–8, rep. in *Voices Against Death: American Opposition to Capital Punishment 1789–1975*, ed. Philip English Mackey (New York: Burt Franklin, 1976), 150–5.

63 Arthur Conan Doyle, *When the World Screamed and Other Stories* (San Francisco: Chronicle Books, 1990), 39. The evil Nemor envisages a larger machine which could disintegrate the population of the Thames valley. Professor Challenger lures him into the device and 'disperses' him.

64 Rockwell, *Rambling Recollections*, 232.

65 Rowbottom and Suskind, *Electricity and Medicine*, 248.

66 Streetcar drivers, often the focus of disputes in the period, occupied a position between skilled and industrial workers, and were subject to early attempts to systematize the selection of personnel when Hugo Münsterberg devised tests for the Boston Electrical Railway Co. in the 1900s. Hugo Münsterberg, 'Scientific Selection of Workmen', *Engineering Record*, 67.7 (February 1913), 171; *Psychology and Industrial Efficiency* (1913). For Dreiser, the episode points forward to the streetcar magnate Cowperwood in *The Titan* (1914).

67 On Dreiser's vitalism, see Ronald E. Martin, *American Literature and the Universe of Force* (Durham: Duke University Press, 1981), ch. 7; on Dreiser and Loeb, Moers, *Two Dreisers*, 240–70; on Loeb, Philip Pauly, *Controlling Life: Jacques Loeb and the Engineering Ideal in Biology* (New York: Oxford University Press, 1987).

68 Theodore Dreiser, *Notes on Life*, ed. Marguerite Tjader and John J. McAleer (University of Alabama Press, 1974), 19 (cf. 79–81, 158–61).

69 Theodore Dreiser, *An American Tragedy* (Cleveland: World Publishing, 1948), 22. Subsequent references in text.

70 The place of 'race' in death-sentencing is reflected in a rich vein of Afro-American writing, from Bessie Smith's 'Send Me to the 'lectric Chair' to the execution ending Richard Wright's *Native Son* (1940). The subject is masterfully reworked in Ralph Ellison's *Invisible Man* (1952), which counters electric control (the electrified rug at the 'Battle Royal' and the ECT in the hospital) with the narrator's subversive theft of electricity from 'Monopolated Light & Power'.

71 N. Katherine Hayles, 'Designs on the body: Norbert Weiner, cybernetics, and the play of metaphor', *History of the Human Sciences*, 3 (1990), 211–28.

72 Thomas Pynchon, *Gravity's Rainbow* (1973; London: Vintage, 1995), 647–55.

73 Gilles Deleuze and Félix Guattari, *Anti-Oedipus: Capitalism and Schizophrenia*, trans. Robert Hurley, Mark Seem, Helen Lane (Minneapolis: University of Minnesota Press, 1983), 41.

74 Theodor W. Adorno, *The Stars Down to Earth and Other Essays on the Irrational in Culture*, ed. Stephen Crook (London: Routledge, 1994), 113–23.

75 See Miriam Hansen, *Babel and Babylon: Spectatorship in American Silent Film* (Cambridge: Harvard University Press, 1991), 47; Lisa Cartwright, *Screening the Body: Tracing Medicine's Visual Culture* (Mineappolis: University of Minnesota Press, 1995), 46.

2 WASTE PRODUCTS

1 Henry James, *The Ivory Tower* (London: W. Collins, 1917), 79. Subsequent references in text.

2 Elizabeth David, *A Book of Mediterranean Food*, rev. edn (London: Penguin Books, 1965), 31, citing James's *A Little Tour in France* (1885).

3 On Fletcher see Hillel Schwartz, *Never Satisfied: A Cultural History of Diets, Fantasies, and Fat* (New York: Free Press, 1986), 124–31; Harvey Green, *Fit For America: Health, Fitness, Sport and American Society* (Baltimore: Johns Hopkins University Press, 1986), ch. 11; James C. Whorton, 'Physiological Optimism: Horace Fletcher and the Hygienic Ideology in Progressive America', *Bulletin of the History of Medicine*, 55 (1981), 59–87.

4 Schwartz, *Never Satisfied*, 130; F. A. Hornibrook, *The Culture of the Abdomen* (1924; London: Icon Books, 1964), 27.

5 On Dickens and hygienic reform, see David Trotter, *Circulation and the Novel* (Basingstoke: Macmillan, 1988).

6 Horace Fletcher, *Glutton or Epicure* (Chicago: Herbert Stone, 1899), 41–53; Whorton, 'Physiological Optimism', 62.

7 Herbert Spencer, 'The Social Organism', in *Essays: Scientific, Political and Speculative*, 3 vols. (London: Williams & Norgate, 1891), I, 290; Cynthia Eagle Russett, *Sexual Science: The Victorian Construction of Womanhood* (Cambridge: Harvard University Press, 1989), 163.

8 Jeremy MacClancy, *Consuming Culture* (London: Chapmans, 1992), 26–31.

9 In *Brewsie and Willie* (New York: Random House, 1946), 78, she reports that GIs prefer 'soft stuff': Americans 'dont except at a little meat we dont really chew'.

10 Alfred Kazin, *On Native Grounds* (New York: Harcourt, Brace and World, 1942), 353.

11 Chronologies for the revisions are provided by Hershel Parker, 'Henry James "In the Wood": Sequence and Significance in His Literary Labours, 1905–1907', *Nineteenth Century Fiction*, 38 (1984),

492–513; Philip Horne, *James and Revision: The New York Edition* (Oxford: Clarendon, 1990), appendix.

12 There are flickering mentions of the metaphor of 'rumination' in Leon Edel's biography, *The Master: 1901–16* (New York: Avon Books, 1972), 250 and in Camille Paglia's *Sexual Personae* (n. 22 below); neither applies it to revision.

13 Horne, *James and Revision*, ch. 3; Anthony J. Mazella, 'James's Revisions', *A Companion to Henry James Studies*, ed. Daniel Mark Fogel (Westport: Greenwood Press, 1993), 312–14.

14 See Mark Anderson, 'Anorexia and Modernism, or How I Learned to Diet in All Directions', *Discourse*, 11.1 (1988), 28–41.

15 *The Art of the Novel: Critical Prefaces by Henry James* (New York: Scribner's, 1934), 339–40.

16 *Ibid.*, 135, 310, 230, 233, 266, 278.

17 *Ibid.*, 154, 196, 201, 10, 84–6; 'The New Novel', Henry James, *Selected Literary Criticism*, ed. Morris Shapira (Cambridge University Press, 1981), 376–7.

18 F. R. Leavis, *The Common Pursuit* (1952; London: Penguin, 1976), 228. Arnold Bennett commented on James's 'fastidiousness', his probably never enjoying a pint of beer, the 'thinness' of his stories, his essays 'packed close with vitamines'. 'A Candid Opinion on Henry James', *Evening Standard*, 27 January 1927.

19 *Henry James Letters*, ed. Leon Edel, vol. IV, 1896–1916 (Cambridge: Belknap Press, 1984), 415. Subsequently cited in notes as *Letters*, IV.

20 *Letters*, IV, 494–5.

21 Dorothy Richardson, 'About Punctuation', in *The Gender of Modernism*, ed. Bonnie Kime Scott (Bloomington: Indiana University Press, 1990), 416. First published in *Adelphi* 1.11 (April 1924).

22 Camille Paglia, *Sexual Personae* (London: Penguin, 1990), 616–17. Paglia describes James's late style as 'a *miasma*, a new version of the female swamp of generation' (621).

23 Philip Horne cites this essay and others in which James struggles, as he put it, 'to keep accretions compressed', particularly in the short story. In such formulae, compression again mediates between the necessary overaccumulation of materials and a final form. 'Henry James and the Economy of the Short Story', *Modernist Writers and the Marketplace*, ed. Ian Willison, Warwick Gould, and Warren Chernaik (London: Macmillan, 1996), 21–2.

24 Thomas M. Leitch, 'The Prefaces', in *A Companion*, ed. Fogel, 65.

25 Quoted by Edel from Case 97 of Mackenzie's *Angina Pectoris* (1923), *Letters*, IV, 518.

26 *Letters*, IV, 299–301.

27 *The Letters of Henry James*, ed. Percy Lubbock, 2 vols. (New York: Scribner's, 1920), II, 96, 104.

28 'The Place of Affectional Facts' (1905), *The Writings of William James: A Comprehensive Edition*, ed. John J. McDermott (University of Chicago Press, 1977), 272, 277.

29 See William James, 'The Experience of Activity' (1905), *Writings*, 277–91.

30 *Letters*, IV, 483, 394; *Art of the Novel*, 337–9, 344–5.

31 Gilbert Seldes, 'The Mind of an Artist', *The Dial*, July 1920, 88.

32 James, *Art of the Novel*, 17.

33 Mark Seltzer, *Bodies and Machines* (New York: Routledge, 1992), 49–90.

34 *Ibid.*, 3ff.

35 William James's attitude to Fletcherism wavered: see e.g. *William James: Selected Unpublished Correspondence 1885–1910*, ed. Frederick J. Down Scott (Colombus: Ohio State University Press, 1986), 329, 351.

36 Green, *Fit for America*, 242–57.

37 Leon Edel, 'The Architecture of Henry James's New York Edition', *New England Quarterly*, 24 (1951), 169–78; Millicent Bell, *Edith Wharton and Henry James: The Story of a Friendship* (New York: Braziller, 1965), 167. On the New York Edition as a marketing strategy, see Michael Anesko, *'Friction with the Market': Henry James and the Profession of Authorship* (New York: Oxford University Press, 1986), and Anne T. Margolis, *Henry James and the Problem of Audience* (Ann Arbor: UMI Research Press, 1985).

38 *Letters*, IV, 250.

39 Mazzella, 'James's Revisions', 314; *Letters*, IV, 498; *Art of the Novel*, 347.

40 Schwartz, *Never Satisfied*, 81.

41 Stuart Ewen, *All Consuming Images: The Politics of Style in Contemporary Culture* (New York: Basic Books, 1988), ch. 8 (179 cited).

42 Cited in Irving Norton Fisher, *My Father Irving Fisher* (New York: Comet Press, 1956), 183–4.

43 Elaine Showalter, *Sexual Anarchy: Gender and Culture at the 'Fin de Siècle'* (London: Bloomsbury, 1981), 16.

44 *Letters*, IV, 380, 415.

45 Anesko, *'Friction with the Market'*, 151.

46 Peter Wollen, *Raiding the Icebox: Reflections on Twentieth-Century Culture* (London: Verso, 1993), 20. On waste and streamlining, see Ellen Lupton and J. Abbott Miller, 'Hygiene, Cuisine and the Product World of Early Twentieth-Century America', *Incorporations* [*Zone* 6], ed. Jonathan Crary and Stanford Kwinter (New York: Urzone, 1992), 497–515.

47 To Robert Herrick, 7 August 1907, *The Selected Letters of Henry James*, ed. Leon Edel (New York: Farrar, Straus and Cudahy, 1955), 159.

48 See e.g. Daniel Bell, *The Cultural Contradictions of Capitalism* (New

York: Basic Books, 1966); Ewen, *All Consuming Images*; David Trotter, 'Too Much of a Good Thing: Fiction and the "Economy of Abundance"', *Critical Quarterly*, 34.4 (1992), 27–41. If, as Mark Seltzer cautions, this story of a fall into 'consumerism' has been positioned at varying points, it is nevertheless true that large-scale shifts in consumption took place in the period and became a focus for comment.

49 See Daniel M. Fox, *The Discovery of Abundance: Simon N. Patten and the Transformation of Social Theory* (Ithaca: Johns Hopkins University Press, 1967); William Leach, *Land of Desire: Merchants, Power, and the Rise of a New American Culture* (New York: Vintage, 1994), ch. 8.

50 Lawrence Birkin, *Consuming Desire: Sexual Science and the Emergence of a Culture of Abundance, 1871–1914* (Ithaca: Johns Hopkins University Press, 1988), 12–13. For an eighteenth-century version of this crisis, see Bryan S. Turner, 'The Government of the Body: Medical Regimes and the Rationalization of Diet', in *Regulating Bodies: Essays in Medical Sociology* (London: Routledge, 1992), 177–95.

51 Fletcher, 'What Sense?', Part II of *Glutton or Epicure*, 5. The same doctrines are expounded in *Fletcherism* (1913).

52 See Anson Rabinbach, 'Neurasthenia and Modernity', *Incorporations*, 178–89.

53 James, *Art of the Novel*, 340.

54 *Ibid.*, 304–5, 341.

55 See Anesko, *Friction with the Market*; Margolis, *Henry James*; and Jonathan Freedman, *Professions of Taste: Henry James, British Aestheticism, and Commodity Culture* (Stanford University Press, 1990).

56 On James and advertising, see Jennifer Wicke, *Advertising Fictions: Literature, Advertisement and Social Reading* (New York: Colombia University Press, 1988), ch. 3.

57 Ezra Pound, 'Henry James' (1918), in *Literary Essays of Ezra Pound*, ed. T. S. Eliot (London: Faber & Faber, 1954), 295–338. Appositely, Pound describes his essay as 'a dull grind' in its digestion of James's corpus.

58 Cf. Seltzer's account of surveillance in *Henry James and the Art of Power* (Ithaca: Cornell University Press, 1984); and John Goode's analysis of character as self-possession in 'Character and Henry James', *New Left Review*, 40 (1966), 55–75.

59 Seltzer, *Bodies and Machines*, 57.

60 See Gillian Brown, 'The Empire of Agoraphobia', *Representations*, 20 (1987), 134–57.

61 Henry James, 'The Art of Fiction', *Literary Criticism: Essays on Literature, American Writers, English Writers*, ed. Leon Edel (New York: Library of America, 1984), 44.

62 Dana J. Ringuette, 'The Self-Forming Subject: Henry James's Pragmatic Revision', *Mosaic*, 23 (1990), 115–30 (119 cited).

63 William C. Spengemann, *A Mirror for Americanists: Reflections on the Idea of American Literature* (Hanover: University Press of New England, 1989), 109.

64 H. G. Wells, *Anticipations* (London: Chapman and Hall, 1901), 81.

65 See G. R. Searle, *The Quest for National Efficiency: A Study in British Politics and Political Thought 1899–1914* (1971; London: Ashfield Press, 1990).

66 See Cecelia Tichi's discussion of waste and efficiency in *Shifting Gears: Technology, Literature and Culture in Modernist America* (Chapel Hill: University of North Carolina Press, 1987).

67 Barnes, introduction to Lorine Prunette, *Women and Leisure: A Study of Social Waste* (New York: E. P. Dutton, 1924), xvi–xvii.

68 Thorstein Veblen, *The Theory of the Leisure Class* (1899; London: Unwin, 1970), 51.

69 Thorstein Veblen, *Absentee Ownership and Business Enterprise in Recent Times: The Case of America* (London: G. Allen & Unwin, 1924), ch. 11.

70 Max Lerner, intro., *The Portable Veblen* (New York: Viking, 1948), 26. Such productive/non-productive oppositions are common in conservative thought: e.g. in the works of Ernst Jünger, coded as German productivity or *kraft* vs. Jewish circulation.

71 *The Portable Veblen*, 58.

72 See John Cawelti, *Apostles of the Self-made Man* (University of Chicago Press, 1965).

73 Werner Sombart, *Luxury and Capitalism*, intro. Philip Siehelman, trans. W. R. Dittmar (1913; Ann Arbor: University of Michigan Press, 1967).

74 Eugene O'Neill, *The Hairy Ape and Other Plays* (London: Jonathan Cape, 1923), scene II.

75 F. Scott Fitzgerald, *Tender is the Night: A Romance*, rev. edn (London: Penguin, 1986), 51.

76 Jackie Vickers points out an antecedant in Paul Bourget's description of Sargent's portrait of Isabella Gardner, wife of the railway magnate Jack Gardner. 'Women and Wealth: F. Scott Fitzgerald, Edith Wharton and Paul Bourget', *Journal of American Studies* 26 (1992), 261–3.

77 See e.g. Stuart Ewen and Elizabeth Ewen, *Channels of Desire: Mass-Images and the Shaping of American Consciousness* (New York: McGraw-Hill, 1982); Leach, *Land of Desire*.

78 H. B. Gray and Samuel Turner, *Eclipse or Empire?* (London: Nisbet, 1916), 146–7, 163.

79 Lupton and Miller, 'Hygiene, Cuisine', 504.

80 Fox, *The Discovery of Abundance*, 71–94, 133.

81 Prunette, *Women and Leisure*, 9.
82 Stuart Chase, *The Tragedy of Waste* (New York: Macmillan, 1925), 2.
    The book originated in a *New Republic* article.
83 Gilbert Seldes, *The Years of the Locust* (Boston: Little, Brown & Co.,
    1933), 25–6.
84 Kenneth Burke, 'Waste – The Future of Prosperity', *New Republic*, 16
    July 1930.
85 Caroline Tisdall and Angelo Bozzolla, *Futurism* (London: Thames &
    Hudson, 1977), 170.
86 Vorticist Manifesto, *Blast*, 1 (1914). For discussions of Pound and
    efficiency, see Hugh Kenner, *The Mechanic Muse* (New York: Oxford
    University Press, 1987); Clarke, *Dora Marsden*, 125; and esp. Tichi,
    Shifting Gears, 91–6. James F. Knapp offers a critique of Tichi in
    Literary Modernism and the Transformation of Work (Evanston:
    Northwestern University Press, 1988), chs. 1–2, pointing out that
    Pound was ambivalent about Taylorism; however he limits his argu-
    ment to modes of production, ignoring such areas as sexuality,
    consumption, and advertising.
87 *The Tradition of Constructivism*, ed. Stephen Bann (New York:
    Penguin, 1974), 9.
88 Pound to Moore, 1 February 1919. The full text of the letter is pub-
    lished in *The Gender of Modernism*, 362–5. Moore reviewed *A Draft of
    XXX Cantos* in *The Criterion*, 13 (April 1934), 482–5.
89 Ezra Pound, *The Cantos* (New York: New Directions, 1971), referred
    to by Canto.
90 Jean-Michel Rabaté, *Language, Sexuality and Ideology in Ezra Pound's
    Cantos* (London: Macmillan, 1986), 218–20, 261–9.
91 Hyacinthe Dubreuil, *Standards* (Paris: Grasset, 1929), 323; cited in
    Doray, *From Taylorism to Fordism*, 69–70.
92 Upton Sinclair, *The Flivver King: A Story of Ford-America* (1937; Bath:
    Cedric Chivers, 1971), 85; Sherwood Anderson, *Perhaps Women*
    (New York: Horace Liveright, 1931), 36–9.
93 'Fatigue . . . revealed two faces of modernity. On the one side it was
    a defense, marking the limits of the body's ability to convert energy
    into work, a limit beyond which the human motor could not func-
    tion. On the other, fatigue was the body's method of economizing
    its energy, acting as a regulator of the body's expenditure of energy'
    (Rabinbach, 'Neurasthenia', 141).
94 Duchamp was, Rosalind Kraus notes, 'enamoured of the body's
    secretions' and 'imagined a transformer . . . that would make use of
    little bits of wasted energy such as "the fall of urine and excrement",
    or "the spill of tears"'. *The Optical Unconscious* (Cambridge: MIT
    Press, 1993), 108.
95 Dora Marsden, 'Views and Comments', *The New Freewoman*, 1 July
    1913, 23; discussed in Bruce Clarke, *Dora Marsden and Early*

Modernism: Gender, Individualism, Science (Ann Arbor: University of Michigan Press, 1996), 125.

96 Wyndham Lewis, *Creatures of Habit and Creatures of Change: Essays on Art, Literature and Society 1914–1956*, ed. Paul Edwards (Santa Rosa: Black Sparrow, 1989), 126.

97 Loy, 'Gertrude Stein', *The Gender of Modernism*, 241. First published in the *Transatlantic Review*, 2.2 (1924).

98 Sandra M. Gilbert and Susan Gubar, *No Man's Land: The Place of the Woman Writer in the Twentieth Century*, vol. II, *Sexchanges* (New Haven: Yale University Press, 1989), 241; *The Yale Gertrude Stein*, ed. Richard Kostelanetz (New Haven: Yale University Press, 1980), 124.

99 Getrude Stein, *Look at Me Now and Here I Am: Writings and Lectures 1909–45*, ed. Patricia Meyerowitz (London: Penguin Books, 1971), 196.

100 Gertrude Stein, *The Making of Americans: Being a History of a Family's Progress* (Paris: Contact Editions, 1925), 586; Lisa Ruddick, *Reading Gertrude Stein: Body, Text, Gnosis* (Ithaca: Cornell University Press, 1990), 77, 243.

101 Sally Shuttleworth, 'Female Circulation: Medical Discourse and Popular Advertising in the Mid-Victorian Era', in *Body/Politics: Women and the Discourses of Science*, ed. Mary Jacobus, Evelyn Fox Keller, and Sally Shuttleworth (Routledge: New York, 1990), 47–68.

102 Eliot to Eleanor Hinkley, 3 January 1915, *The Letters of T. S. Eliot*, vol. I, 1898–1922, ed. Valerie Eliot (London: Harcourt Brace Jovanovich, 1988), 77. Subsequently cited as *Letters*, I.

103 Maud Ellmann, *The Poetics of Impersonality: Eliot and Pound* (Brighton: Harvester, 1987), 93.

104 *The Waste Land: A Facsimile and Transcript of the Original Drafts*, ed. Valerie Eliot (London: Faber & Faber, 1971), 45–7.

105 See Ellmann, *Poetics of Impersonality*; Wayne Koestlenbaum, *Double Talk: The Erotics of Male Literary Collaboration* (New York: Routledge, 1989).

106 Eliot to Richard Aldington, 17 November 1921, *Letters*, I, 488.

107 F. L. Lucas, *New Statesman*, 22 (3 November 1923), 116–18; rep. in *T. S. Eliot: Critical Assessments*, ed. Graham Clarke, 4 vols. (London: Christopher Helm, 1990), II, 118.

108 Eliot to Henry Eliot, 13 December 1921, *Letters*, I, 493.

109 Pound to Eliot, 24 December 1921, *Letters*, I, 497; Forrest Read, ed., *Pound/Joyce: The Letters of Ezra Pound to James Joyce, with Pound's Essays on Joyce* (New York: New Directions, 1967), 146 (Appendix C details Pound's excisions from the Jakes episode in 'Calypso').

110 Eliot to Scofield Thayer, 20 January 1922, *Letters*, I, 502.

111 Eliot to Ottoline Morrell, 15 June 1922, *Letters*, I, 529.

112 Eliot to Pound, 9 and 19 July 1922, *Letters*, I, 539, 550

113 Tichi, *Shifting Gears*, 71.

114 Verdenal to Eliot, 26 December 1912, *Letters*, I, 36.
115 Louis Untermeyer, 'Disillusion vs. Dogma', *Freeman*, 7 January 1923, 453; rep. in *Critical Assessments*, II, 81.
116 *The Waste Land*, 31, 43.
117 *Ibid.*, 37.
118 'I expel *myself,* I spit *myself* out, I abject *myself* within the same motion through which "I" claim to establish *myself.*' Julia Kristeva, *Powers of Horror: An Essay on Abjection*, trans. Leon S. Roudiez (New York: Colombia University Press, 1982), 3.
119 Ellmann comments on waste paper in *Poetics of Impersonality*; my reading pursues a more literal line.
120 Eliot to Charlotte Eliot, 28 April 1918, *Letters*, I, 229–30.
121 *The Waste Land*, 105.
122 Pound to Eliot, 14 March 1922, *Letters*, I, 511, 514.
123 Humbert Wolfe, 'Waste Land and Waste Paper', *Weekly Westminster*, 1 n.s. (November 1923), 94; rep. in *Critical Assements*, II, 120–2.
124 Eliot to Hutchinson, 11 July 1919, *Letters*, I, 317.
125 Lawrence Rainey, 'The Price of Modernism: Reconsidering the Publication of *The Waste Land*', *Critical Quarterly*, 31.4 (1989), 21–47 (25, 43n.16 cited).
126 Pound to Anderson, 12 November 1917, *Pound/The Little Review: The Letters of Ezra Pound to Margret Anderson*, ed. Thomas L. Scott and Melvin J. Friedman (London: Faber & Faber, 1989), 151.
127 Pound to Quinn, 17 May 1917, *Selected Letters of Ezra Pound to John Quinn 1915–1920*, ed. Timothy Materer (Durham: Duke University Press, 1991), 117.
128 Eliot to Pound, 12 March 1922, *Letters*, I, 507.
129 Rainey, 'The Price of Modernism'.
130 Letter to Emily Holmes Coleman, 1936 (Barnes Collection, University of Maryland, Delaware); cited in Bonnie Kime Scott, *Refiguring Modernism*, vol. 1, *The Women of 1928* (Bloomington: Indiana University Press, 1995), 138–9.
131 John Gordon has recently argued that '*The Waste Land* and *Four Quartets* enact a classic opposition between head and heart' or between nerves and blood. Certainly nerves dominate the earlier poem, but the blood of 'Quartets' seems to me much more subminated. 'T.S. Eliot's Head and Heart', *ELH*, 62.4 (1995), 979–1000.

3 PROSTHETIC MODERNISM

1 Freud, *Civilization and its Discontents*, *The Standard Edition of the Complete Psychological Works of Sigmund Freud*, 24 vols., general editor James Strachey (London: Hogarth Press and the Institute for Psycho-Analysis, 1953–73), XXI, 86–92 (all subsequent references

are to this edition). Avital Ronell provides a fascinating reading of this passage in *The Telephone Book: Technology, Schizophrenia, Electric Speech* (Lincoln: University of Nebraska Press, 1989), 84–94.

2 Gerald Heard, *Pain, Sex and Time: A New Hypothesis of Evolution* (London: Cassell, 1939), 60.

3 See Georges Canguilhem, 'Machine and Organism', *Incorporations* [*Zone* 6], ed. Jonathan Crary and Stanford Kwinter (New York: Urzone, 1992), 44–69; from *La Connaissance de la vie* (Paris: Vrin, 1985).

4 *The Philosophical Writings of Descartes*, vol. ii, *The Correspondence*, trans. John Cottingham et al. (Cambridge University Press, 1991), 64, 243.

5 See Anson Rabinbach, *The Human Motor: Energy, Fatigue, and the Origins of Modernity* (New York: Basic Books, 1990).

6 Cf. Elaine Scarry, *The Body in Pain: The Making and Unmaking of the World* (New York: Oxford University Press, 1985), 259.

7 Marl Marx, *Capital*, vol. i, intro. Ernest Mandel, trans. Ben Fowkes (London: Penguin, 1976), 503, 548, 614.

8 Bernard Doray, *From Taylorism to Fordism: A Rational Madness*, trans. David Macey (London: Free Association Books, 1988), 82.

9 I have, here, deliberately skirted the psychodynamics of fetishism, explored e.g. in *Fetishism as Cultural Discourse*, ed. Emily Apter and William Pietz (Ithaca: Cornell University Press, 1993).

10 Klaus Theweleit, 'Circles, Lines and Bits', *Incorporations*, 260.

11 Cited in Eric Mottram, *Blood on the Nash Ambassador: Investigations in American Culture* (London: Hutchinson Radius, 1989), 96.

12 Samuel Butler, *Unconscious Memory* (London: David Bogue, 1880), 227; *Erewhon* (1872; rev. edn London: A. C. Fifield, 1918), 245, 270. Successive drafts of *Erewhon* shifted Butler's position.

13 David F. Channell, *The Vital Machine: A Study of Technology and Organic Life* (New York: Oxford University Press, 1991), 67.

14 See Doray, *Taylorism to Fordism*, 80–2.

15 Canguilhem, 'Machine and Organism', 61; Jeffrey Herf, *Reactionary Modernism: Technology, Culture and Politics in Weimar and the Third Reich* (Cambridge University Press, 1984), 158; A. Fox-Lane Pitt-Rivers, *The Evolution of Culture and Other Essays* (Oxford: Clarendon, 1906), 25.

16 Martin Heidegger 'The Question Concerning Technology' (1953), in *Basic Writings: Martin Heidegger*, ed. David Farrell Krell (London: Routledge, 1978), 311–41; Maurice Merleau-Ponty, *Phenomenology of Perception*, trans. Colin Smith (London: Routledge, 1981), 199.

17 Ronell, *The Telephone Book*, 88; Mark Seltzer, *Bodies and Machines* (New York: Routledge, 1992), 10.

18 Andrew Ure, *The Philosophy of Manufactures* (London: C. Knight, 1835), 13.

19 See Doray, *Taylorism to Fordism*, ch. 3.

20 Henry Adams, *The Education of Henry Adams* (1907; Boston: Houghton Mifflin, 1974), 380.

21 Arthur Keith, *The Engines of the Human Body* (London: Williams & Norgate, 1919), v. I am indebted to Jonathan Sawday, 'The Archeology of the Body: Fiction, Fraud, "Race" and the Story of Piltdown', Bodily Fictions Conference, Brunel University, 9 September 1995.

22 Thomas Edison, 'The Woman of the Future', *Good Housekeeping*, October 1913, 436; cited in David E. Nye, *Electrifying America: Social Meanings of New Technology* (Cambridge: MIT Press, 1990), 242.

23 Gerald Stanley Lee, *Crowds* (London: Curtis Brown, 1913), 65, 247, 199, 259.

24 Early texts include Carl Snyder, *The World Machine* (1911) and George Crile's *Man, an Adaptive Mechanism* (1916). Brian Stableford surveys such writing in *Scientific Romance in Britain 1890–1950* (New York: St. Martin's Press, 1985), 154–65, countering them to the pessimism of Oswald Spengler's *The Decline of the West* (1918) and R. Austin Freeman's *Social Decay and Regeneration* (1921).

25 Huxley, *Essays of a Biologist* (1923), cited in Stableford, *Scientific Romance*, 155.

26 Ronald C. Macfie, *Metanthropos, or the Future of the Body*, Today and Tomorrow series (London: Kegan Paul, Trench, & Trubner, 1928), title of ch. 4.

27 Garet Garrett, *Ouroboros, of the Mechanical Extension of Mankind*, Today and Tomorrow Series (London: Kegan Paul, Trench, & Trubner, 1926), 12.

28 J. D. Bernal, *The World, the Flesh and the Devil*, Today and Tomorrow Series (London: Kegan Paul, Trench, & Trubner, 1929), 39–40.

29 Loren Baritz, *The Servants of Power: A History of the Use of Social Science in American Industry* (Middletown: Wesleyan University Press, 1960), 60ff; Richard Gillespie, *Manufacturing Knowledge: A History of the Hawthorne Experiments* (Cambridge University Press, 1991).

30 See Channell, *The Vital Machine* ; Anthony Wilden, 'Changing Frames of Order: Cybernetics and the Machina Mundi', in *The Myths of Information: Technology and Postindustrial Culture* (London: Routledge & Kegan Paul, 1980).

31 Arnold Bennett, *The Human Machine* (London: New Age Press, 1908), 16.

32 David King Holloway, *Huxley in Hollywood* (London: Bloomsbury, 1989), 167.

33 See e.g. Teresa de Laurentis, Andreas Huyssen and Kathleen Woodward, eds., *The Technological Imagination: Theories and Fictions* (Madison: Coda Press, 1980); Leo Marx, *The Pilot and the Passenger: Essays on Literature, Technology and Culture in the United States* (New York: Oxford University Press, 1988).

34 Joseph W. Slade, 'American Writers and American Inventions: Cybernetic Discontinuity in Pre-World War II Literature', *The Technological Imagination*, 27–47; John F. Kasson, *Civilizing the Machine: Technology and Republican Values in America, 1776–1900* (New York: Penguin, 1977).

35 Ezra Pound, *The Cantos* (New York: New Directions, 1971), Canto 74, 441.

36 *The Tradition of Constructivism*, ed. Stephen Bann (New York: Da Capo, 1974) 9, 110.

37 *Disk* (1923), in *The Tradition of Constructivism*, 99.

38 Wyndham Lewis, 'Shropshire Lads or Robots Again', *New Britain*, 2.34 (10 January 1934), 226–7; rep. in *Creatures of Habit and Creatures of Change: Essays on Art, Literature and Society 1914–1956*, ed. Paul Edwards (Santa Rosa: Black Sparrow, 1989), 190–4; *The Art of Being Ruled*, ed. Reed Way Dasenbock (1926; Santa Rosa: Black Sparrow, 1989), 191.

39 See Peter L. Caracciolo, 'The Metamorphosis of Wyndham Lewis's *The Human Age:* Medium, Intertextuality, Genre', in *Modernist Writers and the Marketplace*, ed. Ian Willison, Warwick Gould and Warren Chernaik (London: Macmillan, 1996), 258–86. Lewis's influence on Marshall McLuhan is noted by Caracciolo and others.

40 Bob Brown, 'The Readies', *transition* 19/20 (June 1930); rep. in *In Transition: A Paris Anthology* (New York: Doubleday, 1990), 59–65.

41 Jerome McGann discusses Brown in *Black Riders: The Visible Language of Modernism* (Princeton University Press, 1993), 84–97.

42 Bob Brown, *Words, I but Bend my Finger in a Beckon and Words, Birds of Words, Hop on it, Chirping* (Paris: Hours Press, 1931), 1,19.

43 Bob Brown, *Gems: A Censored Anthology* (Cagnes-sur-Mer: Roving Eye Press, 1931), 23.

44 Samuel Beckett et al., *Our Exagmination Round His Factification for Incamination of Work in Progress* (1929; London: Faber & Faber, 1972), 190.

45 Wyndham Lewis, *Time and Western Man*, ed. Paul Edwards (1927; Santa Rosa: Black Sparrow, 1993), 88.

46 See *Pound/Joyce: The Letters of Ezra Pound to James Joyce, with Pound's Essays on Joyce*, ed. Forrest Read (New York: New Directions, 1967), 96ff (101–2 cited); George M. Gould, *Biographic Clinics* (Philadelphia: P. Blakiston's Sons, 1903) and *Concerning Lafcadio Hearn* (London: T. Fisher Unwin, 1908). In the former, Gould attributes much of what is diagnosed as neurasthenia to eye-strain; in the latter, he echoes Nordau on the 'pathology of genius' (108).

47 Pound to Quinn, 17 May 1917, *Selected Letters of Ezra Pound to John Quinn 1915–1920*, ed. Timothy Materer (Durham: Duke University Press, 1991), 117.

48 Pound to Quinn, 10 August 1922, *Selected Letters to Quinn*, 216. Pound wrote a short piece on Berman for the *New Age* in 1922.

49 See Ian F. A. Bell, *Critic as Scientist: The Modernist Poetics of Ezra Pound* (London: Methuen, 1981); Celia Tichi, *Shifting Gears: Technology, Literature and Culture in Modernist America* (Chapel Hill: University of North Carolina Press, 1987); Lisa Steinman, *Made in America: Science, Technology and American Modernism* (New Haven: Yale University Press, 1987).

50 Pound, 'Psychology and Troubadours', in *The Spirit of Romance* (1910; London: Peter Owen, 1970), 92; 'The Serious Artist' (1913), in *Literary Essays of Ezra Pound*, ed. T. S. Eliot (London: Faber & Faber, 1954), 41–57.

51 See Glenn S. Burne, *Remy de Gourmont: His Ideas and Influence in England and America* (Carbondale: Southern Illinois University Press 1963); Richard Sieburth, *Instigations: Ezra Pound and Remy de Gourmont* (Cambridge, MA: Harvard University Press, 1978). Gourmont was one source of T. S. Eliot's concept of the 'dissociation of sensibility', a term close to the 'distraction' examined in chapter 7. Jeffrey Mehlman explores Gourmont's preoccupation with 'dissociation' and politicized metaphors of amputation/castration in 'Remy de Gourmont with Freud: Fetishism and Patriotism', *Fetishism as Cultural Discourse*, 84–91.

52 Remy de Gourmont, *The Natural Philosophy of Love*, trans. and intro. Ezra Pound (1926; London: Neville Spearman, 1957), 30. On paedomorphism, see Laura Doyle, *Bordering on the Body: The Racial Matrix of Modern Fiction and Culture* (New York: Oxford University Press, 1994), 65–7.

53 Ezra Pound, 'Postscript to *The Natural Philosophy of Love* by Rémy de Gourmont' (1921), in *Pavannes and Divagations* (New York: New Directions, 1958), 203–14.

54 Ezra Pound, *Instigations of Ezra Pound, together with an Essay on the Chinese Written Character by Ernest Fenollosa* (New York: Boni & Liveright, 1920), 171.

55 Umbro Apollonio, ed., *Futurist Manifestos*, trans R. Brain et al. (London: Thames & Hudson, 1973), 70–4, 93–4.

56 William Carlos Williams, 'Water, Salts, Fat, etc.', *Imaginations*, ed. Webster Schott (London: MacGinnon & Kee, 1970), 357–63.

57 See Silas Weir Mitchell, *Injuries of Nerves* (1872).

58 See J. Gerald Kennedy's *Poe, Death, and the Life of Writing* (New Haven: Yale University Press, 1987), ch. 2.

59 *Collected Works of Edgar Allan Poe*, vol. II, *Tales and Sketches 1831–1842*, ed. Thomas Olive Mabbott (Cambridge: Belknap Press, 1978), 61–82.

60 Poe, *Collected Works*, 376–91.

61 Mark Seltzer, 'Writing Technologies', *New German Critique*, 57 (1992), 171.

62 See Elizabeth Bronfen, *Over Her Dead Body: Death, Femininity and the Aesthetic* (Manchester University Press, 1992), 59–65, 324–36.

63 On Poe and language, see Douglas Tallack, *The Nineteenth Century American Shory Story: Language, Form, and Ideology* (London: Routledge, 1993).

64 D. H. Lawrence, *Selected Literary Criticism*, ed. Anthony Beale (London: William Heinemann, 1955), 330. Kenneth Silverman's *Edgar A. Poe: Mournful and Never-Ending Remembrance* (London: Weidenfeld & Nicholson, 1992) sees the early death of Poe's mother as underlying substitution.

65 Andrew Levy, *The Culture and Commerce of the American Short Story* (Cambridge University Press, 1993).

66 Dickens to Poe, 27 November 1842, *The Letters of Charles Dickens*, vol. III, ed. Madeline House, Graham Storey, and Kathleen Tillotson (Oxford: Clarendon Press, 1974), 385.

67 Kennedy derives the phrase 'using up' from 'the colloquial notion of "using up" or abusing an author in print'; *Poe, Death, and the Life of Writing*, 115.

68 Tzvetan Todorov explores Poe's preference for the detail in *Genres in Discourse* , trans. Catherine Porter (Cambridge University Press, 1990), 93–102.

69 To Charles Anthon, October 1844, *The Letters of Edgar Allen Poe*, 2 vols., ed. John Ward Ostron (Cambridge: Harvard University Press, 1948), I, 268.

70 Edgar Allan Poe, *The Brevities: Pinkidia, Marginalia, Fifty Suggestions and Other Works*, ed. Burton R. Pollin (New York: Gordian Press, 1985), 313. On Poe's late attempts to suggest that his short pieces were part of a 'book-unity', see Michael Allen, *Poe and the British Magazine Tradition* (New York: Oxford University Press, 1969),184–6.

71 Cf. John Irwin on doubling in *American Hieroglyphics: The Symbol of the Egyptian Hieroglyphics in the American Renaissance* (New Haven: Yale University Press, 1980), 98.

72 See Peter Nicholls, *Modernisms: A Literary Guide* (London: Macmillan, 1995), 18–20 (on Poe and Baudelaire).

73 William Carlos Williams, 'Edgar Allan Poe', *In the American Grain*, intro. Horace Gregory (Norfolk, CT: New Directions, 1925), 221–3.

74 Nicholls, *Modernisms*, 122–3; Ernest Hemingway, *A Moveable Feast* (London: Jonathan Cape, 1964), 74.

75 Scarry, *The Body in Pain*, 121.

76 See Joanna Bourke, *Dismembering the Male: Men's Bodies, Britain and the Great War* (London: Reaktion Books, 1996); Stephen Kern, *The Culture of Love: Victorians to Moderns* (Cambridge, MA: Harvard University Press, 1992); Sandra M. Gilbert and Susan Gubar, *No Man's Land: The Place of the Woman Writer in the Twentieth Century*, vol. II, *Sexchanges* (New Haven: Yale University Press, 1989), ch. 7; and, on wounding in war, Scarry, *The Body in Pain*, ch. 2. The limbs destroyed were not, of course, just those of men, a point made by

Rebecca West in her account of women munitions workers, 'Hands that War', *Daily Chronicle*, 1916, in *The Young Rebecca: Writings of Rebecca West 1911–17*, ed. Jane Marcus (Bloomington: Indiana University Press, 1982), 387–90.

77 Paul Virilio, *War and Cinema: The Logistics of Perception*, trans. Patrick Camiller (London: Verso, 1989).

78 Samuel Harber, *Efficiency and Uplift: Scientific Management in the Progressive Era, 1890–1920* (University of Chicago Press, 1964), 119; Daniel Pick, *War Machine: The Rationalization of Slaughter in the Modern Age* (New Haven: Yale University Press, 1993).

79 John Dewey, 'What are we Fighting For?', *Independent*, 94 (1918), 474, 480–83.

80 H. W. Nevinson, *Visions and Memories* (London: Oxford University Press, 1944), 86. Cf. Gino Severini's painting 'Train of the Wounded' (1915).

81 Mark Twain, *The American Claimant* (New York: Charles L. Webster, 1892).

82 Dix's 'Sex Murder' series might be seen as a fetishistic attempt to displace war onto the feminine body (the idealized body in the name of which war is fought).

83 Thomas Richards, *The Commodity Culture of Victorian England: Advertising and Spectacle 1851–1914* (London: Verso, 1990), 241 et passim.

84 See Harvey Green, *The Uncertainty of Everyday Life, 1915–1945* (New York: Harper Collins, 1992), 22–5; Roland Marchand, *Advertising the American Dream: Making Way for Modernity, 1920–1940* (Berkeley: University of California Press, 1985), 356.

85 Marchand, *Advertising the American Dream*, 16–20.

86 Charles Goodrum and Helen Dalrymple, *Advertising in America: The First Two Hundred Years* (New York: Harry N. Abrams, 1990), 67, 128, 149–55.

87 Marchand, *Advertising the American Dream*, 150.

88 Goodrum and Dalrymple, *Advertising in America*, 68–73.

89 Charles H. Willi, *Facial Rejuvenation* (London: Cecil Parker, 1926); Elizabeth B. Margetson, *Living Canvas: A Romance of Aesthetic Surgery*, intro. Charles H. Willi (London: Methuen, 1936), 2, 18, 65. Margetson was a popular novelist and journalist.

90 A related topos is the doll-smashing described by Jane Marcus in novels of the period, 'Laughing at Leviticus: *Nightwood* as Woman's Circus Epic', *Silence and Power: A Reevaluation of Djuna Barnes*, ed. Mary Lynn Broe (Carbondale: Southern Illinois University Press, 1991), 221–50.

91 Jean Rhys, *After Leaving Mr. Mackenzie* (Harmondsworth: Penguin, 1971), 86; Storm Jameson, *Men Against Women*, intro. Elaine Feinstein (London: Virago, 1982), 269; Radcliffe Hall, *The Well of*

Loneliness, intro. Alison Hennegan (London: Virago, 1982), 187; Christina Stead *The Beauties and the Furies*, intro. Hilary Bailey (London: Virago, 1982), 70.

92 Rhys experienced the confluence of textual, commercial, and bodily fragmentation which we saw in Poe: the end of *Voyage in the Dark* (1934) was 'mutilated' by her publisher when the heroine Anna Morgan's death after an abortion was revised to let her survive, thanks to a male doctor.

93 Jean Rhys, *Good Morning, Midnight* (1939; London: Penguin, 1969), 52–3, 120, 156.

94 Wolfgang Fritz Haug, *Critique of Commodity Aesthetics: Appearance, Sexuality and Advertising in Capitalist Society*, trans. Robert Bock (London: Polity, 1986), 90–1.

95 Victor Tausk, 'On the Origin of the "Influencing Machine" in Schizophrenia', *The Psychoanalytic Quarterly*, 2 (1933), 519–56 (529 cited). Despite their ungenerous dismissal of Tausk, his work anticipates the technopoetics of Deleuze and Guattari in *Anti-Oedipus*.

96 Tausk, 'On the Origin', 554, 556.

97 *Ibid.*, 521.

98 Hanns Sachs's 'The Delay of the Machine Age', *The Psychoanalytic Quarterly* 2 (1933): 404–24 (the issue in which Tausk's paper appeared) offered a historicization of the psychoanalytic theory of the machine. Sachs asks why the ancient world did not discover machines as it did mathematics. He concludes that the Greeks saw machines which replaced human bodies as 'uncanny' because of the threatened breaking of ego-boundaries presented by the animated-inanimate. In 'peoples whose narcissism was more strongly developed than ours and more strongly related to the body-ego', there is a shrinking from the mechanical. In modern man, Sachs implies, the desire for narcissistic satisfaction has taken another route, violating bodily integrity in achieving a wider dispersal of libidinal energies.

99 Theodor W. Adorno, *The Stars Down to Earth and Other Essays on the Irrational in Culture*, ed. Stephen Crook (London: Routledge, 1994), 114–15.

4 AUTO-FACIAL-CONSTRUCTION

1 Greg Mullins, 'Nudes, Prudes, and Pygmies: The Desirability of Disavowal in *Physical Culture*', *Discourse* 15.1 (1992), 27.

2 Kenneth Dutton, *The Perfectible Body: The Western Ideal of Physical Development* (London: Cassell, 1995).

3 See Richard Weston, *Modernism* (London: Phaidon, 1996), 129–31.

4 F. Matthias Alexander, *Man's Supreme Inheritance* (London: Methuen, 1910), 136.

5 F. Matthias Alexander, *Conscious Control* (London: Methuen, 1912), 3.

6 F. Matthias Alexander, *Constructive Conscious Control*, intro. John Dewey (London: Methuen, 1924), 92. Similarly, Alexander seeks to circumvent the dialectic of 'concentration' and 'mind wandering' (attention/distraction) described in ch. 7 here.

7 'Introductory Word', *John Dewey: The Middle Works, 1899–1924*, Vol.11: 1918–1919, ed. Jo Ann Boydston (Carbondale: Southern Illinois University Press, 1982), 351.

8 Randolph Bourne, 'Making Over the Body', *New Republic* 15 (1918), 28–9; rep. in Appendix I, *John Dewey: The Middle Works* 11 359–60.

9 John Dewey, 'Reply to a Reviewer', *New Republic* 15 (1918),55; rep. in *John Dewey: The Middle Works* 11 353–55.

10 Wyndham Lewis, *The Art of Being Ruled*, ed. Reed Way Dasenbock (1926; Santa Rosa: Black Sparrow, 1989), 349–50.

11 Wyndham Lewis, *The Complete Wild Body* (Santa Barbara: Black Sparrow Press, 1982), 251–2. On the machine, see 'Machinery and Lions', *The Caliph's Design* (London: The Egoist, 1919).

12 Lewis, 'Call yourself a Man!' *The Art of Being Ruled*, ed. Reed Way Dasenbock (1926; Santa Rosa: Black Sparrow, 1989), 250.

13 An exception was the anti-Taylorist Jean-Marie Lahy in France in 1908, promulgating the radical view that women compositors were as good as men. Anson Rabinbach, *The Human Motor: Energy, Fatigue, and the Origins of Modernity* (New York: Basic Books, 1990), 250.

14 See Lucy Bland, *Banishing the Beast: English Feminism and Sexual Morality, 1885–1914* (London: Penguin, 1995). Laura Doyle examines the figure of the mother in eugenics in *Bordering on the Body: The Racial Matrix of Modern Fiction and Culture* (New York: Oxford University Press, 1994).

15 Bruce Clarke, *Dora Marsden and Early Modernism: Gender, Individualism, Science* (Ann Arbor: University of Michigan Press, 1996), 12–18.

16 Hillel Schwartz, 'Torque: The New Kinaesthetic of the Twentieth Century', *Incorporations* [*Zone* 6], ed. Jonathan Crary and Stanford Kwinter (New York: Urzone, 1992), 71–126. Schwartz opposes this kinaesthetic, with its fluid movements, to the robotic movements of machine-culture; it can, however, be argued that the ideals of frictionless movement and a balanced centre are simply an *internalization* of machine aesthetics.

17 Hillel Schwartz, *Never Satisfied: A Cultural History of Diets, Fantasies and Fat* (New York: Free Press, 1986), 105.

18 Harvey Green, *Fit for America: Health, Fitness, Sport and American Society* (Baltimore: Johns Hopkins University Press, 1986), 257; Schwartz, *Never Satisfied*, 144.

19 Mrs Bagot Stack, *Building the Body Beautiful: The Bagot Stack Stretch-and-Swing System* (London: Chapman and Hall, 1931), 23.

20 Mrs A. J. Cruikshank and Prunella Stack, *Movement is Life* (London: G. Bell & Sons, 1937), 100, 229.

21 Bagot Stack, *Building the Body Beautiful*, 3.

22 Work on Loy includes: Mina Loy, *The Last Lunar Baedeker*, ed. Roger L. Conover (Highlands, N.C.: Jargon Society, 1982) and *The Lost Lunar Baedeker*, ed. Roger L. Conover (New York: Farrar, Straus, Giroux, 1996); Virginia Kouidis, *Mina Loy, American Modernist Poet* (Baton Rouge: Louisiana State University Press, 1980); Carolyn Burke, 'Becoming Mina Loy', *Women's Studies* 7 (1980), 136–150, 'The New Poetry and the New Woman: Mina Loy', in *Coming to Light: American Women Poets in the Twentieth Century*, eds. Diane Wood Middlebrook and Marilyn Yalom (Ann Arbor: University of Michigan Press, 1985) and *Becoming Modern: The Life of Mina Loy* (New York: Farrar, Straus, Giroux, 1996); *The Gender of Modernism: A Critical Anthology*, ed. Bonnie Kime Scott (Bloomington: Indiana University Press, 1980), 230–51; Steven Watson, *Strange Bedfellows: The First American Avant-Garde* (New York: Abbeville Press, 1991); Linda A. Kinnahan, *Poetics of the Feminine: Authority and the Literary Tradition in William Carlos Williams, Mina Loy, Denise Levertov and Kathleen Fraser* (New York: Cambridge University Press, 1994).

23 Djuna Barnes, *Ladies Almanack* (1928; Elmwood Park: Dalkey Archive Press, 1992), 12.

24 Conover's Introduction, Loy, *Last Lunar Baedeker*, xviii.

25 On futurist gender-politics, see Caroline Tisdall and Angelo Bozzolla, *Futurism* (London: Thames & Hudson, 1977), 153–64; Peter Nicholls, *Modernisms: A Literary Guide* (London: Macmillan, 1995), 84–111.

26 *New York Evening Sun*, 17 February 1917.

27 Bridget Elliott and Jo-Anne Wallace, *Women Artists and Writers: Modernist (im)positionings* (London: Routledge, 1994), 151.

28 A full list would include different degrees of 'participation': from the relatively passive (models like Kiki of Montparnasse) to the sexualized collaborator (George Yeats). Watson's *Strange Bedfellows* is interesting here: placing the love-relations between modernists in prominent position, it offers a sense of connectedness and homo-social exchange. On the other hand, in clarifying those structures it occasionally occludes points of resistance.

29 Watson, *Strange Bedfellows*, 265–71, 337–8, 379. She committed suicide in Paris in 1927.

30 See Loy, 'Songge Byrd' and 'Nancy Cunard', *Last Lunar Baedeker*, 238, 259. Loy also worked on a long poem on Duncan, 'Biography of Songge Byrd' (1952), Loy Papers, Beineke Library, Yale University, YCAL MSS 6, Box 5, folder 130.

31 On visibility, see Janet Lyon, 'Women Demonstrating Modernism', *Discourse* 17.2 (1994–5), 6–25.

32 See Nicola Beauman, *A Very Great Profession: The Woman's Novel*

1914–39 (London: Virago, 1983); Alison Light, *Forever England: Femininity, Literature and Conservative Between the Wars* (London: Routledge, 1991).

33 On alternative 'maps' of Modernism, see Elliott and Wallace, *Women Artists and Writers*, esp. 156–62. A useful case-study is Barbara Buhler Lynes, *O'Keefe, Stieglitz and the Critics, 1916–1929* (Chicago: University of Chicago Press, 1989).

34 Scott (ed.), *The Gender of Modernism*, 63–4.

35 See Charlotte Mandel, 'Garbo/Helen: The Self-Projection of Beauty by H. D.', *Womens' Studies* 7 (1980), 127–35.

36 Loy, *Last Lunar Baedeker*, 58. A striking unpublished essay discusses the treatment of the erotic in modernist writers, comparing D'Annunzio, Joyce, Harris, Lawrence, Eliot, Huxley, and others. 'On Literature', YCAL MSS 6, Box 7, folder 190.

37 Loy, 'The Oil in the Machine', YCAL MSS 6, Box 6, folder 168. Cf. an unpublished draft satire, 'Sacred Prostitute' (1916), with two characters jokingly called 'Futurism' and 'Love'. He kisses her mechanically: 'Do-you-like it? Do-you-like-it? Do-you-like it?' YCAL MSS 6, Box 6, folder 176, 13.

38 Loy, 'Brain', YCAL MSS 6, Box 5, folder 80, dated August 1945. I have cited the TS text from Loy's papers, rather than the slightly less positive text in *Last Lunar Baedeker*, 257.

39 Bryher, 'Three Poems', *transition* 3 (1927), rep. in *In Transition: A Paris Anthology* (New York: Doubleday, 1990), 66–7.

40 Loy, 'Island in the Air', TS, YCAL MSS 6, Box 4, folder 58, 11; folder 65, 83–4. Cf. the 'iron busks / of curved corsets', *Last Lunar Baedeker*, 140.

41 Futurism is attacked in her poem 'The Effectual Marriage'; in 'Lion's Jaws'; and in her play *The Pamperers*, inaugurating the 'Modern Forms' section of *The Dial* in 1920.

42 Loy, 'Pazzarella', TS, YCAL MSS 6, Box 6, folder 170–1, 3. It is dedicated to 'the great Tuscan – the most sympathetic of mysoginists [sic?]'. Scrawled at the top is: 'Parody of Gio's work'.

43 Loy, *Lost Lunar Baedeker*, 49.

44 Loy, 'The Stomach', TS, YCAL MSS 6, Box 6, Folder 178, 3.

45 'Pygmaleon and Galatea' ends with the sculptor abandoning his creation:

> But Galatea did not weep and turn to stone again
> As tradition would have you know
> She became a living picture
> And joined the Folly show.

TS, YCAL MSS Box 5, Folder 145, n.d. (annotation reads: 'written eons ago').

46 Loy, *Lost Lunar Baedeker*, 4–8; Julia Kristeva, 'Sabat Mater', *Tales of*

Love, trans. Leon S. Roudiez (New York: Colombia University Press, 1987), 234–63; cf. also Doyle's discussion of the 'intercorporeal' in relation to maternity in *Bordering on the Body*.

47 Mina Loy, 'Gertrude Stein', *transatlantic review*, 2.2 (1924); rep. in *The Gender of Modernism*, 239.

48 Loy, *Lost Lunar Baedeker*, 72.

49 Loy, *Lost Lunar Baedeker*, 145.

50 Loy, *Last Lunar Baedeker*, 147–8.

51 Watson, *Strange Bedfellows*, 301, 31.

52 Loy, *Lost Lunar Baedeker*, 225–8.

53 Mina Loy, *Auto-Facial-Construction*, Sociétaire du Salon d'Automne Paris (Florence: Tipografia Giuntina, 1919); rep. in *Last Lunar Baedeker*, 283–4, 328n and (corrected text) in *Lost Lunar Baedeker*, 165–6.

54 Andrew Michael Roberts, '"How to Be Happy in Paris": Mina Loy and the Objects of Desire', *Objects of Modernism* Conference, Southampton, July 1995.

55 Mina Loy, *Psycho-Democracy A movement to focus human reason on THE CONSCIOUS DIRECTION OF EVOLUTION* (Florence: Tipografia Peri & Rossi, 1920).

56 Mina Loy, *Listen! The Idea-Market Organ of the Psycho-Democratic Party*, n.d. 1 (cover sheet attached to *Psycho-Democracy*).

57 Loy, YCAL MSS 6, Box 7, folder 186 (c.1940?).

58 Loy to Williams, June 1959, cited in *Last Lunar Baedeker*, xiv.

59 Mina Loy, *Insel*, ed. Elizabeth Arnold (Santa Rosa: Black Sparrow Press, 1991), 19, 21, 30, 69, 131.

60 Loy, *Last Luna Baedeker*, 92. On the erotic, see Kinnahan, *Poetics of the Feminine*, 52–7.

61 Loy, 'Arthur Craven is Alive!', *Last Lunar Baedeker*, 317–22 (draft fragment, title supplied by editor).

62 Michael Oriad, *Sporting with the Gods: The Rhetoric of Play and Game in American Culture* (Cambridge: Cambridge University Press, 1991). On Hemingway's boxing and 'self-hardening', see Robert McAlmon and Kay Boyle, *Being Geniuses Together, 1920–1930* (London: Hogarth Press, 1984), 160–2. In *On Boxing* (London: Pan, 1988), Joyce Carol Oates describes boxing as 'the obverse of the feminine' (76).

63 Nathanael West, *The Dream Life of Balso Snell*, in *The Collected Works of Nathanael West* (London: Secker & Warburg, 1957), 31–2; Ezra Pound, *Pavannes and Divagations* (London: Faber & Faber, 1960), 204.

64 West, *Collected Works*, 36.

65 Cited in Patrick Waldberg, *Surrealism* (London: Thames & Hudson, 1965), 63.

66 Loy, 'Sacred Prostitute', 22.

67 *Last Lunar Baedeker*, lii, 330n.

68 Dan Streible, 'A History of the Boxing Film', *Film History* 3 (1989), 235–47. The equation also applies to Soviet cinema: the actor-boxer Boris Barnet made *The House on Trubnaya* (1928) and other films notable for agile camerawork.

69 Cited in Stuart Chase, *Men and Machines* (London: Jonathan Cape, 1929), 258. On sports, advertising and entertainment, see Ann Douglas, *Terrible Honesty: Mongerel Manhattan in the 1920s* (London: Picador, 1996), 64–6.

70 On Barnes's journalism see Mary Lynn Broe, 'Gunga Duhl, the Pen Performer: Djuna Barnes's Early Journalism', *Belle Lettres* 1 (September 1985). The grotesque body in Barnes's work is discussd by Sheryl Stevenson, 'Writing the Grotesque Body: Djuna Barnes's Carnival Parody'; Jane Marcus, 'Laughing at Leviticus: *Nightwood* as Woman's Circus Epic'; both in *Silence and Power: A Reevaluation of Djuna Barnes*, ed. Mary Lynn Broe (Carbondale: Southern Illinois University Press, 1991), 81–91, 221–50.

71 Articles rep. in *New York: Djuna Barnes*, ed. Alyce Barry (London: Virago, 1990), 187 cited.

72 Djuna Barnes, *I Could Never be Lonely without a Husband: Interviews*, ed. Douglas Messerli (1985; London: Virago, 1987), 138.

73 Oates, *On Boxing*, 105–6. See Kasia Boddy, 'Watching the Fight: Women Spectators in Boxing Fiction and Film', *American Bodies*, ed. Tim Armstrong (New York: New York University Press, 1996), 204–212.

74 Barnes, *I Could Never be Lonely*, 286.

75 Barnes, *New York World Magazine*, 23 August 1913; rep. in *New York*, 168–73.

76 Djuna Barnes, *Nightwood* (London: Faber & Faber, 1936), 68, 91, 96–8.

77 See Marcus, 'Laughing at Leviticus'.

78 Barnes, *Nightwood* 33, 27–28.

79 *Ibid.*, 116.

5 SEMINAL ECONOMIES

1 Yeats replied: 'I did consult a physician, and he has restored me to my vigour'. *Frank Pearce Sturm: His Life, Letters and Collected Work*, ed. Richard Taylor (University of Illinois Press, 1969), 103, 105.

2 Yeats to Ethel Mannin, 19 December 1935, *Letters of W. B. Yeats*, ed. Allan Wade (London: Hart-Davis, 1954), 845.

3 Richard Ellmann, *W. B. Yeats's Second Puberty* (Washington: Library of Congress, 1985). Rep. in *Four Dubliners* (London: Hamish Hamilton, 1987).

4 Virginia D. Pruitt and Raymond D. Pruitt, 'Yeats and the Steinach

Operation', *Yeats: An Annual of Critical and Theoretical Studies*, 1 (1983), 104–24. Victor Medvei, *A History of Endochrinology* (Lancaster: MTP Press, 1982), describes its effects as 'transient and even auto-suggestive' (404).

5 Samuel Hynes, 'All the Wild Witches: the Women in Yeats's Poems', *Southern Review*, 85 (1977), 580; Elizabeth Cullingford, 'Yeats and Women: Michael Robartes and the Dancer', *Yeats Annual*, 4 (1986), 29–52.

6 Yeats to Ethel Mannin, 4 March 1935, *Letters*, 831.

7 W. B. Yeats, *Essays and Introductions* (London: Macmillan, 1961), 292–93.

8 See James Longenbach, *Stone Cottage: Pound, Yeats, and Modernism* (Oxford University Press, 1988).

9 Pound, 'The New Therapy', *The New Age*, 3.20 (16 March 1922), 260.

10 Ian F. A. Bell, *Critic as Scientist: The Modernist Poetics of Ezra Pound* (London: Methuen, 1981), 214. See also Richard Sieburth, *Instigations: Ezra Pound and Remy de Gourmont* (Cambridge: Harvard University Press, 1978).

11 Ezra Pound, 'Postscript to *The Natural Philosophy of Love* by Rémy de Gourmont' (1921), in *Pavannes and Divagations* (New York: New Directions, 1958), 203–14 (Yeats owned a copy). Olivia Shakespear read Berman's book and wrote of it to Yeats in 1926, praising its 'chemical–mechanical view of the cosmos', 'Olivia Shakespeare: Letters to W. B. Yeats', ed. John Harwood, *Yeats Annual*, 6 (1988), 67.

12 Pound to John Quinn, 10 March 1916, *Selected Letters of Ezra Pound to John Quinn 1915–1920*, ed. Timothy Materer (Durham: Duke University Press, 1991), 66.

13 Wayne Koestlenbaum, *Double Talk: The Erotics of Male Literary Collaboration* (New York: Routledge, 1989), 120–1.

14 Cf. Christine Battersby, *Gender and Genius* (London: Women's Press, 1989).

15 William Carlos Williams, *I Wanted to Write a Poem* (1958; London: Cape, 1967), 40; 'Walter, Salts, Fats, etc.', *Imaginations*, ed. Webster Schott (London: MacGibbon & Kee, 1970), 359.

16 Janet Oppenheim, *'Shattered Nerves': Doctors, Patients, and Depression in Victorian England* (New York: Oxford University Press, 1991), uses Benson as a running example.

17 Ezra Pound, *The Cantos* (London: Faber & Faber, 1981), 534.

18 *The Variorum Edition of the Poems of W.B Yeats*, ed. Peter Allt and Russell K. Alspach (New York: Macmillan, 1966), 469. Subsequently cited in text as *VP*.

19 Automatic script, 28 May 1919, *Yeats's Vision Papers*, general ed. George Mills Harper, 3 vols. (London: Macmillan, 1992), III, 293.

20 See George Mills Harper, *The Making of Yeats's A Vision: A Study of the Automatic Script*, 2 vols. (Carbondale: Southern Illinois University Press, 1987), I, ch. 1, esp. 1–27. On such silent co-authorship, see Ruth Perry and Martine Watson Brownley, eds., *Mothering the Mind: Twelve Studies of Writers and their Silent Partners* (New York: Holmes and Meier, 1984).

21 Yeats, *Vision Papers*, III, 87.

22 Harper, *The Making of Yeats's A Vision*, 278 n.7 (the passage from Underwood is cited by Myers). The shift towards masculine manipulation of mediums is described by Alex Owen, *The Darkened Room: Women, Power and Spiritualism in Late Victorian England* (London: Virago, 1989); the replacement of the female medium with a discursive *technology* by Friedrich A. Kittler, *Discourse Networks 1800/1900*, trans. Michael Metteer (Stanford University Press, 1990).

23 Yeats, *Essays and Introductions*, 95; *Ah, Sweet Dancer. W. B. Yeats, Margot Ruddock. A Correspondence*, ed. Roger McHugh (London: Macmillan, 1970), 21; W. B. Yeats, *Autobiographies* (London: Macmillan, 1955), 94.

24 See Joseph M. Hassett, *Yeats and the Poetics of Hate* (Dublin: Gill & Macmillan, 1986), ch. 9; Phillip L. Marcus, 'Incarnation in Middle Yeats', *Yeats Annual*, 1 (1982), 68–81.

25 Harper, *The Making of Yeats's A Vision*, 228ff; *Yeats's Vision Papers*, III, 226. We can project that story back to Yeats's first consultation of Elizabeth Radcliffe, about the 'phantom' pregnancy of his mistress Mabel Dickinson.

26 *Uncollected Prose by W. B. Yeats*, vol. II, ed. John P. Frayne and Colton Johnson (London: Macmillan, 1975), 462–3.

27 Taylor quoted by Stan Smith, 'Porphyry's Cup: Yeats, Forgetfulness, and the Narrative Order', *Yeats Annual*, 5 (1987), 29–30.

28 'Parnell's Funeral' is one poem desiring an acknowledgment of history, paternity, and succession: 'Had Cosgrave eaten Parnell's heart, the land's / Imagination had been satisfied' (*VP* 543).

29 Yeats, *Autobiographies*, 182.

30 Yeats to Ethel Mannin, 4 March 1935, *Letters*, 831–2.

31 Cf. *The Variorum Edition of the Plays of W. B. Yeats*, ed. Russell K. Alspach (London: Macmillan, 1966), 1003, and *Essays and Introductions*, 51, where it is suggested that the phrase has its origins in folklore.

32 Yeats to Dorothy Wellesley, 21 December 1935, *Letters*, 846; 11 August 1935, *Letters on Poetry from W. B. Yeats to Dorothy Wellesley* (Oxford University Press, 1964), 19.

33 Sigmund Freud, 'On Narcissism: An Introduction' (1914), *Standard Edition*, XIV.

34 Denis E. Smith and F. A. C. Wilson, 'The Source of Yeats's "What Magic Drum?"' *Papers on Language and Literature*, 9 (1973), 197–201.

35 See Medvei, *History of Endocrinology*, 291–2, 302, 405; Eric J. Trimmer, *Rejuvenation: The History of an Idea* (London: Robert Hale, 1967), ch. 9. Ironically, a recent report speculates that the HIV virus may have entered human populations from African monkeys, not via hunting, the bestiality hinted at in popular accounts, or polio serum, but via Voronoff's operations – a story which links modernist experimentation and postmodern disease.

36 George Drinka, *The Birth of Neurosis: Myth, Malady, and the Victorians* (New York: Simon, 1984), 228.

37 Hillel Schwartz, *Never Satisfied: A Cultural History of Diets, Fantasies, and Fat* (New York: Free Press, 1986), 139.

38 Anson Rabinobach, *The Human Motor: Energy, Fatigue, and the Origins of Modernity* (New York: Basic Books, 1990), 142–5.

39 Handbill folded into a 1932 edition of Hancock's advertising pamplet *The Shadow of the Stork*, placed in turn in a 1930 edition of Marie Stopes's *Married Love*, author's collection.

40 Grace Stuart, *Gland Treatment for Renewal or Rejuvenation of the Body Through Applied New Thought* (London: L. N. Fowler, 1925). Stuart criticizes Steinach's treatment of women.

41 Freud's operation took place on 17 November 1923, after surgery for the cancer in his palate; he reported no effect. Ernst Jones, *The Life and Work of Sigmund Freud*, III (London: Hogarth Press, 1957), 104. Artaud had injections of 'testicular liquid'.

42 See Jeffrey Weeks, *Sex, Politics and Society: The Regulation of Sexuality Since 1800* (London: Longman, 1981); James D. Steakley, *The Homosexual Emancipation Movement in Germany* (New York: Arno Press, 1975).

43 Ethel Mannin, *Young in the Twenties: A Chapter of Autobiography* (London: Hutchinson, 1971), 67.

44 Yeats to Ethel Mannin, 19 December 1935, *Letters*, 845.

45 Robert Huxter, *Reg and Ethel: Reginald Reynolds, his Life and Work and his Marriage to Ethel Mannin* (York: Sessions Book Trust, 1992), 100.

46 Gregorio Marañon, *The Evolution of Sex and Intersexual Conditions*, trans. Warre B. Wells (London: Allen & Unwin, 1932), 68.

47 Norman Haire, *Rejuvenation: The Work of Steinach, Voronoff, and Others* (London: G. Allen & Unwin, 1924).

48 Peter Schmidt, *The Conquest of Old Age: Methods to Effect Rejuvenation and to Increase Functional Activity*, trans. Eden and Cedar Paul (London: Routledge, 1931), 41, 275, 269. Yeats's letter to Sturge Moore, dated July 10 [1934], is in the Sturge Moore Collection, University of London Library, cat. no. 2/76.

49 Schmidt, *The Conquest of Old Age*, 41.

50 G. J. Barker-Benfield, 'The Spermatic Economy: A Nineteenth-Century View of Sexuality', *Feminist Studies*, 1 (1972), 45–74.

51 Spencer cited in Cynthia Eagle Russett, *Sexual Science: The Victorian Construction of Womanhood* (Cambridge: Harvard University Press, 1989), 118.

52 Retaining such energies via *coitus reservatus* remained popular: Havelock Ellis praised the technique, as does Gerald Heard in *Pain, Sex, and Time* (London: Cassell, 1939): the body is strengthened 'by a mobilization of all the endochrine secretions, roused, released within the body and not squandered without it' (198).

53 The tradition extends to Apollo's account of creation in *The Eumenides*: 'The mother is no parent of that which is called her child, but only nurse of the new-planted seed that grows. The parent is he who mounts.' *The Eumenides*, 658–60, in *Aeschylus I: Oresteia*, trans. Richmond Lattimore, ed. David Grene and Richmond Lattimore (New York: Washington Square Press, 1967), 172. D. L. Macdonald, 'The Return of the Dead in "Large Red Man Reading"', *Wallace Stevens Journal*, 12 (1988), 30, quotes this passage and suggests that it reflects a tradition in which 'all writers (psukhai, patrons of seed) are masculine and all readers . . . are feminine'.

54 Thomas Laqueur, *Making Sex: Body and Gender from the Greeks to Freud* (Cambridge: Harvard University Press, 1990) 147, 187.

55 *The Letters of John Addington Symonds*, ed. Herbert M. Schuller and Robert L. Peters (1969), III, 798, 811. This letter is commented on by Sedgwick, *Between Men, English Literature and Male Homosexual Desire* (New York: Columbia University Press, 1985), 211; Koestlenbaum, *Double Talk*, 47. Marie Stopes boldly suggested that *female* orgasm also produces health-enhancing secretions, *Married Love*, 18th edn (London: G. P. Putnam, 1926), 86.

56 Schmidt, *The Conquest of Old Age*, 40.

57 Harvey Green, *Fit for America: Health, Fitness, Sport and American Society* (Baltimore: Johns Hopkins University Press, 1986), 266, 349 n19.

58 Gloria C. Kline, *The Last Courtly Lover: Yeats and the Idea of Woman* (Ann Arbor: UMI Research Press, 1983), 125, argues that Yeats's late relationships recapitulated those with Lady Gregory and Maud Gonne. But, clearly, the balance of power had shifted.

59 Kathleen Woodward, 'The Mirror Stage of Old Age', in *Language, Memory, Desire: Ageing – Literature – Psychoanalysis*, ed. Kathleen Woodward and Murray M. Schwartz (Bloomington: Indiana University Press, 1986), 97–113.

60 Yeats to Dorothy Wellesley, 8 November 1936, *Letters*, 866. The first letter subsequently cited is to Olivia Shakespear, 10 April 1936, *Letters*, 852; the others to Dorothy Wellesley, *Letters on Poetry*, 83, 99, 108, 111.

61 *Variorum Plays,* 779. See A. Norman Jeffares, *A New Commentary on the Poems of W. B. Yeats* (London: Macmillan, 1984), 467–68, for Lady Gregory's translation.

62 J. Laplanche and J.-B. Pontalis, *The Language of Psychoanalysis,* trans. Donald Nicholson-Smith (London: Karnac, 1988), 255. This is not to deny Yeats's apparent sympathies for lesbian sexuality. On hetero-sexuality's need to posit homosexuality as narcissistic, see Michael Warner, 'Homo-Narcissism; or, Heterosexuality', in *Engendering Men: The Question of Male Feminist Criticism,* ed. Boon and Cadden (New York: Routledge, 1990), 190–206.

63 Yeats to Olivia Shakespear, 24 July 1934, *Letters,* 824.

64 Peter Nicholls, 'Apes and Familiars', *Textual Practice,* 6.3 (1992), 426.

65 2 July, 1936, *Letters on Poetry,* 71.

66 21 July, 1936; *Letters on Poetry,* 82.

67 The cover of *The Secret Rose* (London: Lawrence and Bullen, 1897), shows two entwined rose trees, a complex design which in part alludes to the story of 'Costello the Proud, of Oona the daughter of Dermott and of the Bitter Tongue'. See *The Secret Rose, Stories by W. B. Yeats: A Variorum Edition,* ed. Phillip L. Marcus, Warwick Gould, and Michael J. Sidnell (Ithaca: Cornell University Press, 1981), 61–81. Cf. also 'Baile and Aillinn', and *VP* 554.

68 Patricia Parker, 'Gender Ideology, Gender Change: The Case of Marie Germain', *Critical Inquiry,* 19 (1993), 345; A. M. Garab, 'Fabulous Artifice: Yeats's "Three Bushes" Sequence', *Criticism,* 7 (1965), 238.

69 July, 1936; *Letters on Poetry,* 73.

70 For an example see Warwick Gould, '"Portrayed Before His Eyes": An Abandoned Late Poem', *Yeats Annual,* 6 (1988), 214–21.

71 See Terence Brown, *Ireland: A Social and Cultural History, 1922–79* (London: Fontana, 1981), 124.

72 Phyllis Grosskurth, *Havelock Ellis: A Biography* (New York University Press, 1985), 377–8; Annette Kuhn, *Cinema, Censorship and Sexuality, 1909–1925* (London: Routledge 1988), 77–96.

73 David Bradshaw, 'The Eugenics Movement in the 1930s and the Emergence of *On the Boiler*', *Yeats Annual,* 9 (1992), 189–215.

74 Even Elizabeth Cullingford's lucid discussion of these songs in *Yeats, Ireland, and Facism* (London: Macmillan, 1981), ch. 11. shows some reluctance to deal with what is, paradigmatically, Facist thought.

75 Jeffares, *A New Commentary,* 499–500.

76 Klaus Theweleit, *Male Fantasies I: Women, Floods, Bodies, History,* trans, Stephen Conway, Erica Carter, and Chris Turner (Oxford: Polity Press, 1985).

77 W. B. Yeats, *On the Boiler* (Dublin: Cuala Press, 1939), 19.

78 Medvei, *A History of Endochrinology,* 801.

79 Magnus Hirshfeld, *Racism,* trans. and ed. Eden and Cedar Paul (London: Gollancz, 1938), 305.

6 MAKING A WOMAN

1 Patrice Petro, *Joyless Streets: Women and Melodramatic Representation in Weimar Germany* (Princeton University Press, 1989), 114.

2 See Billie Melman, *Women and the Popular Imagination in the Twenties: Flappers and Nymphs* (London: Macmillan, 1988).

3 Peter Brooks, *Body Work: Objects of Desire in Modern Narrative* (Cambridge, MA: Harvard University Press, 1993), 223.

4 See e.g. Regenia Gagnier, *Idylls of the Marketplace: Oscar Wilde and the Victorian Public* (Aldershot: Scolar Press, 1987); Eve Kosofsky Sedgwick, *Epistemology of the Closet* (Berkeley: University of California Press, 1990); Ed Cohen, *Talk on the Wilde Side: Toward a Genealogy of a Discourse on Male Sexualities* (New York: Routledge, 1993); Amy Koritz, 'Salomé: Exotic Woman and the Transcendent Dance', in *Gender and Discourse in Victorian Literature and Art,* ed. Anthony H. Harrison and Beverley Taylor (DeKalb: Northern Illinois University Press, 1992), 251–73. Gagnier and Koritz both argue that Salomé must be seen as more than simply a *femme fatale;* she exemplifies the autonomy of female sexuality, and the political use of that sexuality against the 'mouthpiece of God'.

5 See Richard Dellamora: Traversing the Feminine in Oscar Wilde's Salomé', in *Victorian Sages and Cultural Discourse,* ed. Thais E. Morgan (New Brunswick: Rutgers University Press, 1990), 246–64.

6 Rita Felski, 'The Counterdiscourse of the Feminine in Three Texts by Wilde, Huysmans, and Sacher-Masoch', *PMLA* 106 (1991), 1098.

7 Cf. Elizabeth Bronfen, *Over Her Dead Body: Death, Femininity and the Aesthetic* (Manchester University Press, 1992). On Wilde's treatment of the executed man in terms of homosexual culture, see Kevin R. Kopleston, 'Wilde's Love-Deaths', *The Yale Journal of Criticism,* 5.3 (1992), 32–60.

8 As Gagnier points out, the play also parodies Christian discourse by incorporating it into the language of Salomé's triumphant desire (*Idylls,* 168–9).

9 Gagnier, *Idylls,* 168.

10 Robert Sherard, *The Real Oscar Wilde* (London: T. Werner Laurie, 1917), 328–32.

11 Vance Thompson, *The Two Deaths of Oscar Wilde* (San Francisco: The Leaflet, 1930).

12 Neil Bartlett, *Who Was that Man? A Present for Mr Oscar Wilde* (London: Serpent's Tail, 1988), 28.

13 Gagnier, *Idylls,* 153–4, 199–204; Michael Kettle, *Salomé's Last Veil: The Libel Case of the Century* (London: Hart-Davis MacGibbon, 1977).

14 Hester Travers Smith, *Psychic Messages from Oscar Wilde*, preface by Sir William Barrett (London: T. Werner Laurie, 1924), 5.

15 Smith, *Psychic Messages*, 9.

16 Yeats was afraid that he could not finish his revisions to *A Vision* and Thomas of Dorlowicz returned via Dolly to reassure him: 'You have time'. Yeats to Olivia Shakespear, 9 July 1928, *The Letters of W. B. Yeats*, ed. Allan Wade (London: Hart-Davis, 1954), 744.

17 Smith, *Psychic Messages*, 7, 13, 10.

18 *The Collected Letters of W. B. Yeats*, vol. 1, ed. John Kelly (Oxford: Clarendon, 1986), 375n.

19 *The Ghost Epigrams of Oscar Wilde, as taken down through Automatic Writing by Lazar* (New York: Covici Friede, 1928).

20 On medical hostility to mediumship and accusations of hysteria, see Janet Oppenheim, *The Other World: Spiritualism and Psychical Research in England, 1850–1914* (New York: Cambridge University Press, 1985); Judith R. Walkowitz, *City of Dreadful Delight: Narratives of Sexual Danger in Late-Victorian London* (University of Chicago Press, 1992), 171ff.

21 Koestenbaum, *Double Talk*, 176. As Leon Surette points out, Pound cut a good deal of the draft's occult material, derived from Jessie Weston. *The Birth of Modernism: Ezra Pound, T. S. Eliot, W. B. Yeats, and the Occult* (Montreal: McGill Queen's University Press, 1993), 236, 240, 262ff.

22 T. S. Eliot, *Four Quartets* (1944; London: Faber & Faber, 1959), 43.

23 Ethel Mannin, *Privileged Spectator* (London: Jarrolds, 1939), 39. See her description of 'the dark little hotel' in her short story 'Maiden Lady' (in *Dryad*). In 1963, the hotel was re-developed, with a night in Wilde's rooms an attraction.

24 *Man into Woman* was first published in Danish as *Fra Mand til Kvinde* (Copenhagen: Hage & Clausen, 1931), and translated into German with a title which suggests the origins of the story in masculine fantasy: *Ein mensch wechselt sein geschlecht* (a man changes his sex). The English edition was entitled *Man into Woman: An Authentic Record of a Change of Sex. The true story of the miraculous transformation of the Danish painter Einar Wegener – Andreas Sparre* (London: Jarrolds, 1931); the American edition was published by E. P. Dutton the same year. It was republished in the USA for the Popular Library in 1953 (cashing in on the Jorgensen case). Sandy Stone briefly discusses the book's generic status in 'The *Empire* Strikes Back: A Posttranssexual Manifesto', in *Body Guards: The Cultural Politics of Gender Ambiguity*, ed. Julian Epstein and Kristina Straub (New York: Routledge, 1991), 280–304.

25 Jan Morris, *Conundrum* (London: Coronet, 1975), 48; Marjorie Garber, *Vested Interests: Cross-Dressing and Cultural Anxiety* (New York: Routlege, 1992), 112 (on Richards).

26 Judith Shapiro comments that with the Jorgensen case 'Transsexualism first captured the popular imagination', 'Transsexualism: Reflections on the Persistence of Gender and the Mutability of Sex', *Body Guards*, 249. Popular perceptions are similar: see e.g. Sally Vincent, 'Lost Boys', *The Guardian Weekend*, 16 October 1993, 4–8, 37. Raymond's critique of transsexual surgery, *The Transsexual Empire* (London: Virago, 1980), sees it as symptomatic of masculine envy and gender-appropriation. While she has been attacked both by libertarians defending the individual's right to body-manipulation and by feminist critics working from less essentialist standpoints, some *institutional* aspects of the Lili Elbe case fit her critique well.

27 Norman Haire, *An Encyclopedia of Sexual Knowledge* (London: Encyclopedia Press, 1952), 402–4. See also the account of the cases of 'Dora R.' and 'Toni E.' in F. Abraham, 'Genitalumwandlung an zwei männlichen Transvestiten', *Zeitschrift für Sexualwissenschaft*, 18 (1931), 223–6.

28 I am grateful to Rainer Herrn of the Magnus Hirschfeld Gesellschaft for this information, and for confirmation that the book's 'Dr. Hardenfeld' – who completes the psychological appraisal of Andreas – is almost certainly Hirschfeld. See Herrn's 'Vom Geschlechtsverwandlungswahn zur Geschlechtsumwandlung', *Pro Familia Magazin*, February 1995, 14–18. The first operation was castration. A Berlin plastic surgeon, Professor Gohrbandt (the book's 'Gebhard'), was involved in early operations, though the identity of the 'Professor Kreutz' who masterminds the subsequent operations at the Women's Clinic in Dresden (removal of penis, implantation of ovarian tissue, formation of a vagina) is unclear.

29 Charlotte Wolff, *Magnus Hirschfeld: A Portrait of a Pioneer in Sexology* (London: Quartet, 1986); James D. Steakley, *The Homosexual Emancipation Movement in Germany* (New York: Arno Press, 1975). Steinach was invited to join the Institute when it was set up in 1919.

30 Andrew Field, *The Formidable Miss Barnes: A Biography of Djuna Barnes* (London: Secker & Warburg, 1983), 117; Robert McAlmon and Kay Boyle, *Being Geniuses Together, 1920–1930*, rev. edn (London: Hogarth Press, 1984), 95–8.

31 Christopher Isherwood, *Christopher and his Kind*. I am grateful to Norman Page for allowing me to see the chapter on Hirschfeld in his unpublished study of Isherwood and Auden's Berlin years.

32 See Eugen Steinach and Josef Loebel, *Sex and Life: Forty Years of Biological and Medical Experiments* (London: Faber & Faber, 1940).

33 F. A. E. Crew, 'Abnormal Sexuality in Animals. III. Sex Reversal', *Quarterly Review of Biology*, 2 (1927), 427–41.

34 See Freud's 1920 paper 'The Psychogenesis of a Case of Female Homosexuality', where Steinach is placed at the limits of psychoanalytic knowledge, where 'it leaves the rest to biological research'

(*Standard Edition*, XVIII, 171–2); and the long footnote on Steinach in the first of the 'Three Essays on the Theory of Sexuality', added 1920, where Freud follows Fleiss in believing that the experiments of Steinach, Lipschütz, and others failed to invalidate the theory of 'the general bisexual disposition of the higher animals'.

35 The use of slides to show a blurring of gender-distinctions parodies Galton's photographic 'composites', which aimed to differentiate racial and physical 'types': see Allan Sekula, 'The Body and the Archive', *October*, 39 (1987), 3–64.

36 Steakley's taxonomy has been mapped onto contemporary and sub-sequent debates in the Anglo-American context: see Sedgwick, *Epistemology*, 88–90; Elaine Showalter, *Sexual Anarchy: Gender and Culture at the 'Fin de Siècle'* (London: Bloomsbury, 1981), 172–4.

37 Wolff, *Magnus Hirschfeld*, 148–51.

38 See Thewleit, *Male Fantasies*; and, on androgyny and the post-1932 return to 'proper' gender-roles, Petro, *Joyless Streets*, chs. 2, 3. Also useful is Linda Mizejewski's *Divine Decadence: Fascism, Female Spectacle, and the Making of Sally Bowles* (Princeton University Press, 1992).

39 Atina Grossman, 'The New Woman and the Rationalization of Sexuality in Weimar Germany', in *Powers of Desire: The Politics of Sexuality*, ed. Ann Snitow, Christine Stansell, and Sharon Thompson (New York: Monthly Review Press, 1983).

40 Petro, *Joyless Streets*, 121.

41 Gregorio Marañon, *The Evolution of Sex and Intersexual Conditions*, trans. Warre B. Wells (London: Allen & Unwin, 1932), 300, 329.

42 Cf. Angela Carter's *The Passion of New Eve* (1977), with its shift from the romantic transvestitism of Tristessa to Evelyn/Eve's violently imposed transsexual surgery.

43 For convenience, I refer to the text throughout as Wegener's, though it is sometimes compiled from his journals and letters, and sometimes ventriloquized in such a way that the source is unclear.

44 Garber, *Vested Interests*, 100.

45 Rachel Bowlby, 'Promoting Dorian Gray', *OLR*, 9 (1987), 147–62; rep. in *Shopping with Freud* (London: Routledge, 1993), 7–24.

46 *Dansk Biografisk Leksikon* (Copenhagen: Glydendal, 1984), xv, 355–6. There is no entry on Einar Wegener.

47 G. B., *The Studio* 89 (1925), 350.

48 Ernst Renan, *The Poetry of the Celtic Races and Other Studies* (1896; London: Kennikat Press, 1970), 72.

49 Thomas Laqueur, *Making Sex: Body and Gender from the Greeks to Freud* (Cambridge, MA: Harvard University Press, 1990), 37.

50 Many of these somatic effects seem symbolic: adult castration does not change the voice.

51 Suzanne J. Kessler, 'The Medical Construction of Gender: Case Management of Intersexual Infants', *Signs*, 16 (1990), 3–26.

52 Kreutz's (woman) assistant comments: 'Your case is a novelty for us

here. And what adds to the interest which we take in you for scientific reasons is the fact that you are an artist, an intellectual, and therefore able to analyse your own feelings, your own emotional life. You will experience the unprecedented and incredible thing: first to have lived and felt as a man, and then to live and feel as a woman' (121).

53 On Freud's position, see Robert J. Stoller, *The Transsexual Experiment* (London: Hogarth Press, 1975).

54 In a letter of 13 January 1914, Dorothy Wellesley commented to Pound that she was reading Flaubert's *Salammbo*, noting the story's potential: 'it is an unholy Stodge, I do think – but I suppose quite fairly Imagiste?' *Ezra Pound and Dorothy Shakespear: Their Letters 1909–1914*, ed. Omar Pound and A. Walton Litz (London: Faber & Faber, 1984), 300. On Pound's revision of Laforgue, see Scott Hamilton, *Ezra Pound and the Symbolist Inheritance* (Princeton University Press, 1992), 107–11.

55 Ezra Pound, 'Our Tetrarchal Précieuse', *Pavannes and Divagations* (London: Peter Owen, 1960), 189–200 (199 cited).

56 *The Variorum Edition of the Plays of W. B. Yeats*, ed. Russell K. Alspach (London: Macmillan, 1966), 1311.

57 To Olivia Shakespear, 7 August 1934, *Letters of W. B. Yeats*, ed. Allan Wade (London: Hart-Davis, 1954), 827. Cf. Yeats's preface of 30 May 1935, *Variorum Plays*, 1311.

58 Garber, *Vested Interests*, 342.

59 Yeats, *A Full Moon in March*, lines 192–7, *The King of the Great Clock Tower*, lines 193–8; *Variorum Plays*, 989, 1006.

60 Genevieve Brennan, '"The Binding of the Hair" and Yeats's Reading of Eugene O'Curry', *Yeats Annual*, 5 (1987), 220; F. A. C. Wilson, *W. B. Yeats and Tradition* (London: Methuen, 1968), 70.

61 Cited in Showalter, *Sexual Anarchy*, 182.

62 Helene Cixous, 'Castration or Decapitation?', trans. Annette Kuhn, *Signs*, 7 (1981), 50.

63 The term 'organ-inferiority' (*minderwertigkeit*) is Adler's, and Freud was uncomfortable with it. Nevertheless, it fits the stress on power-relations here.

64 See Teresa Brennan, *The Interpretation of the Flesh: Freud and Femininity* (New York: Routledge, 1992), 47.

65 Sigmund Freud, 'Some Psychical Consequences of the Anatomical Distinctions between the Sexes' (1925), *Standard Edition*, XIX, 252.

66 Juliet Mitchell comments that 'For Freud the absence of the penis in women is significant only in that it makes meaningful the father's prohibition of incestuous desires.' *Feminine Sexuality: Jacques Lacan and the école freudienne*, ed. Juliet Mitchell and Jacqueline Rose (New York: Pantheon Books, 1982), 17.

67 In the article cited earlier, Dellamora criticizes Richard Ellmann's reading of the play for bolstering a Freudian reading akin to that

here, and thus excluding the feminine perspective embodied in *Salomé* ('Traversing the Feminine', 250–1). My point, however, is simply that the play contains a *structure* of masculine self-assertion like Freud's – even if that structure is troubled by other possibilities. It thus explores the masculine fantasy of difference which Dellamora sees Ellmann as attempting to stabilize.

68 *A Full Moon in March*, lines 154–61, *Variorum Plays*, 987.

69 See Peter Nicholls, 'Violence, Recognition, and Some Versions of Modernism', *Parataxis*, 4 (1993), 19–35.

70 Butler borrows the term from Roy Schafer; Judith Butler, *Gender Trouble: Feminism and the Subversion of Identity* (New York: Routledge, 1990), 69–70.

71 Butler, *Gender Trouble*, 114.

72 Anne Balsamo, 'On the Cutting Edge: Cosmetic Surgery and the Technological Production of the Gendered Body', *Camera Obscura*, 28 (1992), 206–37.

73 Cf. Peter Wollen's discussion of batchelor machines, *Raiding the Icebox: Reflections on Twentieth-Century Culture* (London: Verso, 1993), 44–7.

7 DISTRACTED WRITING

1 William Barrett, *On the Threshold of the Unseen* (London: Kegan Paul, 1920). F. W. Myers referred to techniques like hypnotism as an 'expansion of human faculty'. Myers, *Human Personality: Its Survival of Bodily Death*, 2 vols. (London: Longmans, Green, 1903), I, 221.

2 For a deconstruction of that tradition see Jonathan Goldberg, *Writing Matters: From the Hands of the English Renaissance* (Stanford University Press, 1990).

3 W. B. Yeats, 'The Manuscript of "Leo Africanus"', ed. Steve L. Adams and George Mills Harper, *Yeats Annual*, 1 (1982), 3–47 (29 cited).

4 Ezra Pound, 'Affirmations II. Vorticism', *New Age*, 14 January 1915, 278.

5 K. P. S. Jochum, 'Yeats's Vision Papers and the Problem of Automatic Writing: A Review Essay', *English Literature in Transition*, 36 (1993), 323–36 (325 cited).

6 See *William James on Psychical Research*, ed. Gardner Murphy & Robert Ballou (New York: Viking, 1960), 29ff; Janet Oppenheim, *The Other World: Spiritualism and Psychical Research in England, 1850–1914* (Cambridge University Press, 1985); Alex Owen, *The Darkened Room: Women, Power and Spiritualism in Late Victorian England* (London: Virago, 1989).

7 Frederic W. H. Myers, 'Automatic Writing', *Proceedings of the Society for Psychical Research*, 3 (1885), 23–63; 'Multiple Personality', *The Nineteenth Century*, 20 (1886), 648–66.

8 Anne Harrington, *Medicine, Mind, and the Double Brain: A Study in*

Nineteenth Century Thought (Princeton University Press, 1987). As she points out, more holistic psychologies succeeded until the debate was revived in the 1960s. See also Robert M. Young, *Mind, Brain and Adaptation in the Nineteenth Century: Cerebral Localization and its Biological Context from Gall to Ferrier* (Oxford: Clarendon, 1970).

9 Henri F. Ellenberger, *The Discovery of the Unconscious: The History and Evolution of Dynamic Psychiatry* (New York: Basic Books, 1970), 126. The phenomenon of split or multiple personalities is more complex: see Ian Hacking, *Rewriting the Soul: Multiple Personality and the Sciences of Memory* (Princeton University Press, 1995). Mikkel Borch-Jacobsen's reflections on recent enthusiasms for Multiple Personality Disorder are also relevant to what follows here, focusing attention on the pragmatics which elicits such diagnoses, and depicting the self, disconnected from the reflexiveness of the *cogito*, as a switching-device. 'Who's Who? Introducing Multiple Personality', in *Supposing the Subject*, ed. Joan Copjec (London: Verso, 1994), 45–63.

10 Henry Adams, *The Education of Henry Adams*, ed. Earnest Samuels (1907; Boston: Houghton Mifflin, 1973), 433.

11 Alfred Binet, *On Double Consciousness* (Chicago: Open Court, 1890), 40, 52, 55, 77, 81; cf. Pierre Janet's *L'Automatisime psychologique* (1889).

12 Remy de Gourmont, *Decadence and Other Essays on the Culture of Ideas*, trans. W. A. Bradley (New York: Harcourt, Brace, 1921), 189–90.

13 *Ibid.*, 200.

14 Stevenson to Myers, 14 July 1892, Upoho, Samoa; in Myers, *Human Personality*, ii, 301–3.

15 Frederic W. H. Myers, *Science and the Future Life* (London: Macmillan, 1893), 23.

16 Myers, *Human Personality*, ii, 117–18.

17 Frederic W. H. Myers, 'Automatic Writing – II', *Proceedings of the Society for Psychical Research*, 3 (1885), 227–8.

18 Robert Louis Stevenson, *The Strange Case of Dr. Jekyll and Mr. Hyde*, ed. Jenni Calder (1886; London: Penguin, 1979), 86, 90. Subsequent references in text.

19 W. T. Stead, 'The Man of Dreams', *Borderland*, 2 (1895), 20; cf. 'Two Doubles I Have Seen', *Borderland*, 3 (1896), 25. Stead's attitude to the double is confused: in some cases he suggests that it represents 'alternating personality' (two entities in one body); in others it is a separate embodied being.

20 Stead, 'The Man of Dreams', 18–19. *Borderland* often foregrounds the hand: there is a graphological analysis of a Mark Twain letter, and, elsewhere, a picture of his physical hand with an analysis of its lines, offering both indexical and iconic clues.

21 Friedrich A. Kittler, *Discourse Networks 1800/1900*, trans. Michael Metteer (Stanford University Press, 1990), 223.

22 Louis Aragon, *Treatise on Style* (1928), trans. Alyson Waters (Lincoln: University of Nebraska Press, 1991), 18–19.

23 Paul Balan, ed., *Attention: An Enduring Problem in Psychology* (New York: D. Van Nostrad, 1966).

24 Jonathan Crary, 'Unbinding Vision', *October*, 68 (1994), 21–44.

25 William James, *The Principles of Psychology*, 2 vols. (London: Macmillan, 1910), I, 404. For debates on the conceptualization of attention, see e.g. W. B. Pillsbury, *Attention* (New York: Macmillan, 1908), and Edward B. Tichner's response in *Lectures on the Elementary Psychology of Feeling and Attention* (New York: Macmillan, 1908), 171–206.

26 L. R. Geissler, 'The Measurement of Attention', *American Journal of Psychology*, 20 (1909), 473–529. For a synoptic discussion of the term 'distraction', see John E. Evans, 'The Effect of Distraction on Reaction Time', *Archives of Psychology*, 37 (1916), 1–106. On 'rhythmicisation', see E. Neil McQueen, *The Distribution of Attention* (Cambridge University Press, 1917).

27 Oppenheim, *The Other World*, 77.

28 Myers, *Human Personality*, I, 217–18.

29 Sigmund Freud, *Jokes and their Relation to the Unconscious* (1905), *Standard Edition*, 8. Freud discusses the attention/distraction coupling elsewhere, notably in *The Psychopathology of Everyday Life* (1901), where his consideration of attention and slips of the tongue or pen is indebted to Wundt.

30 J. Laplanche and J.-B. Pontalis, *The Language of Psycho-Analysis*, trans. Donald Nicholson-Smith (London: Karnac Books, 1988), 44.

31 Crary, 'Unbinding Vision', 22, 32.

32 Yeats, 'Leo Africanus', 13, 24–27.

33 See *Yeats's Vision Papers*, general editor George Mills Harper, 3 vols. (London: Macmillan, 1992), II, 35ff (sessions for 31 August 1918 and subsequent weeks).

34 Leon M. Solomons and Gertrude Stein, 'Studies from the Psychological Laboratory of Harvard University. II. Normal Motor Automatism', *Psychological Review*, 3 (1896), 492–512; Gertrude Stein, 'Cultivated Motor Automatism; A Study of Character in its Relation to Attention', *Psychological Review*, 5 (1898), 295–306.

35 B. F. Skinner, 'Has Gertrude Stein a Secret?' *Atlantic Monthly*, January 1934, 50–7.

36 Sherwood Anderson, 'Gertrude Stein', *American Spectator*, 2 (April 1934), 3; rep. in *Sherwood Anderson/Gertrude Stein, Correspondence and Personal Essays*, ed. Ray Lewis White (Chapel Hill: University of North Carolina Press, 1972), 80–4. Many follow Anderson in condemning Skinner's thesis: e.g. Elizabeth Sprigge dismisses it as 'a complete error' in her introduction to Gertrude Stein, *Look at Me Now and Here I Am: Writing and Lectures 1909–45*, ed. Patricia Meyerowitz (London: Penguin Books, 1971), 15. More positive

comments are provided (briefly) by Randa Dubrick, *The Structure of Obscurity: Gertrude Stein, Language, Cubism* (Urbana: University of Illinois Press, 1984), 105–6; Wendy Steiner, *Exact Resemblance to Exact Resemblance: The Literary Portraiture of Gertrude Stein* (New Haven: Yale University Press, 1980), 48–9; and by Jayne Walker, *The Making of a Modernist: Gertrude Stein from 'Three Lives' to 'Tender Buttons'* (Amhurst: University of Massachusetts Press, 1984). The most sympathetic treatment of the controversy, connecting Stein to the mechanistic biology of Jacques Loeb, is that of medical essayist Gerald Weissman, 'Gertrude Stein on the Beach', *The Doctor with Two Heads and Other Essays* (New York: Vintage, 1991), 80–97.

37 See e.g. Conrad Aiken, 'We Ask for Bread', *New Republic*, 78 (4 April 1934), 219, rep. in *A Reviewer's ABC: Collected Criticism of Conrad Aiken*, ed. Rufus A. Blanshard (London: W. H. Allen, 1961), 364–7. Like Skinner, Aiken distinguishes between narrative texts like *Melanctha* and 'automatic' writings which he sees as 'aesthetic miscalculation'.

38 Lisa Ruddick, for example, writes that there is 'an idea of long standing about Stein, that she did not believe in the idea of an unconscious. This notion arose partly from her own comments in 1936 to the effect that her work was not produced through unconscious process, or "automatic writing" – comments prompted by an article by B. F. Skinner.' Ruddick cites Stein's reply, in *Everyone's Autobiography*, that writing should be 'exact' and conscious. As we will see, the purpose of Stein's automatic writing experiments was *not* to suggest that the unconscious would write the script, but rather to test the mechanism of automatism in such a way that would suggest that no 'other self' was present. Lisa Ruddick, *Reading Gertrude Stein: Body, Text, Gnosis* (Ithaca: Cornell University Press, 1990), 92.

39 Wilma Koutstaal, 'Skirting the Abyss: A History of Experimental Explorations of Automatic Writing in Psychology', *Journal of the History of the Behavioral Sciences*, 28 (1992), 5–26.

40 Jutta Spillmann and Lothar Spillmann, 'The Rise and Fall of Hugo Münsterberg', *Journal for the History of Behavioral Psychology*, 29 (1993), 330.

41 Other psychologists also doubted the need to hypothesize a secondary personality, for example William McDougal in *Mind*, October 1903 (reflecting on Myers).

42 Stein, 'Cultivated Motor Automatism', 298.

43 Solomons and Stein, 'Normal Motor Automatism', 501–2.

44 Janet Hobhouse, *Everybody Who Was Anybody: A Biography of Gertrude Stein* (London: Weidenfeld & Nicholson, 1975), 70–1.

45 Stein, *Look at Me Now*, 86. Where possible I cite this, currently the most available selection of Stein's writings.

46 Gertrude Stein, *The Geographical History of America or the Relation of Human Nature to the Human Mind*, intro. Thornton Wilder (New York: Random House, 1936), 115.

47 Skinner, 'Has Gertrude Stein a Secret?', 55.

48 See Anson Rabinbach, *The Human Motor: Energy, Fatigue, and the Origins of Modernity* (New York: Basic Books, 1990), 93–4; and, for a discussion of time in relation to bodily technologies, Mary Ann Doane, 'Temporality, Storage, Legibility: Freud, Marey and the Cinema', *Critical Inquiry*, 22 (1996), 313–43.

49 Gertrude Stein, 'How Writing is Written' (1935), in *Previously Uncollected Writings*, Vol. II, ed. Robert Bartlett Haas (Los Angeles: Black Sparrow Press, 1974), 155.

50 Stein, 'Portaits and Repetition', *Look at Me Now*, 108.

51 Gertrude Stein, *Everyone's Autobiography* (1937; London: Virago, 1985), 231.

52 On the taxonomy of Stein's styles, see Marjorie Perloff, *Poetic Licence: Essays on Modernist and Postmodernist Lyric* (Evanston: Northwestern University Press, 1990), 145–60.

53 'Miss Furr and Miss Skeene', *A Stein Reader*, ed. Ulla E. Dydo (Evanston: Northwestern University Press, 1993), 259. Originally pub. in *Geography and Plays* (Boston: Four Seas, 1922).

54 Umbro Appolloni, ed., *Futurist Manifestos*, trans. R. Brain et al. (London: Thames & Hudson, 1973), 98. On Khlebnikov, see Peter Nicholls, *Modernisms: A Literary Guide* (Houndmills: Macmillan, 1995), 126–35. Compare, too, Aragon in his *Traité du Style*: 'I trample syntax because it must be trampled . . . Faulty or defective sentences, misbehaving parts, forgetting what has been said and no foresight of what is to come, lack of agreement, disregarding rules, run-on sentences, inaccurate expressions, steering wheels out of kilter, clauses out of whack, confusion of tenses, figures of speech in which a preposition is replaced by a conjunction without shifting gears' (17).

55 Ruddick, *Reading Gertrude Stein*, 193.

56 William H. Gass, 'Gertrude Stein and the Geography of the Sentence', *The World Within the Word* (Boston: Nonpareil Books, 1979), 63–123.

57 Cf. Harriet Scott Chessman, *The Public is Invited to Dance: Representation, the Body and Dialogue in Gertrude Stein* (Stanford University Press, 1989), 91.

58 Stein, *Look at Me Now*, 21.

59 André Breton, *Manifesto of Surrealism* (1924), in *Manifestos of Surrealism*, trans. Richard Seaver and Helen R. Lane (Ann Arbor: University of Michigan Press, 1972), 12, 19, 33–5, 47. On the intellectual background see Anna Balakian, *André Breton: Magus of Surrealism* (New York: Oxford University Press, 1971).

60 André Breton, *The Magnetic Fields*, trans. David Gascoyne (London: Athlone, 1985), 14–15.
61 André Breton, 'The Automatic Message' (1933), *The Surrealists Look at Art* (Venice, California: Lapis Press, 1990), 140.
62 Breton, *Manifesto of Surrealism*, 29–30.
63 *Ibid.*, 26.
64 Breton, 'The Automatic Message', 142.
65 Aragon cited by David Gascoyne, intro. to Breton, *The Magnetic Fields*, 17; Aragon, *Treatise on Style*, 94.
66 Breton, 'The Automatic Message', 147.
67 Kittler, *Discourse Networks*, 228.
68 In the second Surrealist Manifesto, Breton – for all his dislike of the split personality – advocated detachment ('dédoublement') , splitting the self into *scriptor* and *lector* with the latter exerting an editorial function in order to avoid cliché. This however, can be seen as a pragmatics: the source of the material remains unquestioned. For an account stressing conscious control, see J. H. Matthews, *Surrealism, Insanity and Poetry* (New York: Syracuse University Press, 1982).
69 Michel Foucault, *Death and the Labyrinth: The World of Raymond Roussel*, trans. Charles Ruas, into. John Ashbery (1963; London: Athlone Press, 1987), 38–9.
70 F. T. Martinetti, 'Destruction of Syntax – Imagination without Strings – Words-in-Freedom' (1913), in Umbro Appolloni, ed., *Futurist Manifestos*, trans. R. Brain et al. (London: Thames & Hudson, 1973), 105; Roger Shattuck, *The Innocent Eye: On Modern Literature and the Arts* (1984; New York: Washington Square Press, 1986), 182–205.
71 Rebecca West, *The Strange Necessity: Essays and Reviews* (1928; London: Virago, 1987), 85, 124–7.
72 William Carlos Williams, *I Wanted to Write a Poem* (1958; London: Cape, 1967), 60; 'The Work of Gertrude Stein' and 'Prologue' to *Kora in Hell*, in *Imaginations*, ed. Webster Schott (London: MacGibbon & Kee, 1970), 14, 348.
73 Eliot to Waterlow, 19 December 1921, *The Letters of T. S. Eliot*, vol. I, 1898–1922, ed. Valerie Eliot (London: Harcourt Brace Jovanovich, 1988), 495; T. S. Eliot, *The Use of Poetry and the Use of Criticism: Studies in the Relation of Criticism to Poetry in England* (1933; London: Faber & Faber, 1964), 144–5. Eliot's co-ordinates here are partly those supplied by Brémond and the 'pure poetry' debate, but he also cites A. E. Housman, echoing Nordau and others, on poetry being a 'morbid secretion' produced by poor health.
74 Others using forms of automatic writing include Radcliffe Hall (a psychic researcher); H. D.; David Gascoyne; the creators of the 'Ern Malley' poems in Australia; the Beats; William Burroughs; the artists Jackson Pollock and Cy Twombly; James Merrill, whose *The Changing Light at Andover* recycles table-rapping as camp. On

Pollock, see Rosalind E. Kraus, *The Optical Unconscious* (Cambridge, MA: MIT Press, 1993), 282–308.

75 Skinner, 'Has Gertrude Stein a Secret?', 54.

76 Skinner, citing Stein, 'Has Gertrude Stein a Secret?'.

77 B. F. Skinner, *The Shaping of a Behaviorist* (New York: Knopf, 1979), 253.

78 B. F. Skinner *About Behaviorism* (New York: Knopf, 1974), 17.

79 Stein, 'How Writing is Written', 157.

80 B. F. Skinner, *Particulars of My Life* (London: Jonathan Cape, 1976), 128–9, 202.

81 Skinner, *Particulars*, 216–17.

82 Skinner, *Shaping*, 207.

83 Skinner's wife, Yvonne, seems to have acted as a conduit for the 'other': she had worked for 'a newspaper handwriting expert' and introduced him to Morton Prince's *Dissociation of a Personality*. Marriage itself, he reports, seemed like two personalities in one.

84 Skinner, *Shaping*, 207–8, 224–55, 251–2.

85 In *Everyone's Autobiography*, Stein insists that no automatic writing had been produced at Harvard, and adds that 'writing should be very exact and one must realize what there is inside in one and then in some way it comes into words and the more exactly the words fit the emotion the more beautiful the words'(231–2). This explanation continues the intentionalist line of Stein's thinking of the 1930s, as we will see.

86 Stein, *Everyone's Autobiography*, 230–1.

87 Skinner, 'Has Gertrude Stein a Secret?'; Stein, 'How Writing is Written', 155.

88 Richard Bridgeman, *Gertrude Stein in Pieces* (New York: Oxford University Press, 1970), 135.

89 Gertrude Stein, *Narration* (University of Chicago Press, 1935), 51; cited in *Look at Me Now*, 273. Cf. Aragon in his *Treatise on Style*:

> If the man who holds the pen does not know what he will write, what he is writing, and he discovers as he rereads what he has written, if he feels alien to what has come to life by his hand (whose secrets remain hidden to him), and consequently he thinks he has written any old thing, it would be quite wrong to conclude that what has taken shape here is really just any old thing. It is when you write a letter *because* you have something to say that you are writing any old thing. You give in to your own arbitrariness. But in surrealism all is rigor. Inevitable rigor. The meaning is formed outside of you. (95–6)

90 Marjorie Perloff attempts to link the poem to a new modernist 'moment', arguing that it is closer to Huget's original than Stein scholars admit. '"Barbed-Wire Entanglements": The "New American Poetry" 1930–1932', *Modernism–Modernity*, 2.1 (1995), 145–75.

91 Stein, *Everyone's Autobiography*, 71.

92   Stein approaches Bakhtin here: Shakespeare's sonnets made 'one sound', as against the 'three sounds' of any two words in the play; the 'lively sound' of the plays contrasts with the 'smooth sound' of the sonnets.

93   Gertrude Stein, *Look at Me Now*, 297. Stein makes the same distinction elsewhere: e.g. 'What is English Literature?' (1935) posits 'disconnection' as characteristic of American literature.

94   Stein, *Look at Me*, 300.

95   Janet Hobhouse, Introduction, *Everyone's Autobiography*, xii.

96   On Downey (1875–1932) see Koutstaal, 'Skirting the Abyss', and *In Memoriam June Etta Downey* (Laramie: University of Wyoming, 1934). She varied techniques, combining psychometrics with introspective reports.

97   The 'Downey Will-Temperature Test' was designed to reveal, though motor activity, a typology of the personality. June Etta Downey, 'Muscle-Reading: A Method of Investigating Involuntary Movements and Mental Types', *Psychological Review*, 16 (1909), 257–301; 'Automatic Phenomenon of Muscle-reading', *Journal of Philosophy, Psychology and Scientific Method*, 5 (1908), 650–7; *Graphology and the Psychology of Handwriting* (Baltimore: Warwick and York, 1919); *The Will-Temperature and Its Testing* (Yonkers-on-Hudson: World Book Co., 1923).

98   June Etta Downey, 'Control Processes in Modified Handwriting', *Psychological Review*, 9 (1908), 1–148 (54–5 cited).

99   Downey, 'Control Processes', 102.

100 June E. Downey and John E. Anderson, 'Automatic Writing', *American Journal of Psychology*, 26 (1915), 161–95 (193–5 cited).

101 Edwin E. Slosson and June E. Downey, *Plots and Personalities: A New Method of Testing and Training the Creative Imagination* (New York: Century, 1922), 74–5 (the chapter cited was written by Downey).

102 June E. Downey, 'The Psychology of Figures of Speech', *American Journal of Psychology*, 30 (1919), 103–15.

103 June E. Downey, *Creative Imagination: Studies in the Psychology of Literature* (London: Kegan Paul, Trench, & Trubner, 1929), 60.

104 *Ibid.*, 63–74.

105 *Ibid.*, 192–6.

106 Harrington, *Medicine, Mind*, 142–5; André Breton, *Les vases communicants* (1955; Paris: Gallimard, 1970).

107 Boris Sidis, *The Psychology of Suggestion: A Research into the Subconscious Nature of Man and Society*, intro. William James (New York: D. Appleton, 1898), 161, 268; Boris Sidis and Simon Goodhart, *Multiple Personality: An Experimental Investigation into the Nature of Human Individuality* (New York: D. Appleton, 1905), 364, 268.

108 Sidis, *Multiple Personality*, 296.

109 David P. Kuna, 'The Concept of Suggestion in the Early History of

Advertising Psychology', *Journal of the History of the Behavioral Sciences*, 12 (1976), 347–53.

110 Sidis and Goodhart, *Multiple Personality*, 328.

111 Yeats, *Vision Papers*, III, 229.

112 Sigfied Kracauer, 'Cult of Distraction: On Berlin's Picture Palaces', *The Mass Ornament*, trans. Thomas Y. Levin (Cambridge, MA: Harvard University Press, 1995), 326.

113 Kracauer in *The Street*, 3 February 1924; cited in Miriam Hansen, 'Decentric Perspectives: Kracauer's Early Writings on Film and Mass Culture', *New German Critique*, 54 (1991), 49. See also Hansen, '"With Skin and Hair": Kracauer's Theory of Film, Marseilles 1940', *Critical Inquiry*, 19 (1993), 437–69.

114 Walter Benjamin, *Understanding Brecht*, trans. Anna Bostock, intro. Stanley Mitchell (London: New Left Books, 1973), 100.

115 *Ibid.*, 103.

116 Benjamin, 'The Work of Art in the Age of Mechanical Production', *Illuminations*, ed. Hannah Arendt, trans. Harry Zohn (1968; London: Fontana, 1973), 237.

117 Benjamin, *Illuminations*, 239–42.

118 Benjamin uses two words which his English translators render as 'distraction'. *Ablenkung* is distraction in the sense of an interruption or diversion of attention; Benjamin uses it slightly earlier in the essay when writing of the 'vehement distraction' employed by Dada. *Zerstreuung* (cognate with James's *Zerstreutheit*, and the term Kracauer uses), usually signals distraction in the sense of entertainment – Benjamin writes of *die Zerstreute Masse*, and of the opposition of attention or composure (*Sammlung*) and distraction.

119 Benjamin, *Illuminations*, 238.

120 *Ibid.*, 242–3.

121 *Ibid.*, 177. Virginia Woolf's 1926 essay 'The Cinema' has a similar evocation of 'the chaos of the streets . . . some momentary assembly of colour, sound, movement' when she reaches for a sense of what film might become when it has mastered its art. Virginia Woolf, *The Captain's Death Bed and Other Essays* (London: Hogarth Press, 1950), 171.

8 FILM FINDS A TONGUE

1 Mary Ann Doane, 'Technology's Body: Cinematic Vision in Modernity', *Differences*, 5.2 (1993), 1–23 (13 cited).

2 Jonathan Crary, *Techniques of the Observer: On Vision and Modernity in the Nineteenth Century* (Cambridge, MA: MIT Press, 1990). On medicine, the body, and film, see Lisa Cartwright, *Screening the Body: Tracing Medicine's Visual Culture* (Minneapolis: University of Minnesota Press, 1995).

3 On the concept of 'suture' as the binding of the cinematic subject into a discursive system, see Stephen Heath, *Questions of Cinema* (Bloomington: Indiana University Press, 1981).

4 Noël Birch, *Life to those Shadows*, trans. Ben Brewster (London: British Film Institute, 1990), 234–42. The aim of producing sound accompanied cinema from Edison – in the Kinetophone, Animatograph, Cinephone, Vivaphone, Phonofilm, Photophone, etc. – though developments in amplification technology in the 1920s were also important. See Harry M. Geduld, *The Birth of the Talkies: From Edison to Jolson* (Bloomington: Indiana University Press, 1975), 299–303; and on technological succession, Peter Wollen, 'Cinema and Technology: A Historical Overview', *Semiotic Counter-Strategies: Readings and Writings* (London: Verso, 1982), 169–77.

5 William C. de Mille, *Hollywood Saga* (New York: E. P. Dutton, 1939), 269; cited in Alexander Walker, *The Shattered Silents: How the Talkies Came to Stay* (London: Elm Tree Books, 1978), 56–7. On the 'thrill', see Tom Gunning, 'An Aesthetic of Astonishment: Early Film and the (In)Credulous Spectator', *Art & Text*, 34 (1989), 31–45.

6 Fitzhugh Green, *The Film Finds its Tongue* (New York: G. P. Putnam's, 1929).

7 Walker, *The Shattered Silents*, 44.

8 This essay thus offers a commentary, pursuing rather different material, on Silverman's thesis in *The Acoustic Mirror: The Female Voice in Psychoanalysis and Cinema* (Bloomington: Indiana University Press, 1988), that 'Hollywood's sound regime is another mechanism, analogous to suture, whereby the female subject is obliged to bear a double burden of lack – to absorb the male subject's castration as well as her own' (63).

9 Cited by Terry Ramsaye, *A Million and One Nights: A History of the Motion Picture*, 2 vols. (New York: Simon & Schuster, 1926), I, lxviii. He adds that 'one may say that just as electricity may be called the one fundamental energy so we may call the motion picture the one fundamental art'.

10 *Life*, 23 January 1925; cited in Walker, *The Shattered Silents*, 29.

11 Gary Allighan, *The Romance of the Talkies* (London: Claude Stacey, 1929), 7.

12 An article on 'colour-music' appeared in London on the cusp of sound, in 1929, noting the fashion for elaborate lighting systems in cinemas. Vernon J. Clancey, 'Colour-Music', *The Realist*, 1.4 (July 1929), 138–47. The futurists also advocated colour–sound equivalents, e.g. Enrico Prampolini's 'Chromophony' manifesto (1913).

13 Green, *The Film Finds its Tongue*, 42–3, 46.

14 James R. Cameron, *Motion Pictures with Sound* (New York: Cameron Publishing Co., 1929), 21.

15 Investigating the limits of sound perception in *The Sensations of Tone* (1863), Helmholtz argues that perceptions of tonal divisions and

sound-spectra are more finely tuned and broader in bandwidth than sight. Moreover 'the auditory nerve is far superior to the optic nerve'. Hermann von Helmholtz, 'The Facts of Perception' (1878), *Helmholtz on Perception*, ed. Richard M. Warren and Roslyn P. Warren (New York: John Wiley, 1968), 211–12.

16 Silverman, *The Acoustic Mirror*, 42–3; Michel Chion, *Audio-Vision: Sound on Screen*, trans. Claudia Gorbman, foreword by Walter Murch (New York: Colombia University Press, 1990), 16–17, 170.

17 *The Talkies: Articles and Illustrations from Photoplay Magazine, 1928–1940*, ed. Richard Griffith (New York: Dover, 1971), 280; *Moving Picture World*, 28 May 1927, cited in Geduld, *Birth of the Talkies*, 174.

18 Walker, *The Shattered Silents*, 11.

19 *Ibid.*, 25.

20 Green, *The Film Finds its Tongue*, 68, 141.

21 *Ibid.*, 12.

22 King Vidor, *A Tree is a Tree* (London: Longmans, Green, 1954), 120.

23 Benchley in *Opportunity*, April 1929; cited in Donald Bogle's introduction to *A Separate Cinema: Fifty Years of Black Cast Posters*, ed. John Kisch and Edward Mapp (New York: Noonday Press, 1992), xviii–xx; cf. Thomas Cripps, *Slow Fade to Black: The Negro in American Film, 1900–1942* (New York: Oxford University Press, 1977), chs. 9–10.

24 Vidor, *A Tree is a Tree*, 119.

25 Dorothy Richardson, 'Dialogue in Dixie', *Close Up*, v 3 (September 1929), 211–18.

26 Doane, 'Technology's Body', 19–20 comments briefly on related issues.

27 Cripps, *Slow Fade*, 247.

28 Kish & Mapp, eds., *A Separate Cinema*, 28–9.

29 Barry Salt, *Film Style and Technology: History and Analysis*, 2nd rev. edn (London: Starword, 1992), 107–8, 189, 212ff; Robert Sklar, *Film: An International History of the Medium* (London: Thames & Hudson, 1993), ch. 8.

30 Tom Gunning, 'The Cinema of Attraction: Early Film, Its Spectator and the Avant–Garde', *Wilde Angle*, 8.3–4 (1986), 63–70 (66 cited). Alan Speigel argues more broadly that 'no other art form . . . represents a more accurate embodiment of a modernist and relativist metaphysics than cinematographic form'. Alan Spiegel, *Fiction and the Camera Eye: Visual Consciousness in Film and the Modern Novel* (Charlottesville: Virginia University Press, 1976), 32.

31 Virginia Woolf, 'The Cinema', *The Captain's Death Bed and Other Essays* (London: Hogarth Press, 1950), 166–71 (169 cited).

32 Sabine Hake, *The Cinema's Third Machine: Writing on Film in Germany, 1907–1933* (Lincoln: University of Nebraska Press, 1993), 77–8, 101.

33 *Ibid,*, 82–3.

34 Jean Epstein, 'The Senses I(b)' (1921), in Richard Abel, *French Film Theory and Criticism, a History/Anthology 1907–1939*, 2 vols. (Princeton University Press, 1988), I, 243, 205; Paul Willemen, 'On Reading Epstein on *Photogénie*', *Afterimage*, 10 (Autumn 1981), 44–5.

35 Vertov cited in Richard Weston, *Modernism* (London: Phaidon, 1996), 157.

36 Abel, *French Film*, I, 83.

37 Sergei Eisenstein, 'A Course in Treatment' (1932), in *Film Form*, trans. Jay Leyda (London: Denis Dobson, 1951), 106 (cf. his 'Beyond the Shot'); Vachel Lindsay, *The Art of the Moving Picture* (New York: Macmillan, 1915; 2nd rev. edn 1922), xxxvi. For other examples, see Miriam Hansen, 'Mass Culture as Hieroglyphic Writing: Adorno, Derrida, Kracauer', *New German Critique*, 56 (1992), 43–75.

38 Hillel Schwartz, 'Torque: The New Kinaesthetic of the Twentieth Century', *Zone*, 6, 'Incorporations', ed. Jonathan Crary and Sanford Kwinter (New York: Urzone, 1992), 101. Béla Balázs, *Theory of the Film*, trans. Edith Bone (New York: Roy, 1953), 40.

39 H. D., 'The Borderline Pamphlet' (1930), in *The Gender of Modernism: A Critical Anthology*, ed. Bonnie Kime Scott (Bloomington: Indiana University Press, 1990), 112, 114. On the cinematic in H. D., see Charlotte Mandel, 'The Redirected Image: Cinematic Dynamics in the Style of H. D.', *Literature/Film Quarterly*, 11 (1983), 36–45.

40 H. D., 'The Borderline Pamphlet', 120.

41 Ramsaye, *A Million and One Nights*, I, lxi, lxvii, lxviii.

42 Aldous Huxley, 'Silence is Golden', *Do What You Will* (London: Chatto & Windus, 1929), 52–61 (61 cited); Peter Wollen, *Raiding the Icebox: Reflections on Twentieth-Century Culture* (London: Verso, 1993), 54.

43 Elmer Rice, *Seven Plays* (New York: Viking, 1950), 67–9.

44 Huxley, 'Silence is Golden', 54.

45 *The Film Factory: Russian and Soviet Cinema in Documents*, ed. and trans. Richard Taylor, co-ed. and intro. Ian Christie (Cambridge, MA: Harvard University Press, 1988), 309.

46 Rudolph Arnheim, 'A New Laocoon', rep. in *Film as Art* (London: Faber & Faber, 1983).

47 René Crevel and Paul Eluard, 'Un Film commercial', *Le Surréalisme au service de la révolution*, 4 (December 1931), 29; cited in Herbert S. Gershman, *The Surrealist Revolution in France* (Ann Arbor: University of Michigan Press, 1969), 33.

48 Ernest Betts, *Heraclitus, of the Future of Films*, Today and Tomorrow Series (London: Kegan Paul, Trench, & Trubner, 1928), 86–8. Betts also wrote for *Close Up*.

49 Hansen, 'Mass Culture', 55.
50 See Richter's comments, written in the 1930s, in *The Struggle for the Film*, trans. Ben Brewster (Aldershot: Woldwood House, 1986), 109.
51 Sergei Eisenstein, Vsevolod Pudovkin, and Grigori Alexandroff, 'Statement on Sound', *The Film Factory*, 234–35. Published in *Zhizn' iskusstva*, 5 August 1928, the declaration was reprinted in *Close Up* and elsewhere.
52 *The Film Factory*, 280, 328, 266.
53 Viktor Shklovsky, 'The Script Laboratory' (1930), *The Film Factory*, 295, 307.
54 *Close Up*, 3.2 (August 1928), 32; *Close Up*, 3.3 (September 1928), 16.
55 *Close Up*, 5.1 (July 1929); 5.3 (September 1929), 169, 179, 187; 218.
56 *Close Up*, 4.6 (June 1929), 31.
57 Richardson, 'Dialogue in Dixie', 213–144. In a piece on 'Musical Accompaniment' in the August 1927 issue of *Close Up* she had praised well-integrated live music.
58 Dorothy Richardson, 'Continuous Performance. A Tear for Lycidas', *Close Up*, 7.3 (September 1930), 196–202 (200 cited).
59 Neither did H. D. comment on sound after *Borderland*: the last of several articles and reviews for *Close Up* was in December 1929: see Michael Boughn, *H. D. – A Bibliography* (Charlottesville: University Press of Virginia, 1993).
60 Robert de Traz, *Silent Hours*, trans. Dorothy M. Richardson (London: G. Bell, 1934), 131.
61 Grant Allen is briefly discussed in the Introduction (above).
62 Walter Reich, in *Sound and the Cinema: The Coming of Sound to American Film* (Pleasantville, NY: Redgrave Publishing, 1980), 110.
63 Christie, 'Soviet Cinema', 43–5.
64 On 'inner speech', see Ian Christie, 'Making Sense of Early Soviet Sound', *Inside the Film Factory: New Approaches to Russian and Soviet Cinema*, ed. Richard Taylor and Ian Christie (London: Routledge, 1991), 176–92; and Paul Willemen, 'Cinematic Discourse – The Problem of Inner Speech', *Screen*, 22.3 (1981), 63–93.
65 Dorothy Richardson, 'The Continuous Performance: The Film Gone Male', *Close Up*, 9.1 (March 1932), 36–8; rep. in *The Gender of Modernism*, 423–5.
66 Cited by Miriam Hansen, '"With Skin and Hair": Kracauer's Theory of Film, Marseilles 1940', *Critical Inquiry*, 19 (1993), 458.
67 Kracauer, *Theory of Film*, 109.
68 F. Scott Fitzgerald, 'Handle With Care', *The Crack-Up*, ed. Edmund Wilson (New York: New Directions, 1945), 78.
69 Ian Hamilton, *Writers in Hollywood, 1915–1951* (London: Harper Collins, 1990), 43. See also Richard Alan Fine, *Hollywood and the Profession of Authorship, 1928–1940* (Ann Arbor: UMI Research

Press, 1985); Judith Mayne, *Private Novels, Public Films* (Athens: University of Georgia Press, 1988).

70 Chandler to Dale Warren, 7 November 1951, *Selected Letters of Raymond Chandler*, ed. Frank McShane (London: Jonathan Cape, 1981), 298.

71 Gregory D. Black, *Hollywood Censored: Morality Codes, Catholics, and the Movies* (Cambridge University Press, 1994), ch. 4.

72 Richard Gray, 'They Worship Death Here: Faulkner, *Sanctuary* and Hollywood', B A A S Conference, Leeds, April 1996. On Faulkner in Hollywood, see Hamilton, *Writers in Hollywood*, 191–209; Gene D. Phillips, *Fiction, Film, and Faulkner: the Art of Adaptation* (Knoxville: University of Tennessee Press, 1988).

73 The details of censorship here and below are drawn from Black, *Hollywood Censored*, 97; Lea Jacobs, *The Wages of Sin: Censorship and the Fallen Woman, 1928–1942* (Madison: University of Wisconsin Press, 1991), 36–9.

74 Hamilton, *The Writer in Hollywood*, 158.

75 Thomas Strychacz, *Modernism, Mass Culture, and Professionalism* (Cambridge University Press, 1993), 188. Strychacz brilliantly unpicks the contradictory ways in which West's text engages with the discourse of Hollywood. See also Rita Barnard, '"When You Wish Upon a Star": Fantasy, Experience and Mass Culture in Nathanael West', *American Literature*, 66:2 (1994): 325–51; Richard Simon, 'Between Capra and Adorno: West's *Day of the Locust* and the Movies of the 1930s', *Modern Language Quarterly*, 54.4 (1993), 513–34.

76 Nathanael West, *The Day of the Locust* (1939), in *The Complete Works of Nathanael West* (London: Secker & Warburg, 1957), 261.

77 Strychacz, *Modernism*, 195. Strychacz argues that Tod's painting 'does indeed frame or "contain" chaos', but he also notes that the picture jerks, film-like, into life at the book's end.

78 *The Day of the Locust*, 363, 365.

79 See e.g. Miriam Hansen, *Babel and Babylon: Spectatorship in American Silent Film* (Cambridge, MA: Harvard University Press, 1991); Richard Maltby, 'The Social Evil, the Moral Order, and the Melodramatic Imagination, 1890–1915', *Melodrama: Stage, Picture, Screen*, ed. Jacky Bratton, Jim Cook, Christine Gledhill (London: British Film Institute, 1994), 214–30.

80 Barbara Low, 'The Cinema in Education: Some Psychological Considerations', *Contemporary Review* (November 1925), 638–35; reprinted as 'Mind-Growth or Mind-Mechanization: The Cinema in Education', *Close Up*, 3 (September 1927), 44–52. The piece was influential: Ramsaye cites it, as does Gilbert Seldes in *An Hour with the Movies and Talkies* (Philadelphia: J. B. Lippincott, 1929), 62.

81 Low, 'The Cinema in Education', 629–35.

82 Hugo Münsterberg, *The Photoplay: A Psychological Study* (New York: D. Appleton, 1916), 220–1, 227.

83 On British novels, see Billie Melman, *Women and the Popular Imagination in the Twenties: Flappers and Nymphs* (London: Macmillan, 1988); American parallels are surveyed by Michael Oriard on women 'playing the game', *Sporting With the Gods: The Rhetoric of Play and Game in American Culture* (Cambridge University Press, 1991), 421.

84 Lewis Jacobs, *The Rise of the American Film* (New York: Harcourt, Brace, 1939), 400, 410.

85 Richard Maltby, '"Baby Face" or How Joe Breen Made Barbara Stanwyck Atone for Causing the Wall Street Clash', *Screen*, 27.2 (1986), 22–45 (28 cited).

86 See Lynne Kirby, 'Gender and Advertising in American Silent Film: From Early Cinema to the Crowd', *Discourse*, 13.2 (1991), 3–20.

87 Hansen, *Babel and Babylon*, 85.

88 Eric Rhode, *A History of the Cinema: From its Origins to 1970* (London: Allen Lane, 1976), 319–20.

89 Gilles Deleuze, *Cinema 2: The Time-Image*, trans. Hugh Tomlinson and Robert Galeta (London: Athlone Press, 1989), 225.

90 As Mary Ann Doane notes, 'the addition of sound to the cinema introduces the possibility of re-presenting a fuller (and organically unified) body, and of confirming the status of speech as an individual property right'. 'The Voice in the Cinema: The Articulation of Body and Space', in *Film Sound: Theory and Practice*, ed. Elizabeth Weiss and John Betton (New York: Colombia University Press, 1985), 163.

91 Alan Williams, 'Historical and Theoretical Issues in the Coming of Sound', *Sound Theory, Sound Practice*, ed. Rick Altman (New York: Routledge, 1992), 126–37 (135 cited). Williams operates with a rather restricted definition of melodrama.

92 Their predecessors were the Ziegfeld Follies and the British Tiller Girls, popular in Berlin in the 1920s and linked by Kracauer to the machine-aesthetic of Fordism. Kracauer, *The Mass Ornament*, 75–86; Wollen, *Raiding the Icebox*, 54–8.

93 See Lucy Fischer, 'The Image of Woman as Image: The Optical Politics of *Dames*', *Film Quarterly*, 30 (1976), 2–11; rep. in *Genre: The Musical*, ed. Rick Altman (London: Routledge & Kegan Paul/British Film Institute, 1981), 70–84. See also David Martin, *The Films of Busby Berkeley* (San Francisco: David Martin, 1965).

94 Doane, 'Technology's Body', 3.

95 Clive Hirschorn, *Gene Kelly: A Biography* (London: W.H. Allen, 1974), 218.

96 Peter Wollen, *Singin' in the Rain* (London: British Film Institute, 1992), 55–6.

97 Wollen and Silverman both note a deconstructive irony here: Reynold's voice 'as' Lina was in fact the real voice of Hagen.

98 Clifford Howard, 'Talk and Speech', *Close Up*, 6.5 (May 1930), 395.

99 Mark Roth, 'Some Warners Musicals and the Spirit of the New Deal', *Velvet Light Trap* 17 (1977), 1–7.

100 For an exploration of cinematic writing stressing the legacy of such ideas, from Alexandre Astruc's '*caméra-stylo*' in the late 1940s to *auteur* theory, see Tom Conley, *Film Hieroglyphs: Ruptures in Classical Cinema* (Minneapolis: University of Minesota Press, 1991).

Index

'acute' pleasures (Grant Allen), 8, 233
Adams, Henry, 82, 85, 189
addiction, 26–31, 40–1
Adorno, Theodor, 4, 9, 40, 104; and
	Horkheimer, 230
advertising, 25, 29, 59, 61, 92, 98–100
AE (George Russell), 138
agamogenesis, 117; *see also* self-
	insemination
Aitken, Conrad, 288 n. 37
Aldington, Richard, 89
Alexander, F. M., 5–6; Alexander
	Technique, 107–8; Huxley and, 85;
	Mina Loy and, 121
Allen, Grant, *Physiological Aesthetics*, 8
Anderson, Sherwood, *Perhaps Women*, 65;
	defence of Stein, 197
Anesko, Michael, 52
anorexia, 56
Aragon, Louis, 194, 289 n. 54
Arnheim, Rudolph, 230
attention *see* distraction
Auden, W. H., 166
Auto-Facial-Construction (Mina Loy),
	120–2
automatic writing, 187–219; June Etta
	Downey on, 212–14; and Eliot, 204,
	290 n. 73; and Gertrude Stein,
	197–202, 209–11; and *Jekyll and Hyde*;
	mediums, 162–4, 188; and
	Surrealism, 201–3; William Carlos
	Williams on; other exponents of, 290
	n. 74

Bagot Stack, Mary (exerciser), 110–11
Bakhtin, M., 292 n. 92
Baldick, Chris, 18
Barnes, Djuna, 74, 125–9, 166; and
	boxing, 126–8; *Lady's Almanac*, 112;
	Nightwood, 128–9
Barney, Natalie, 113
Barrett, Sir William, 187

Barrymore, John, 223
Bartlett, Neil, 162
Bates, W. H. (sight-cure exponent), 85
'Battle of the Systems' *see* electricity
Beard, George M., on nerves, 15, 17, 31,
	35, 147; on language, 196
Beardsley, Aubrey, 160, 172
Behaviourism, 206
Beichman, Arnold, 34
Bell, Ian, 7, 135
belly-ache, Pound and, 64–5
Benchley, Robert, 225
Benda, Julien, 153
Benedikt, Moritz, 18
Benjamin, Walter, on distraction and film,
	216–19
Bennett, Arnold, 44, 145; *Riceyman Steps*,
	30
Benson, A. C., 136
Berkeley. Busby, 243, 246
Berman, Louis (endochrinologist), 70,
	135
Bernal, J. D., *The World, the Flesh and the
	Devil*, 83–4
Besant, Annie, *Thought Power*, 85
Betts, Ernest, *Heraclitus, or the Future of
	Films*, 227, 230
Bezier, Janet, 6
Binet, Alfred, 188–9
Birkin, Lawrence, 9
birth, 116–19, 135, 169
Blüher, Hans, 167
Boccioni, Umberto, 90, 122
body, in advertising, 98–100; cinematic
	body, 220–47; electric body, 14–41;
	fragmented body, 91–5, 105, 227;
	gendering of, 159, 164–9, 173–6,
	180–3; as habitus, 7, 107, 111; limits
	of, 3–5, 187, 193–7; as machine, 2,
	15, 18, 50, 62, 66, 78–90, 95, 101–5;
	114–16, 193–4, 228, 269 n. 98;
	radiant or specular body, 98, 111–12;

301

Flexner Report, 2
Flint, F. S., 89
Food and Drug Act (1906), 99
Foote, Edward B., 17
Fordism, 44, 65
Forster, E. M., 'The Machine Stops', 82
Foucault, Michel, 8, 203
Freud, Sigmund, 5, 17, 20, 94, 102, 108,
	139, 159, 166, 176, 201, 241, 282–3
	n. 34; on attention and distraction,
	195, 216, 287 n. 29; on gender,
	180–1; on narcissism, 151; on
	prosthesis, 77–8
Freytag-Loringhoven, Elsa von, 113–14
Friedman, Susan Stanton, 114
Frost, Robert, 206
Fuller, Loie, 110
Futurism, and bodily efficiency, 63, 106;
	Mina Loy on, 114–19; and organ-
	extension, 90; and technology, 86;
	and war, 96, 98; and words, 200–1,
	203

Gagnier, Regenia, 161
Galsworthy, John, 163
Galvani, Luigi, 14
Garber, Marjorie, 170, 177
Garrett, Garet, *Ouroboros*, 83
Gass, William H., 201
Geddes, Patrick, and J. Arthur Thomson,
	The Evolution of Sex, 20, 48, 149
gender, and bodily energies, 5, 9; and
	bodily reform, 108–11; in cinema,
	233, 236–43, 245–6; and Modernism,
	114, 152–3, 164; *see also* femininity,
	hormones, masculinity, surgery
Gerry, Elbridge T., 34
Giddens, Anthony, 4
Gilbert, Sandra M. and Susan Gubar, 67
Gilbreth, Frank and Lilian (time-and-
	motion researchers), 220, 243
Gilman, Charlotte Perkins, 18
goat-glanding, and cinema, 221–6, 244–7
Godden, Richard, 20
gold-digging, *see* cinema
Gonne, Maud, 152
Gordon, John, 262 n. 131
Gould, George H. (sight-cure exponent),
	88–9, 265 n. 46
Gourmont, Remy de, 89–90, 109, 266 n.
	51; *The Natural Philosophy of Love*, 135,
	'Subconscious Creation', 190
gramaphone, 115, 229
Grant, Madison, 106
graphosomatology, 6–7; *see also*
	handwriting

Gray, H. B., and Samuel Turner, *Eclipse or
	Empire?*, 61
Gray, Richard, 235
Green, Alfred, *Baby Face*, 242
Green, Fitzhugh, 222, 224
Green, Harvey, 149
Greenslade, Roy, 8
Gregory, Lady Augusta, 151
Guattari, Félix, 21, 40
Gully, James (doctor), 15
Gunning, Tom, 226
Gunther, Hans, *Der nordischer Gedanke*, 158

habitus., 7, 111; *see also* Bourdieu
Hacking, Ian, 286 n. 9
Hagen, Jean, 221, 244
Haire, Norman, 133, 144–5, 165, 167
Hake, Sabine, 227
Haldane, J. R., *Daedalus*, 83, 86
Hall, Radcliffe, *The Well of Loneliness*, 100–1
Hamilton, Ian, 235
Hamnet, Nina, 113
handwriting, 7, 187–8; and rejuvenation,
	146; in *Jekyll and Hyde*, 191–2; *see also*
	automatic writing
Hanna, Rev. (double personality), 190
Hansen, Miriam, 230
Hardy, Thomas, 34
Harraway, Donna, 169
Harrington, Anne, 189
Haug, F. M., *Critique of Commodity Aesthetics*,
	101
Haugmard, Louis, 227
Hawthorne experiments (General
	Electric), 84
Hays, Will, 224; Hays Office, 235
H. D. (Hilda Dolittle), 89, 114; and
	Borderline, 228
Heard, Gerald, *Pain, Sex and Time*, 62, 78,
	278 n. 52
Heidegger, Martin, 81
Hellman, Lilian, 234
Hellpach, Willy, 17
Helmholtz, Hermann von, 8, 15, 199, 223,
	294–5 n. 15
Hemingway, Ernest, 95, 123, 194
Herf, Jeffrey, 81
hieroglyphics, and film, 227–8
Hirschfeld, Magus,144–5, 155, 157–8,
	166–7
HIV virus, 288 n. 35
Hobhouse, Janet, 198
Hofmannsthal, Hugo von, 227
Hogben, Thomas (endochrinologist), 70
homosexuality, conceptualization of, 151,
	166–7